BIRDS

of

GEORGIA

Happy Birding!

Dr. John W. Parrish, Jr.
Giff Beaton
Gregory Kennedy

Dr. John W. Parrish, Jr.

with contributions from
Chris Fisher & Andy Bezener

Lone Pine Publishing International

Distributed by Lone Pine Publishing
1808 B Street NW, Suite 140
Auburn, WA USA 98001

Website: www.lonepinepublishing.com

Library and Archives Canada Cataloguing in Publication

Parrish, John (John W.), 1941–
      Birds of Georgia / John Parrish, Giff Beaton, Gregory Kennedy.

Includes bibliographical references and index.
ISBN-13: 978-976-8200-05-1
ISBN-10: 976-8200-05-7

      1. Birds—Georgia—Identification. I. Beaton, Giff, 1959–
II. Kennedy, Gregory, 1956– III. Title.

QL684.G4P37 2006   598'.09758   C2005-907749-2

Illustrations: Gary Ross, Ted Nordhagen, Ewa Pluciennik
Cover Illustration: Pileated Woodpecker, by Gary Ross
Scanning & Digital Film: Elite Lithographers Co.

PC: P13

CONTENTS

ACKNOWLEDGMENTS

It was extraordinarily grati-fying working with Giff Beaton on this book. His wealth of knowledge of the birds of Georgia made this joint project feasible. As with all projects of this magnitude, I must thank the multitude of devout birders in Georgia who gather the infor-mation to make a book such as this possible. I am indebted to those who participate in Christmas Bird Counts, Breeding Bird Surveys and other projects, who diligently report their "bird-finds" to *The Oriole* and other ornithological literature. A special apprecia-tion goes to the coauthors of the past edi-tions of the *Annotated Checklist of Georgia Birds* (ACOGB) for maintaining such excel-lent records of the state's birds. Thanks especially to Paul W. Sykes, Jr., a recent coauthor, for his

Purple Gallinule

unstinting efforts with the ACOGB. Thanks also to Jim Ozier and Brad Winn, of the Nongame-Endangered Wildlife Program at the Wildlife Resources Division of the Georgia Department of Natural Resources, who were helpful in providing data on some species. The superb editorial assistance and support of Nicholle Carrière, Genevieve Boyer, Krista Kagume and Gary Whyte, all of Lone Pine, made work on this book a thoroughly enjoyable and rewarding experience. In addition, thank you to Gary Ross, Ted Nordhagen and Ewa Pluciennik, whose skilled illustrations have brought each page to life.

I am forever grateful to my major professor, Dr. Elden W. Martin of Bowling Green State University, for introducing me to the joys of avian research and the study of ornithology. Thanks also to my dozens of undergraduate and graduate students for making the study of birds truly exciting. I thank the following for support of my research on ultraviolet vision, bioenergetics, hematology and the demographics of birds: Emporia State University, Georgia Southern University, Cornell University, Kansas Department of Wildlife and Parks, Georgia Department of Natural Resources, Arcadia Wildlife Preserve Inc., Georgia Power Co., Avian Powerline Interaction Committee, Barnes Lumber, Weyerhaeuser, Frito-Lay and Coca Cola Inc. A special thanks for my wife's loving support during this project.

—John W. Parrish, Jr.

I would like to thank my wife Becky for all her love and encouragement during my many years of traversing Georgia looking for birds. In addition to all the help already mentioned by John Parrish, I enjoyed working with John and all the great people at Lone Pine.

—Giff Beaton

Greater White-fronted Goose
size 30 in • p. 35

Snow Goose
size 31 in • p. 36

Ross's Goose
size 23 in • p. 37

Canada Goose
size 35 in • p. 38

Wood Duck
size 17 in • p. 39

Gadwall
size 20 in • p. 40

American Wigeon
size 20 in • p. 41

American Black Duck
size 22 in • p. 42

Mallard
size 24 in • p. 43

Mottled Duck
size 21 in • p. 44

Blue-winged Teal
size 15 in • p. 45

Northern Shoveler
size 19 in • p. 46

Northern Pintail
size 23 in • p. 47

Green-winged Teal
size 14 in • p. 48

Canvasback
size 20 in • p. 49

Redhead
size 20 in • p. 50

Ring-necked Duck
size 16 in • p. 51

Greater Scaup
size 17 in • p. 52

Lesser Scaup
size 16 in • p. 53

Surf Scoter
size 18 in • p. 54

White-winged Scoter
size 21 in • p. 55

Black Scoter
size 19 in • p. 56

Long-tailed Duck
size 18 in • p. 57

Bufflehead
size 14 in • p. 58

Common Goldeneye
size 18 in • p. 59

Hooded Merganser
size 17 in • p. 60

Red-breasted Merganser
size 23 in • p. 61

Ruddy Duck
size 15 in • p. 62

GROUSE & ALLIES

Chachalaca
size 22 in • p. 63

Ruffed Grouse
size 17 in • p. 64

Wild Turkey
size 39 in • p. 65

Northern Bobwhite
size 10 in • p. 66

DIVING BIRDS

Red-throated Loon
size 25 in • p. 67

Common Loon
size 32 in • p. 68

Pied-billed Grebe
size 13 in • p. 69

Horned Grebe
size 14 in • p. 70

Red-necked Grebe
size 19 in • p. 71

Eared Grebe
size 13 in • p. 72

Black-capped Petrel
size 16 in • p. 73

Cory's Shearwater
size 20 in • p. 74

Greater Shearwater
size 19 in • p. 75

Audubon's Shearwater
size 12 in • p. 76

Wilson's Storm-Petrel
size 7 in • p. 77

Northern Gannet
size 36 in • p. 78

American White Pelican
size 63 in • p. 79

Brown Pelican
size 48 in • p. 80

Double-crested Cormorant
size 29 in • p. 81

Anhinga
size 33 in • p. 82

Magnificent Frigatebird
size 39 in • p. 83

HERONLIKE BIRDS

American Bittern
size 25 in • p. 84

Least Bittern
size 13 in • p. 85

Great Blue Heron
size 51 in • p. 86

Great Egret
size 39 in • p. 87

HERONLIKE BIRDS

Snowy Egret
size 24 in • p. 88

Little Blue Heron
size 24 in • p. 89

Tricolored Heron
size 26 in • p. 90

Reddish Egret
size 30 in • p. 91

Cattle Egret
size 20 in • p. 92

Green Heron
size 18 in • p. 93

Black-crowned Night-Heron
size 24 in • p. 94

Yellow-crowned Night-Heron
size 24 in • p. 95

White Ibis
size 22 in • p. 96

Glossy Ibis
size 23 in • p. 97

Roseate Spoonbill
size 32 in • p. 98

Wood Stork
size 38 in • p. 99

Black Vulture
size 25 in • p. 100

Turkey Vulture
size 28 in • p. 101

BIRDS OF PREY

Osprey
size 23 in • p. 102

Swallow-tailed Kite
size 23 in • p. 103

Mississippi Kite
size 14 in • p. 104

Bald Eagle
size 37 in • p. 105

Northern Harrier
size 20 in • p. 106

Sharp-shinned Hawk
size 12 in • p. 107

Cooper's Hawk
size 17 in • p. 108

Red-shouldered Hawk
size 19 in • p. 109

Broad-winged Hawk
size 16 in • p. 110

Red-tailed Hawk
size 22 in • p. 111

Golden Eagle
size 35 in • p. 112

BIRDS OF PREY

American Kestrel
size 10 in • p. 113

Southeastern Kestrel
size 8 in • p. 114

Merlin
size11 in • p. 115

Peregrine Falcon
size 17 in • p. 116

RAILS, COOTS & CRANES

Black Rail
size 6 in • p. 117

Clapper Rail
size 14 in • p. 118

King Rail
size 15 in • p. 119

Virginia Rail
size 10 in • p. 120

Sora
size 9 in • p. 121

Purple Gallinule
size 13 in • p. 122

Common Moorhen
size 13 in • p. 123

American Coot
size 14 in • p. 124

Sandhill Crane
size 45 in • p. 125

Whooping Crane
size 56 in • p. 126

SHOREBIRDS

Black-bellied Plover
size 12 in • p. 127

American Golden-Plover
size 10 in • p. 128

Wilson's Plover
size 8 in • p. 129

Semipalmated Plover
size 7 in • p. 130

Piping Plover
size 7 in • p. 131

Killdeer
size 10 in • p. 132

American Oystercatcher
size 18 in • p. 133

Black-necked Stilt
size 14 in • p. 134

American Avocet
size 17 in • p. 135

Greater Yellowlegs
size 14 in • p. 136

Lesser Yellowlegs
size 10 in • p. 137

Solitary Sandpiper
size 8 in • p. 138

Willet
size 15 in • p. 139

Spotted Sandpiper
size 7 in • p. 140

Upland Sandpiper
size 12 in • p. 141

Whimbrel
size 18 in • p. 142

Long-billed Curlew
size 23 in • p. 143

Marbled Godwit
size 18 in • p. 144

Ruddy Turnstone
size 9 in • p. 145

Red Knot
size 10 in • p. 146

Sanderling
size 8 in • p. 147

Semipalmated Sandpiper
size 6 in • p. 148

Western Sandpiper
size 6 in • p. 149

Least Sandpiper
size 5 in • p. 150

White-rumped Sandpiper
size 7 in • p. 151

Baird's Sandpiper
size 7 in • p. 152

Pectoral Sandpiper
size 9 in • p. 153

Purple Sandpiper
size 9 in • p. 154

Dunlin
size 8 in • p. 155

Stilt Sandpiper
size 8 in • p. 156

Buff-breasted Sandpiper
size 8 in • p. 157

Short-billed Dowitcher
size 11 in • p. 158

Long-billed Dowitcher
size 12 in • p. 159

Wilson's Snipe
size 11 in • p.160

American Woodcock
size 11 in • p. 161

Wilson's Phalarope
size 9 in • p. 162

Red-necked Phalarope
size 7 in • p. 163

Red Phalarope
size 9 in • p. 164

Pomarine Jaeger
size 22 in • p. 165

Parasitic Jaeger
size 18 in • p. 166

Laughing Gull
size 16 in • p. 167

Franklin's Gull
size 14 in • p. 168

Bonaparte's Gull
size 13 in • p. 169

Ring-billed Gull
size 19 in • p. 170

Herring Gull
size 24 in • p. 171

Lesser Black-backed Gull
size 21 in • p. 172

Glaucous Gull
size 27 in • p. 173

Great Black-backed Gull
size 30 in • p. 174

Black-legged Kittiwake
size 17 in • p. 175

Gull-billed Tern
size 14 in • p. 176

Caspian Tern
size 21 in • p. 177

Royal Tern
size 20 in • p. 178

Sandwich Tern
size 15 in • p. 179

Common Tern
size 14 in • p. 180

Forster's Tern
size 15 in • p. 181

Least Tern
size 9 in • p. 182

Bridled Tern
size 15 in • p. 183

Sooty Tern
size 16 in • p. 184

Black Tern
size 9 in • p. 185

Black Skimmer
size 18 in • p. 186

Rock Pigeon
size 12 in • p. 187

Eurasian Collared-Dove
size 12 in • p. 188

White-winged Dove
size 12 in • p. 189

Mourning Dove
size 12 in • p. 190

Common Ground-Dove
size 7 in • p.191

Black-billed Cuckoo
size 12 in • p.192

Yellow-billed Cuckoo
size 12 in • p.193

OWLS

Barn Owl
size 15 in • p. 194

Eastern Screech-Owl
size 8 in • p. 195

Great Horned Owl
size 21 in • p. 196

Barred Owl
size 20 in • p. 197

Short-eared Owl
size 15 in • p. 198

NIGHTHAWKS, SWIFTS & HUMMINGBIRDS

Common Nighthawk
size 9 in • p. 199

Chuck-will's-widow
size 12 in • p. 200

Whip-poor-will
size 10 in • p. 201

Chimney Swift
size 5 in • p. 202

Ruby-throated Hummingbird
size 4 in • p. 203

Black-chinned Hummingbird
size 3 in • p. 204

Rufous Hummingbird
size 3 in • p. 205

Belted Kingfisher
size 13 in • p. 206

WOODPECKERS

Red-headed Woodpecker
size 9 in • p. 207

Red-bellied Woodpecker
size 10 in • p. 208

Yellow-bellied Sapsucker
size 8 in • p. 209

Downy Woodpecker
size 6 in • p. 210

Hairy Woodpecker
size 9 in • p. 211

Red-cockaded Woodpecker
size 8 in • p. 212

Northern Flicker
size 13 in • p. 213

Pileated Woodpecker
size 17 in • p. 214

FLYCATCHERS

Olive-sided Flycatcher
size 7 in • p. 216

Eastern Wood-Pewee
size 6 in • p. 217

Yellow-bellied Flycatcher
size 6 in • p. 218

Acadian Flycatcher
size 6 in • p. 219

Willow Flycatcher
size 6 in • p. 220

Least Flycatcher
size 5 in • p. 221

Eastern Phoebe
size 7 in • p. 222

Vermilion Flycatcher
size 6 in • p. 223

FLYCATCHERS

Great Crested Flycatcher
size 8 in • p. 224

Western Kingbird
size 8 in • p. 225

Eastern Kingbird
size 8 in • p. 226

Gray Kingbird
size 9 in • p. 227

Scissor-tailed Flycatcher
size 10 in • p. 228

SHRIKES & VIREOS

Loggerhead Shrike
size 9 in • p. 229

White-eyed Vireo
size 5 in • p. 230

Yellow-throated Vireo
size 5 in • p. 231

Blue-headed Vireo
size 5 in • p. 232

Warbling Vireo
size 5 in • p. 233

Philadelphia Vireo
size 5 in • p. 234

Red-eyed Vireo
size 6 in • p. 235

JAYS & CROWS

Blue Jay
size 12 in • p. 236

American Crow
size 18 in • p. 237

Fish Crow
size 15 in • p. 238

Common Raven
size 24 in • p. 239

LARKS & SWALLOWS

Horned Lark
size 7 in • p. 240

Purple Martin
size 7 in • p. 241

Tree Swallow
size 5 in • p. 242

Northern Rough-winged Swallow
size 5 in • p. 243

Bank Swallow
size 5 in • p. 244

Cliff Swallow
size 5 in • p. 245

Barn Swallow
size 7 in • p. 246

CHICKADEES, NUTHATCHES & WRENS

Carolina Chickadee
size 5 in • p. 247

Tufted Titmouse
size 6 in • p. 248

Red-breasted Nuthatch
size 4 in • p. 249

CHICKADEES, NUTHATCHES & WRENS

White-breasted Nuthatch
size 6 in • p. 250

Brown-headed Nuthatch
size 5 in • p. 251

Brown Creeper
size 5 in • p. 252

Carolina Wren
size 5 in • p. 253

House Wren
size 5 in • p. 254

Winter Wren
size 4 in • p. 255

Sedge Wren
size 4 in • p. 256

Marsh Wren
size 5 in • p. 257

KINGLETS, BLUEBIRDS & THRUSHES

Golden-crowned Kinglet
size 4 in • p. 258

Ruby-crowned Kinglet
size 4 in • p. 259

Blue-gray Gnatcatcher
size 5 in • p. 260

Eastern Bluebird
size 7 in • p. 261

Veery
size 7 in • p. 262

Gray-cheeked Thrush
size 7 in • p. 263

Swainson's Thrush
size 7 in • p. 264

Hermit Thrush
size 7 in • p. 265

STARLINGS, MIMICS & WAXWINGS

Wood Thrush
size 8 in • p. 266

American Robin
size 10 in • p. 267

Gray Catbird
size 9 in • p. 268

Northern Mockingbird
size 10 in • p. 269

Brown Thrasher
size 11 in • p. 270

European Starling
size 8 in • p. 271

American Pipit
size 6 in • p. 272

Cedar Waxwing
size 7 in • p. 273

WOOD-WARBLERS & TANAGERS

Blue-winged Warbler
size 5 in • p. 274

Golden-winged Warbler
size 5 in • p. 275

Tennessee Warbler
size 5 in • p. 276

Orange-crowned Warbler
size 5 in • p. 277

Nashville Warbler
size 5 in • p. 278

Northern Parula
size 4 in • p. 279

Yellow Warbler
size 5 in • p. 280

Chestnut-sided Warbler
size 5 in • p. 281

Magnolia Warbler
size 5 in • p. 282

Cape May Warbler
size 5 in • p. 283

Black-throated Blue Warbler
size 5 in • p. 284

Yellow-rumped Warbler
size 5 in • p. 285

Black-throated Green Warbler
size 5 in • p. 286

Blackburnian Warbler
size 5 in • p. 287

Yellow-throated Warbler
size 5 in • p. 288

Pine Warbler
size 5 in • p. 289

Prairie Warbler
size 5 in • p. 290

Palm Warbler
size 5 in • p. 291

Baybreasted Warbler
size 5 in • p. 292

Blackpoll Warbler
size 5 in • p. 293

Cerulean Warbler
size 5 in • p. 294

Black-and-white Warbler
size 5 in • p. 295

American Redstart
size 5 in • p. 296

Prothonotary Warbler
size 5 in • p. 297

Worm-eating Warbler
size 5 in • p. 298

Swainson's Warbler
size 6 in • p. 299

Ovenbird
size 6 in • p. 300

Northern Waterthrush
size 6 in • p. 301

Louisiana Waterthrush
size 6 in • p. 302

Kentucky Warbler
size 5 in • p. 303

Connecticut Warbler
size 6 in • p. 304

Mourning Warbler
size 5 in • p. 305

Common Yellowthroat
size 5 in • p. 306

Hooded Warbler
size 5 in • p. 307

Wilson's Warbler
size 5 in • p. 308

Canada Warbler
size 5 in • p. 309

Yellow-breasted Chat
size 7 in • p. 310

Summer Tanager
size 7 in • p. 311

Scarlet Tanager
size 7 in • p. 312

Eastern Towhee
size 8 in • p. 313

Bachman's Sparrow
size 6 in • p. 314

Chipping Sparrow
size 6 in • p. 315

Clay-colored Sparrow
size 6 in • p. 316

Field Sparrow
size 6 in • p. 317

Vesper Sparrow
size 6 in • p. 318

Lark Sparrow
size 6 in • p. 319

Savannah Sparrow
size 6 in • p. 320

Grasshopper Sparrow
size 5 in • p. 321

Henslow's Sparrow
size 5 in • p. 322

Le Conte's Sparrow
size 5 in • p. 323

Nelson's Sharp-tailed Sparrow
size 5 in • p. 324

Saltmarsh Sharp-tailed Sparrow
size 5 in • p. 325

Seaside Sparrow
size 6 in • p. 326

Fox Sparrow
size 7 in • p. 327

Song Sparrow
size 6 in • p. 328

Lincoln's Sparrow
size 5 in • p. 329

Swamp Sparrow
size 5 in • p. 330

White-throated Sparrow
size 7 in • p. 331

White-crowned Sparrow
size 6 in • p. 332

SPARROWS, GROSBEAKS & BUNTINGS

Dark-eyed Junco
size 6 in • p. 333

Northern Cardinal
size 8 in • p. 334

Rose-breasted Grosbeak
size 8 in • p. 335

Blue Grosbeak
size 7 in • p. 336

Indigo Bunting
size 5 in • p. 337

Painted Bunting
size 5 in • p. 338

Dickcissel
size 6 in • p. 339

BLACKBIRDS & ALLIES

Bobolink
size 7 in • p. 340

Red-winged Blackbird
size 8 in • p. 341

Eastern Meadowlark
size 10 in • p. 342

Yellow-headed Blackbird
size 9 in • p. 343

Rusty Blackbird
size 9 in • p. 344

Brewer's Blackbird
size 9 in • p. 345

Common Grackle
size 12 in • p. 346

Boat-tailed Grackle
size 15 in • p. 347

Shiny Cowbird
size 8 in • p. 348

Brown-headed Cowbird
size 7 in • p. 349

Orchard Oriole
size 7 in • p. 350

Baltimore Oriole
size 8 in • p. 351

FINCHLIKE BIRDS

Purple Finch
size 6 in • p. 352

House Finch
size 6 in • p. 353

Red Crossbill
size 6 in • p. 354

Pine Siskin
size 5 in • p. 355

American Goldfinch
size 5 in • p. 356

Evening Grosbeak
size 8 in • p. 357

House Sparrow
size 6 in • p. 358

INTRODUCTION

BIRDING IN GEORGIA

In recent decades, birding has evolved from an eccentric pursuit practiced by a few dedicated individuals to a continent-wide activity that boasts millions of professional and amateur participants. A survey by the U.S. Fish and Wildlife Service at the beginning of the 21st century estimated that about 46 million Americans were involved in birding in one form or another, and that they collectively spent more than 32 billion dollars on travel, equipment and other expenses related to birding. If you are reading this, either you're already a birder or you think that birding is something you might like to try. Regardless, there are many reasons why birding has become so popular. Many birders find birding simple and relaxing, whereas others enjoy the outdoor exercise that it affords. Some see it as a rewarding learning experience, an opportunity to socialize with like-minded people and a way to monitor the health of the local environment. Still others watch birds to reconnect with nature. A visit to any of our state's premier birding locations, such as the coastal beaches, any of the large lakes or one of the mountain balds, would doubtless uncover still more reasons why people watch birds.

Georgia birders are incredibly fortunate! Our state—the largest east of the Mississippi River—encompasses a great diversity of habitats. We have the Mountains region to the north, the rolling hills of the Piedmont in the upper middle part of the state, the expansive Coastal Plain below the Fall Line (which extends from Augusta southwest through Macon and ends near Columbus). And of course, we have a marvelous maritime coastline with a bonanza of barrier islands that jut out into the sea. In addition to supporting a wide range of breeding birds and year-round residents, our state hosts a large number of spring and fall migrants that move through our area on the way to their breeding and wintering grounds. In all, 405 bird species have been seen and recorded in Georgia (plus 8 provisional and 4 extirpated species). Of these, 322 species make regular appearances in the state.

Christmas bird counts, breeding bird surveys, nest box programs, migration monitoring and birding lectures and workshops all provide a chance for novice, intermediate and expert birders to interact and share their enthusiasm for the wonder of birds. So, whatever your level, there is ample opportunity for you to get involved!

BEGINNING TO LEARN THE BIRDS

The Challenge of Birding

Birding (also known as "birdwatching") can be extremely challenging and getting started is often the most difficult part. Learning to recognize all the birds in Georgia is a long process. But fear not! The species pictured in this guide will help you get started. Although any standard North American field guide will help you identify local birds, such guides can be daunting because they cover the entire continent and present an overwhelming number of species. By focusing specifically on the bird life of Georgia, we hope to make the introduction to the world of birding a little less intimidating.

Do not expect to become an expert overnight. To be able to identify any bird at a glance, you will have to spend more than a few hours in the field with binoculars and this guide. It could conceivably take a lifetime of careful study to master the art of birding. After all, only a small number of birders and ornithologists in our state can identify all of our species with confidence. Nevertheless, almost everyone finds the continual learning process of birding to be enjoyable, if not downright thrilling. If possible, try to locate some experienced birders in your area. Go to the Georgia Ornithological Society website (www.gos.org), where there are lists of birding groups throughout the state with contact information, or turn to page 28 for a list of Georgia birding organizations. Birders always enjoy helping someone new to the sport and can help you get your "birding lifelist" started on a local field trip.

CLASSIFICATION: THE ORDER OF THINGS

To an ornithologist (a biologist who studies birds), the species is the fundamental unit of classification because the members of a single species look most alike and they naturally interbreed with one another. Each species has a scientific name, usually derived from Latin or Greek, that designates the genus and species, (which is always italicized or underlined) and a single accredited common name, so that the different vernacular names of a species do not cause confusion. A bird has been properly identified only when it has been identified "to species," and most ornithologists use the accredited common name. For example, "American Coot" is an accredited common name, even though some people call this bird the "Mudhen." *Fulica americana* is the American Coot's scientific name. (*Fulica* is the genus, or generic name, and *americana* is the species, or specific name).

To help make sense of the hundreds of bird species in our region, scientifically oriented birders lump species into recognizable groups. The most commonly used groupings, in order of increasing scope, are genus, family and order. The American Coot and Common Moorhen are different species that do not share a genus (their generic names are different), but they are both members of the family Rallidae (the rail family). The rail, limpkin and crane families are in turn grouped within the order Gruiformes, which comprises a number of "chickenlike" birds.

Ornithologists have arranged all of the orders to make a standard sequence. It begins with the geese, swans and ducks (order Anseriformes), which are thought by many to be most like the evolutionary ancestors of modern birds. This sequence ends with those species, such as the finches, that are thought to have been most strongly modified by evolutionary change and most departed from the ancestral form. We have organized this book according to this standard evolutionary sequence.

TECHNIQUES OF BIRDING

Being in the right place at the right time to see birds in action involves both skill and luck. Although there is always a bit of serendipity involved in meeting a unique and interesting bird, the more you know about a bird—its range, preferred habitat, food preferences and hours and seasons of activity—the better your chances will be of seeing it. It is much easier to find an Eastern Screech-Owl in the forest than elsewhere, especially at night in spring when adults are calling for mates. In contrast, an Eastern Meadowlark would be most likely seen during the day in an open meadow, pasture or agricultural field.

Generally, spring and fall are the busiest birding times, as many breeding birds migrate from their winter homes to nest in Georgia and others move through the state to and from their summer and winter habitats north and south of our state.

Temperatures are moderate during these times of the year, and a great number of birds are on the move, often heavily populating small patches of habitat before moving on. Male songbirds are easy to identify on spring mornings as they belt out their courtship songs. Throughout much of the year, diurnal birds are most visible in the early morning hours when they are foraging, but during winter they are often more active in the day when milder temperatures prevail. Timing is crucial because summer foliage often conceals birds and cold weather drives many species farther south for winter. Try to find out where the International Migratory Bird Day (the second Saturday in May) might be celebrated in your area, join the group and enjoy the thrills of birding.

OPTICS

John James Audubon, one of the most famous American bird painters, shot the birds before he painted them, which is how early birding was often undertaken. With the development of sophisticated optical equipment, today ornithologists use binoculars and spotting scopes to easily identify birds and to appreciate the beauty and fine details of their plumages without harming them.

Binoculars

Binoculars come in two basic types: porro-prism (in which there is a distinct, angular bend in the body of the binoculars) and roof-prism (in which the body is straight). Each has its distinct advantages, but without going into painstaking details, roof-prism binoculars are probably the best choice for most birders. This type of binocular is usually lighter, smaller and easier to hold steady while viewing birds.

The optical power of binoculars is described with a two-number code. For example, a compact pair of binoculars might be "8 x 21," and a larger pair might have "8 x 40" stamped on it. In each case, the first number states the magnification, and the second number indicates the diameter, in millimeters, of the front lenses. Eight-power binoculars are the easiest to hold and to use for finding birds; 10-power binoculars give a more magnified view but are harder to hold steady. Larger lenses gather more light, so a 35 mm or 40 mm lens will perform much better at dusk than a 20 mm or 30 mm lens of the same magnification.

For a beginner, eight-power, porro-prism binoculars with front lenses at least 35 mm in diameter (thus 8 x 35 or 8 x 40) are suitable. Some binoculars have a wider field of view than others, even if the two-number code is identical. We recommend the wider field of view, because many beginners have trouble finding birds in compact, narrow-view binoculars.

Look at many types of binoculars before making a purchase. Talk to other birders about their binoculars and ask to try them. Go to a store that specializes in birding—the sales people there will know from personal experience which models perform best in the field. An excellent pair of binoculars can be

Eastern Screech-Owl

had for as little as $250. For birding, don't buy a cheap pair from a sporting goods or merchandise store, because you will likely find those binoculars to be inadequate in the field.

When birding, lift the binoculars up while keeping your eyes on the bird. This way you will not lose the bird in the magnified view. You can also note an obvious landmark near the bird (a bright flower or a dead branch, for example) and then use the landmark as a reference point to find the bird with the binoculars.

Spotting Scopes

The spotting scope (a small telescope with a sturdy tripod) is designed to help you view birds that are beyond the range of binoculars, such as ducks floating off the coastal shore. Good scopes can be purchased for about the same cost as a pair of binoculars. For most birders, a spotting scope with a 20x magnification will prove adequate. Some scopes will even allow you to take photographs through them with a 35 mm single-lens reflex (SLR) or a digital camera.

Cameras

Hoping to photograph even backyard birds is a tremendous challenge, even for the professionals. But keeping a camera with you when you bird makes it more likely that you will finally be able to get that great shot that you may have been trying to capture for weeks or months.

If you intend to photograph birds, you should buy a 35 mm single-lens reflex (SLR) camera with a telephoto lens measuring at least 300 mm. The recent surge in production of digital SLR cameras with smaller than 35 mm CCD or CMOS detectors provide a boon for the would-be bird photographer. For example, if you purchase a 300 mm lens and the camera has a 2x magnification factor, that 300 mm lens functionally becomes a 600 mm lens. Now you have a decent chance to get that perfect bird picture. As with a spotting scope, a solid tripod is essential for the camera.

BIRDING BY EAR

All birders start by learning to identify birds visually, then they often increase their birding skills by learning the songs and calls of the birds. Recognizing birds by their vocalizations can greatly enhance your birding experience. When experienced birders conduct breeding bird surveys in summer, they make nearly 90 percent of their bird identifications by songs and calls, because listening is far more efficient.

There are numerous tapes and CDs that can help you learn bird songs, and a portable MP3 or tape player with headphones can let you quickly compare a live bird with a recording.

The old-fashioned way to remember bird songs is to make up words for them. We have given you some of the classic renderings in the species accounts that follow, such as *who cooks for you? who cooks for you-all?* for the Barred Owl, as well as some nonsense syllables, such as *tsit tsit tsit* for the Blackpoll Warbler.

Black-bellied Plover

Some of these approximations work better than others; birds often add or delete syllables from their calls, and very few pronounce consonants in a recognizable fashion. Be aware that songs usually vary from place to place as well.

WATCHING BIRD BEHAVIOR

Once you are confident identifying birds and remembering their common names, you can begin to appreciate their behavior. Studying birds involves keeping notes and records. The timing of bird migrations is an easy thing to record, as are details of feeding, courtship and nesting behavior if you are willing to be patient. Flocking birds can also provide fascinating opportunities to observe and note social interactions, especially when individual birds can be recognized. Such observations have contributed greatly toward our knowledge of birds. However, casual note taking should not be equated with more standardized, scientific methods of study.

Blackpoll Warbler

Birding, for most people, is a peaceful, nondestructive recreational activity. One of the best ways to watch bird behavior is to look for a spot rich with avian life, and then sit back and relax. If you become part of the scenery, the birds, at first startled by your approach, will soon resume their activities and allow you into their world.

BIRDING BY HABITAT

From an avifaunal perspective, Georgia can be separated into five broad physiographic regions: Mountains, Piedmont, Coastal Plain, Coast and adjacent Offshore waters. The relative abundance, temporal and spatial distribution and breeding range of the species in this book are described with reference to these physiographic regions. Each physiographic region is composed of a number of different habitats. Each habitat is a community of plants and animals supported by the infrastructure of water and soil and regulated by the constraints of topography, climate and elevation.

Simply put, a bird's habitat is the place in which it normally lives. Some birds prefer the open water, some are found in cattail marshes, others like mature coniferous forests and still others prefer abandoned agricultural fields overgrown with tall grass and shrubs. Knowledge of a bird's habitat increases the chances of identifying the bird correctly.

Habitats are just like neighborhoods: if you associate friends with the suburb in which they live, you can just as easily learn to associate specific birds with their preferred habitats. Only in migration, especially during inclement weather, do some birds leave their usual habitat.

TOP BIRDING SITES IN GEORGIA

Georgia has so many great birding sites that it's impossible to list all of them, but here is a list of the 50 top sites. They have been selected to represent a broad range of bird communities and habitats, with an emphasis on accessibility. It is generally a good idea to check local regulations concerning access and also find out when hunting may be permitted (so you know to avoid the site during this time).

There are many other sites, including just about any local or state park and all the wildlife management areas and national wildlife refuges, but this list will give you a place to start. For a more extensive discussion of birding areas, refer to *Birding Georgia* by Giff Beaton.

GEORGIA'S TOP 50 BIRDING SITES

Sites listed in **bold face** have an expanded write-up following the list.

Mountain Region
1. Crockford-Pigeon Mountain WMA
2. Cloudland Canyon SP
3. Arrowhead Wildlife Education Area
4. **Pine Log WMA**
5. Cohutta WMA
6. **Ivy Log Gap**
7. Neel's Gap
8. **Brasstown Bald**
9. Rabun Bald
10. **Burrell's Ford**

Piedmont Region
11. West Point Lake and Dam
12. Oxbow Meadows
13. Sweetwater Creek SP
14. **Kennesaw Mountain National Battlefield Park**
15. Chattahoochee River NRA
16. **E.L. Huie Land Application Facility**
17. Charlie Elliott Wildlife Education Center
18. Dawson Forest WMA
19. Lake Lanier
20. **Piedmont NWR**
21. Central City Park and Lower Poplar Street in Macon
22. Ocmulgee NM
23. Watson Spring
24. Dyar Pasture WMA
25. Merry Brothers Brickyards Ponds
26. **Phinizy Swamp Nature Park**
27. Augusta Levee

Coastal Plain
28. **Eufaula NWR and Lake Walter F. George**
29. **Lake Seminole WMA**
30. Chickasawhatchee WMA
31. Reed Bingham SP
32. Paradise Public Fishing Area
33. Grand Bay WMA
34. **Beaverdam WMA**
35. River Bend WMA
36. Okefenokee NWR
37. Big Hammock WMA
38. Titan Turf (formerly East Georgia Turf Farm)
39. Altamaha River Overlook
40. Paulks Pasture WMA

Coast
41. Tybee Island and Fort Pulaski
42. Savannah-Ogeechee Canal
43. Youman's Pond
44. **Harris Neck NWR**
45. Sapelo Island
46. **Altamaha WMA**
47. **St. Simons Island**
48. Andrews Island
49. **Jekyll Island**
50. Cumberland Island

NM	= National Monument
NRA	= National Recreation Area
NWR	= National Wildlife Refuge
SP	= State Park
WMA	= Wildlife Management Area

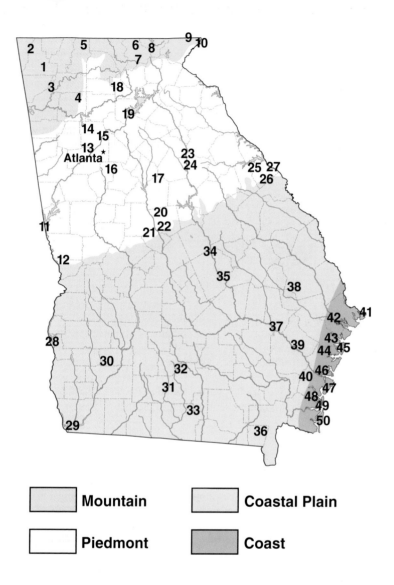

Mountain	**Coastal Plain**
Piedmont	**Coast**

Pine Log WMA

At this leased wildlife management area just northeast of Cartersville, you can find a number of interesting breeding and wintering species. It is one of the only places in Georgia where Red Crossbills are known to breed, although they are few in number. In summer, the combination of forested areas and more open areas provide a good variety of species to look for. At least 14 warbler species breed here, including the Ovenbird and the Black-throated Green Warbler, and this site is the most southerly spot where you can find both species regularly. Access is easy on several gravel or dirt roads, but it can be muddy here after periods of rain.

Ivy Log Gap

This site is simply a dirt road through the Blue Ridge Mountains, but it is easy to drive with a passenger car and you can see many otherwise very difficult-to-find species along the road. The main attraction here is the 18 or so warbler species, including the Cerulean Warblers that breed along the road or nearby in spring and early summer. There are also many interesting vireos, flycatchers, tanagers and other beautiful neotropical migrant songbirds. One of the bonuses is that the road runs along the side of a hill for much of its length, so you can view canopy species at eye level without suffering from "warbler neck!"

Brasstown Bald

This bald is the highest mountain in Georgia at 4784 feet, and here you can get very close to otherwise inaccessible higher-elevation species just by driving a good paved road up to the parking lot near the top of the mountain. Watch for Common Ravens cavorting above you in the thermals, along with Broad-winged Hawks and other raptors in summer. Also check the edges

Ruffed Grouse

of the parking lot for breeding Canada Warblers. There are several great hiking trails that start from the parking lot, and you can see Ruffed Grouse along them if you are both quiet and lucky! Many other interesting species breed on this mountain, around the parking lot or trails to the top, including the Rose-breasted Grosbeak and the Veery, two species you cannot see elsewhere in the state without hiking.

Burrell's Ford

This site is reached by driving along Forest Road 646 for about 7 miles to the Chattooga River and the South Carolina border, and both sides of the river are great for birding, especially in summer. One of the real attractions here is that this is one of the last remaining areas with old-growth, white pine–hemlock habitat in Georgia, and several species occur here that are really rare in the south. This is one of the only places in the south to reliably find Red-breasted Nuthatches year-round, and there is a possibility that both Brown Creepers and Golden-crowned Kinglets may breed here in very low numbers. In summer there are many songbirds breeding here, including such warblers as Swainson's, Black-throated Green and Worm-eating. In winter, there have been a few sightings of the unbelievably cute Northern Saw-whet Owl along this road, but it's not clear how often this owl is here.

Kennesaw Mountain National Battlefield Park

Kennesaw Mountain is a small mountain just northwest of Atlanta, but it has a well-deserved reputation for being a superb spot during songbird migration in spring and fall. Peak numbers of birds are found from April 15th to May 5th and from August 15th to October 10th. Birding is easy: you just walk up and down the 1.5-mile-long paved road to the summit and back. Warbler counts of up to 30 species on a spring morning have been made here, with up to 22 species on a fall morning. These numbers don't include all the tanagers, thrushes, vireos, flycatchers and other goodies found here. There are often other birders around to help with identification for beginners, and there is a helpful visitor's center with books about nature and about the Civil War battle that is commemorated here.

E.L. Huie Land Application Facility

This site is really two great spots in one. First is a huge complex of wastewater treatment ponds that is simply one of the best places in the whole state for watching shorebirds in season (depending on water levels in the settling ponds) and for observing waterfowl in migration and winter. There are a few nest boxes here for Tree Swallows and Purple Martins, and just about all species of swallows can be seen here during migration. Second is the Newman Wetland Center, just 2 miles down the road, with a superb education center and a great boardwalk and walking trail year-round. This is a great spot for many local permanent residents such as Brown-headed Nuthatches, Red-headed Woodpeckers and Red-shouldered Hawks and for breeding summer residents such as Green Herons and Louisiana Waterthrushes, as well as for Winter Wrens and sparrows in winter.

Piedmont National Wildlife Refuge

Piedmont National Wildlife Refuge is not only the easiest place in Georgia to see a Red-cockaded Woodpecker, it's 35,000 acres of great habitat. In addition to the mature loblolly pine forest that houses the woodpeckers and many other interesting species, there are ponds, fields and streams to explore. Though most often birded in spring and summer for breeding neotropical migrants and residents such as Bachman's Sparrows and Brown-headed Nuthatches, this huge refuge has wonderful birding year-round, and its central location in the state makes it easy to get to from anywhere. The visitor center has interesting exhibits and always has the latest info on where to see the woodpeckers.

Phinizy Swamp Nature Park

Phinizy Swamp Nature Park has been open for only about five years, but it has quickly become one of the most popular and rewarding birding spots in the state. Located near Augusta, this park is a working wastewater treatment facility, and it has dozens of large vegetated cells (ponds) with easy walking access to all of them. Whether you are interested in waterfowl and sparrows in winter, passerine migrants in the forested edges, shorebirds in spring and fall, or rails and bitterns of some kind almost year-round, there are always great birds here. With a well-stocked visitor center and educational programs instructing thousands of students each year, this site serves the community in many ways in addition to just birding access.

Eufaula National Wildlife Refuge and Lake Walter F George

These two sites are located right on the Georgia–Alabama state line. Most of the refuge is actually situated within Alabama and is well worth visiting. The part in Georgia is called the Bradley Unit, and it's great for ducks in fall and winter (but call ahead to avoid hunting dates). After parking in the lot, there is a 5-mile loop along a dike road that you can walk while you savor the beauty of this spot. There are wonderful breeding birds here too, from songbirds such as Prothonotary Warblers to waterbirds such as Purple Gallinules, King Rails and Least Bitterns. Late summer and fall bring an ample assortment of wading birds, and in winter you can find hordes of sparrows here, including the elusive Le Conte's.

Lake Seminole Wildlife Management Area

Located in the extreme southwest corner of the state, this wildlife management area is split up into many different parcels all around the lake. There are portions along both main rivers entering the lake, good for both migrant and resident land birds, as well as parcels accessing the main lake and the numerous ponds around it. This lake has the largest population of Bald Eagles away from the coast in the state, and in winter the lake is covered with waterfowl (mostly American Coots), which is probably why all the eagles are here! Wood Ducks and other ducks can be found on the ponds and main lake, and the main lake supports the largest numbers of Canvasbacks in winter.

Beaverdam Wildlife Management Area

This wildlife management area is located just north of Dublin in the upper Coastal Plain, and it offers easy access to great riparian habitat along the Oconee River and several feeder creeks. This spot is really wonderful for breeding passerines of the lower half of the state, such as Swainson's Warblers, Prothonotary Warblers and Acadian Flycatchers. Mississippi Kites also breed here, and you can often see them feeding above the forest canopy on summer mornings. The open areas are great for sparrows in winter and for Common Ground-Doves year-round. With all the mature hardwood forest along the river corridor, this spot is also an excellent one for migration in spring and fall.

Harris Neck National Wildlife Refuge

Harris Neck is a huge refuge right along the coast, and it has many exciting types of habitat to explore at any time of year. In winter, many northern species of songbirds overwinter in the forest and abundant fields of this former World War II–era training base. Summer brings its own interesting southern species, including the magnificent Painted Bunting. Woody Pond is named for the many Wood Storks that nest there, easily viewed from a dike just off the main loop road, and this pond is managed just for this species. The same conditions that attract Wood Storks also bring in many other species of waders in summer and fall, and many of these birds stay to spend the winter in the relatively benign climate here. There are always a few ducks on the ponds in winter too, to round out your visit.

Altamaha Wildlife Management Area

Altamaha Wildlife Management Area is located just off I-95 on the coast and is a huge series of diked impoundments, with a few patches of forest for songbirds and also some fields for sparrows in winter. The impoundments are now being managed for optimum bird attractiveness in all seasons, with lower water levels for shorebirds in spring and fall and higher water levels in winter for ducks. There are two observation towers to help you scan all of the available areas, and you can walk around miles and miles of dikes also. In fall, multitudes of sparrows work the brushy areas along these dikes, including such local rarities as White-crowned Sparrows and Clay-colored Sparrows. These ponds teem with rails in winter also, though they are difficult to spot.

St. Simons Island

This barrier island is moderately developed, but an area called East Beach has some of the best coastal bird viewing in the entire state. From one position you can scan several areas of beach and mudflat, depending on season and tide, and view 40 or 50 species all at the same time! Shorebirds, gulls, terns, waders and who knows what else may fly into your view. Birds of special interest here at various times of year include Piping Plovers, Red Knots, Marbled Godwits, Whimbrels, Least Terns, Lesser Black-backed Gulls and Reddish Egrets. It's best to be here on a falling or rising tide; avoid dead low tide when the birds will be too far away to see.

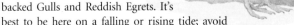

Piping Plover

Jekyll Island

This single spot has probably hosted more super-rare birds than any other site in the state, and it is a top destination for birders year-round. At any time of year the beaches and areas just offshore are teeming with gulls and terns. In spring and fall especially, areas such as the south beach are excellent spots to look for just about any shorebird that passes through the state in migration, and many of these shorebirds stay in winter, including Western Sandpipers and Dunlins. Gull numbers are highest in winter, and a viewing area just off the north end annually hosts a flock of sea ducks. There are always both species of scaup here in winter, also usually Buffleheads and Black Scoters, and sometimes the other scoters or other species. In summer, duck, shorebird and gull numbers are reduced, but other favorites such as Painted Buntings in the scrub areas and Gray Kingbirds at the Convention Center delight.

BIRD LISTING

Keeping a list of birds seen is immensely popular among birders and can take many forms. Some birders maintain a "life-list" of all birds seen, whereas others maintain lists for their state, county or simply the backyard. Listing is so popular that the American Birding Association publishes a regular bulletin of its member's "listing" accomplishments. One of the nation's Top Listers, for example, is Dr. Paul Sykes, who is a resident of Georgia. Keeping a recorded list of birds and the numbers seen on a trip or over a period of time serves a purpose—it provides records that can be submitted to *The Oriole*, the official journal of the Georgia Ornithological Society, to track bird migrations, nesting activities or unusual sightings. Nearly all birders list the species they have seen during excursions or at home. It is up to you to decide what kind of list—systematic or casual—you will keep, and you may choose not to make lists at all. However, lists may prove rewarding in unexpected ways. For example, after you visit a new area, your list becomes a souvenir of your experiences there. By reviewing the list, you can recall memories and details that you might otherwise have forgotten. Keeping regular, accurate lists of birds in your neighborhood can also be useful for local researchers. It can be interesting to compare the arrival dates and last sightings of hummingbirds and other seasonal visitors, or to note the first sighting of a new visitor to your area.

Although there are programs available for listing birds on computers, many naturalists simply keep records in field notebooks. Waterproof books and waterproof pens work well on rainy days, though many birders prefer to use a pocket recorder in the field and to transcribe their observations into a dry notebook at home. Find a notebook you like, and personalize it with field sketches, observations, poetry or whatever you wish.

BIRDING ACTIVITIES
Birding Groups

A great way to increase the pleasure of birding is to join birding groups in your area. We recommend that you join in on such activities as Christmas bird counts, birding festivals and the meetings of your local birding or natural history club. Meeting other people with the same interests can make birding even more pleasurable, and there is always something to be learned when birders of all levels gather. If you are interested in bird conservation and environmental issues, natural history groups and conscientious birding stores can keep you informed about the situation in your area and what you can do to help. Bird hotlines provide up-to-date information on the sightings of rarities, which are often easier to relocate than you might think. The following is a brief list of contacts that will help you get involved:

Organizations

American Birding Association
P.O. Box 6599
Colorado Springs, CO 80934-6599
Phone: (800) 850-2373
Website: www.americanbirding.org

National Audubon Society
700 Broadway
New York, NY 10003
Phone: (212) 979-3000
Website: www.audubon.org (lists local chapters within Georgia)

Briar Creek Bird Club
1982 Burkhalter Road
Statesboro, GA 30458

Georgia Ornithological Society
P.O. Box 181
High Shoals, GA 30645
Rare Bird Hotline: (770) 493-8862
Website: www.gos.org

Okefenokee Bird Club
326 Pineview Drive
Waycross, GA 31501

Seven Hills Birdwatchers
Rome, GA

Toccoa Bird Club
5668 Fernside Drive
Toccoa, GA 30577

Palm Warbler

Bird Conservation

Georgia abounds with bird life. There are still large areas of wilderness here, including parks, wildlife refuges and public lands. Nevertheless, agriculture, forestry and development for housing threaten viable bird habitat throughout the state. It is hoped that more people will learn to appreciate nature through birding, and that those people will do their best to protect the natural areas that remain. Many bird enthusiasts support groups such as the Georgia Ornithological Society and the Georgia Nature Conservancy, which help birds by providing sanctuaries or promoting conservation of the natural world.

Landscaping your own property to provide native plant cover and natural foods for birds is an immediate and personal way to ensure the conservation of bird habitat. The cumulative effects of such urban "nature-scaping" can be significant. If your yard is to become a bird sanctuary, you may want to keep the neighborhood cats out—cats kill an estimated one billion birds each year in the U.S., alone. Check with the local Humane Society for methods of protecting both your feline friends and wild birds. Ultimately, for protection of birds, cats are best kept indoors.

Bird Feeding

Many people set up backyard bird feeders or plant native berry- or seed-producing plants in their garden to attract birds to their yard. The kinds of food available will determine which birds visit your yard. Staff at birding stores can suggest which foods will attract specific birds. Hummingbird feeders are popular in summer to attract the Ruby-throated Hummingbird and are filled with a simple sugar solution made from one part sugar to four parts water (do not add food coloring—it is harmful to the birds).

Contrary to popular opinion, birds do not become dependent on feeders, nor do they subsequently forget to forage naturally. Winter is when birds appreciate feeders the most, but it is also difficult to find food in spring before flowers bloom, seeds develop and insects hatch. Birdbaths will also entice birds to your yard at any time of year, and heated birdbaths are particularly appreciated in the colder months. Avoid birdbaths that have exposed metal parts because wet birds can accidentally freeze to them in winter. There are many good books written about feeding birds and landscaping your yard to provide natural foods and nest sites.

Eastern Bluebird

Nest Boxes

Another popular way to attract birds is to set out nest boxes. Birds that commonly use nest boxes in the backyard include the Eastern Bluebird, Carolina Chickadee, Tufted Titmouse, sometimes the Brown-headed Nuthatch and of course, the Purple Martin. Larger nest boxes in appropriate habitats can attract kestrels, owls and cavity-nesting ducks.

Cleaning Feeders and Nest Boxes

Nest boxes and feeding stations must be kept clean to prevent birds from becoming ill or spreading disease. Old nesting material may harbor a number of parasites, as well as their eggs. Once the birds have left for the season, remove the old nesting material and wash and scrub the nest box with detergent or a 10 percent bleach solution (1 part bleach to 9 parts water). You can also scald the nest box with boiling water. Rinse it well and let it dry thoroughly before you remount it. However, some studies have shown that bluebirds prefer nest boxes that are not cleaned each year.

Feeding stations should be cleaned monthly. Feeders can become moldy and any seed, fruit or suet that is moldy or spoiled must be removed. Unclean bird feeders can also be contaminated with salmonellosis and possibly other avian diseases. Clean and disinfect feeding stations with a 10 percent bleach solution, scrubbing thoroughly. Rinse the feeder well and allow it to dry completely before refilling it. Discarded seed and feces on the ground under the feeding station should also be removed. We advise that you wear rubber gloves and a mask when cleaning nest boxes or feeders.

West Nile Virus

Since the West Nile Virus first surfaced in North America in 1999, it has caused fear and misunderstanding—some people have become afraid of contracting the disease from birds, and health departments in some communities have advised residents to eliminate feeding stations and birdbaths. To date, the disease affects 138 species of birds. Corvids (crows, jays and ravens) and raptors have been the most obvious victims because of their size, though the disease also affects some smaller species. The virus is transmitted to birds and to humans (as well as some other mammals) by mosquitoes that have bitten infected birds. Humans cannot contract the disease from casual contact with infected birds and birds do not get the disease from other birds. As well, not all mosquito species can carry the disease. According to the Centers for Disease Control and Prevention (CDC), only about 20 percent of people who are bitten and become infected will develop any symptoms at all and less than 1 percent will become severely ill.

Because mosquitoes breed in standing water, birdbaths have the potential to become mosquito breeding grounds. Birdbaths should be emptied and the water changed at least weekly. Drippers, circulating pumps, fountains or waterfalls that keep water moving may not prevent mosquitoes from laying their eggs in the water. Consider purchasing a product that contains *Bacillus thuringiensis*, which will kill the mosquito larvae within 24 hours. This bacterium will not harm birds, fish or pets. There are also other bird-friendly products available to treat water in birdbaths. You can contact your local nature store or garden center, or do some research on-line, for more information on these products.

Boat-tailed Grackle

ABOUT THE SPECIES ACCOUNTS

This book gives detailed accounts of 322 species of birds that are listed as regular by the Georgia Ornithological Society's Checklist and Bird Records Committee; these 322 species can be expected on an annual basis. Thirty occasional species and species of special note are briefly mentioned in an illustrated appendix. Georgia birders can expect to see small numbers of these occasional species every few years, brought here either because of anticipated range expansion, migration or well-documented wandering tendencies. The order of the birds and their common and scientific names follow the American Ornithologists' Union's *Check-list of North American Birds* (7th edition, July 1998 and supplements through to *The Forty-fifth Supplement 2005*).

Bobolink

As well as discussing the identifying features of a bird, each species account also attempts to bring a bird to life by describing its various character traits. Personifying a bird helps us to relate to it on a personal level. However, the characterizations presented in this book are based on the human experience and most likely fall short of truly defining the way birds perceive the world. The characterizations should not be mistaken for scientific propositions. Nonetheless, we hope that a lively, engaging text will communicate our scientific knowledge as smoothly and effectively as possible.

One of the challenges of birding is that many species look different in spring and summer than they do in fall and winter. Many birds have breeding and nonbreeding plumages, and immature birds often look different from their parents. This book does not try to describe or illustrate all the plumages of a species; instead, it focuses on the forms that are most likely to be seen in our area. So, for permanent and summer resident birds, the illustrations show the bird's colorful breeding plumages, whereas for winter and migrant birds, the illustrations often feature nonbreeding plumage.

ID: It is difficult to describe the features of a bird without being able to visualize it, so this section is best used in combination with the illustrations. Where appropriate, the description is subdivided to highlight the differences between male and female birds, breeding and nonbreeding birds and immature and adult birds. The descriptions use as few technical terms as possible and favor easily understood language. Birds may not have "jaw lines," "eyebrows" or "chins," but these, and other scientifically inaccurate terms are easily understood by all readers. Some of the most common features of birds are pointed out in the Glossary illustration (p. 369).

Size: The size measurement, the average length of the bird's body from bill to tail, is an approximate measurement of the bird as it is seen in nature. The size of larger birds is often given as a range, because there is variation among individuals. In addition, wingspan (from wing tip to wing tip) is given for all birds in the book. Please note that birds with long tails often have large length measurements that do not necessarily reflect "body" size.

Status: A general comment, such as "common," "uncommon" or "rare" is usually sufficient to describe the relative abundance of a species. Wherever possible, we have also indicated status at different times of the year. Situations are bound to vary somewhat because migratory pulses, seasonal changes and centers of activity tend to concentrate or disperse birds.

Habitat: The habitats we have listed describe where each species is most commonly found. In most cases, it is a generalized description, but if a bird is restricted to a specific habitat, the habitat is described precisely. Because of the freedom flight gives them, birds can turn up in almost any type of habitat, especially during migration. However, they will usually be found in environments that provide the specific food, water, cover, and in some cases, nesting habitat, they need to survive.

Nesting: The reproductive strategies used by different bird species vary: in each species account, nest location and structure, clutch size, incubation period and parental duties are discussed. Remember that birding ethics prohibit the disturbance of active bird nests. If you disturb a nest, you may drive off the parents during a critical period or expose defenseless young to predators. The nesting behavior of birds that do not nest in our region is not described.

Feeding: Birds spend a great deal of time foraging for food. If you know what a bird eats and where the food is found, you will have a good chance of finding the bird you are looking for. Birds are frequently encountered while they are foraging; we hope that our description of their feeding styles and diets provides valuable identifying characteristics, as well as interesting dietary facts.

Voice: You will hear many birds, particularly songbirds, which may remain hidden from view. Memorable paraphrases of distinctive sounds will aid you in identifying a species. These paraphrases only loosely resemble the call, song or sound produced by the bird. Should one of our paraphrases not work for you, feel free to make up your own—the creative exercise will reinforce your memory of the bird's vocalizations.

Similar Species: Easily confused species are discussed briefly. If you concentrate on the most relevant field marks, the subtle differences between species can be reduced to easily identifiable traits. You might find it useful to consult this section when finalizing your identification; knowing the most relevant field marks will speed up the identification process. Even experienced birders can mistake one species for another.

Brown Creeper

Best Sites: If you are looking for a particular bird, you will have more luck in some locations than in others, even within the range shown on the range map. There are many excellent sites in Georgia; unfortunately we cannot list them all. We have listed places that, besides providing a good chance of seeing a species, are easily accessible. As a result, many nature centers, state game areas and state and national parks are mentioned.

Range Maps: The range map for each species represents the overall range of the species in an average year. Most birds will confine their annual movements to this range, although each year some birds wander beyond their traditional boundaries. Areas of a range with good habitat will support a denser population than areas with poorer habitat. These maps cannot show small pockets within the range where the species may actually be absent, or how the range may change from year to year. In general, the closer you get to the edge of the mapped range, the lower the density of that species is likely to be. We have used cross-hatching to indicate areas where a species is regular but rare to casual in occurrence.

Unlike most other field guides, we have attempted to show migratory pathways—areas of the region where birds may appear while en route to nesting or winter habitat. Many of these migratory routes are "best guesses," which will no doubt be refined as new discoveries are made. The representations of the pathways do not always distinguish high-use migration corridors from areas that are seldom used.

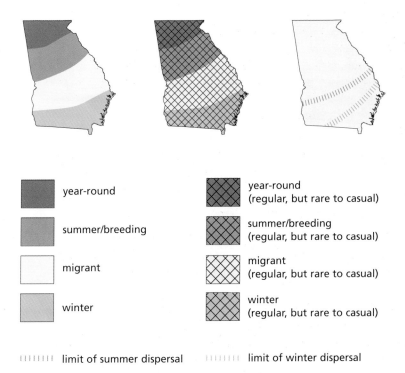

year-round

summer/breeding

migrant

winter

year-round
(regular, but rare to casual)

summer/breeding
(regular, but rare to casual)

migrant
(regular, but rare to casual)

winter
(regular, but rare to casual)

IIIIIIII limit of summer dispersal

IIIIIIII limit of winter dispersal

NONPASSERINES

Nonpasserine birds represent 17 of the 18 orders of birds found in Georgia, about 58 percent of the species in our state. They are grouped together and called "nonpasserines" because, with few exceptions, they are easily distinguished from the "passerines," or "perching birds," which make up the 18th order. Being from 17 different orders, however, means that nonpasserines vary considerably in their appearance and habits—they include everything from the 5-foot-tall Great Blue Heron to the 4-inch-long Ruby-throated Hummingbird.

Generally speaking, nonpasserines do not "sing." Instead, their vocalizations are referred to as "calls." There are also other morphological differences. For example, the muscles and tendons in the legs of passerines are adapted to grip a perch, and the toes of passerines are never webbed. Many nonpasserines are large, so they are among our most notable birds. Waterfowl, raptors, gulls, shorebirds and woodpeckers are easily identified by most people. Some of the smaller nonpasserines, such as doves, swifts and hummingbirds, are frequently thought of as passerines by novice birders and can cause those beginners some identification problems. With a little practice, however, these birds will become recognizable as nonpasserines. By learning to separate the nonpasserines from the passerines at a glance, birders effectively reduce by half the number of possible species for an unidentified bird.

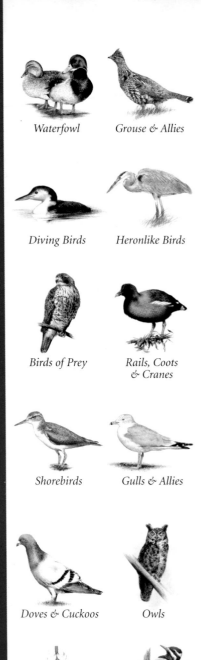

Waterfowl

Grouse & Allies

Diving Birds

Heronlike Birds

Birds of Prey

Rails, Coots
& Cranes

Shorebirds

Gulls & Allies

Doves & Cuckoos

Owls

Nightjars, Swifts
& Hummingbirds

Woodpeckers

GREATER WHITE-FRONTED GOOSE

Anser albifrons

Greater White-fronted Geese breed on the arctic tundra and winter in the southern U.S. and Mexico. They are uncommon stragglers into Georgia in winter, and they are usually seen foraging on aquatic plants along coastal mudflats, feeding on waste grain in plowed fields or eating grass shoots in pastures. • Watch for Greater White-fronted Geese among flocks of Canada Geese or Snow Geese. The slightly smaller Greater White-fronted Geese can be best distinguished by their bright orange feet, which shine like beacons as the birds stand on mudflats or fields, and by the laughing notes they utter in flight. • The Greater White-fronted Goose has an almost circumpolar arctic distribution. It is the only North American representative of the five species of gray geese found in Eurasia. Like most geese, the White-front is a long-lived bird that mates for life, with both parents caring for the young. • Albifrons is Latin for "white forehead," a key identifying characteristic of this goose.

ID: brown overall; black speckling on belly; pinkish bill; white around bill and on forehead; white hindquarters; black band on uppertail; orange feet. *Immature:* pale belly without speckles; little or no white on face.
Size: *L* 27–33 in; *W* 4½–5 ft.
Status: rare to uncommon migrant and winter visitor to the Coastal Plain from November to April; rare in the Piedmont in winter; accidental along the Coast.
Habitat: croplands, fields, open areas and shallow marshes.

Nesting: does not nest in Georgia.
Feeding: dabbles in water and gleans the ground for grass shoots, sprouting grain, waste grain and occasionally aquatic invertebrates.
Voice: high-pitched "laugh."
Similar Species: *Canada Goose* (p. 38): white "chin strap"; black neck; pale belly lacks speckling. *Greylag Goose:* domesticated or barnyard goose; somewhat larger; paler brown; lacks black belly markings. *Snow Goose* (p. 36): blue morph has white head and upper neck and all-dark breast and belly.
Best Sites: Eufaula NWR (HC: 24); Harris Neck NWR (HC: 25); Wassaw NWR; Altamaha WMA.

SNOW GOOSE

Chen caerulescens

Snow Geese grub for their food, often targeting the belowground parts of plants. Their strong, serrated bills are well designed for pulling up the rootstocks of marsh plants and gripping slippery grasses. In recent years, Snow Goose populations have increased dramatically in North America, with these geese taking advantage of human-induced changes in the landscape and in the food supply. Because of their large numbers, there is concern that they may be degrading the sensitive tundra environment that they use for nesting. • Georgia does not receive the staggering numbers of Snow Geese found in other areas, though the birds occasionally visit in fall and winter. In recent years, small numbers have begun to remain year-round. Watch farm ponds or lagoons for individuals or small flocks of these noisy geese. • Unlike Canada Geese, which fly in "V" formations, migrating Snow Geese usually form oscillating, wavy lines. • Until 1983, this species' two color morphs, a white and a blue, were considered different species. The scientific name *caerulescens* means "bluish" in Latin and was coined to describe the blue morph.

blue morph

ID: white overall; black wing tips; pink feet and bill; dark "grinning patch" on bill; plumage is occasionally stained rusty red. *Blue morph:* white head and upper neck; dark blue-gray body. *Immature:* gray or dusty white plumage; dark bill and feet.
Size: *L* 28–33 in; *W* 4½–5 ft.
Status: rare to uncommon from October to March.
Habitat: shallow wetlands, lakes and fields.

Nesting: does not nest in Georgia.
Feeding: grazes on waste grain and new sprouts; also eats aquatic vegetation, grasses, sedges and roots.
Voice: loud, nasal, constant *houk-houk* in flight.
Similar Species: *Ross's Goose* (p. 37): smaller; shorter neck; lacks black "grinning patch." *Tundra Swan* (p. 359): larger; white wing tips. *American White Pelican* (p. 79): much larger bill and body.
Best Sites: St. Simons I. (HC: 81); E.L. Huie; Eufaula NWR.

ROSS'S GOOSE

Chen rossii

This small goose looks so similar to the Snow Goose that inexperienced birders can easily get the two confused. The Ross's Goose is often overlooked, particularly when individuals are mixed within large flocks of migrating Snow, Canada or domestic geese. The Mallard-sized Ross's Goose was first reported in Georgia in 1989 at Eufaula National Wildlife Refuge, and this goose has been seen almost yearly since then. The Ross's Goose has also been seen in the Coastal Plain at Tattnall County and in the mountains at Walker County, with one goose taking up permanent residence in Madison County. The increase in recent records is indicative of the range expansion of this species, which is also evident in other southeastern states. • Most of the world population of Ross's Goose nests along the remote arctic coastline of northeastern Canada. • This bird was named after Bernard Rogan Ross, a former chief factor (manager of a trading post) for the Hudson's Bay Company and a correspondent of the Smithsonian Institute.

ID: white overall; black wing tips; dark pink feet and bill; lacks "grinning patch"; small bluish or greenish "warts" on base of bill; plumage is occasionally stained rusty by iron in water. *Blue morph* (very rare): white head; blue-gray body plumage. *Immature:* gray plumage; dark bill and feet.
Size: *L* 23 in; *W* 3¾ ft.
Status: accidental to rare (increasing) visitor to all regions except the Coast from November to May.
Habitat: *Breeding:* tundra, marshes, agricultural fields, lakes and ponds.

In migration: shallow lakes and ponds, freshwater marshes, flooded fields and other agricultural areas.
Nesting: does not nest in Georgia.
Feeding: grazes on waste grain and new sprouts; also eats aquatic vegetation, grasses, sedges and roots.
Voice: high-pitched *keek* call in flight.
Similar Species: *Snow Goose* (p. 36): larger; longer neck; dark "grinning patch" on bill. *Tundra Swan* (p. 359): much larger; white wing tips. *American White Pelican* (p. 79): much larger bill and body.
Best Sites: Eufaula NWR; shallow lakes and ponds or flooded agricultural fields.

CANADA GOOSE

Branta canadensis

Previously, thousands of Canada Geese descended on Georgia each winter, but these large flocks now overwinter farther north. Canada Geese have cut short their migration to enjoy the abundant food supply found in the corn and grainfields that now cover the Midwest. Though a few of these migratory geese regularly visit Georgia each year, there are now many more resident nonmigratory individuals and flocks. • Few people realize that at one time Canada Geese were hunted almost to extinction. Populations have since been reestablished, and in recent decades these large, bold geese have inundated urban waterfronts, picnic sites, golf courses and city parks. Today, many people even consider them pests. • Canada Goose pairs mate for life, and unlike most birds, the parents do not sever bonds with their young until the beginning of the next year's nesting, almost a year after the young are born, thus increasing the chance for survival of young birds. Fuzzy goslings seem to compel people, especially children, to get closer. Unfortunately, goose parents can harm unwelcome strangers. Hissing sounds and low, outstretched necks are signs that you should give these birds some space.

ID: long, black neck; white "chin strap"; white undertail coverts; light brown underparts; dark brown upperparts; short, black tail.
Size: *L* 21–48 in; *W* 3½–5 ft.
Status: permanent breeding resident from April to June; few migrants.
Habitat: lakeshores, riverbanks, ponds, farmlands and city parks.
Nesting: on an island or shoreline; usually on the ground but may use a heron rookery; female builds a nest of plant materials lined with down; female incubates 3–8 white eggs for 25–28 days while the male stands guard.

Feeding: grazes on new sprouts, aquatic vegetation, grass and roots; tips up for aquatic roots and tubers.
Voice: loud, familiar *ah-honk,* often answered by other Canada Geese.
Similar Species: other geese lack white "chin strap." *Greater White-fronted Goose* (p. 35): brown neck and head; orange legs; white around base of bill; dark speckling on belly. *Brant* (p. 359): white "necklace"; black upper breast. *Snow Goose* (p. 36): blue morph has white head and upper neck. *Double-crested Cormorant* (p. 81): lacks white "chin strap" and undertail coverts; crooked neck in flight.
Best Sites: E.L. Huie; Lake Lanier; other ponds and lakes.

WOOD DUCK

Aix sponsa

The male Wood Duck is one of the most colorful waterbirds in North America, and books, magazines, postcards and calendars routinely celebrate its beauty. • Wood Ducks are truly birds of the forest and will nest in trees that are a mile or more from the nearest body of water. Forced into the adventures of life at an early age, newly hatched ducklings often jump 20 feet or more out of their nest cavity in a tree to follow their mother to the nearest body of water. The little bundles of down are not exactly feather light, but they bounce fairly well and seldom sustain injury. • Landowners with a tree-lined small pond or other suitable wetland may attract a family of Wood Ducks by building a nest box with a predator guard and lining it with sawdust. The nest box should be erected close to the wetland shoreline at a reasonable height, usually at least 5 feet above the ground or water, but too many nests in an area can be detrimental. • The scientific name *sponsa* is Latin for "promised bride," suggesting that the male appears formally dressed for a wedding. • The Wood Duck accounts for nearly 50 percent of ducks hunted in Georgia.

ID: *Male*: glossy, green head with some white streaks; crest is slicked back from crown; white "chin" and throat; white-spotted, purplish chestnut breast; black and white shoulder slash; golden sides; dark back and hindquarters. *Female:* white, teardrop-shaped eye patch; mottled brown breast is streaked with white; gray-brown upperparts; white belly.

Size: *L* 15–20 in; *W* 30 in.

Status: common permanent breeding resident, except uncommon in the Mountains; common winter resident south of the Fall Line.

Habitat: swamps, ponds, marshes and lakeshores with wooded edges.

Nesting: in a hollow or tree cavity; may be as high as 30 ft; also in an artificial nest box; usually near water; cavity is lined with down; female incubates 9–14 white to buff eggs for 25–35 days.

Feeding: gleans the water's surface and tips up for aquatic vegetation, especially duckweed, aquatic sedges and grasses; eats more fruits and nuts than other ducks.

Voice: *Male:* ascending *ter-wee-wee*. *Female:* squeaky *woo-e-e-k*.

Similar Species: *Hooded Merganser* (p. 60): slim, black bill; black and white breast; male has black head with white crest patch.

Best Sites: almost any large pond; also on rivers; Rum Creek WMA; Big Hammock WMA.

GADWALL

Anas strepera

Male Gadwalls lack the striking plumage of most other male ducks, but they nevertheless have a dignified appearance and a subtle beauty. Once you learn their field marks—a black rump and white wing patches—Gadwalls are surprisingly easy to identify. • Ducks in the genus *Anas*, the dabbling ducks, are most often observed tipping up their hindquarters and submerging their heads to feed, but Gadwalls dive more often than others of this group. These ducks feed equally during the day and night, a strategy that reduces the risk of predation because the birds avoid spending long periods of time sleeping or feeding. • Gadwall numbers have greatly increased in Georgia in recent years, and this duck has expanded its range throughout North America. The majority of Gadwalls winter on the Gulf Coast of the United States and Mexico, although increasing numbers overwinter on inland lakes across the country. • In Georgia, Gadwalls are generally common winter residents, with accidental summer reports in recent years in the Piedmont and the coast.

ID: white speculum; white belly. *Male:* mostly gray; black hindquarters; dark bill. *Female:* mottled brown; brown bill with orange sides.
Size: *L* 18–22 in; *W* 33 in.
Status: uncommon to common winter resident from September to May; accidental statewide in summer.
Habitat: shallow wetlands, lake borders and beaver ponds.
Nesting: does not nest in Georgia.
Feeding: dabbles and tips up for aquatic plants; also eats aquatic invertebrates, tadpoles and small fish; grazes on grass and waste grain during migration; one of the few dabblers to dive routinely for food.

Voice: *Male:* simple, singular quack; often whistles harshly. *Female:* high *kaak kaaak kak-kak-kak*, in series and oscillating in volume.
Similar Species: *American Wigeon* (p. 41): green speculum; male has white forehead and green swipe trailing from each eye; female lacks black hindquarters. *Mallard* (p. 43), *Northern Pintail* (p. 47) and *other dabbling ducks* (pp. 40–48): generally lack white speculum, black hindquarters of male Gadwall, and orange-sided bill of female.
Best Sites: Lake Seminole WMA (HC: 3000+); E.L. Huie; Altamaha WMA; Rum Creek WMA.

AMERICAN WIGEON

Anas americana

The male American Wigeon's characteristic, piping, three-syllabled whistle sets it apart from the wetland orchestra of buzzes, quacks and ticks. Listen carefully to the female and you'll realize where toy makers got the sound for rubber duckies. • Although this bird frequently dabbles for food, nothing seems to please a wigeon more than the succulent stems and leaves of pond-bottom plants. These plants grow far too deep for a dabbling duck, so wigeons often pirate from accomplished divers, such as American Coots, Canvasbacks, Redheads and scaups. In contrast to other ducks, the American Wigeon is a good walker and is commonly observed grazing on shore. • The American Wigeon nests farther north than any other dabbling duck, with the exception of the Northern Pintail. Pair bonds are strong and last well into incubation. • Because of the male's bright white crown and forehead, some people call this bird "Baldpate."

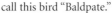

ID: large, white upper-wing patch; cinnamon breast and sides; white belly; black-tipped, blue-gray bill; green speculum; white "wing pits." *Male:* white fore-head; green swipe extends back from eye. *Female:* grayish head; brown underparts.
Size: *L* 18–22½ in; *W* 32 in.
Status: uncommon to common winter resident on the Coast and uncommon winter resident elsewhere from September to May; accidental in summer in the Piedmont and the upper Coastal Plain.
Habitat: shallow wetlands, lake edges and ponds.
Nesting: does not nest in Georgia.

Feeding: dabbles and tips up for the leaves and stems of pondweeds and other aquatic plants; also grazes and uproots young shoots in fields; may eat some invertebrates; occasionally pirates food from other birds.
Voice: *Male:* nasal, frequently repeated whistle: *whee WHEE wheew. Female:* soft, seldom-heard quack.
Similar Species: *Gadwall* (p. 40): white speculum; lacks large, white wing patch; male lacks green eye swipe; female has orange swipes on bill. *Eurasian Wigeon:* gray "wing pits"; male has rufous head, cream forehead and rosy breast; lacks green eye swipe; female usually has browner head.
Best Sites: Lake Seminole WMA (HC: 3000+); Savannah NWR; Eufaula NWR; Harris Neck NWR.

AMERICAN BLACK DUCK

Anas rubripes

During the cool winter months, the American Black Duck can be seen paddling through the waters of northern Georgia. Come spring, this duck takes off for breeding grounds in the northeastern United States and Canada. • In recent years, the eastern expansion of the Mallard has come at the expense of this species. A male Mallard will aggressively pursue a female American Black Duck, and if she can't find a male of her own kind, she will often accept the offer. Hybrid offspring are less fertile and are usually unable to reproduce. To the abundant Mallard, it is not a loss, but to the declining American Black Duck population, it is a further setback. • This dark, dabbling duck usually feeds in the shallows, where it probes the mud and searches below the water's surface for aquatic plants and insects, often with only its rump remaining above the surface. • Male and female American Black Ducks are remarkably similar in appearance, which is unusual for waterfowl.

ID: dark brownish black body; light brown head and neck; bright orange feet; violet speculum. *Male:* yellow olive bill. *Female:* dull green bill mottled with gray or black. *In flight:* whitish underwings; dark body.
Size: *L* 20–24 in; *W* 35 in.
Status: uncommon migrant and winter resident from September to April; declining numbers in recent years.
Habitat: lakes, wetlands, rivers and agricultural areas.
Nesting: does not nest in Georgia.

Feeding: tips up and dabbles in shallows for the seeds and roots of pondweeds; also eats aquatic invertebrates, larval amphibians and fish eggs.
Voice: *Male:* a croak. *Female:* a loud quack.
Similar Species: *Mottled Duck* (p. 44): paler warm brown; body feathers have buffy edge with internal buffy markings. *Mallard* (p. 43): white belly; blue speculum bordered with white; female is lighter overall and has white outer tail feathers. *Gadwall* (p. 40): black hindquarters; white speculum.
Best Sites: Savannah NWR (HC: 8000); J. Strom Thurmond Reservoir (HC: 1700+); Harris Neck NWR; Blanton Creek WMA; E.L. Huie.

MALLARD
Anas platyrhynchos

The male Mallard, with his iridescent, green head and chestnut brown breast, is the classic wild duck. Mallards can be seen almost any day of the year, often in flocks and always near open water. These confident ducks have even been known to take up residence in local swimming pools. • Wild Mallards will freely hybridize with domestic ducks, which were originally derived from Mallards in Europe. The resulting offspring, often seen in city parks, are a confusing blend of both parents. • Male ducks molt after breeding, losing much of their extravagant plumage. This "eclipse" plumage camouflages them during their flightless period and they usually molt again into their breeding colors by early fall. • The body heat generated by a brooding hen is enough to increase the growth rate of nearby grasses, which she will then manipulate to further conceal her precious nest. • The wild Mallard is an uncommon to common winter resident over the entire state, but introduced or feral populations are breeding in many local areas throughout Georgia.

ID: dark blue speculum bordered by white; orange feet. *Male:* glossy, green head; yellow bill; chestnut brown breast; white "necklace"; gray body plumage; black tail feathers curl upward. *Female:* mottled brown overall; orange bill is spattered with black.
Size: *L* 20–27½ in; *W* 35 in.
Status: uncommon to common winter resident; introduced birds are local permanent residents.
Habitat: lakes, wetlands, rivers, city parks, agricultural areas and sewage lagoons.
Nesting: in tall vegetation or under a bush, often near water; nest of grass and other plant material is lined with down; female incubates 7–10 light green to white eggs for 26–30 days.
Feeding: tips up and dabbles in shallows for the seeds of sedges, willows and pondweeds; also eats insects, aquatic invertebrates, larval amphibians and fish eggs.
Voice: *Male:* deep, quiet quacks. *Female:* loud quacks; very vocal.
Similar Species: *Northern Shoveler* (p. 46): much larger bill; male has white breast. *American Black Duck* (p. 42): darker than female Mallard; purple speculum lacks white border. *Common Merganser* (p. 360): blood red bill and white underparts; male lacks chestnut breast.
Best Sites: statewide; E.L. Huie; Lake Lanier.

MOTTLED DUCK

Anas fulvigula

This bird's striking resemblance to a female Mallard has led some experts to argue that it is only a race of Mallard rather than a separate species in its own right. Only birdwatchers that live in South Carolina, Georgia or along the Gulf Coast need to be concerned with distinguishing this look-alike bird from its close relatives the Mallard and the American Black Duck. The key to identification is to watch for the blue speculum bordered by black—a feature that can sometimes be seen when the bird is at rest or in flight. • The Mottled Duck is primarily nonmigratory. The warm, productive waters of the Gulf Coast provide all the nutrients and structure it needs to survive and successfully raise young. • Recent introductions of the Mottled Duck into coastal South Carolina have resulted in increased numbers of this bird in Georgia.

ID: back feathers have wide, pale brown edges and buffy internal markings; blue speculum bordered by black; lacks white on tail; small black mark on bill at base, without larger black mark in the center.

Size: *L* 20–22 in; *W* 30 in.

Status: uncommon permanent breeding resident; numbers increasing in recent years.

Habitat: marshes; also found in flooded rice fields and wet prairies.

Nesting: shallow bowl of grasses, rushes, reeds or aquatic vegetation concealed by surrounding vegetation on dry ground usually close to water; female incubates 8–12 whitish to buffy olive eggs for 24–28 days.

Feeding: dabbles just below the water's surface or tips up for aquatic vegetation and invertebrates.

Voice: loud *quack* similar to the Mallard's.

Similar Species: *Female Mallard* (p. 43): is paler; has black mark in center of bill; white on tail; blue speculum bordered by white. *American Black Duck* (p. 42): all-dark back feathers with very thin, brown edges; purple speculum.

Best Sites: Altamaha WMA (HC: 100); Savannah NWR; Harris Neck NWR.

BLUE-WINGED TEAL

Anas discors

The small, speedy Blue-winged Teal is renowned for its aviation skills. This teal can be identified in flight by its small size and by the sharp twists and turns that it executes with precision. • Despite the similarity of their names, the Green-winged Teal is not the Blue-winged Teal's closest relative. The Blue-winged Teal is more closely related to the Northern Shoveler and the Cinnamon Teal (*A. cyanoptera*). These birds all have broad, flat bills, pale blue forewings and green speculums. Female Cinnamon Teals and female Blue-winged Teals are so similar in appearance that even expert birders have difficulty distinguishing them in the field. • Blue-winged Teals migrate farther than most ducks, summering as far north as the Canadian tundra and wintering mainly in Central and South America. • The scientific name *discors* is Latin for "without harmony," which might refer to this bird's call as it takes flight, or to its contrasting plumage. • This teal is a common winter and fall migrant in Georgia, with a half-dozen breeding records for the Coastal Plain in Atkinson, Lee and Richmond counties in recent years.

ID: *Male:* blue-gray head; white crescent on face; darker bill than female; black-spotted breast and sides. *Female:* mottled brown overall; white throat. *In flight:* blue forewing patch; green speculum.
Size: *L* 14–16 in; *W* 23 in.
Status: common migrant from March to June and from August to October; uncommon in winter south of the Fall Line; rare in winter in the Piedmont.
Habitat: shallow lake edges and wetlands; prefers areas of short but dense emergent vegetation.
Nesting: in grass along shorelines and in meadows; nests built with grass and

considerable amounts of down; female incubates 8–13 white eggs (may be tinged with olive) for 23–27 days.
Feeding: gleans the water's surface for sedge and grass seeds, pondweeds, duck-weeds and aquatic invertebrates.
Voice: *Male:* soft *keck-keck-keck*. *Female:* soft quacks.
Similar Species: *Cinnamon Teal* (p. 360): female is virtually identical to female Blue-winged Teal, but brown is richer and eye line is less distinct. *Green-winged Teal* (p. 48): female has smaller bill, black and green speculum and lacks blue forewing patch. *Northern Shoveler* (p. 46): much larger bill with paler base; male has green head and lacks spotting on body.
Best Sites: any pond or lake during migration; Altamaha WMA; Eufaula NWR.

NORTHERN SHOVELER

Anas clypeata

At first glance, the male Northern Shoveler looks like a male Mallard with an extremely long, spoonlike bill. A closer look, however, will reveal other differences—the Northern Shoveler has a white breast and chestnut flanks, whereas the Mallard has white flanks and a chestnut breast. • The extra large, spoon-like bill allows this handsome duck to strain small invertebrates from the water and from the bottoms of ponds. This duck eats much smaller organisms than do most other waterfowl, and its intestines are elongated to prolong the digestion of hard-bodied invertebrates. The Northern Shoveler's specialized feeding strategy means that it is rarely seen tipping up; it is more likely to be found in the shallows of ponds and marshes where the mucky bottom is easiest to access. • The scientific name *clypeata*, Latin for "furnished with a shield," possibly refers to the chestnut patches on the flanks of the male. This species was once placed in its own genus, *Spatula*, the meaning of which needs no explanation.

ID: large, spatulate bill; blue forewing patch; green speculum. *Male:* green head; yellow eyes; white breast; chestnut brown flanks. *Female:* mottled brown overall; orange-tinged bill.

Size: *L* 18–20 in; *W* 30 in.

Status: uncommon migrant from August to June; in winter, rare north of the Fall Line, but more common south of the Fall Line.

Habitat: shallow marshes, bogs and lakes with muddy bottoms and emergent vegetation, usually in open and semi-open areas.

Nesting: does not nest in Georgia.

Feeding: dabbles in shallow and often muddy water; strains out plant and animal matter, especially aquatic crustaceans, insect larvae and seeds; rarely tips up.

Voice: generally quiet; occasionally a raspy chuckle or quack, most often heard during spring courtship.

Similar Species: *Mallard* (p. 43): blue speculum bordered by white; lacks pale blue forewing patch; male has chestnut brown breast and white flanks. *Blue-winged Teal* (p. 45): much smaller bill; smaller overall; male has spotted breast and sides.

Best Sites: Savannah NWR (HC: 500); Altamaha WMA (HC: 300+); E.L. Huie.

NORTHERN PINTAIL

Anas acuta

The trademark of the elegant Northern Pintail is the drake's long, tapering tail feathers, which make up one quarter of his body length. The elongated tail feathers are easily seen in flight and point skyward when he dabbles. Long-tailed Ducks are the only other ducks with a similar tail, but they also have a much shorter neck and are rarely found in Georgia. • Northern Pintails were once one of the most numerous ducks in North America, but populations have declined steadily in recent decades. Though drought, wetland drainage and loss of grassland habitat are serious threats for many waterfowl species, the Northern Pintail population has suffered more than most. These ducks are especially susceptible to lead poisoning, often mistaking the lead shot left behind by hunters for the hard seeds that they regularly eat. A single ingested pellet contains enough lead to poison a bird. • These ducks use shallow wetlands, intertidal habitats and estuaries throughout our region, but rarely stay in one place for long. Check for visiting Northern Pintails at E.L. Huie (Clayton County) or Lake Horton (Fayette County), and Merry Brothers Brickyard Ponds in Richmond County.

ID: long, slender neck; dark, glossy bill. *Male:* chocolate brown head; long, tapering tail feathers; white of breast extends up sides of neck; dusty gray body plumage; black and white hindquarters. *Female:* mottled light brown overall. *In flight:* slender body; brownish speculum with white trailing edge.

Size: *L* 21–25 in; *W* 34 in.

Status: uncommon migrant and winter resident from September to May.

Habitat: coastal areas, shallow wetlands, fields and lake edges.

Nesting: does not nest in Georgia.

Feeding: tips up and dabbles in shallows for the seeds of sedges, willows and pondweeds; also eats aquatic invertebrates and larval amphibians; eats waste grain in agricultural areas during migration; diet is more varied than that of other dabbling ducks.

Voice: generally silent in Georgia. *Male:* soft, whistling call. *Female:* rough quack.

Similar Species: male is distinctive. *Mallard* (p. 43) and *Gadwall* (p. 40): females are chunkier, usually have dark or 2-tone bills and lack tapering tail and long, slender neck. *Blue-winged Teal* (p. 45): green speculum; blue forewing patch; female is smaller. *Long-tailed Duck* (p. 57): head is not uniformly dark; all-dark wings.

Best Sites: above-mentioned sites; Savannah NWR (HC: 5000); Altamaha WMA (HC: 500); Eufaula NWR.

GREEN-WINGED TEAL

Anas crecca

One of the speediest and most maneuverable of waterfowl, the Green-winged Teal, with its red head, green "mask" and amazing flying speed, might bring to mind a comic book superhero. • When intruders cause these small ducks to rocket up from the wetland's surface, the birds circle quickly overhead in small, tight-flying flocks, returning to the water only when the threat has departed. A predator's only chance of catching a healthy teal is to snatch it from the water or from a nest. • Green-winged Teals often undertake a partial migration before molting into their postbreeding, "eclipse" plumage. In this plumage they can't fly because they do not possess a full set of flight feathers. • The name "teal" possibly originated from the medieval English word *tele* or the old Dutch word *teling*, both of which mean "small," and which originally referred to the Green-winged Teal's Eurasian counterpart.

ID: small bill; green and black speculum. *Male:* chestnut brown head; green swipe extends back from eye; white shoulder slash; creamy breast is spotted with black; pale gray sides. *Female:* mottled brown overall; light belly.
Size: *L* 12–16 in; *W* 23 in.
Status: uncommon to common migrant from September to April; common winter resident along the Coast; less common in the Coastal Plain, but rare north of the Fall Line.

Habitat: shallow lakes, wetlands, beaver ponds and meandering rivers.
Nesting: does not nest in Georgia.
Feeding: dabbles in shallows, particularly on mudflats, for aquatic invertebrates, larval amphibians, marsh plant seeds and pondweeds.
Voice: *Male:* crisp whistle. *Female:* soft quack.
Similar Species: *American Wigeon* (p. 41): male lacks white shoulder slash and chestnut brown head. *Blue-winged Teal* (p. 45) and *Cinnamon Teal* (p. 360): female has blue forewing patch.
Best Sites: Macon Brickyard Ponds (HC: 700); Onslow I. (HC: 400); E.L. Huie.

CANVASBACK

Aythya valisineria

Most male ducks sport richly decorated backs, but the male Canvasback has a bright, clean back that, appropriate to its name, appears to be wrapped in white canvas. In profile, the Canvasback casts a noble image—the long bill meets the forecrown with no apparent break in angle, allowing birds of either sex to be distinguished at long range. This bird's back and unique profile are unmistakable field marks. • Canvasbacks are diving ducks that are typically found on large areas of open water. Because these birds prefer large lakes and bays and the deepest areas of wetlands, birders often need binoculars to admire the male's wild red eyes and mahogany head. Canvasbacks may be found throughout Georgia, but these birds are quite rare. Some birds converge on wetlands in the Lake Seminole Wildlife Management Area. • The scientific name *valisineria* refers to one of the Canvasback's favorite foods, wild celery (*Vallisneria americana*).

ID: head slopes upward from bill to forehead. *Male:* canvas white back and sides; chestnut brown head; black breast and hindquarters; red eyes. *Female:* profile is similar to male's; duller brown head and neck; gray back and sides. **Size:** *L* 19–22 in; *W* 29 in.
Status: rare to uncommon migrant and local winter resident in the interior from October to May; uncommon winter resident on the Coast from November to February; most winter residents are found at Lake Seminole WMA.

Habitat: marshes, ponds, shallow lakes and other wetlands.
Nesting: does not nest in Georgia.
Feeding: dives to depths of up to 30 ft (average is 10–15 ft); feeds on roots, tubers, the basal stems of plants, including pondweeds and wild celery, and bulrush seeds; occasionally eats aquatic invertebrates.
Voice: generally quiet in Georgia.
Similar Species: *Redhead* (p. 50): rounded rather than sloped forehead; male has gray back and bluish bill.
Best Sites: Lake Seminole WMA (HC: 6000+); Savannah NWR (HC: 500+); Piedmont NWR; Phinizy Swamp Nature Park.

REDHEAD

Aythya americana

Redheads arrive in Georgia in October but are difficult ducks to find. Small flocks are most commonly seen along the coast, surfing just offshore with scaups or scoters. • To distinguish a Redhead from the similar-looking and equally rare Canvasback, most birders will tell you to contrast the birds' profiles, but the most obvious difference between them is the color of their backs—the Canvasback has a white back, while the Redhead's is gray. • On their prairie nesting grounds, female Redheads usually incubate their own eggs and brood their young as other ducks do, but where they are found along with Blue-winged Teals and Red-necked Ducks, they also may lay their eggs in the nests of these other ducks. This behavior is called "egg dumping." • The Redhead is a diving duck, but it will occasionally feed on the surface of a wetland like a dabbler. Seagrass and shoal grass form a large part of its winter diet.

ID: black-tipped, blue-gray bill. *Male:* rounded, red head; black breast and hindquarters; gray back and sides. *Female:* dark brown overall; lighter "chin" and "cheek" patches.

Size: *L* 18–22 in; *W* 29 in.

Status: uncommon migrant and rare to uncommon winter resident from October to May.

Habitat: coastal areas; inland on large wetlands, ponds, lakes, bays and rivers.

Nesting: does not nest in Georgia.

Feeding: dives to depths of 10 ft; eats primarily aquatic vegetation, especially pondweeds, duckweeds and the leaves and stems of plants; occasionally eats aquatic invertebrates.

Voice: generally quiet in Georgia.

Similar Species: *Canvasback* (p. 49): clean white back; bill slopes onto forehead. *Ring-necked Duck* (p. 51): female has a more prominent white eye ring, white ring on bill and peaked head. *Lesser Scaup* (p. 53) and *Greater Scaup* (p. 52): male has dark head and whiter sides; female has more white at base of bill.

Best Sites: Blackbeard NWR (HC: 200); Lake Walter F. George (HC: 150+); Jekyll I.; Lake Blackshear; West Point L.; E.L. Huie.

RING-NECKED DUCK

Aythya collaris

The Ring-necked Duck is common in migration and winter over most of Georgia, with higher numbers associated with cypress swamps in the coast and Coastal Plain. Its distinctive white bill markings and angular head are field marks that immediately strike an observer. After seeing the Ring-necked Duck in the wild, you may wonder why it was not named the "Ring-billed Duck," and you would not be the first birder to ponder this perplexing puzzle. The official appellation is derived from the scientific name *collaris* (collar), which originated with an ornithologist looking at an indistinct cinnamon "collar" on a museum specimen, not a birder looking at a live duck through binoculars. • Ring-necked Ducks are diving ducks, like scaups, Redheads and Canvasbacks, but they prefer to feed in shallower shoreline waters, frequently tipping up for food like a dabbler. They ride high on the water and tend to carry their tails clear of the water's surface. Ring-necks are generalized feeders, which allows them to capitalize on the low resources found in the subarctic and boreal settings where they commonly nest. They can even nest in boggy areas where a pickier eater would find it hard to eke out a living.

ID: *Male:* angular, dark purple head; black breast, back and hindquarters; white shoulder slash; gray sides; blue-gray bill with black and white bands at tip; thin, white border around base of bill. *Female:* dark brown overall; white eye ring; dark bill with black and white bands at tip; pale crescent on front of face.

Size: *L* 14–18 in; *W* 25 in.

Status: common migrant and winter resident; two recent breeding records near Augusta.

Habitat: wooded ponds, swamps, marshes and sloughs with emergent vegetation; small lakes.

Nesting: on a floating island or hummock; rarely on a shoreline; frequently over water; bulky nest of grass and moss is lined with down; female incubates 8–10 olive tan eggs for 25–29 days.

Feeding: dives under water for aquatic vegetation, including seeds, tubers and pondweed leaves; also eats aquatic invertebrates and mollusks.

Voice: seldom heard in Georgia. *Male:* low-pitched, hissing whistle. *Female:* growling *churr.*

Similar Species: *Lesser Scaup* (p. 53): lacks white ring near tip of bill; male lacks white shoulder slash and black back; female has broad, clearly defined white border around base of bill. *Greater Scaup* (p. 52): lacks white ring near tip of bill; male has greenish black head and white sides; female has broad, clearly defined white border around base of bill. *Redhead* (p. 50): rounded rather than peaked head; less white on front of face; female has a less prominent eye ring.

Best Sites: Lake Seminole WMA (HC: 19,000+); Piedmont NWR (HC: 3000+); cypress swamps in the south.

GREATER SCAUP

Aythya marila

In winter, Greater Scaups are uncommon along Georgia's coastlines, where they are often seen in the company of, and easily confused with, Lesser Scaups. In flight, watch for the Greater Scaup's longer, white wing stripe that extends into the primary feathers. Also, the Greater Scaup's rounder head is green, whereas the Lesser Scaup's peaked head has a lavender iridescence. The color of each duck's head corresponds with the first letter of its name, a feature that may help you remember which scaup is which. However, light conditions in the field, combined with the scaup's habit of rafting far out in the water, often make specific identification nearly impossible. • Scaups are diving ducks, and thus have a heavier bone structure than dabbling ducks and also require a longer running start across the surface of the water to take off.

ID: rounded head; golden eyes. *Male:* dark, iridescent green head (may appear black); black breast; white belly, sides and flanks; light gray back; dark hindquarters; black-tipped, blue bill. *Female:* brown overall; well-defined white patch at base of bill and often secondary white patch in "cheek." *In flight:* white flash through wing extends well into primary feathers.
Size: *L* 16–19 in; *W* 28 in.
Status: rare to uncommon migrant and winter resident along the Coast from November to April; rare inland in winter.
Habitat: prefers coastal areas. *In migration:* inland on lakes, large marshes and reservoirs; usually far from shore.

Nesting: does not nest in Georgia.
Feeding: dives under water, to greater depths than other *Aythya* ducks, for aquatic invertebrates and vegetation; favors freshwater mollusks in winter.
Voice: generally quiet in Georgia; alarm call is a deep *scaup*. *Male:* may issue a 3-note whistle and a soft *wah-hooo. Female:* may give a subtle "growl."
Similar Species: *Lesser Scaup* (p. 53): slightly smaller; shorter white wing-flash in flight; slightly smaller bill; male has peaked, purplish black head; female has peaked head. *Ring-necked Duck* (p. 51): black back; white shoulder slash; white ring around base of bill. *Redhead* (p. 50): female has less white at base of bill; male has red head and darker sides.
Best Sites: Jekyll I. and other barrier islands; inland at E.L. Huie.

LESSER SCAUP

Aythya affinis

Large groups of Lesser Scaups may gather along the coast and near offshore in winter, especially near Jekyll Island. In fact, flotillas of migrating Lesser Scaups can number over 25,000 individuals off the coast of Georgia. But if you don't live near the coast, don't despair—these birds may also appear inland. • A member of the *Aythya* genus of diving ducks, the Lesser Scaup leaps up neatly before diving under water, where it propels itself with powerful strokes of its feet. • The scientific name *affinis* is Latin for "adjacent" or "allied"—a reference to this scaup's close association to other diving ducks. "Scaup" might refer to a preferred winter food of this duck—shellfish beds are called "scalps" in Scotland—or, more likely, it might be a phonetic imitation of one of this bird's calls. • Both the Lesser Scaup and the Greater Scaup are known by the nickname "Bluebill."

ID: yellow eyes. *Male:* purplish black head; black breast and hindquarters; dusty white sides; grayish back; black-tipped, blue-gray bill. *Female:* dark brown overall; well-defined white patch at base of bill.
Size: *L* 15–18 in; *W* 25 in.
Status: common inland and abundant on the Coast from October to June; rare in summer with more than 24 nonbreeding records.
Habitat: coastal areas; common inland on large lakes and wetlands.
Nesting: does not nest in Georgia.

Feeding: dives under water for aquatic invertebrates, mostly mollusks, amphipods and insect larvae; occasionally eats aquatic vegetation.
Voice: generally silent in Georgia; alarm call is a deep *scaup*.
Similar Species: *Greater Scaup* (p. 52): rounded head; slightly larger bill; longer, white wing-flash; male's head is greenish black. *Ring-necked Duck* (p. 51): male has white shoulder slash and black back; female has white-ringed bill. *Redhead* (p. 50): female has less white at base of bill; male has red head and darker sides.
Best Sites: offshore of southern barrier islands, especially St. Catherines I. (HC: 25,500); inland at Piedmont NWR and Rum Creek WMA (HC: 1100+).

53

SURF SCOTER
Melanitta perspicillata

Surf Scoters are uncommon along the Georgia coast in winter, but they are more numerous offshore, occasionally surfing in large, mixed rafts along the north end of Jekyll Island. Most scoters spend their winters just beyond the breaking surf on both the Atlantic and Pacific coasts, and they are well adapted to life on rough water. When spring storms whip up whitecaps on the Atlantic, these ducks ride comfortably among the crashing waves. • The Surf Scoter is the only scoter that breeds and winters exclusively in North America. Like other far northern breeders, Surf Scoters pair up before arriving on their summer breeding grounds to take advantage of the precious little summer available to them. • The Surf Scoter has the unfortunate distinction of being one of the least-studied waterbirds in North America. Much of the information that is known of its behavior and distribution was documented for the first time only in the latter part of the 20th century. • Although these birds are only casual inland, small numbers are sometimes seen on the Chattahoochee River lakes.

1st winter

ID: large, stocky duck; large bill; sloping forehead; all-black wings. *Male:* black overall; white forehead and nape; orange bill and legs; black spot, outlined in white, at base of bill. *Female:* brown overall; dark gray bill; 2 whitish patches on sides of head.
Size: *L* 16–20 in; *W* 30 in.
Status: uncommon winter resident on the Coast, and more numerous Offshore, from October to May; rare in the Coastal Plain (October to March) and accidental in the Mountains in migration.
Habitat: coastal areas; rarely inland on large lakes or wetlands.
Nesting: does not nest in Georgia.

Feeding: dives to depths of 30 ft; eats mostly mollusks; also takes aquatic insect larvae, crustaceans and some aquatic vegetation.
Voice: generally quiet in Georgia; infrequently utters low, harsh croaks. *Male:* occasionally gives a low, clear whistle. *Female:* guttural *krraak krraak.*
Similar Species: *White-winged Scoter* (p. 55): white wing patches; male lacks white on forehead and nape. *Black Scoter* (p. 56): male is all black; female has well-defined, pale "cheek."
Best Sites: offshore of barrier islands, such as St. Simons I. (HC: 150+), Tybee I. (HC: 34) and St. Catherines I.; inland at Lake Walter F. George (HC: 8).

WHITE-WINGED SCOTER

Melanitta fusca

When White-winged Scoters race over the ocean, their flapping wings reveal a key identifying feature—the white innerwing patches strike a sharp contrast to the bird's otherwise black plumage. Scoters have small wings relative to the weight of their bodies, so they require long stretches of water for takeoff. • The White-winged Scoter is the largest and most abundant of the three species of scoters in North America, but it is the least likely to be seen in Georgia. • The White-winged Scoter often eats hard-shelled clams and shellfishes whole. It relies upon its remarkably powerful gizzard to crush shells that would require a hammer for us to open. • The name "scoter" may be derived from the way this bird scoots across the water's surface. Scooting can be a means of traveling quickly from one foraging site to another. The name "coot" has also been incorrectly applied to all three species of scoter because of their superficial resemblance to this totally unrelated species.

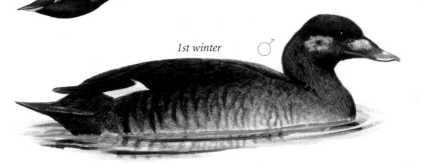

1st winter

ID: stocky body; large, bulbous bill; sloping forehead; base of bill is fully feathered. *Male:* black overall; white patch below eye. *Female:* brown overall; gray-brown bill; 2 whitish patches on sides of head. *In flight:* white wing patches.

Size: *L* 18–24 in; *W* 34 in.

Status: rare to uncommon winter resident off the Coast, and more numerous Offshore, from October to May; rare in the Piedmont and the Coastal Plain in winter; accidental in the Mountains in winter.

Habitat: coastal areas; rarely inland on large lakes or rivers.

Nesting: does not nest in Georgia.

Feeding: deep, underwater dives last up to 1 minute; eats mostly mollusks; may also take crustaceans, aquatic insects and some small fish.

Voice: generally quiet in Georgia.

Similar Species: *Surf Scoter* (p. 54): lacks white wing patches; male has white forehead and nape. *Black Scoter* (p. 56): lacks white patches on wings and around eyes. *American Coot* (p. 124): whitish bill and nasal "shield"; lacks white patches on wings and around red eyes.

Best Sites: offshore, especially Sapelo I. (HC: 100), Jekyll I. and St. Catherines I.

BLACK SCOTER
Melanitta nigra

Dark plumage and a bright yellow-orange bulge on the bill makes this sea duck easy to identify. Scoters use their sturdy bills to wrench shellfish off underwater rocks. They swallow mollusks whole and grind the shells in their muscular gizzards. • While floating on the water's surface, Black Scoters tend to hold their heads high, unlike other scoters, which generally gaze downward. The male is the only North American duck that is uniformly black. • Black Scoters are the most vocal of the scoters, and they often reveal their presence with plaintive, mellow, whistling calls from far out on open water. You may also hear a whistling sound as a group of scoters flies overhead, but in this case the sound comes from the wings, not from the syrinx (vocal cords). • Of the three Scoter species found in Georgia, the Black Scoter is the most common, even though numbers fluctuate annually.

1st winter

ID: *Male:* black overall; large yellow-orange knob on bill. *Female:* light "cheek"; dark "cap"; brown overall; dark gray bill.
Size: *L* 17–20 in; *W* 28 in.
Status: common winter resident off the Coast, but abundant Offshore, from October to May; accidental in the Coastal Plain and Piedmont in winter; accidental nonbreeder on the Coast in summer at Tybee I.
Habitat: shallow coastal waters.
Nesting: does not nest in Georgia.

Feeding: dives under water; eats mostly mollusks and aquatic insect larvae; occasionally eats aquatic vegetation and small fish.
Voice: generally quiet in Georgia; infrequently an unusual *cour-loo;* wings whistle in flight.
Similar Species: *White-winged Scoter* (p. 55): white wing patches; male has white slash below eye. *Surf Scoter* (p. 54): male has white on head; female has 2 whitish patches on sides of head.
Best Sites: offshore barrier islands, including Jekyll I. (HC: 6000), Tybee I., St. Catherines I., Sapelo I. and Cumberland I.; accidental inland at large lakes and reservoirs.

LONG-TAILED DUCK

Clangula hyemalis

This ancient mariner can survive violent winter gales and storms that send even the most high-spirited captains to harbor. It is an irregular visitor in winter, when it tends to remain in deeper coastal waters, well away from shore. So observers are usually limited to brief glimpses of this bird's winter finery and the long, slender tail feathers for which this duck is named. • The Long-tailed Duck is among the world's deepest-diving waterfowl—it makes regular dives to depths of more than 200 feet. • The breeding and nonbreeding plumages of these arctic-nesting sea ducks are like photo-negatives of each other: the winter plumage is mostly white with dark patches, whereas the spring breeding plumage is mostly dark with white highlights. • Long-tailed Ducks are among the noisiest breeders on the arctic tundra and are constantly squabbling about something. However, in winter when they are in Georgia they remain relatively silent. • Until recently, this duck was officially called "Oldsquaw," a name that many people still use.

nonbreeding

nonbreeding

ID: *Breeding male:* dark head with white "eye patch"; dark neck and upperparts; white belly; dark bill; long, dark central tail feathers. *Breeding female:* short tail feathers; gray bill; dark crown, throat patch, wings and back; white underparts. *Nonbreeding male:* pale head with dark patch; pale neck and belly; dark breast; long, white patches on back; pink bill with dark base; long, dark central tail feathers. *Nonbreeding female:* similar to breeding female, but generally lighter, especially on head.
Size: *L* 17–20 in; *W* 28 in.

Status: irregular winter visitor on the Coast from November to May; rare in the Piedmont and Coastal Plain regions; accidental in the Mountains.
Habitat: coastal waters; occasionally inland on large, deep lakes and wetlands.
Nesting: does not nest in Georgia.
Feeding: dives for mollusks, crustaceans and aquatic insects; occasionally eats roots and young shoots; may also take some small fish.
Voice: generally quiet in Georgia.
Similar Species: *Northern Pintail* (p. 47): thin, white line extends up sides of neck; gray sides.
Best Sites: offshore barrier islands, such as Sapelo I. (HC: 15), St. Catherines I. and Jekyll I.; inland at Augusta ponds (HC: 7), E.L. Huie and Columbus.

BUFFLEHEAD

Bucephala albeola

The simple, bold pattern of the Bufflehead is easy to notice bobbing among piers and wharfs in saltwater bays. Males are strikingly dressed in black and white, their most characteristic feature a great white patch on the back of the head. Females are somber but appealing, their sooty heads ornamented with a pretty, white "cheek" spot. • Tiny Buffleheads are right at home in coastal bays and estuaries amid their larger relatives. During their winter stay in Georgia, Buffleheads dive for mollusks, mostly snails. If you are lucky, you may even see a whole flock dive at the same time. • The scientific name *Bucephala*, meaning "ox-headed" in Greek, refers to the shape of this bird's head; *albeola* is Latin for "white," a reference to the male's plumage.

ID: very small, rounded duck; white speculum in flight; short, gray bill; short neck. *Male:* white wedge on back of head; head is otherwise iridescent, dark green or purple, usually appearing black; dark back; white neck and underparts. *Female:* dark brown head; white, oval ear patch; light brown sides.
Size: *L* 13–15 in; *W* 21 in.
Status: uncommon to common migrant and winter resident, more common on the Coast, from October to May.
Habitat: sheltered coastal waters; occasionally on open water of lakes, large ponds and rivers.

Nesting: does not nest in Georgia.
Feeding: dives for aquatic invertebrates; takes water boatmen and mayfly and damselfly larvae in summer; favors mollusks, particularly snails, and crustaceans in winter; also eats some small fish and pondweeds.
Voice: generally quiet in Georgia. *Male:* growling call. *Female:* harsh quack.
Similar Species: *Hooded Merganser* (p. 60): white crest is outlined in black. *Common Goldeneye* (p. 59): males are larger and have white patch between eye and bill. *Other diving ducks* (pp. 49–62): females are much larger.
Best Sites: offshore barrier islands at Wassaw I. (HC: 1800+); inland at Callaway L. (HC: 100+).

COMMON GOLDENEYE

Bucephala clangula

Around white patch contrasted against a dark head easily identifies the Common Goldeneye. Named for its bright yellow eyes, this squat duck is a rare visitor to our region in winter and is one of the more difficult ducks to locate. State parks and wetlands have become increasingly important for the Common Goldeneye, because much of its winter habitat has been altered or lost. • During the winter, Common Goldeneyes dive to catch crustaceans, fish and mollusks, but in the summer they dine mainly on aquatic invertebrates. • Courtship begins in winter, soon after the birds leave Georgia. The male's courtship display looks much like an avian slapstick routine, although to the male it is surely a serious matter. He performs a number of odd postures and vocalizations, often in front of seemingly disinterested females. In one common routine, he arches his puffy, iridescent head backward until his forehead seems to touch his back. Then he suddenly catapults his neck forward like a coiled spring, while giving a painful-sounding *peent*.

ID: steep forehead with peaked crown; black wings with large, white patches; golden eyes. *Male:* dark, iridescent green head; round, white "cheek" patch; dark bill; dark back; white sides and belly. *Female:* chocolate brown head; lighter breast and belly; gray-brown body plumage; dark bill is tipped with yellow in spring and summer.
Size: *L* 16–20 in; *W* 26 in.
Status: rare to uncommon migrant and winter resident from October to May; accidental inland in late spring.

Habitat: open water of lakes, large ponds and rivers.
Nesting: does not nest in Georgia.
Feeding: dives for crustaceans, mollusks and aquatic insect larvae; may also eat tubers, leeches, frogs and small fish.
Voice: generally silent in Georgia.
Similar Species: *Hooded Merganser* (p. 60): white crest is outlined in black. *Bufflehead* (p. 58): males are smaller and have white wedge on back of head.
Best Sites: Lake Seminole WMA (HC: 100+); West Point Dam (HC: 41); E.L. Huie.

59

HOODED MERGANSER
Lophodytes cucullatus

Extremely attractive and exceptionally shy, the Hooded Merganser is one of the most sought-after ducks from a birder's perspective. Most of the attention is directed toward the handsome male: in moments of arousal or agitation he quickly unfolds his brilliant crest, which is usually held flat, to attract a mate or to signal approaching danger. The drake displays his full range of colors and athletic abilities in elaborate, late-winter courtship displays and chases. In Georgia, the Hooded Merganser is most likely to be seen on the coast in winter, and some birds may stay to nest in the Coastal Plain and less often the Piedmont. • All mergansers have thin bills with small, toothlike serrations to help the birds keep a firm grasp on slippery prey. The smallest of the mergansers, Hoodies have a more diverse diet than their larger relatives. They supplement their usual diet of fish with crustaceans, insects and even acorns. • Unusually, female Hooded Mergansers have been known to share incubation of eggs with female Wood Ducks and goldeneyes.

ID: slim body; crested head; dark, thin, pointed bill. *Male:* black head and back; bold, white crest is outlined in black; white breast with 2 black slashes; rusty sides. *Female:* dusky brown body; shaggy, reddish brown crest. *In flight:* small, white wing patches.
Size: *L* 16–18 in; *W* 24 in.
Status: common migrant and winter resident from October to May; rare to uncommon summer breeder, primarily in the Coastal Plain but also in the Piedmont.
Habitat: forest-edged ponds, wetlands, lakes and rivers.
Nesting: usually in a tree cavity 15–40 ft above the ground; may also use nest boxes; cavity is lined with leaves, grass and down; female incubates 10–12 spherical, white eggs for 29–33 days; some females lay their

eggs in another bird's nest, including nests of other species.
Feeding: very diverse diet; dives for small fish, caddisfly and dragonfly larvae, snails, amphibians and crayfish.
Voice: generally silent in Georgia; occasionally low grunts and croaks. *Male:* froglike *crrrrooo* in courtship display. *Female:* occasionally a harsh *gak* or a croaking *croo-croo-crook*.
Similar Species: *Bufflehead* (p. 58): male lacks black crest outline and black shoulder and breast slashes. *Red-breasted Merganser* (p. 61) and *Common Merganser* (p. 360): females have much longer, orange bill and gray back. *Other diving ducks* (pp. 49–62): females lack crest.
Best Sites: Okefenokee NWR (HC-winter: 300+); Ocmulgee WMA; Piedmont NWR. *Winter:* Glynn Co. (HC: 400+); Monroe Co. lakes and ponds (HC: 300+).

RED-BREASTED MERGANSER

Mergus serrator

A glossy, slicked-back crest and wild red eyes give the Red-breasted Merganser the disheveled, wave-bashed look of an adrenalized windsurfer. This species was formerly called "Sawbill" and "Sea-Robin," and it's a good thing that bird names are now standardized—who knows what we would be calling this punk-haired bird today. • At home in salt water, Red-breasted Mergansers are common along our coast in winter. During peak migration, thousands of these birds may congregate along inshore waters to rest and refuel. • Unlike the other two merganser species, Red-breasts prefer to nest on the ground. This bird's lack of dependence on trees enables it to nest where related cavity-nesting species cannot. Shortly after their mates have begun incubating, males fly off to join large offshore rafts for the duration of summer. During this time, a brief molt makes the males largely indistinguishable from their female counterparts. • Red-breasts will sometimes fish cooperatively, funneling fishes for easier capture.

ID: large, elongated body; red eyes; thin, serrated, orange bill; shaggy, slicked-back head crest. *Male:* green head; light rusty breast spotted with black; white "collar"; gray sides; black and white shoulders. *Female:* gray-brown overall; reddish head; white "chin," foreneck and breast. *In flight:* male has large, white wing patch crossed by 2 narrow, black bars; female has 1 dark bar that separates white speculum from white upperwing patch.

Size: *L* 19–26 in; *W* 30 in.

Status: uncommon to common migrant and winter resident inland, sometimes in large flocks on large reservoirs, from October to June; common winter resident on the Coast; some nonbreeders in summer.

Habitat: coastal waters and estuaries. *In migration:* lakes and large rivers, especially those with rocky shorelines and islands.

Nesting: does not nest in Georgia.

Feeding: dives under water for small fish; also eats aquatic invertebrates, fish eggs and crustaceans.

Voice: generally silent in Georgia.

Similar Species: *Common Merganser* (p. 360): male has clean white breast and blood red bill and lacks head crest; female's rusty foreneck contrasts with white "chin" and breast.

Best Sites: on the coast at Jekyll I. (HC: 1200+) and Sapelo I. (HC: 800); inland at Lake Walter F. George (HC: 300), West Point L. (HC: 200).

RUDDY DUCK

Oxyura jamaicensis

Ruddy Ducks are the epitome of decorum when they visit Georgia each winter. They spend hours with their heads tucked into their back feathers and their tails flattened against the water. At this time of year, they keep flights to a minimum. Takeoff requires full use of a Ruddy Duck's legs and wings, so diving is a preferred option to avoid predators. • In contrast to their wintertime modesty, Ruddies are the clowns of the northern wetlands in summer. They display energetic courtship behavior with comedic enthusiasm. The small males vigorously pump their bright blue bills, almost touching their breasts. The *plap, plap, plap-plap-plap* of the display increases in speed to its hilarious climax: a spasmodic jerk and a sputter. • From mid-October until the end of April, Ruddies are relatively common along our coast, but numbers fluctuate annually and may be decreasing. These unusual ducks find walking on land extremely difficult, so chances are you will see them in the water.

breeding

nonbreeding

ID: large bill and head; short neck; long, stiff tail feathers (often held upward). *Breeding male:* white "cheek"; chestnut red body; blue bill; black tail and crown. *Female:* brown overall; dark "cheek" stripe; darker crown and back. *Nonbreeding male:* similar to female but with white "cheek."

Size: *L* 15–16 in; *W* 18½ in.

Status: uncommon to common migrant and winter resident from September to June; uncommon winter resident in rivers and fresh water along the Coast; rare nonbreeder in summer.

Habitat: sewage lagoons and lakes with open, shallow water.

Nesting: does not nest in Georgia.

Feeding: dives to the bottom of wetlands for seeds of pondweeds, sedges and bulrushes and for the leafy parts of aquatic plants; also eats a few aquatic invertebrates.

Voice: generally silent in Georgia.

Similar Species: *Cinnamon Teal* (p. 360): lacks white "cheek" and blue bill. *Other diving ducks* (pp. 49–62): females lack long, stiff tail and dark facial stripe.

Best Sites: Lake Varner (HC: 300+); Macon industrial area (HC: 300); Altamaha WMA (HC: 300); E.L. Huie.

PLAIN CHACHALACA

Ortalis vetula

The Plain Chachalaca resembles a cross between a turkey and a roadrunner. Surprisingly, this mix makes for a very agile tree inhabitant. The long, broad tail aids in balancing on precariously small branches, and the short wings will not get in the way of a Chachalaca flying through dense brush. • The Plain Chachalaca is the only member of the chickenlike Cracidae family to venture out of the tropics and into the United States. These tree-dwelling birds have expanded northward from Mexico into the riparian woodlands and scrub of southern Texas. They were introduced to Georgia's Sapelo Island in the 1920s, with a current population of about 30 to 40 birds. • These secretive birds are not common, but groups are easy to locate once they begin to call. Chachalacas are very social in nature and are especially noisy during the breeding season. To attract a mate, a lone male will begin with his low pitched call, and soon the female will chime in with her higher, screechy reply. • *Vetula* is Latin for "little old woman," and supposedly refers to the bird's constant calling. The common name is onomatopoetic and imitates the *cha-cha-laca* call.

ID: gray-brown upperparts; buffy underparts; long, scaly legs with long talons; dark gray-blue face; long, dark brown tail with white tip. *Breeding male:* red patch of skin on throat.
Size: *L* 22 in; *W* 24–28 in.
Status: uncommon permanent breeding resident on Sapelo I. (see arrow).
Habitat: riparian woodlands and woody thickets near water.
Nesting: up to 15 ft high in a tree or shrub close to water; sometimes built on top of another species old nest; nest is a loose bed of sticks, vines and twigs lined with Spanish moss; a small depression in the center holds 2–3 eggs; female incubates for 25 days.
Feeding: takes food in trees and on the ground; primarily eats berries, seeds, green vegetation and flower buds; sometimes takes insects and other invertebrates.
Voice: flocks of up to 20 birds will call together, creating a constant, rough *cha-cha-lac-a;* males have a lower tone than females; during courtship males will call first.
Similar Species: none.
Best Sites: Sapelo I. (HC: 25).

RUFFED GROUSE

Bonasa umbellus

The Ruffed Grouse is a common and widespread grouse in North America, inhabiting a wide variety of woodland habitats ranging from small deciduous woodlots and suburban riparian woodlands to vast expanses of mixedwood and boreal forest. Georgia's mountainous region falls at the southernmost tip of the Ruffed Grouse's range, so these birds just barely nest in our state. • There is no mistaking the reverberating "drumming" of a Ruffed Grouse. To proclaim his territory, the male struts along a fallen log with his tail fanned and his neck feathers ruffed, periodically beating the air with accelerating wing strokes. This nonvocal method of communication is ideal for the habitat in which this bird lives—lower frequency sounds are less attenuated by dense woodlands, and thus, travel farther. • During winter, scales grow out along the sides of this bird's feet, giving the Ruffed Grouse temporary "snowshoes." • This secretive grouse is probably more common than reported in Georgia.

♂

rufous morph

ID: small head crest; mottled, gray-brown overall; black feathers on sides of lower neck (visible when fluffed out in courtship displays); gray- or reddish-barred tail has broad, dark, subterminal band and white tip. *Female:* incomplete subterminal tail band.
Size: L 15–19 in; W 22 in.
Status: uncommon and local breeding resident in the Mountains, mostly above about 1800 ft; rare visitor to upper Piedmont.
Habitat: deciduous and mixed forests and riparian woodlands; in many areas it favors young, second-growth stands with birch and poplar.
Nesting: in a shallow depression among leaf litter; often beside boulders, under a log or at the base of a tree; female incubates 9–12 buff-colored eggs for 23–25 days.
Feeding: gleans from the ground and vegetation; omnivorous diet includes seeds, buds, flowers, berries, catkins, leaves, insects, spiders and snails; may take small frogs.
Voice: *Male:* uses his wings to produce a hollow, drumming courtship sound of accelerating, deep booms. *Female:* clucks and "hisses" around her chicks.
Similar Species: *Northern Bobwhite* (p. 66): conspicuous throat patch and broad "eyebrow"; short tail lacks dark subterminal band.
Best Sites: Rabun Bald; Brasstown Bald.

WILD TURKEY

Meleagris gallopavo

The Wild Turkey was once very common throughout most of eastern North America, but during the 20th century, habitat loss and overharvesting took a toll on this bird. Today, efforts at restoration have reestablished the Wild Turkey in the woodlands of the East and the Midwest. • Although turkeys prefer to feed on the ground and travel by foot—they can run faster than 19 miles per hour—they can fly short distances and they roost in trees at night. • This charismatic bird is the only native North American animal that has been widely domesticated. The wild ancestors of most other domestic animals came from Europe. • The Wild Turkey is a wary bird with acute senses and a highly developed social system. Early in life both male and female turkeys gobble. The females eventually outgrow this practice, leaving males to gobble competitively for the honor of mating. • If Congress had taken Benjamin Franklin's advice in 1782, our national emblem would be the Wild Turkey, instead of the majestic Bald Eagle.

ID: *Male:* naked, blue-red head; dark, glossy, iridescent body plumage; barred, copper-colored tail; largely unfeathered legs; long, central breast tassel; colorful head and body; red wattles. *Female:* smaller; blue-gray head; less iridescent body.

Size: *Male:* L 3–3½ ft; W 5½ ft. *Female:* L 3 ft; W 4 ft.

Status: uncommon to common permanent breeding resident.

Habitat: deciduous, mixed and riparian woodlands; occasionally eats waste grain and corn in late fall and winter.

Nesting: in a woodland or at a field edge; in a depression on the ground under thick cover; nest is lined with grass and leaves; female incubates 10–12 brown-speckled, pale buff eggs for up to 28 days.

Feeding: in fields near protective woods; forages on the ground for seeds, fruits, bulbs and sedges; also eats insects, especially beetles and grasshoppers; may take small amphibians.

Voice: wide array of sounds; courting male gobbles loudly; alarm call is a loud *pert*; gathering call is a cluck; contact call is a loud *keouk-keouk-keouk*.

Similar Species: all other grouse and grouselike birds are much smaller.

Best Sites: Rum Creek WMA & Piedmont NWR; Callaway Gardens (HC: 100+); across the Coastal Plain.

NORTHERN BOBWHITE

Colinus virginianus

The Northern Bobwhite is the official designated game bird of Georgia and is the only quail native to eastern North America. The male's characteristic, whistled *bob-white* call, usually issued in spring, is often the only evidence of this bird's presence among the dense, tangled vegetation of its rural, woodland home. • Throughout fall and winter, Northern Bobwhites typically travel in large family groups called "coveys," collectively seeking out sources of food and huddling together during cool nights. When they huddle, members of the covey all face outward, enabling the group to detect danger from any direction. With the arrival of summer, breeding pairs break away from their coveys to perform elaborate courtship displays in preparation for another nesting season. • Bobwhites benefit from habitat disturbance, using the early successional habitats created by fire, agriculture and forestry.

ID: mottled brown, buff and black upperparts; white crescents and spots edged in black on chestnut brown sides and upper breast; short tail. *Male:* white throat; broad, white "eyebrow." *Female:* buff throat and "eyebrow." *Immature:* smaller and duller overall; lacks black on underparts.
Size: *L* 10 in; *W* 13 in.
Status: locally uncommon to common permanent breeding resident, and more common south of the Fall Line over last 10 years; numbers have declined; rare and local in the Mountains to about 3200 ft.
Habitat: farmlands, open woodlands, woodland edges, grassy fencelines, roadside ditches and brushy, open country; on managed hunting preserves in the Coastal Plain.

Nesting: in a shallow depression on the ground, often concealed by surrounding vegetation or a woven, partial dome; nest is lined with grass and leaves; pair incubates 12–16 white to pale buff eggs for 22–24 days.
Feeding: eats seasonally available seeds, berries, leaves, roots and nuts; also takes insects and other invertebrates.
Voice: whistled *hoy* is given year-round. *Male:* a whistled, rising *bob-white* in spring and summer.
Similar Species: *Ruffed Grouse* (p. 64): lacks conspicuous throat patch and broad "eyebrow"; long, fan-shaped tail has broad, dark subterminal band; black patches on sides of neck.
Best Sites: Callaway Gardens (HC: 291); across the Coastal Plain.

RED-THROATED LOON

Gavia stellata

The Red-throated Loon typically swims low in the water with its bill held high. Our smallest loon, the Red-throat can leap up from the water directly into flight, stand upright on land and even take off from land. No other loon has these abilities—other loons require 330 feet or more of runway on open water to gain flight. • Native Americans have long considered Red-throated Loons to be reliable meteorologists—these birds often become very noisy before the onset of foul weather, possibly sensing changes in barometric pressure. • Red-throated Loons breed in the Arctic and winter along the Atlantic and Pacific coasts. Look for them along the northern coast near Tybee Island in winter, or inland, on the lakes of western Georgia, during migration. • The scientific name *stellata* refers to the starlike, white speckles on this bird's back in its nonbreeding plumage.

nonbreeding

nonbreeding

ID: slim bill is held upward. *Breeding:* red throat; gray face and neck; black and white stripes from nape to back of head; plain, brownish back. *Nonbreeding:* white-speckled back; white face; dark gray on crown and back of head. *In flight:* hunched back; legs trail behind tail; rapid wingbeats.
Size: *L* 23–27 in; *W* 3½ ft.
Status: erratic visitor along the Coast and Offshore from October to May; rare in the Piedmont and accidental in the Coastal Plain from October to May.

Habitat: coastal waters; occasionally estuaries. *In migration:* large freshwater lakes.
Nesting: does not nest in Georgia.
Feeding: dives deeply and captures small fish; occasionally eats aquatic insects and amphibians; may eat aquatic vegetation in early spring.
Voice: Mallard-like *kwuk-kwuk-kwuk-kwuk* in flight; distraction call is a loud *gayorwork*.
Similar Species: *Common Loon* (p. 68): larger; heavier bill; lacks white speckling on back in nonbreeding plumage.
Best Sites: off Tybee I. (HC: 200+) and other barrier islands; West Point L.; Lake Walter F. George; other large inland reservoirs.

67

COMMON LOON

Gavia immer

The quavering wail of the Common Loon is an uncommon sound on Georgia's large lakes, but seeking out this beautiful bird and hearing its haunting call is well worth the effort. Loons float very low on the water, disappearing behind swells, then reappearing like ethereal guardians of the lakes. • Common Loons are well adapted to their aquatic lifestyle. These divers have nearly solid bones that make them less buoyant (most birds have hollow bones), and their feet are placed far back on their bodies for underwater propulsion. Small bass, perch, sunfish, pike and white-fish are all fair game for these excellent underwater hunters. On land, however, their rear-placed legs make walking seem difficult, and their heavy bodies and small wing size means they require a lengthy sprint over water before taking off. It is thought that "loon" is derived from the Scandinavian word *lom*, meaning "clumsy person," in reference to this bird's clumsiness on land.

nonbreeding

nonbreeding

ID: *Breeding:* green-black head; stout, thick, black bill; white "necklace"; white breast and underparts; black and white "checkerboard" upperparts; red eyes. *Nonbreeding:* much duller plumage; sandy brown back; light underparts. *In flight:* long wings beat constantly; hunchbacked appearance; legs trail behind tail.

Size: *L* 28–35 in; *W* 4–5 ft.

Status: common winter resident on the Coast and Offshore from September to May; uncommon inland at large reservoirs from September to May; very rare nonbreeder in all regions in summer.

Habitat: open ocean; lakes with open water.

Nesting: does not nest in Georgia.

Feeding: pursues small fish under water to depths of 180 ft; occasionally eats large, aquatic invertebrates and larval and adult amphibians.

Voice: alarm call is a quavering tremolo, often called "loon laughter"; contact call is a long but simple wailing note *where aaare you?;* breeding notes are soft, short hoots; male territorial call is an undulating, complex yodel.

Similar Species: *Red-throated Loon* (p. 67): smaller; slender bill; sharply defined white face and white-spotted back in nonbreeding plumage.

Best Sites: offshore of many barrier islands, especially Cumberland I. (HC: 600+); inland at Lake Lanier (HC: 1000+), Lake Hartwell and West Point L.

PIED-BILLED GREBE
Podilymbus podiceps

The odd, exuberant chortle of the Pied-billed Grebe fits right in with the boisterous cacophony of Georgia's wetland communities. Heard more frequently than seen, the Pied-billed Grebe is the smallest, shyest and least colorful of our grebes. It is an extremely wary bird but is easy to find on almost any pond or lake in Georgia. It tends to swim inconspicuously in shallow waters of quiet bays and rivers or flooded fields, only occasionally voicing its strange chuckle or whinny. • These grebes build their floating nests among sparse vegetation, so that they can see their numerous predators—including Great Blue Herons, small turtles and water snakes—approaching from far away. When frightened by an intruder, they cover their eggs and slide under water, leaving a nest that looks like nothing more than a mat of debris. A Pied-billed Grebe can slowly submerge up to its head, so that only its nostrils and eyes remain above the water.

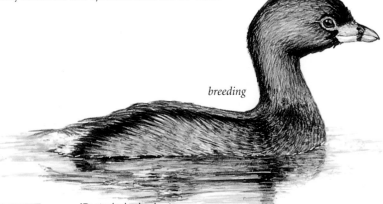

breeding

ID: stocky body; short, laterally compressed "chicken bill." *Breeding:* all-brown body; black ring on pale bill; black throat; very short tail; white undertail coverts; pale belly; pale eye ring. *Nonbreeding:* yellow eye ring; yellow bill lacks black ring; white "chin" and throat; brownish crown.

Size: *L* 12–15 in; *W* 16 in.

Status: common migrant and winter resident from September to May; rare during the breeding season from March to May, except on the Coast where uncommon.

Habitat: ponds, marshes, impoundments and backwaters with sparse emergent vegetation; flooded agricultural lands; rarely on salt water.

Nesting: among sparse vegetation in sheltered bays, ponds and marshes; floating platform nest, made of wet and decaying plants, is anchored to or placed among emergent vegetation; pair incubates 4–5 white to buff eggs for about 23 days and raises the striped young together.

Feeding: makes shallow dives and gleans the water's surface for aquatic invertebrates, small fish and adult and larval amphibians; occasionally eats aquatic plants.

Voice: loud, whooping call begins quickly, then slows down: *kuk-kuk-kuk cow cow cow cowp cowp cowp*.

Similar Species: *Eared Grebe* (p. 72): seldom seen in summer; red eyes; black and white head; golden "ear" tufts and chestnut flanks in breeding plumage. *Horned Grebe* (p. 70): seldom seen in summer; red eyes; black and white head; golden "ear" tufts and red neck in breeding plumage. *American Coot* (p. 124): all-black body; pale bill extends onto forehead.

Best Sites: *In migration:* most freshwater habitats. *Winter:* Rum Creek WMA & Piedmont NWR (HC: 150+); Garden Lakes, Rome (HC: 100+).

69

HORNED GREBE

Podiceps auritus

Along the coast and at large inland reservoirs in Georgia, this compact little grebe can be seen riding high in the water. It has a rounded head outline, with slightly puffed "cheeks," and its neck is somewhat curved or thrust forward when swimming. • This grebe catches its food in long dives that may last up to three minutes, and it can travel as far as 400 feet under water. The bird starts the dive with a pronounced upward and forward leap, and propels itself under water solely with its feet. Unlike the fully webbed front toes of most swimming birds, grebe toes are individually webbed, or "lobed"—the three forward-facing toes have individual flanges that are not connected to the other toes. • The Horned Grebe flies more readily than most grebes, with a strong, direct, loonlike flight that reveals a large white patch at the rear of the inner wing. • This bird's common name and its scientific name, *auritus* (eared), refer to the golden feather tufts, or "horns," that these grebes acquire in breeding plumage.

nonbreeding

ID: *Breeding:* rufous neck and flanks; black head; golden "ear" tufts; black back; white underparts; red eyes; flat crown. *Nonbreeding:* lacks "ear" tufts; black upperparts; white "cheek," foreneck and underparts. *In flight:* wings beat constantly; hunchbacked appearance; legs trail behind tail.
Size: *L* 12–15 in; *W* 18 in.
Status: uncommon to common migrant and winter resident from September to May; accidental nonbreeder in summer at Lake Lanier and Richmond Co.
Habitat: wetlands and large lakes.

Nesting: does not nest in Georgia.
Feeding: makes shallow dives and gleans the water's surface for aquatic insects, crustaceans, mollusks, small fish and adult and larval amphibians.
Voice: silent in migration and winter.
Similar Species: *Eared Grebe* (p. 72): black neck in breeding plumage; black "cheek" and darker neck in nonbreeding plumage. *Pied-billed Grebe* (p. 69): thicker, stubbier bill; mostly brown body. *Red-necked Grebe* (p. 71): larger; dark eyes; lacks "ear" tufts; white "cheek" in breeding plumage.
Best Sites: West Point Dam (HC: 200+); Lake Lanier (HC: 200+); Jekyll I. (HC: 100+); Savannah NWR; Rum Creek WMA.

RED-NECKED GREBE

Podiceps grisegena

In winter, the few Red-necked Grebes that stray into Georgia spend most of their time swimming and diving along our coastlines. They prefer to stay close to shore, searching for small fish in estuaries, bays or inlets. Red-necked Grebes are sociable birds and will join other grebes or waterfowl to hunt. • A grebe will capture its prey under water with a quick snap of its bill. Small prey are swallowed under water but larger fish are taken to the surface to be eaten. When thirsty, a grebe will fill its bill with water and then tilt its head back to drink. All grebes feed, sleep and court on water, and they even carry their newly hatched young on their backs. The striped young can stay aboard even when the parents dive under water. • The Red-necked Grebe is one of the largest North American grebes. The scientific name *grisegena* means "gray cheek"—a distinctive field mark of this bird in nonbreeding plumage.

nonbreeding

ID: *Breeding:* rusty neck; whitish "cheek"; black crown; straight, heavy bill is dark above and yellow underneath; black upperparts; light underparts; dark eyes. *Nonbreeding:* grayish white foreneck, "chin" and "cheek."
Size: *L* 17–22 in; *W* 24 in.
Status: rare migrant and winter resident on the Coast or in the Piedmont from November to April; accidental in the Coastal Plain and the Mountains.
Habitat: open, deep lakes.
Nesting: does not nest in Georgia.
Feeding: dives and gleans the water's surface for small fish, aquatic invertebrates and crustaceans.

Voice: silent in migration.
Similar Species: *Horned Grebe* (p. 70): smaller; dark "cheek" and golden "horns" in breeding plumage; red eyes, all-dark bill and bright white "cheek" in nonbreeding plumage. *Eared Grebe* (p. 72): smaller; black neck in breeding plumage; black "cheek" in nonbreeding plumage. *Pied-billed Grebe* (p. 69): smaller; thicker, stubbier bill; mostly brown body. *Western Grebe:* red eyes; black and white neck in breeding plumage. *Ducks* (pp. 35–62): all lack the combination of white "cheek" and red neck.
Best Sites: off any barrier island; Rum Creek WMA & Piedmont NWR; Lake Lanier (HC: 3); West Point L.

EARED GREBE

Podiceps nigricollis

Eared Grebes undergo cyclical periods of atrophy and hypertrophy throughout the year, meaning that their internal organs and pectoral muscles shrink or swell, depending on whether or not the birds need to migrate. This strategy leaves Eared Grebes flightless for a longer period—nine to ten months over the period of a year—than any other flying bird in the world. • Like other grebes, the Eared Grebe eats feathers. The feathers often pack the digestive tract, and it is thought that they protect the stomach lining and intestines from sharp fish bones or parasites, or perhaps they slow the passage of food, allowing more time for complete digestion. • The Eared Grebe inhabits parts of Europe, Asia, Central Africa and South America, making it the most abundant grebe not only in North America, but also in the world. • The scientific name *nigricollis* means "black neck," a characteristic feature of this bird's breeding plumage.

nonbreeding

ID: *Breeding:* black neck, "cheek," forehead and back; red flanks; fanned-out, golden "ear" tufts; white underparts; thin, straight bill; red eyes; slightly raised crown. *Nonbreeding:* dark "cheek" and upperparts; light underparts; dusky upper foreneck and flanks. *In flight:* wings beat constantly; hunchbacked appearance; legs trail behind tail.

Size: *L* 11½–14 in; *W* 16 in.

Status: rare to uncommon migrant and winter resident in the Piedmont from November to May; accidental in other regions, mostly from August to October and from January to May.

Habitat: wetlands, larger lakes and sewage disposal ponds.

Nesting: does not nest in Georgia.

Feeding: makes shallow dives and gleans the water's surface for aquatic insects, crustaceans, mollusks, small fish and larval and adult amphibians.

Voice: usually quiet outside the breeding season.

Similar Species: *Horned Grebe* (p. 70): rufous neck in breeding plumage; white "cheek" in nonbreeding plumage. *Pied-billed Grebe* (p. 69): thicker, stubbier bill; mostly brown body. *Red-necked Grebe* (p. 71): larger overall; longer bill; red neck and whitish "cheek" in breeding plumage; dusky white "cheek" in nonbreeding plumage.

Best Sites: Rum Creek WMA (HC: 11), Lake Burton; Carters L.; Eufaula NWR; Lake Walter F. George; E.L. Huie; Jekyll I.

BLACK-CAPPED PETREL

Pterodroma hasitata

O nly about 2000 Black-capped Petrels are believed to exist worldwide, and relatively little is known about them. • These medium-sized seabirds usually fly high over the water, rolling from side to side as they glide. They are generally found far out to sea, usually off the north coast of Georgia and the Carolinas. They grace Atlantic waters on the edge of the Gulf Stream from spring to fall, then haunt Caribbean breeding colonies in winter. • Because the colonial nesting sites of Black-capped Petrels are located on far removed islands and these birds only visit their nesting burrows at night, they are difficult birds to study. The small population is believed to be declining, because of habitat degradation and egg predation by humans and also because of introduced species including cats, rats and mongooses. • On its native islands in the Caribbean, the Black-capped Petrel is called *Diablotin* or "little devil" for its eerie nocturnal calls.

ID: dark gray upper-parts; white under-parts; black "cap"; stubby, black bill; thick, white "collar." *In flight:* long, pointy wings held in an "M" shape; triangular, black bar on white underwing; prominent white rump.
Size: *L* 16 in; *W* 3 ft.
Status: uncommon Offshore and Gulf Stream visitor from February to December; best seen in July, August and October.
Habitat: open ocean, usually 100–155 mi. offshore.

Nesting: does not nest in Georgia.
Feeding: picks squid and crustaceans off the water's surface.
Voice: generally silent on the open sea.
Similar Species: *Cory's Shearwater* (p. 74): pale brown upperparts; brown head; yellow bill; lacks white "collar"; broad, white tail band; hunched, sweeping wings. *Greater Shearwater* (p. 75): thin bill; dark "collar"; clean black "cap"; holds wings straight in flight. *Manx Shearwater* (rare, p. 360) and *Audubon's Shearwater* (p. 76): lack white "collar" and rump.
Best Sites: boating far offshore of barrier islands (HC: 100+).

CORY'S SHEARWATER

Calonectris diomedea

This stalwart shearwater was first spotted off the coast of New England in 1880 by Charles Barney Cory, who believed it to be a new species. Further investigation revealed this seabird as the North Atlantic race of the Mediterranean Shearwater. With nesting grounds on the rocky shores of Mediterranean islands, the Cory's Shearwater is the only shearwater that breeds as well as overwinters in the Northern Hemisphere. Following the breeding season, individuals disperse hundreds of miles to the Indian Ocean or the Atlantic Coast.
• Because these gregarious birds rarely investigate marine vessels, spotting a Cory's Shearwater can be challenging. • *Diomedea* is a form of the name Diomedes, a Trojan War hero whose companions were turned into birds when their ship was lost at sea. *Calonectris* is Greek for "beautiful swimmer," but with a broad wingspan and slow wingbeats, this bird most often exhibits grace in the air by soaring on the ocean breezes.

ID: gray-brown above; white below; dark wing tips and tail tip; white neck and lower "cheek" blends with pale brown head; small, white rump patch; large yellow bill with small "tube" above upper mandible. *In flight*: wings slightly bent while gliding.
Size: L 18–21 in; W 3¾ ft.
Status: common far Offshore from April to November.
Habitat: open ocean; favors warm waters; flocks gather near food sources.

Nesting: does not nest in Georgia.
Feeding: will follow large, fish-eating fish and feed on the small prey that are forced to the water's surface; at night will take squid and crustaceans.
Voice: usually silent at sea; occasionally utters a hoarse, nasal cry.
Similar Species: *Greater Shearwater* (p. 75): white "collar" extends around nape; dark upperparts and white underparts are more contrasted; smudging on belly; darker bill.
Best Sites: boating far offshore of barrier islands, such as St. Simons I. (HC: 360).

GREATER SHEARWATER

Puffinus gravis

Fishing boats are often mobbed by Greater Shearwaters fighting over the opportunity to grab a free meal. These shearwaters also forage together with whales and dolphins. • Greater Shearwaters migrate to the North Atlantic for summer, but they do not breed here. In fact, considering their abundance here it is surprising that they breed in such a small area: Gough Island and islands in the Tristan da Cunha group in the South Atlantic. • Greater Shearwaters are most common over the outer part of the continental shelf—they tend to avoid near-shore and mid-ocean areas. However, when small fish move to beaches to spawn, Greater Shearwaters will follow them. At such times, and in very calm or foggy weather, huge flocks may appear off headlands. In dead calm conditions, takeoff can be achieved only with great difficulty, and the birds are effectively grounded.

Habitat: open ocean; favors cold waters; most common over the outer portion of the continental shelf; drawn inshore by weather conditions and prey abundance.

Nesting: does not nest in Georgia.

Feeding: seizes prey from the surface of the water or dives to 30 ft; eats mainly small fish and squid but may also eat crustaceans.

Voice: a bleating *waaan* like a lamb; generally silent in Georgia.

Similar Species: *Cory's Shearwater* (p. 74): lacks brown "collar," belly and undertail coverts; yellow bill. *Manx Shearwater* (p. 360): darker upperparts; white belly and undertail coverts. *Jaegers* (pp. 165–66): wing flashes more prominent; longer tails; central tail feathers project out in flight.

Best Sites: boating far offshore of barrier islands (HC: 50+); Cumberland I.; St. Simons I.; Jekyll I.

ID: dark brown upperparts; white underparts, except for brown belly, brown undertail coverts and incomplete brown "collar"; usually 1 narrow, white band at base of tail. *In flight:* straight, narrow, pointed wings; dark "wing pits" and wing linings; dark trailing edge of wings; some molting birds have jaegerlike white wing patch.

Size: *L* 19 in; *W* 3½ ft.

Status: rare to uncommon far Offshore from May to December; accidental from the shore of the barrier islands.

AUDUBON'S SHEARWATER

Puffinus lherminieri

Quick, choppy wingbeats broken by short glides distinguish the Audubon's Shearwater from the similar-looking Manx Shearwater. This short-winged bird is the smallest shearwater to regularly visit North Atlantic waters in summer and often joins large, mixed-species flocks. • While pursuing small fish or squid, the Audubon's Shearwater skims the surface of the water, alternately flapping, gliding and diving. Unlike other seabirds, this shearwater does not follow fishing vessels but rather wanders the seas at will, usually remaining close to its breeding areas. • During the nesting season these birds feed at night then return to their nesting burrows by day. Audubon's Shearwaters nest on tropical islands around the world, including the Atlantic, Pacific and Indian oceans, as well as the Persian Gulf.

ID: dark brownish black above; pale underparts; white throat. *In flight:* short wings, quite long tail; quick wingbeats and short glides.
Size: *L* 12 in; *W* 27 in.

Status: uncommon visitor far Offshore in the Gulf Stream from April to December; 2 winter sightings Offshore in February.

Habitat: open ocean.
Nesting: does not nest in Georgia.
Feeding: dives for fish, squid and other small marine animals.
Voice: generally silent on the open sea; sometimes utters high, whiny notes.
Similar Species: *Manx Shearwater* (p. 360): larger, with slower wingbeats and longer and more frequent glides.
Best Sites: boating far offshore of barrier islands, primarily in outershelf and Gulf Stream (HC-summer: 150+).

WILSON'S STORM-PETREL

Oceanites oceanicus

This long-legged storm-petrel dances over the surface of the water, feet daintily pattering as it hovers, stirring up the small shrimp, amphipods and fish that it feeds on. The outer portion of the continental shelf is where you are most likely to see it, but this storm-petrel occasionally wanders close to land in summer. Like many marine birds, the Wilson's Storm-Petrel follows fishing boats, grabbing whatever scraps of food it can. • This long-distance migrant must eat well—it travels from the Antarctic to the edge of the Arctic and back again each year. It nests on islands and cliffs in the Antarctic region and near southern South America, and otherwise spends its time at sea. The Wilson's Storm-Petrel is occasionally spotted off our coast between May and September, during the Southern Hemisphere's winter, but the majority of these birds winter in the North Atlantic. • According to Greek mythology, "Oceanites" were sea nymphs that, like storm-petrels, spent their lives at sea. • Despite their small size, storm-petrels can live to be more than 20 years old.

ID: dark brown overall, with white on rump and undertail coverts; square tail. *In flight:* shallow, stiff wingbeats, suggesting a swallow; toes extend beyond end of tail.

Size: *L* 7 in; *W* 16½ in.

Status: uncommon far Offshore visitor from April to September; accidental onshore.

Habitat: open ocean, especially over the continental shelf, but occasionally wanders close to land along the coast.

Nesting: does not nest in Georgia.

Feeding: hovers over the water with its feet touching the surface, grabbing food items from the surface; takes shrimp, amphipods, small fish, small squid and marine worms.

Voice: usually silent; soft peeping or chattering may be heard from groups of feeding birds.

Similar Species: *Shearwaters* (pp. 74–76, 360) and *Black-capped Petrel* (p. 73): much larger; glide much more often and rarely flap.

Best Sites: boating far offshore and in the Gulf Stream (HC: 50).

NORTHERN GANNET

Morus bassanus

Unfortunately, the Northern Gannet's spectacular feeding behavior is often demonstrated far from the sight of land. Squadrons of gannets soaring at heights of more than 100 feet above the ocean's surface will suddenly arrest their flight by folding their wings back and simultaneously plunge headfirst into the ocean depths in pursuit of schooling fish. The gannet's reinforced skull has evolved to cushion the brain from diving impacts. • Northern Gannets spend most of the year feeding and roosting at sea but may be blown close to shore on windy days. In some years they are common off the coast of Georgia, especially from December to March. • Only during the brief summer breeding season do these birds seek the stability of land to lay eggs and raise young in large sea-cliff colonies in Atlantic Canada. They often mate for life, reestablishing pair bonds each year at their nest sites by indulging in elaborate face-to-face nest-duty exchange sequences that involve wing raising, tail spreading, bowing, sky-pointing and preening. • "Gannet" is derived from the Anglo-Saxon (c. 450–c.1200) word "ganot," meaning "little goose." This bird was once classified taxonomically and popularly with the geese and is still known as "Solan Goose" *juvenile* in Europe.

ID: thick, tapered bill; long, narrow wings; pointed tail; white overall with black wing tips and feet; buffy wash on nape. *Immature:* various stages of mottled gray, black and white.
Size: *L* 3 ft; *W* 6 ft.
Status: uncommon to common winter resident far Offshore and along the Coast from October to May.
Habitat: roosts and feeds in coastal and open ocean waters most of year; often seen well offshore.

Nesting: does not nest in Georgia.
Feeding: often forages by submerging its head while floating on the water's surface, then diving to pursue prey; eats fish, including herring and mackerel, and sometimes squid; may steal from other birds or scavenge from fishing boats.
Voice: generally silent.
Similar Species: *Snow Goose* (p. 36): shorter, pinkish bill; broader wings and long, extended neck in flight.
Best Sites: boating offshore of barrier islands (HC: 600+); along the coast of St. Catherines I. (HC: 600+), Tybee I., Sapelo I., Cumberland I., St. Simons I. and Jekyll I.

AMERICAN WHITE PELICAN
Pelecanus erythrorhynchos

The American White Pelican is a majestic wetland presence with a wingspan only a foot shy of the height of a basketball hoop. Its porous, bucketlike bill is dramatically adapted for feeding. As the pelican lifts its bill from the water, the fish are held within its flexible pouch while the water drains out. In a single scoop, a pelican can hold over 3 gallons of water and fish, which is about two to three times as much as its stomach can hold. This impressive feat confirms Dixon Lanier Merritt's quotation: "A wonderful bird is a pelican, His bill will hold more than his belican!" • The pelican's black wing tips contain a pigment called melanin that makes the feathers stronger and more resistant to wear. All other large, white birds with black wing tips fly with their necks extended—the American White Pelican is the only one to fly with its neck pulled back toward its wings. • Groups of foraging pelicans deliberately herd fish into schools, then dip their bills and scoop up the prey. American White Pelicans eat about 4 pounds of fish per day, but because they prefer nongame fish they do not pose a threat to the potential catches of fishermen.

nonbreeding

ID: very large, stocky, white bird; long, orange bill and throat pouch; black primary and secondary wing feathers; short tail; naked orange skin patch around eye. *Breeding:* small, keeled plate develops on upper mandible; pale yellow crest on back of head. *Nonbreeding* and *immature:* white plumage is tinged with brown.
Size: *L* 4½–6 ft; *W* 9 ft.
Status: rare to uncommon visitor on the Coast, mostly from October to May; rare on the Coast in summer; rare in the Coastal Plain in migration and winter; accidental in the Piedmont.
Habitat: large lakes or rivers.
Nesting: does not nest in Georgia.
Feeding: surface-dips for small fish and amphibians; small groups of pelicans often feed cooperatively by herding fish into large concentrations.
Voice: generally quiet; adults rarely issue piglike grunts.
Similar Species: no other large, white bird has a long bill with a pouch.
Best Sites: St. Marys R. (HC: 100+); Andrews I. (HC: 100+); inland at E.L. Huie (HC: 30) and Lake Lanier.

BROWN PELICAN

Pelecanus occidentalis

Despite its abundance and its ease of flight, the Brown Pelican is seldom encountered away from marine or intertidal habitats in Georgia. Unlike the American White Pelican, which occurs in freshwater areas throughout most of its range, the Brown Pelican is strictly a coastal species. • Just about everyone sees Brown Pelicans where they are numerous. They are among the most conspicuous waterbirds, perching on beaches, rocks and pilings or coursing the troughs in single file. • The Brown Pelican forages by a unique plunge-dive method: it folds its wings, pulls back its head and dives headfirst into the water. Only the Brown Pelican forages this way; other pelican species scoop up their prey. • In the 1950s and 1960s, DDT-related reproductive failures caused Brown Pelicans to nearly disappear in California and in many areas of the southeastern United States. Since then, these highly persistent pesticides have been banned, and pelican populations have recovered.

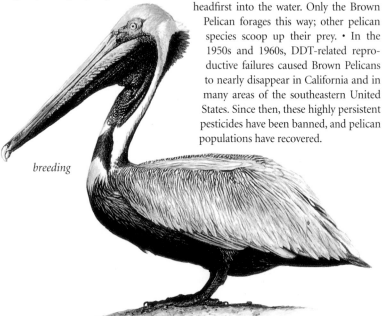

breeding

ID: grayish brown body; very large bill. *Nonbreeding:* white neck; head washed with yellow; pale yellowish pouch. *Breeding:* yellow head; white foreneck; dark brown hindneck; grayish pouch. *1st year:* uniformly dusky; buff-tipped head and neck contrast with pale underparts.
Size: *L* 4 ft; *W* 7 ft.
Status: endangered (federal); common breeding resident along the Coast; first breeding record in Georgia in 1988.
Habitat: coastal and estuarine waters, over the continental shelf in some areas; visits offshore islands; roosts on protected islets, sea stacks, sandbars and piers.

Nesting: nests on the ground or in mangroves; nest may be a scrape or an elaborate platform woven from sticks and lined with vegetation; pair incubates 2–3 bright, chalky-white eggs under footwebs for 29–32 days; pair cares for young.
Feeding: forages almost exclusively for fish, which are caught by diving headfirst into the water from heights of up to 60 ft; fish are held in the flexible pouch until water is drained; concentrations feeding over extensive schools of fish commonly number in the hundreds.
Voice: generally silent.
Similar Species: *American White Pelican* (p. 79): all-white body with extensive black in wings.
Best Sites: *Breeding:* Egg Island Bar (several thousand pairs) and the mouth of Satilla R. (several hundred pairs).

DOUBLE-CRESTED CORMORANT

Phalacrocorax auritus

The Double-crested Cormorant's beauty can take longer to appreciate than that of other birds. This slick-feathered bird often appears disheveled, and extra-close encounters typically reveal the foul stench of fish oil. Nevertheless, its mastery of the aquatic environment is virtually unsurpassed. The absence of water-proofing feather structures in the Double-crested Cormorant helps it during underwater dives by decreasing the bird's buoyancy. Instead of floating upon the water after a bout of diving, the Double-crested Cormorant is often seen perched in a tree with its wings partially spread in an attempt to dry its feathers. The cormorant's long, rudderlike tail, excellent underwater vision and sealed nostrils also contribute to the success of its aquatic lifestyle.
• Once believed to compete with fishermen for the same fish, it is now known that cormorants also take undesirables such as alewives, sticklebacks and sculpins.

juvenile

breeding

ID: all-black body; long, crooked neck; thin bill, hooked at tip; blue eyes. *Breeding:* throat pouch becomes intense orange-yellow; fine, black plumes trail from "eye-brows." *Immature:* brown upperparts; buff throat and breast; yellowish throat patch. *In flight:* rapid wingbeats; kinked neck.

Size: *L* 26–32 in; *W* 4½ ft.

Status: uncommon to common permanent resident; rare breeding records inland and on the Coast.

Habitat: coastal areas and estuaries; swamps, large lakes and wide, meandering rivers.

Nesting: colonial; on the ground on a low-lying island, often with terns and gulls, or precariously high in a tree; nest platform is made of sticks, aquatic vegetation and guano; pair incubates 2–7 bluish white eggs for 25–29 days; young are fed by regurgitation.

Feeding: long underwater dives to depths of 30 ft or more to capture small schooling fish or, rarely, amphibians and invertebrates; uses its bill to grasp prey and bring it to the surface.

Voice: generally quiet; may issue piglike grunts or croaks, especially near nesting colonies.

Similar Species: *Great Cormorant:* white "chin strap" borders yellow throat patch; larger head and body; thicker neck. *Anhinga* (p. 82): black body streaked with silver and white; long, curved neck; fanlike tail, red eyes; swims submerged. *Magnificent Frigatebird* (p. 83): forked tail; red throat patch on male; female and immature have white breast.

Best Sites: inland at E.L. Huie and Lake Juliette; along the coast at Chatham Co. and Camden Co., Tybee I. (HC: 2500), St. Catherines I. (HC: 1600+) and Lake Oconee (HC: 650). *Winter:* Savannah R. and Chattahoochee R.

ANHINGA
Anhinga anhinga

The Tupi natives of Brazil named this bird Anhinga, or "devil bird—evil spirit of the woods." Once you see the Anhinga in action, you can start to understand this perception. With dense bones and easily waterlogged feathers, the "Snakebird" swims almost completely submerged, holding its curved neck just above water, making it an ominous presence in Georgia's freshwater ponds and canals. One quick lunge and a stab of the Anhinga's long, sharp bill will finish off a frog or fish. Serrations on the top of the bill keep the prey from flopping off until the Anhinga flips its catch in the air and swallows the meal headfirst. • Following a swim, the Anhinga must dry out its feathers and warm up. Perching on a protruding snag, it unfolds its silver-decorated wings in a royal display, while its black plumage glints green in the sunlight. Watch for sunbathing Anhingas along canals or in cypress swamps. • On warm days Anhingas will soar on rising thermals, fanning their large tails.

breeding

ID: black body with silver and white streaking; long, curved neck; fanlike tail; red eyes. *Breeding*: blue-green eye rims; heavier streaking (not attained until third year). *Female and immature*: buffy from neck up; less streaking.
Size: *L* 30–36 in; *W* 4 ft.
Status: common, local breeding resident; uncommon in winter.
Habitat: quiet, sheltered, slowly moving or still freshwater ponds, lakes and rivers.
Nesting: in a tree above or near calm water; in colonies with other large birds (cormorants, herons); male brings sticks but female builds nest or may use an abandoned egret or heron nest; pair incubates 2–5 whitish eggs for 25–29 days.
Feeding: will swim submerged or perch motionless and stab prey, including fish, frogs, leeches and snakes.
Voice: descending metallic clicks while perched.
Similar Species: *Double-crested Cormorant* (p. 81): thicker, black body; heavy bill with hook; blue eye; yellow throat patch; dives for prey. *Magnificent Frigatebird* (p. 83): forked tail; red throat patch on male; female and immature have white breast.
Best Sites: Merry Brothers Brickyard Ponds and Phinizy Swamp Nature Park (HC: 42); Savannah NWR; Okefenokee NWR; Lake Seminole WMA.

MAGNIFICENT FRIGATEBIRD

Fregata magnificens

Kleptoparasitism, or piracy feeding, is a strategy often employed by the Magnificent Frigatebird. Flying gulls, terns, shorebirds and other birds carrying food are harassed in mid-flight until they drop or regurgitate their meal. Once food is dropped, the frigatebird swoops down to snatch the falling item before it hits the water or the ground. This agile aerial acrobat is even capable of snatching food directly from the bill of another bird during a spectacular aerial dogfight. • When compared to body weight, the Magnificent Frigatebird has the largest wing surface area of any bird alive. With great wings and a deeply forked tail, the frigatebird is virtually unsurpassed at soaring and aerial maneuvers. • During courtship, groups of males put on a unique performance for onlooking females. The males inflate gular sacs like large, red balloons and simultaneously raise their bills, vibrate their wings and shake their heads, uttering hoarse, cackling calls. The only known Magnificent Frigatebird breeding colonies in the United States occur in the Florida Keys and the Dry Tortugas. Other breeding sites are found in the Caribbean, Central America and South America.

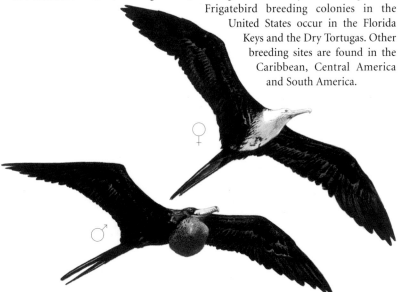

ID: long, forked tail; long, narrow wings; long, hooked bill. *Male:* glossy black plumage with red-orange (inflatable) throat patch. *Female:* blackish brown plumage with white breast. *Immature:* varying amount of white on head and breast.
Size: *L* 3–3½ ft; *W* 7–8 ft.
Status: rare visitor on the Coast from April to November; accidental inland, usually after hurricanes.
Habitat: nests among mangroves, trees or dense shrubs on coastal islands; feeds along coastal waters and occasionally far Offshore.
Nesting: does not nest in Georgia.
Feeding: forages from the air, swooping to snatch prey off the water's surface or coastal land; also feeds by kleptoparasitism; eats mostly fish but occasionally eats small birds, eggs, jellyfish and crustaceans.
Voice: hoarse cackling call.
Similar Species: *Anhinga* (p. 82), *Double-crested Cormorant* (p. 81) and *Great Cormorant:* lack forked tail, red throat patch of male and white breast of female and immature.
Best Sites: Jekyll I.

AMERICAN BITTERN

Botaurus lentiginosus

At the approach of an intruder, this bittern's first reaction is to freeze with its bill pointed skyward—its vertically streaked, brown plumage blends perfectly with its surroundings. An American Bittern will always face an intruder, moving ever so slowly to keep its camouflaged breast toward danger. In most cases, intruders simply pass by without noticing the bird. But this defensive reaction can sometimes result in an unfortunate comical turn for the bittern—it will try to mimic a reed even in an entirely open field! Although the camouflage fools potential predators, the cryptic plumage is most likely an adaptation to reduce this bird's visibility to prey while hunting. The American Bittern prefers to hunt in dim light situations, at dawn or dusk, when its camouflage is most effective.

• American Bitterns are rare in Georgia but are occasionally found near the coast in winter or along the Coastal Plain during migration. Late mornings and early afternoons are the best times to locate these secretive birds, though the chances of actually seeing one are quite slim. The American Bittern's distinctive pumplike breeding call is rarely heard in Georgia.

nonbreeding

ID: brown upperparts; brown streaking from "chin" through breast; straight, stout bill; yellow legs and feet; black outer wings; black streaks from bill down neck to shoulder; short tail.

Size: *L* 23–27 in; *W* 3½ ft.

Status: uncommon migrant and winter resident inland, mostly south of the Fall Line, from August to May; rare in the Mountains and the Piedmont.

Habitat: marshes, wetlands and lake edges with tall, dense grass, sedges, bulrushes and cattails.

Nesting: does not nest in Georgia.

Feeding: patient stand-and-wait predator; strikes at small fish, crayfish, amphibians, reptiles, mammals and insects.

Voice: generally silent in Georgia; deep, slow, resonant, repetitive *pomp-er-lunk* or *onk-a-BLONK;* most often heard in the evening or at night in spring.

Similar Species: *Black-crowned Night-Heron* (p. 94), *Yellow-crowned Night-Heron* (p. 95): immatures have dark brown upperparts, flecked with white. *Least Bittern* (p. 85) and *Green Heron* (p. 93): immatures lack dark streak from bill to shoulder.

Best Sites: Grand Bay WMA (HC: 10+); Altamaha WMA; Harris Neck NWR.

LEAST BITTERN

Ixobrychus exilis

The Least Bittern is the smallest of the herons and is one of the most seclusive marsh birds in North America. It inhabits marshes where tall, impenetrable stands of cattails conceal most of its movements. This bird moves about with ease, its slender body passing freely and unnoticed through dense marshland habitat. An expert climber, the Least Bittern can often be seen 3 feet or more above water, clinging to vertical stems and hopping about without getting its feet wet. This technique allows it to forage over much deeper water, although only at the water's surface. • Least Bittern sightings tend to be rare, owing in part to this bird's secretive behavior and solitary lifestyle.

nonbreeding

ID: rich buff flanks and sides; streaking on foreneck; white underparts; mostly pale bill; yellowish legs; short tail; dark primary and secondary feathers. *Male:* black crown and back. *Female and immature:* chestnut brown head and back; immature has darker streaking on breast and back. *In flight:* large, buffy shoulder patches.

Size: *L* 11–14½ in; *W* 17 in.

Status: uncommon breeding resident on the Coast, and locally common elsewhere as far north as the lower Piedmont, from April to October; rare in the Mountains.

Habitat: freshwater marshes with cattails and other dense emergent vegetation.

Nesting: mostly the male constructs a platform of dry plant stalks on top of bent marsh vegetation; nest site is usually well concealed within dense vegetation; pair incubates 4–5 pale green or blue eggs for 17–20 days; pair feeds the young by regurgitation.

Feeding: stabs prey with its bill; eats mostly small fish; also takes large insects, tadpoles, frogs, small snakes, leeches and crayfish; may build a hunting platform.

Voice: *Male:* guttural *uh-uh-uh-oo-oo-oo-ooah. Female:* a ticking sound. Both issue a *tut-tut* call or a *koh* alarm call.

Similar Species: *American Bittern* (p. 84): larger; bold brown streaking on underparts; black streak from bill to shoulder. *Black-crowned Night-Heron* (p. 94) and *Yellow-crowned Night-Heron* (p. 95): immatures have dark brown upperparts with white flecking. *Green Heron* (p. 93): immature has dark brown upperparts.

Best Sites: Altamaha WMA (HC: 25); Savannah NWR; Eufaula NWR.

GREAT BLUE HERON

Ardea herodias

The sight of a majestic Great Blue Heron is always memorable, whether you are observing its stealthy, often motionless hunting strategy or tracking its graceful wingbeats. Large colonies of Great Blue Herons nest in communal treetop nests, known as rookeries, that are usually located on isolated islands or wooded swamps. Colonies are sensitive to human disturbance, so be careful to observe the birds' behavior from a distance. • Herons are often mistaken for similar-sized cranes. Unlike a crane, which holds its neck outstretched in flight, the Great Blue folds its neck back over its shoulders in an S-shape. • These birds use their bills to spear fish or frogs, then swallow their catch whole. Anglers occasionally catch a fish with distinctive triangular scars—evidence that it once survived a heron attack. Though Great Blue Herons mostly eat fish and are commonly found near water, these birds may also be found stalking fields in search of rodents.

breeding

breeding

ID: large, blue-gray bird; long, curving neck; long, dark legs; blue-gray back and wing coverts; straight, yellow bill; chestnut brown thighs. *Breeding:* richer colors; plumes streak from crown and throat. *In flight:* neck folds back over shoulders; legs trail behind body; slow, steady wingbeats. *White morph ("Great White Heron"):* rare; has all white plumage.
Size: *L* 4–4½ ft; *W* 6 ft.
Status: common breeding resident, with higher abundance in the southwest Coastal Plain; less common north of the Fall Line year-round; common south of the Fall Line in winter; the white morph is a rare visitor to the Coastal Plain and along the Coast.
Habitat: forages along edges of rivers, lakes, marshes, mangroves, estuaries, fields and wet meadows.
Nesting: colonial; flimsy to elaborate stick and twig platform is built in a tree, snag, tall bush or marsh vegetation and can be up to 4 ft in diameter; pair incubates 3–5 pale, bluish green eggs for 28 days.
Feeding: patient stand-and-wait predator; strikes at small fish, amphibians, small mammals, aquatic invertebrates and reptiles; rarely scavenges.
Voice: usually quiet away from the nest; occasionally a deep, harsh *frahnk frahnk frahnk,* usually during takeoff.
Similar Species: *Green Heron* (p. 93), *Black-crowned Night-Heron* (p. 94) and *Yellow-crowned Night-Heron* (p. 95): much smaller; shorter legs. *Great* (p. 87), *Snowy* (p. 88) and *Cattle* (p. 92) *egrets:* all are predominantly white. *Sandhill Crane* (p. 125): red "cap"; flies with neck outstretched. *Little Blue Heron* (p. 89): dark overall; purplish head; lacks yellow on bill. *Tricolored Heron* (p. 90): smaller; darker upperparts; white underparts.
Best Sites: the southwest Coastal Plain and the Piedmont, more common in winter than in summer.

GREAT EGRET

Ardea alba

The plumes of the Great Egret and Snowy Egret were widely used to decorate hats in the early 20th century. An ounce of egret feathers cost as much as $32—more than an ounce of gold at that time—and, as a result, egret populations began to disappear. Some of the first conservation legislation in North America was enacted to outlaw the hunting of Great Egrets. These egrets are now recovering and expanding their range, probably to where they formerly nested. In 2003, we celebrated the 100th anniversary of Teddy Roosevelt's establishment of the nation's first National Wildlife Refuge: Pelican Island, Florida. On this small island it was made illegal to hunt egrets for the feather trade.

nonbreeding

breeding

• Egrets are actually herons, but were given their name for their impressive breeding plumes, referred to as "aigrettes." The aigrettes of a Great Egret can grow up to 4½ feet long! • Great Egrets are capable swimmers and will follow schools of fish into deep water. They will also hunt by standing motionless in shallow water, a behavior that makes them vulnerable to alligator attacks. • The Great Egret is the symbol for the National Audubon Society, one of the oldest conservation organizations in the United States.

ID: white plumage; black legs; yellow bill. *Breeding:* white plumes trail from throat and rump; green skin patch between eyes and base of bill. *In flight:* neck folds back over shoulders; legs extend backward.
Size: *L* 3–3½ ft; *W* 4 ft.
Status: common to abundant breeding resident in the Coastal Plain and abundant on the Coast; rare to uncommon visitor to the Piedmont and the Mountains year-round.
Habitat: marshes, open riverbanks, irrigation canals and lakeshores.

Nesting: colonial, but may nest in isolated pairs; in a tree or tall shrub; pair builds a platform of sticks and incubates 3–5 pale blue green eggs for 23–26 days.
Feeding: patient stand-and-wait predator; occasionally stalks slowly, stabbing at frogs, lizards, snakes and small mammals.
Voice: rapid, low-pitched, loud *cuk-cuk-cuk*.
Similar Species: *Snowy Egret* (p. 88): smaller; black bill; yellow feet. *Cattle Egret* (p. 92): smaller; stockier; orange bill and legs. *Whooping Crane* (p. 126): extremely rare; much larger; red crown; black and red "mask"; black primaries.
Best Sites: widespread south of the Fall Line and along the coast. *Fall* and *winter:* Okefenokee NWR (HC: 2000); Kings Bay Submarine Base (HC: 300+); Macon (HC: 200+).

SNOWY EGRET

Egretta thula

The Snowy Egret is distinguished by its small size and spotless white plumage. The black legs and yellow feet of adult egrets stand out even more. • Herons and egrets, particularly Snowy Egrets, use a variety of feeding techniques. By poking their bright yellow feet in the muck of shallow wetlands, these birds spook potential prey out of hiding places. In an even more devious hunting strategy, Snowy Egrets are known to create shade by extending their wings over open water. When a fish succumbs to the attraction of the cooler shaded spot, it is promptly seized and eaten. Some paleontologists have even suggested that this was one of the original functions of bird wings. • The Snowy Egret was even more affected by plume hunters than the Great Egret, because it was more abundant and widespread, and because its plumes were softer and more delicate.

breeding

nonbreeding

ID: white plumage; black bill and legs; bright yellow feet. *Breeding:* long plumes on throat and rump; erect crown; red-orange lores. *Immature:* similar to adult but with more yellow on legs. *In flight:* yellow feet are obvious.

Size: *L* 22–26 in; *W* 3½ ft.

Status: common breeding resident on the Coast; rare to uncommon breeding resident in the Coastal Plain; uncommon summer visitor to the Piedmont and the Mountains; in winter, fairly common on the Coast but rare inland.

Habitat: open edges of rivers, lakes and marshes.

Nesting: colonial, often with other wading birds, but may nest in isolated pairs; in a tree or tall shrub; pair builds a platform of sticks and incubates 3–5 pale blue-green eggs for 23–26 days.

Feeding: patient stand-and-wait predator; occasionally stalks slowly, stabbing at frogs, lizards, snakes and small mammals.

Voice: rapid, low-pitched, loud *cuk-cuk-cuk*.

Similar Species: *Great Egret* (p. 87): larger; yellow bill; black feet. *Cattle Egret* (p. 92): yellow-orange legs and bill.

Best Sites: Augusta ponds (HC: 15); Savannah NWR; Harris Neck NWR; Altamaha WMA; Okefenokee NWR.

LITTLE BLUE HERON

Egretta caerulea

With dark plumage and a lack of aigrette plumes, the Little Blue Heron was only occasionally taken by plume hunters in the 19th century. As a result, this heron did not suffer the same population decimation as many of its close relatives. • Little Blue Herons are common along the Atlantic Coast throughout the year, and also along the Coastal Plain in summer. Although adults are quite distinct, immature Little Blues are white like Snowy Egrets and Cattle Egrets, making identification confusing. It takes two years for Little Blue Herons to reach the completely dark plumage of adult birds. • Feeding behavior is often the best way to distinguish herons. Larger herons seem graceful even when lunging for a fish, but Little Blue Herons often seem tentative and stiff while hunting, jabbing awkwardly at prey.

breeding

nonbreeding

ID: medium-sized heron; slate blue overall. *Breeding:* shaggy, maroon-colored head and neck; black legs and feet. *Nonbreeding:* smooth, purple head and neck; dull green legs and feet. *Immature:* white, dusky-tipped primaries; yellowish olive legs; blue-gray bill; spotted blue and white when molting to adult plumage.
Size: *L* 24 in; *W* 3½ ft.
Status: common permanent breeding resident on the Coast; rare breeder inland on the Coastal Plain; rare in summer in the Piedmont; accidental in the Mountains in spring.
Habitat: marshes, ponds, lakes, streams and meadows.
Nesting: nests in a shrub or tree above water; female uses sticks collected by the

male to build a bulky platform nest; pair incubates 3–5 pale, greenish blue eggs for 22–24 days.
Feeding: patient stand-and-wait predator, but may wade slowly to stalk prey; eats mostly fish, crabs and crayfish; also takes grasshoppers and other insects, frogs, lizards, snakes and turtles.
Voice: generally silent.
Similar Species: *Snowy Egret* (p. 88): black bill; black legs; bright yellow feet; immature has yellow lores, entirely dark bill, black legs, greenish yellow feet and lacks dusky primary tips. *Cattle Egret* (p. 92): short, yellow bill; yellow legs and feet; immature is similar to adult but has black feet.
Best Sites: Savannah NWR; Harris Neck NWR; Altamaha WMA; Okefenokee NWR. *Summer:* Augusta ponds (HC: 500+).

TRICOLORED HERON

Egretta tricolor

Tricolored Herons are named for the plumage of immature birds, which sport a motley three-toned combination of grayish blue, cinnamon and white feathers. Originally this bird was named the "Louisiana Heron" by Alexander Wilson, the Father of American Ornithology, who favored naming species after the place where the original specimen was found. Captains Meriwether Lewis and William Clark of the legendary Lewis and Clark expedition were responsible for collecting the first specimen, not in the state of Louisiana, but within the vast tract of land obtained in the Louisiana Purchase. Years later, the name Tricolored Heron emerged victoriously over Wilson's former offering.

breeding

nonbreeding

• Although Tricolored Herons often forage in brackish or salt water, they can shift hunting strategies to feed in a wide variety of wetland habitats. These birds may dash after swimming schools of fish or stalk freshwater prey by stepping out gingerly onto floating mats of thick vegetation. Another feeding strategy involves stirring bottom sediments with one foot, attempting to scare up something edible.

ID: *Breeding:* long, slender bill, neck and legs; purplish- to grayish-blue plumage; white underparts and foreneck; pale rump; long plumes appear on head and back. *Immature:* chestnut on hindneck and wing coverts.

Size: *L* 26 in; *W* 3 ft.

Status: common permanent breeding resident on the Coast; rare breeder inland, recently in Brooks Co.; rare summer visitor to the Piedmont; accidental in the Mountains in late summer.

Habitat: coastal saltwater and freshwater marshes, mangrove swamps, estuaries, protected bays, lakes and rivers.

Nesting: colony nester; often found in multispecies colonies; female uses sticks and vegetation collected by the male to build a bulky platform nest in a tree, shrub or mangrove (rarely on the ground); pair incubates 3–4 greenish blue eggs for 21–25 days; pair raises the young.

Feeding: primarily feeds on fish; may also eat crustaceans, large insects, amphibians and small reptiles; forages alone along the shore or in shallow water by wading slowly or standing motionless.

Voice: generally silent outside of the breeding season; alarm call is a harsh *aaah* call; gives *cuhl-cuhl* when courting.

Similar Species: *Reddish Egret* (p. 91): shaggy reddish head and neck; dark underparts. *Little Blue Heron* (p. 89): nonbreeding plumage is all dark; breeding plumage has shaggy pinkish neck and dark underparts.

Best Sites: Savannah NWR; Harris Neck NWR; barrier islands, especially St. Catherines I. (HC-winter: 450+).

REDDISH EGRET

Egretta rufescens

When foraging for fish among the saltwater habitats of the southern coast, the Reddish Egret reveals itself as one of the most entertaining birds of North America. Its most distinctive—and most typical—foraging technique involves lurching through shallow water in a weaving half-run while stabbing its bill in all directions, attempting to catch a fish off guard. Standing motionless, holding its wings out to the side is another strategy—the shade provides better visibility by reducing the sun's glare and may also attract fish seeking shelter from the sun. The Reddish Egret also rakes the water substrate with its feet to expose bottom-dwelling prey. • Reddish Egrets spend much of their time hunting in the shallows of coastal mudflats. They also perch on large tree branches to wait out high tide.

breeding

dark morph

ID: gray with rusty brown neck and head; dark bluish legs; dark bill; pale eye. *Breeding:* shaggy neck plumes; pinkish bill with black tip. *Immature:* gray with cinnamon color on head, neck and inner wing; dark bill. *White morph:* rare in Georgia; all-dark legs and feet; pinkish bill with black tip in breeding plumage.
Size: *L* 27–32 in; *W* 3¾ ft.
Status: rare to uncommon nonbreeding visitor to the Coast year-round; accidental inland at Okefenokee NWR.
Habitat: coastal lagoons, salt marshes, tidal flats, estuaries and mangrove swamps.
Nesting: does not nest in Georgia.

Feeding: various feeding behaviors; eats mainly small fish; also eats tadpoles and crustaceans.
Voice: territorial low clucking notes; guttural croaks during nesting.
Similar Species: *Tricolored* (p. 90), *Little Blue* (p. 89) and *Great Blue* (p. 86) *herons:* all lack rusty brown neck; lack bill with dark tip in breeding plumage. *Immature Snowy Egret* (p. 88) and *Little Blue Heron* (p. 89): lack the all-dark legs and feet of adult white-morph Reddish Egret.
Best Sites: on the coast and barrier islands; St. Simons I.; Cumberland I.; Sapelo I.; mouth of Altamaha R. (HC-fall: 11).

91

CATTLE EGRET

Bubulcus ibis

Over the last century—and without help from humans—the Cattle Egret has dispersed from Africa to inhabit pastures and roadsides on every continent except Antarctica. Like most herons, the Cattle Egret is a natural wanderer. It spread from Africa to Brazil, through the Caribbean and, by the 1940s, to Florida, then across the United States. Cattle Egrets have even been sighted as far north as southern Alaska and near Great Slave Lake in Canada's Northwest Territories. • The Cattle Egret gets its name from its habit of following grazing animals. Unlike other egrets, its diet consists of terrestrial invertebrates—it feeds on the insects and other small creatures found around ungulates. When foraging, the Cattle Egret sometimes uses a "leapfrog" feeding strategy in which birds leap over one another, stirring up insects for the birds that follow. The Cattle Egret is mistakenly reputed to remove ticks from grazing animals, but the majority of its prey is taken from the ground. • This bird's scientific name *Bubulcus* means "belonging to or concerning cattle." The locals in Georgia often mistakenly call the Cattle Egret a "cowbird," a name that is officially restricted to Shiny Cowbirds and Brown-headed Cowbirds, two species in the blackbird family that also follow cattle.

breeding

breeding

ID: mostly white; yellow-orange bill and legs. *Breeding:* long plumes on throat and rump; buff orange throat, rump and crown; orange-red legs and bill; purple lores. *Immature:* similar to adult but with black feet and dark bill.
Size: *L* 19–21 in; *W* 3 ft.
Status: abundant summer breeding resident and rare in winter south of the Fall Line; uncommon visitor to the Piedmont in migration; rare in the Mountains in migration.
Habitat: agricultural fields, ranchlands and marshes.
Nesting: colonial; often among other herons; in a tree or tall shrub; male supplies sticks for the female who builds a platform or shallow bowl; pair incubates 3–4 pale blue eggs for 21–26 days.
Feeding: picks grasshoppers, other insects, worms, small vertebrates and spiders from fields; often associated with livestock.
Voice: generally silent away from the breeding colony; most common call is an unmusical *rick-rack*.
Similar Species: *Great Egret* (p. 87): larger; black legs and feet. *Snowy Egret* (p. 88): black legs; yellow feet. *Little Blue Heron* (p. 89): immature has blue-gray bill and yellowish olive legs. *Gulls* (pp. 167–75): do not stand as erect; generally have gray mantle.
Best Sites: on the Coastal Plain in fields and pastures, especially those with cattle; Cypress L. heronry; Laurens Co. (HC-fall: 11,000+).

GREEN HERON

Butorides virescens

This crow-sized heron prefers to hunt for frogs and small fish in shallow, weedy wetlands, where it often perches just above the water's surface. While hunting, Green Herons sometimes drop small debris, including twigs, vegetation and feathers, onto the water's surface as a form of bait to attract fish within striking range. • Unlike most herons, the Green Heron nests singly rather than communally, although it can sometimes be found in loose colonies. • If the light is just right, you may be fortunate enough to see a glimmer of green on the back and outer wings of this bird. Most of the time, however, this magical shine is not apparent, especially when the Green Heron often stands frozen under the shade of dense marshland vegetation. • The scientific name *virescens* is Latin for "growing or becoming green," and refers to this bird's transition from a streaky brown juvenile to a greenish adult.

nonbreeding

ID: stocky; green-black crown; chestnut face and neck; white foreneck and belly; blue-gray back and wings mixed with iridescent green; relatively short, yellow-green legs; bill is dark above and greenish below; short tail. *Breeding male:* bright orange legs. *Immature:* heavy streaking along neck and underparts; dark brown upperparts.

Size: *L* 15–22 in; *W* 26 in.

Status: common summer breeder statewide, especially in the Coastal Plain, from March to October; rare in winter in the Piedmont and Coastal Plain; rare to uncommon along the Coast in winter.

Habitat: marshes, lakes and streams with dense shoreline or emergent vegetation and mangroves.

Nesting: nests singly or in small, loose groups; male begins and female completes construction of a stick platform in a tree or shrub, usually very close to water; pair incubates 3–5 pale blue-green eggs for 19–21 days; young are fed by regurgitation.

Feeding: stabs prey with its bill after slowly stalking or standing and waiting; eats mostly small fish; also takes frogs, tadpoles, crayfish, insects, small rodents, snakes, snails and worms.

Voice: generally silent; alarm and flight call are a loud *kowp, kyow* or *skow;* aggression call is a harsh *raah.*

Similar Species: *Black-crowned Night-Heron* (p. 94): larger; white "cheek"; pale gray and white neck; 2 long, white plumes trail down from crown; immature has streaked face and white flecking on upperparts. *Least Bittern* (p. 85): buffy yellow shoulder patches, sides and flanks. *American Bittern* (p. 84): larger; more tan overall; black streak from bill to shoulder.

Best Sites: Savannah NWR; Harris Neck NWR; small, thicketed bodies of water (creek ditches and ponds); Augusta (HC: 187), Glynn Co. (HC: 11).

BLACK-CROWNED NIGHT-HERON

Nycticorax nycticorax

When the setting sun has sent most wetland waders to their nightly roosts, Black-crowned Night-Herons arrive to hunt the marshy waters and to voice their hoarse squawks. These herons patrol the shallows for prey, which they can see in the dim light with their large, light-sensitive eyes. They remain alongside water until morning, when they flap off to treetop roosts. • The Black-crowned Night-Heron is the most abundant heron in the world, occurring virtually worldwide. • A popular hunting strategy for day-active Black-crowned Night-Herons is to sit motionless atop a few bent-over cattails. Anything passing below the perch becomes fair game—even ducklings, small shorebirds or young muskrats. • Young night-herons are commonly seen around large cattail marshes in fall. Because of their heavily streaked underparts, immatures are easily confused with American Bitterns and other young herons. • *Nycticorax*, meaning "night raven," refers to this bird's distinctive nighttime calls.

immature

breeding

ID: black "cap" and back; white "cheek," foreneck and underparts; gray neck and wings; dull yellow legs; stout, black bill; large, red eyes. *Breeding:* 2 white plumes trail down from crown. *Immature:* lightly streaked underparts; brown upperparts with white flecking.
Size: *L* 23–26 in; *W* 3½ ft.
Status: uncommon to common permanent breeding resident near the Coast; uncommon to common breeder in the Coastal Plain (nests inland to Long Co. and Jenkins Co.); rare migrant north of the Fall Line.
Habitat: shallow cattail and bulrush marshes; lakeshores and along slow rivers.
Nesting: colonial; in a tree or shrub; male gathers the nest material; female builds a loose nest platform of twigs and sticks and lines it with finer materials; pair incubates 3–4 pale green eggs for 21–26 days.
Feeding: often at dusk; patient stand-and-wait predator; stabs for small fish, amphibians, aquatic invertebrates, reptiles, young birds and small mammals.
Voice: deep, guttural *quark* or *wok*, often heard as the bird takes flight.
Similar Species: *Great Blue Heron* (p. 86): much larger; longer legs; blue-gray back. *Yellow-crowned Night-Heron* (p. 95): white crown and "cheek" patch, otherwise black head; gray back; immature is very similar to Black-crowned immature. *Green Heron* (p. 93): chestnut brown face and neck; blue-gray back with green iridescence; immature has heavily streaked underparts. *American Bittern* (p. 84): similar to immature night-heron, but bittern has black streak from bill to shoulder and is lighter tan overall.
Best Sites: Harris Neck NWR (HC–winter: 177); Savannah NWR; Youman's Pond; barrier islands; Cypress L. heronry. *Winter:* inland at Augusta and Eufaula NWR.

YELLOW-CROWNED NIGHT-HERON

Nyctanassa violacea

Although night-herons are named for their habit of hunting from dusk until dawn, the Yellow-crowned Night-Heron also hunts during daylight hours, particularly when there are hungry mouths to feed. However, the Yellow-crowned Night-Heron's choice of dense habitat and its slow, nearly imperceptible movement makes this secretive bird a challenge to locate and observe.
• Unlike the Black-crowned Night-Heron, which relies primarily on fish, the Yellow-crowned Night-Heron specializes in catching crustaceans. With a thick bill and powerful neck muscles, the heron can quickly crack open the hard exoskeleton of a crayfish or a crab. • To catch up on sleep and replenish energy reserves, Yellow-crowneds roost-away in the safety of high tree branches.

immature

breeding

ID: black head with white "cheeks," white crown and yellowish forehead; stout black bill with pale base of lower mandible; slate gray neck and body; yellow legs. *Breeding:* long white head plumes extend down back of neck. *Immature:* brown plumage with white spotting; greenish yellow legs. *In flight:* legs extend well behind tail.
Size: *L* 24 in; *W* 3½ ft.
Status: uncommon to locally common permanent breeding resident on the Coast and in the lower Coastal Plain; rare in winter.
Habitat: swamps, bayous, estuaries, riparian thickets, shallow salt marshes, mangroves and other aquatic habitats with thick shoreline cover.

Nesting: along rivers and creeks with permanent water; nests singly or in colonies; occasionally with other wading birds; in a shrub or tree; builds a platform above the ground or water; pair incubates 2–4 pale bluish-green eggs for 21–25 days; pair raises young.
Feeding: eats crustaceans, primarily crayfish and crabs; will also take amphibians, fish, insects and mollusks; feeding tactics include standing and waiting as well as slow, methodical walking or wading.
Voice: rarely given call is a high, short *quok!*
Similar Species: *Black-crowned Night-Heron* (p. 94): black crown and back; lower half of face and undersides are white; immatures have dark streaking on buffy undersides.
Best Sites: along creeks and rivers in the Coastal Plain, including Youman's Pond (HC: 200+); inland at Ocmulgee River (HC: 26 pairs); Cypress L. heronry; Augusta Levee.

WHITE IBIS

Eudocimus albus

From April to November, White Ibises congregate on our coastline, picking slowly through the mud for tasty crabs or crayfish. This highly social species is one of the most common wading birds in Georgia, and regional colonies can number in the thousands. Because of its popularity as a game species, the White Ibis population has declined from historical levels. • Known as an opportunistic thief, this ibis will steal food from other wading birds and even snatch nest-building material from other ibises in its own colony. • Breeding is heavily dependent on the rainy season of May and June, because freshwater pools, which are formed at this time, are necessary for feeding salt-sensitive young. During or immediately following the rains, "bachelor parties" of hopeful males are commonly seen preening, soaring in circles or performing graceful acrobatics. Pairs form when the female accepts the male's offering of a stick. Although White Ibises roost in tight colonies, males are territorial and will jab or bite at challengers. • These highly nomadic birds commute between nesting and feeding areas in long, cohesive lines or "V" patterns.

breeding

nonbreeding

ID: white body; red face and legs; long, red, downcurved bill. *Breeding:* tip of bill becomes dark. *Immature:* brown-gray head, neck and upper sides; white rump and belly. *In flight:* dark wing tips; outstretched neck.

Size: *L* 22 in; *W* 3 ft.

Status: common breeding resident south of the Fall Line to the Coast and less common in winter; rare migrant or late summer wanderer to the Piedmont and the Mountains.

Habitat: shallow water; estuaries, mangroves, flooded fields and swamps.

Nesting: colonial, with up to 50 pairs in mangroves, thickets or forested swamps; will nest from ground level to 15 ft; nest is a platform of sticks, cordgrass or reeds; pair incubates 2–4 brown-splotched eggs for 21–22 days; pair cares for the young.

Feeding: sweeps and probes for varied crustaceans while walking in the shallows; also eats snakes, frogs and small fish.

Voice: mostly silent; throaty alarm or flight call: *hungk-hungk-hungk.*

Similar Species: *Glossy Ibis* (p. 97): same size and shape as immature but no white at all. *Curlews* (p. 143): streaked, brown bodies; black, downcurved bills; dark legs.

Best Sites: Grand Bay WMA (HC: 1000); Augusta (HC: 100+); Savannah NWR; causeways of St. Simons I. and Jekyll I.; Cypress Lake heronry; Harris Neck NWR.

GLOSSY IBIS

Plegadis falcinellus

The exotic look of the Glossy Ibis hints of its distant origins. The powerful trade winds that drew Christopher Columbus to North America are also most likely responsible for guiding these birds to the warm, productive Caribbean only a few centuries ago. Since the 1930s, the Glossy Ibis has quickly established stable breeding populations throughout the east coast of North America from its previously small, confined population in the rich coastal marshes of Florida. Sporadic breeding records along the coast of Maine and southeastern Canada suggest that this expansion will continue northward. • The Glossy Ibis is most often seen sweeping its head back and forth through the water, skillfully using its long, sickle-shaped bill like a precision instrument to probe the marshland mud for unseen prey. Its refined form and graceful movements are similar to those of its Eurasian relative, the Sacred Ibis, which is depicted as a worshipped deity in the hieroglyphic carvings of the ancient Egyptians.

breeding

nonbreeding

ID: long, downcurved bill; long legs; dark skin in front of brown eye is bordered by 2 pale stripes. *Breeding:* chestnut head, neck and sides; green and purple sheen on wings, tail, crown and face. *Nonbreeding:* dark, grayish brown head and neck streaked with white. *In flight:* neck fully extended; legs trail behind tail; hunchbacked appearance; flocks fly in lines or V-formation.

Size: *L* 22–25 in; *W* 3 ft.

Status: local breeding resident and rare in winter on the Coast; rare in the Coastal Plain from March to November; accidental in the Piedmont.

Habitat: freshwater and saltwater marshes, swamps, flooded fields and estuaries shallow enough for wading and with adequate shoreline vegetation for nesting.

Nesting: nests only on Altamaha R. and Satilla R.; in colonies, often intermixed with egrets and herons in rookeries; bulky platform of marsh vegetation and sticks is built over water, on the ground or on top of tall shrubs or small trees; new material is added to the nest until young fledge; 3–4 pale blue or green eggs are incubated by both sexes for approximately 21 days.

Feeding: wades through shallow water; probes and gleans for aquatic and terrestrial invertebrates, including insects (adults and larvae) and crayfish; may also eat amphibians (adults and larvae), snakes, leeches, crabs and small fish.

Voice: cooing accompanies billing and preening during nest relief.

Similar Species: *White Ibis* (p. 96): immature is dull brown with white belly and rump. *Double-crested Cormorant* (p. 81): much larger, with an upright gait and a straight, hooked bill.

Best Sites: Altamaha WMA (HC: 100+); Okefenokee NWR (HC-fall: 14); Satilla R.

ROSEATE SPOONBILL

Platalea ajaja

Roseate Spoonbills sport a bizarre mix of flamingo pink attire, an almost grotesque featherless head and a long paddle-shaped bill reminiscent of duck-billed dinosaur fossils. Ironically, this bird almost went the way of the dinosaurs after plume hunters of the 1800s hunted Roseate Spoonbills almost to extinction, marketing the rosy wings as fashionable fans for high society ladies. Only 30 spoonbills remained in Florida in 1939! Fortunately, enough of the birds survived among the thick mangroves of Florida and the Gulf Coast for populations to rebuild. • Typically, this bird is seen in small groups, often with other shorebirds. It may be found year-round along the coast of southern Florida or Texas, and rarely along the coast of Georgia. Some populations migrate south to the Caribbean during the cooler winter months. If you have the chance to visit the Roseate Spoonbill's mangrove haunts in Florida during the breeding season, you may be fortunate enough to witness its interesting courtship rituals, which include aggressive displays, romantic bill clasping and stick exchanging.

breeding

ID: long, reddish legs and long, paddle-shaped bill; generally pink plumage; white neck and back; red shoulders and rump; orange tail; greenish, unfeathered head may turn buff when breeding. *Immature:* mostly white with pink wings; white, feathered head; yellow-brown legs.
Size: *L* 32 in; *W* 4 ft.
Status: uncommon nonbreeding visitor to the southern Coast from March to October; rare visitor to the Coastal Plain from June to October; accidental elsewhere.
Habitat: saltwater and inland marshes, mangrove swamps and coastal islands, lagoons and mudflats.

Nesting: not known to nest in Georgia.
Feeding: aquatic invertebrates and fish are caught by feel when sweeping the slightly opened bill from side to side while wading through shallow water; invertebrate diet includes shrimp, mollusks, crabs, crayfish and aquatic insects; may eat some aquatic plant material.
Voice: generally silent.
Similar Species: *Wood Stork* (p. 99): all white with dark flight feathers; sickle-shaped bill.
Best Sites: Andrews I. (HC-fall: 60); Jekyll I.; Brunswick.

WOOD STORK

Mycteria americana

The Wood Stork is a denizen of swampy cypress woodlands in the Deep South. This large wader's choice of habitat, lack of attractive plumes and wary, elusive nature helped it to survive the ravages of early plume hunters. Unfortunately, water management projects such as diking, ditching and draining for land development in southern coastal states have more recently imperiled this bird's vital feeding and nesting habitats. • Wood Storks are protected nationwide as an endangered species. Because these storks have specific habitat needs, they are considered an indicator species. Monitoring one or more indicator species allows scientists to judge the state of an ecosystem without untangling every detail. In other words, a change in the size or the health of the Wood Stork population could indicate a change in the environment. • The prominent legend that storks bring forth human babies is many centuries old. The origin of this myth is somewhat of a mystery but most likely derived from the White Stork *(Ciconia ciconia)* of the Eastern Hemisphere, a bird that is still encouraged to nest on European rooftops.

ID: white plumage with black flight feathers and tail; naked, blackish gray head and neck; long, thick, dark, downcurved bill. *Immature:* yellow bill; feathered head and neck are gray-brown.

Size: *L* 3–3¼ ft; *W* 5–5½ ft.

Status: endangered (federal; state); uncommon breeder on the Coast and the Coastal Plain and rare elsewhere; rare in winter on the Coast and the Coastal Plain.

Habitat: lagoons, shallow marshes, cypress swamps, ponds, mangroves and flooded fields.

Nesting: colonial; flimsy stick platform lined with leaves and twigs is built high among cypress or mangroves; male brings nest material to the building female; pair alternate incubation of 2–5 white eggs over 28–32 days; pair feeds the young.

Feeding: partly open bill is inserted into water while wading and snaps shut upon contact with prey; prey is also located by sight; eats mostly fish; will also eat amphibians, reptiles, small mammals, crustaceans, aquatic insects and seeds.

Voice: adults are generally silent but may hiss at nest; young are raucous.

Similar Species: *White-faced Ibis:* white, feathered neck; red face; thin, reddish, downcurved bill. *Roseate Spoonbill* (p. 98): pink and red coloration; long, spatulate bill. *Whooping Crane* (p. 126): heronlike bill; red "cap."

Best Sites: the largest colonies are at Brooks Co. (400 pairs), Harris Neck NWR (300 pairs) and Jenkins Co. (150 pairs); smaller inland colonies are in Screven, Long, Brantley, Charlton, Lowndes and Worth counties.

BLACK VULTURE

Coragyps atratus

Much maligned for morbid feeding habits and sour looks verging on the hideous, this large scavenger is a vital part of a balanced ecosystem. Feeding primarily on carrion, the vulture helps to convert remnants of the dead into nutrients that support the living. In fact, without the Black Vulture's caretaking efforts in this critical cycle, a walk in the woods might be a less than delightful olfactory experience! • Look for these large birds soaring high amongst the clouds, scouring the earth below for signs of their next meal. • There is some evidence to suggest that smell is not as well developed in the Black Vulture as it is in the Turkey Vulture, and that Black Vultures may rely more on their keen vision to find "road-kills." Even if they don't arrive first, they are more aggressive than Turkey Vultures, and often get to eat first.

ID: black plumage with grayish head, legs and feet; bases of primaries are whitish.
Size: *L* 25 in; *W* 4¾ ft.
Status: common permanent breeding resident below about 1800 ft; less common in the Piedmont; rare in the Mountains.
Habitat: forages over open country but tends to roost and nest in forested areas.
Nesting: eggs are laid in a large tree cavity or on the ground in cave, thicket, abandoned building or other sheltered site; no nest material is used; pair incubates 1–3 pale, whitish eggs with some markings for 37–48 days; pair raises the young.
Feeding: carrion forms the bulk of the diet, which is supplemented with eggs, small reptiles, amphibians, small mammals, food wastes from garbage dumps and occasionally some plant material.
Voice: generally silent; may hiss or grunt at nest sites or around communal food sources.
Similar Species: *Turkey Vulture* (p. 101): pink head; 2-toned wings (dark wing linings and light flight feathers); longer, narrower wings and tail; wings usually held in a shallow V-shape.
Best Sites: roadsides; soaring overhead in wind currents; Rum Creek WMA & Piedmont NWR (HC-winter: 200+); Forsyth Co. (HC-winter: 200+).

TURKEY VULTURE

Cathartes aura

Turkey Vultures are unmatched at using updrafts and thermals—they can tease lift from the slightest pocket of rising air and patrol the skies when other soaring birds are grounded. • The Turkey Vulture eats carrion almost exclusively, so its bill and feet are not nearly as powerful as those of eagles, hawks and falcons, which kill live prey. Its red, featherless head may appear grotesque, but this adaptation allows the bird to remain relatively clean while feeding on messy carcasses. • Vultures seem to have mastered the art of regurgitation. This ability allows parents to transport food over long distances to their young and also enables engorged birds to repulse an attacker or "lighten up" for an emergency takeoff. • Mercaptans, the substances added to natural gas to give it its smell, are naturally produced in rotting organisms. It's common practice for Alaskan gas pipeline engineers to find cracks in a pipeline by looking for areas with vultures circling overhead. • Recent DNA molecular studies have shown that our two American vultures are more closely related to storks than to hawks and falcons, as was previously thought. The molecular similarities with storks, and the shared tendency to defecate on their own legs to cool down, strongly support this taxonomic reclassification.

ID: all black; bare, red head. *Immature:* gray head. *In flight:* head appears small; silver gray flight feathers; black wing linings; wings are held in a shallow "V"; rocks from side to side when soaring.
Size: *L* 26–32 in; *W* 5½–6 ft.
Status: common permanent breeding resident statewide.
Habitat: usually seen flying over open country, shorelines or roads; rarely seen over forested areas.
Nesting: in a cave crevice or among boulders; sometimes in a hollow stump or log; no nest material is used; female lays 2 dull white eggs, spotted and blotched with reddish brown; pair incubates the eggs for 38–41 days; young are fed by regurgitation.
Feeding: entirely on carrion (mostly mammalian); sometimes seen at roadkills.
Voice: generally silent; occasionally produces a hiss or grunt if threatened.
Similar Species: *Golden Eagle* (p. 112) and *Bald Eagle* (p. 105): lack silvery gray wing linings; wings are held flat in flight; do not rock when soaring; head is more visible in flight. *Black Vulture* (p. 100): gray head; silvery tips on otherwise black wings.
Best Sites: roadsides feeding on carrion; soaring overhead in wind currents. *In migration:* Forsyth Co. (HC: 300+); Columbus (HC: 270+); Decatur (HC: 300+); Jekyll I. (HC: 300+).

101

OSPREY

Pandion haliaetus

The Osprey eats fish exclusively and is found near water. While hunting, an Osprey will survey waterways from the air—its white belly makes it hard for fish to see it hovering far above the water's surface. The Osprey's dark eye line blocks the glare from the water, enabling it to spot a slowly moving shadow or a flash of silver near the water's surface. Once it has spotted a fish in the water, the Osprey folds its wings and hurls itself in a headfirst dive toward its target. An instant before striking the water, the bird rights itself and thrusts its feet forward to grasp the slippery prey, often striking the water with a tremendous splash. The Osprey's feet are specialized to prevent its catch from making a squirmy escape—two toes face forward, two face backward and the toes have sharp spines to help the Osprey clamp tightly onto even the slipperiest of fish. The Osprey always carries the fish it catches with the fish oriented parallel to its body when flying—the most aerodynamic position.
• The Osprey has been recently reclassified in the same family as the kites, hawks and eagles, but is the only species in its subfamily. One of the most widely distributed birds in the world, it is found on every continent except Antarctica.

ID: dark brown upperparts; white underparts; dark eye line; yellow eyes; light crown. *Male:* all-white throat. *Female:* fine, dark "necklace." *In flight:* long wings are held in a shallow "M"; dark "wrist" patches; brown-and-white-banded tail.
Size: *L* 22–25 in; *W* 4½–6 ft.
Status: uncommon to locally common breeder on the Coast and the Coastal Plain; increasing abundance in the Piedmont on large lakes and along major rivers; uncommon migrant elsewhere; uncommon to rare in winter, except more common along the Coast.
Habitat: lakes and slowly flowing rivers and streams.
Nesting: on a treetop, usually near water; may also use a specially made platform, utility pole or tower up to 100 ft high; massive stick nest is reused over many years; pair incubates 2–4 yellowish eggs,

spotted and blotched with reddish brown, for about 38 days; pair feeds the young, but the male hunts more.
Feeding: dramatic, feet-first dives into the water; fish, averaging 2 lbs, make up almost all of the diet.
Voice: series of melodious ascending whistles: *chewk-chewk-chewk;* also an often-heard *kip-kip-kip.*
Similar Species: *Bald Eagle* (p. 105): larger; holds its wings straighter while soaring; larger bill with yellow base; yellow legs; adult has clean white head and tail on otherwise dark body; lacks white underparts and dark "wrist" patches. *Rough-legged Hawk* (p. 361): smaller; hovers with wings in an open "V"; light phase has whitish wing linings and light tail band.
Best Sites: Lake Seminole WMA; Savannah NWR; Harris Neck NWR; Cumberland I. (HC-spring: 385).

SWALLOW-TAILED KITE

Elanoides forficatus

Gliding and swooping gracefully above the treetops, the striking black and white Swallow-tailed Kite is a breathtaking master of flight. Its incredible flying maneuverability is a product of powerful, swept-back wings and a strong, forked tail. These traits combine with a keen sense of sight and razor-sharp talons to produce a larger and more deadly version of the common Barn Swallow. • Swallow-tailed Kites tend to be early migrants, often arriving in Georgia in early March and departing for their southern wintering grounds in early fall. Once found as far north as the Great Lakes, their breeding range is now confined to the cypress swamps and riparian areas of the Deep South. Occasionally, adults that have completed their seasonal breeding responsibilities may wander into more northerly states. • Most Swallow-tailed Kites winter in South America, where they may add fruit to their typical diet.

ID: white head, undersides and underwing linings; black upperparts and dark eye; long, deeply forked tail. *Immature:* similar to adult with white-tipped primary feathers and shorter tail. *In flight:* never hovers.
Size: *L* 23 in; *W* 4 ft.
Status: uncommon to locally common breeding summer resident of the Coast and southeastern Coastal Plain from March to October.
Habitat: open pine woodlands near water; cypress swamps and riparian, swampy forests; prairie and agricultural land; requires tall trees (more than 60 ft) for nesting.
Nesting: usually on a tall pine tree, often near a cypress swamp; platform of sticks is lined with lichens and Spanish moss; both parents incubate 3–4 eggs for 28–31 days; pair feeds young.
Feeding: large insects, amphibians, lizards, snakes and small birds are caught on the wing or snatched from foliage or the ground with a swooping flight; often eats prey while flying; drinks while flying, skimming the water's surface like a swallow.
Voice: generally silent; alarm call is a rapid *kee-kee-kee-kee-kee.*
Similar Species: *Mississippi Kite* (p. 104): lacks forked tail; has grayer body and red eye. *Immature Magnificent Frigatebird* (p. 83): dark sides create an "open vest"; dark undertail coverts; long bill.
Best Sites: along Savannah, Ogeechee and Altamaha rivers; Big Hammock WMA (HC–late summer: 50+).

MISSISSIPPI KITE

Ictinia mississippiensis

Constantly fanning and twisting its long, rudderlike tail, the Mississippi Kite can swiftly adjust its position in the airy heights. This beautiful bird catches flying insects on the wing or hawks them out of the air. Dragonflies, cicadas, beetles and grasshoppers are favorite prey items and are often eaten in flight, straight from the bird's clutches. Occasionally, blazing, acrobatic aerial pursuits end in the successful capture of larger prey items, including bats, swallows and swifts. • This sociable inhabitant of southern Georgia's moist woodlands relies on the protection of tall trees for nesting and nighttime roosting but requires adjacent areas of open country for hunting. • In fall, large flocks of Mississippi Kites funnel through Texas and Mexico on their way to wintering grounds in southern South America. Typically, breeding Mississippi Kites arrive back in Georgia in April, and they often breed in quiet urban areas with tall trees. The breeding range of this native of the southeastern states seems to be expanding, and sightings now occur as far north as southern New England.

ID: long, swept-back wings with obviously shorter first primaries and pale secondaries; dark gray upperparts; dark tail; pale gray head and underparts; chestnut at base of primaries is often inconspicuous. *Immature:* darkly brownish upperparts; streaky brown underparts; pale translucent bands in dark tail. *In flight:* never hovers; often migrates in small flocks.

Size: *L* 14½ in; *W* 35 in.

Status: uncommon to common summer breeding resident of the Coast and the Coastal Plain, north to the Fall Line, from April to October; rare to uncommon nonbreeder in the Piedmont and the Mountains.

Habitat: riparian woodlands, swamps, woodlot groves and shelterbelts close to open country.

Nesting: nests in small, loose colonies; pair constructs a flimsy stick platform lined with leaves in a relatively tall tree or shrub near the edge of a wooded area; pair incubates 2 eggs and raises young.

Feeding: prey is caught on the wing or in a swooping flight; large flying insects form bulk of diet; small mammals, small birds, frogs, toads, lizards, turtles, snakes and bats are taken; may scavenge roadkill.

Voice: generally silent; call is a high-whistled *pee-weeeeeeee;* disturbed birds give an alarm call: *kee kew, kee kew.*

Similar Species: *Male Northern Harrier* (p. 106): white rump patch; dark wing tips; facial disc. *Swallow-tailed Kite* (p. 103): long, deeply forked tail. *Peregrine Falcon* (p. 116): dark "helmet" and finely barred undersides.

Best Sites: swamp areas of Ocmulgee, Altamaha, Ogeechee and Savannah rivers; Big Hammock WMA; occasionally suburban areas. *In migration:* Augusta (HC: 50); Lake Seminole WMA (HC: 100+); Crawford Co. and Taylor Co. (HC: 30).

BALD EAGLE

Haliaeetus leucocephalus

Bald Eagle nesting pairs perform dramatic aerial displays. In the most impressive display, the two birds fly to a great height, lock talons and then tumble perilously toward the earth. They break off at the last second, just before crashing into the ground. • Bald Eagles generally mate for life. They renew their pair bonds each year by adding new sticks and branches to their massive nests, which are the largest of any North American bird. As of 2005, there were over 80 active Bald Eagle nests in our state, with many on the barrier islands. • As part of the sea eagle group, the Bald Eagle feeds mostly on fish and scavenged carrion. Sometimes an eagle will steal food from an Osprey, resulting in a spectacular aerial chase. • Bald Eagles do not mature until their fourth or fifth year, only then receiving their characteristic white head and tail plumage.

immature

ID: white head and tail; dark brown body; yellow bill and feet. *1st year:* dark overall; dark bill; some white in underwings. *2nd year:* dark "bib"; white in underwings. *3rd year:* mostly white plumage; yellow at base of bill; yellow eyes. *4th year:* light head with dark facial streak; variable pale and dark plumage; yellow bill; paler eyes. *In flight:* broad wings are held flat.

Size: *L* 30–43 in; *W* 5½–8 ft.

Status: threatened (federal); endangered (state); uncommon local breeding resident on the Coast, the Coastal Plain and the southern Piedmont, but rare in the Mountains; uncommon migrant and local winter resident statewide.

Habitat: large lakes and rivers.

Nesting: usually in a tree bordering a large water body, but may be far from water; huge stick nest, up to 15 ft across, is reused for many years; pair incubates 1–3 white eggs for 34–36 days; pair feeds the young; young remain in the nest until they can fly, often for more than 2 months.

Feeding: eats waterbirds, small mammals and fish captured at the water's surface; frequently feeds on carrion.

Voice: thin, weak squeal or gull-like cackle: *kleek-kik-kik-kik* or *kah-kah-kah.*

Similar Species: adult is distinctive. *Golden Eagle* (p. 112): dark overall, except for golden nape; tail may appear faintly banded with white; immature has prominent white patch on wings and at base of tail. *Osprey* (p. 102): like a 4th-year Bald Eagle, but has dark "wrist" patches, dark bill, and M-shaped wings in flight.

Best Sites: Eufaula, Sinclair, Juliette and West Point lakes; Lake Seminole WMA (HC-winter: 11); St. Catherines I. (HC-winter: 8).

NORTHERN HARRIER

Circus cyaneus

The Northern Harrier may be the easiest raptor to identify on the wing because no other midsized bird routinely flies so close to the ground, displaying its prominent white rump and holding its wings in a slight "V" position. It cruises low over fields, meadows and marshes, grazing the tops of long grasses and cattails, and relying on sudden surprise attacks to capture prey. Interestingly, the Northern Harrier uses its ears almost as effectively as the owl to find its prey while hunting (note its owl-like facial pattern, which enhances sound collection).

• The Northern Harrier was once known as the "Marsh Hawk" in North America, and it is still called "Hen Harrier" in Europe. Britain's Royal Air Force was so impressed by this bird's maneuverability that it named its Harrier aircraft after it.

• Northern Harriers are fairly common winter residents in Georgia, but in recent years the North American population has declined in numbers, owing to the loss of wetland habitat. Look for these majestic birds flying low over weedy fields or coastal marshes.

ID: long wings and tail; white rump; black wing tips. *Male:* blue-gray to silver gray upperparts; white underparts; indistinct tail bands, except for 1 dark subterminal band. *Female:* dark brown upperparts; streaky brown and buff underparts. *Immature:* rich, reddish brown plumage; dark tail bands; streaked breast, sides and flanks.

Size: *L* 16–24 in; *W* 3½–4 ft.

Status: common winter resident, but uncommon in the Mountains.

Habitat: open country, including fields, wet meadows, cattail marshes, bogs and croplands.

Nesting: does not nest in Georgia.

Feeding: hunts in low, rising and falling flights, often skimming the top of vegetation; eats small mammals, birds, amphibians, reptiles and some invertebrates.

Voice: generally quiet in Georgia.

Similar Species: *Rough-legged Hawk* (p. 361): broader wings; dark "wrist" patches; black tail with wide, white base; dark belly. *Red-tailed Hawk* (p. 111): lacks white rump and long, narrow tail.

Best Sites: flying low over old fields, agricultural fields and coastal marshes; Cobb Owl Fields (HC: 30); Cumberland I. (HC: 60).

SHARP-SHINNED HAWK

Accipiter striatus

After a successful hunt, the small Sharp-shinned Hawk usually perches on a favorite "plucking post," grasping a meal in its razor-sharp talons. This hawk preys almost exclusively on small birds, pursuing them in high-speed chases. With exceptionally long talons and large eyes, the "Sharpie" can catch its fast-moving prey in flight. You may spot a Sharpie feeding on smaller birds at a rural feedlot or pasture, or even at your backyard bird feeder, where it can take birds as large as doves.
• Though male hawks are often much smaller than females, the Sharp-shinned Hawk is the most sexually dimorphic of all North American raptors. On average, the male weighs just slightly more than half that of the female.
• Accipiters, named after their genus, are woodland hawks. Their short, rounded wings, long, rudderlike tails and flap-and-glide flight pattern give them the maneuverability necessary to negotiate a maze of forest foliage at high speeds.

ID: short, rounded wings; long, straight, heavily barred, square-tipped tail; dark barring on pale underwings; blue-gray back; red, horizontal bars on underparts; red eyes. *Immature:* brown overall; dark eyes; vertical, brown streaking on breast and belly. *In flight:* flap-and-glide flier; very agile in wooded areas.

immature

Size: *Male: L* 10–12 in; *W* 20–24 in. *Female: L* 12–14 in; *W* 24–28 in.
Status: uncommon permanent breeding resident in the Piedmont and the Mountains; common fall migrant on the Coast and in the Mountains from August to April; uncommon winter resident statewide.
Habitat: dense to semi-open forests and large woodlots; occasionally along rivers and in urban areas; favors bogs and dense, moist coniferous forests for nesting.
Nesting: in conifers; builds a new stick nest each year or might remodel an abandoned corvid nest; female incubates 4–5 brown-blotched, bluish white eggs for 34–35 days; male feeds the female during incubation; nestlings fed by both parents until fledging at 24–27 days.

Feeding: pursues small birds through forests; rarely takes small mammals, amphibians and insects.
Voice: silent except during the breeding season, when an intense and often repeated *kik-kik-kik-kik* can be heard.
Similar Species: *Cooper's Hawk* (p. 108): larger; more rounded tail tip has broader terminal band; crown is darker than nape and back. *American Kestrel* (p. 113–14): long, pointed wings; 1 dark "tear streak" and 1 dark "sideburn"; typically seen in open country. *Merlin* (p. 115): pointed wings; rapid wingbeats; 1 dark "tear streak"; brown streaking on buff underparts; dark eyes.
Best Sites: *Fall migration:* along the coast; Jekyll I. (HC: 1000+). *Winter:* Savannah NWR; Harris Neck NWR; Cumberland I.

COOPER'S HAWK

Accipiter cooperii

Larger and heavier than the Sharp-shinned Hawk, the Cooper's Hawk glides silently along swamps and flood plains, using surprise and speed to snatch its prey from midair. Females can seize and decapitate birds as large as chickens, a trait that has earned this species the nickname "Chicken Hawk." • These birds are protected by law in all states and the use of DDT has been banned throughout North America, with the result that the Cooper's Hawk is increasing in numbers and slowly recolonizing former habitats in the region. • Distinguishing the Cooper's Hawk from the Sharp-shinned Hawk is challenging, and the challenge is heightened by the nearly identical sizes of the female Sharpie and the male Cooper's. In flight, the Cooper's has a shallower, stiffer-winged flight, whereas the Sharpie has deeper wingbeats with more bending in the wings. Also, Sharpies have a square tail, whereas the Cooper's tail is more rounded.

immature

Status: uncommon permanent breeding resident; more numerous in fall migration and winter.

Habitat: mixed woodlands, riparian woodlands and urban woodlots.

Nesting: nest of sticks and twigs is built 20–26 ft up in a deciduous tree; often near a stream or pond; might use abandoned crow nest; female incubates 3–5 bluish white eggs for 34–36 days; male feeds the female during incubation.

Feeding: pursues prey in flights through forests; eats mostly songbirds but occasionally takes squirrels and chipmunks; uses "plucking post" or nest for eating.

Voice: fast *cac-cac-cac-cac.*

Similar Species: *Sharp-shinned Hawk* (p. 107): smaller; less rounded tail tip; thinner terminal tail band. *American Kestrel* (p. 113–14): smaller; long, pointed wings; 1 dark "tear streak" and 1 dark "sideburn"; typically seen in open country. *Merlin* (p. 115): smaller; pointed wings; rapid wingbeats; 1 dark "tear streak"; brown streaking on buff underparts; dark eyes.

Best Sites: *Winter:* Harris Neck NWR; Cumberland I.; Jekyll I.; inland at Eufaula NWR, Rum Creek WMA and Athens (HC-winter: 10).

ID: short, rounded wings; long, straight, heavily barred, rounded tail; dark barring on pale undertail and underwings; squarish head; blue-gray back; red, horizontal barring on underparts; red eyes; white terminal tail band. *Immature:* brown overall; dark eyes; vertical brown streaks on breast and belly. *In flight:* flap-and-glide flier.

Size: *Male: L* 15–17 in; *W* 27–32 in. *Female: L* 17–19 in; *W* 32–37 in.

RED-SHOULDERED HAWK

Buteo lineatus

The Red-shouldered Hawk nests in mature trees, usually around river bottoms and in lowland tracts of woods alongside creeks. As spring approaches and pair bonds are formed, this normally quiet hawk utters loud, shrieking *key-yair* calls. Be forewarned that Blue Jays have mastered an impressive impersonation of the Red-shouldered Hawk's vocalizations.
• In summer, the dense cover of this hawk's forested breeding habitat allows few viewing opportunities. However, in migration the Red-shouldered Hawk can be found hunting from exposed perches. Some individuals may hunt even as far as one-half mile from the nearest stand of trees. Fortunately for birders, this hawk's seasonal use of telephone poles and fence posts for hunting gives observers a better glimpse into its otherwise private life. • If left undisturbed, Red-shouldered Hawks will remain faithful to productive nesting sites, returning yearly. After the parents die, one of the young will carry on the family nesting tradition.

immature

ID: chestnut red shoulders on otherwise dark brown upperparts; reddish underwing linings; narrow, white bars on dark tail; barred, reddish breast and belly; reddish undertail coverts.
Immature: large, brown "teardrop" streaks on white underparts; whitish undertail coverts. *In flight:* light and dark barring on underside of flight feathers and tail; white crescents or "windows" at base of primaries.
Size: *L* 19 in; *W* 3½ ft.
Status: locally common permanent breeding resident; more common on the Coast and the Coastal Plain.
Habitat: mature deciduous and mixed forests, wooded riparian areas, swampy woodlands and large, mature woodlots.
Nesting: breeds to 1700 ft and in many quiet urban areas; pair assembles a bulky nest of sticks and twigs, usually 15–80 ft above the ground in the crotch of a deciduous tree (prefers mature maple, ash and beech trees); nest is often reused; female incubates 2–4 darkly blotched, bluish white eggs for about 33 days; pair raises the young.
Feeding: prey is usually detected from a fence post, tree or telephone pole and caught in a swooping attack; may catch prey flushed by low flight; eats small mammals, birds, reptiles and amphibians.
Voice: repeated series of high *key-yair* notes.
Similar Species: *Broad-winged Hawk* (p. 110): lacks reddish shoulders; wings are broader, more whitish and dark-edged underneath; wide, white tail bands. *Red-tailed Hawk* (p. 111): lacks barring on tail and light "windows" at base of primaries.
Best Sites: wetland or riparian areas; Okefenokee NWR (HC-winter: 42); Lake Lanier; Harris Neck NWR; Phinizy Swamp Nature Park; Rum Creek WMA; Big Hammock WMA.

BROAD-WINGED HAWK

Buteo platypterus

The generally shy and secretive Broad-winged Hawk shuns the open fields and forest clearings favored by other buteos, such as the Red-shouldered Hawk, to seclude itself in dense, often wet forests. In this habitat, its short, broad wings and highly flexible tail help it to maneuver in the heavy growth. • Most hunting is done from a high perch with a good view. After being flushed from its perch, the Broad-winged Hawk will return and resume its vigilant search for a meal. • At the end of the nesting season, "kettles" of buteos and other hawks spiral up from their forest retreats, testing thermals for the opportunity to head south. Broad-winged Hawks are often the most numerous species in these flocks. • Broad-winged Hawks are commonly seen on utility poles or wires, resting and watching for rodents. • This hawk will often breed in quiet urban areas with tall trees.

dark morph

ID: broad, black and white tail bands; broad wings with pointed tips; heavily barred, rufous brown breast; dark brown upperparts. *Immature:* dark brown "teardrop" streaks on white breast, belly and sides; buff and dark brown tail bands. *In flight:* pale underwings are outlined with dark brown.
Size: *L* 14–19 in; *W* 32–39 in.
Status: uncommon to common summer breeding resident in the Piedmont and the Mountains from February to November; rare local breeder in the Coastal Plain; uncommon to locally abundant migrant, especially in fall in northwestern Georgia.
Habitat: dense mixed and deciduous forests and woodlots. *In migration:* escarpments and shorelines; also uses riparian and deciduous forests and woodland edges.

Nesting: usually in a deciduous tree, often near water; bulky stick nest is built in a crotch 20–40 ft above the ground; usually builds a new nest each year; mostly the female incubates 2–4 brown-spotted, whitish eggs for 28–31 days; pair raises the young.
Feeding: swoops from a perch for small mammals, amphibians, insects and young birds; often seen hunting from roadside telephone poles in northern areas.
Voice: high-pitched, whistled *peeeo-wee-ee;* generally silent during migration.
Similar Species: Other *buteo hawks* (pp. 109, 111, 361): lack broad banding on tail and broad, dark-edged wings with pointed tips. *Accipiter hawks* (pp. 107–08): long, narrow tails with less distinct banding.
Best Sites: Brasstown Bald; Rabun Bald; Rum Creek WMA. *Fall:* Lake Allatoona Dam (HC: 2100); Chattahoochee R. (HC: 600+); Kennesaw Mt. (HC: 236).

RED-TAILED HAWK

Buteo jamaicensis

Throughout much of North America, Red-tailed Hawks are the most common hawks around. Red-tails use pockets of warm air to soar—rising air currents, known as thermals and updrafts, hold the hawks up and help them to glide. These masters of the skies are so adept at teasing lift out of air currents that during migration they may fly almost 2 miles without flapping once. On cool days without much lift, hawks save energy by scanning the fields from a high perch. During their spring courtship, excited Red-tailed Hawks dive at each other, sometimes locking talons and tumbling through the air together before breaking off to avoid crashing to the ground. • The Red-tailed Hawk's impressive piercing call is often paired with the image of an eagle in TV commercials and movies. • This hawk's tail does not obtain its brick red coloration until the bird matures into a breeding adult, usually by its second year.

immature

ID: red tail; dark upperparts with some white highlights; dark brown band of streaks across belly. *Immature:* extremely variable; lacks red tail; generally darker; band of streaks on belly. *In flight:* fan-shaped tail; white or occasionally tawny brown underside and underwing linings; dark leading edge on underside of wing; light underwing flight feathers with faint barring.

Size: *Male: L* 18–23 in; *W* 4–5 ft. *Female: L* 20–25 in; *W* 4–5 ft.

Status: common permanent breeding resident statewide; more common in winter.

Habitat: open country with some trees; also roadsides, fields, woodlots, hedgerows, mixed forests and moist woodlands.

Nesting: in woodlands adjacent to open habitat; usually in a deciduous tree; rarely on a cliff or in a conifer; bulky stick nest is usually added to each year; pair incubates 2–4 brown-blotched, whitish eggs for 28–35 days; male brings food to the female and young.

Feeding: scans for food while perched or soaring; drops to capture prey; rarely stalks prey on foot; eats voles, mice, rabbits, chipmunks, birds, amphibians and reptiles; rarely takes large insects.

Voice: powerful, descending scream: *keeearrrr* is given year-round.

Similar Species: *Rough-legged Hawk* (p. 361): white tail base; dark "wrist" patches on underwings; broad, dark, terminal tail band. *Broad-winged Hawk* (p. 110): broadly banded tail; broader wings with pointed tips; lacks dark "belt." *Red-shouldered Hawk* (p. 109): reddish wing linings and underparts; reddish shoulders.

Best Sites: almost anywhere, even cities and college campuses. *Winter:* Athens (HC: 61).

GOLDEN EAGLE

Aquila chrysaetos

The Golden Eagle is a western bird associated with mountainous areas, and is therefore a rare treat for eastern birders. Previously thought to be nonmigratory, it in fact does migrate, and its migration route along the Rocky Mountains was discovered in 1992. • The Georgia Department of Natural Resources has released over 100 young in recent years on the Lookout Plateau at Crockford-Pigeon Mountain Wildlife Management Area, where breeding has occurred. • The Golden Eagle is actually more closely related to the buteos than it is to the Bald Eagle. Unlike the Bald Eagle, the Golden Eagle is an active, impressive predator, taking prey as large as foxes, cranes and geese. This fantastic flier can soar high above mountain passes for hours, sometimes stooping at great speeds—150 to 200 miles per hour—for prey or for fun. Few people ever forget the sight of a Golden Eagle soaring overhead—the average wingspan of an adult exceeds 6 feet! • Perceived as a threat to livestock, this noble bird was once the victim of a lengthy persecution. Bounties were offered, encouraging the shooting and poisoning of this regal bird. Today, like all other migratory birds, the Golden Eagle is protected under the Migratory Bird Act.

immature

ID: very large; brown overall with golden tint to neck and head; brown eyes; dark bill; brown tail has grayish white bands; yellow feet; fully feathered legs. *Immature:* white tail base; white patch at base of underwing primary feathers. *In flight:* relatively short neck; long tail; long, large, rectangular wings.
Size: *L* 30–40 in; *W* 6½–7½ ft.
Status: uncommon to rare migrant and winter visitor statewide from September to April; recently reintroduced into northwestern Georgia, where breeding has occurred.
Habitat: semi-open woodlands and fields.

Nesting: usually in a tree in open habitats, especially in the Mountains; huge stick nest is reused for many years; pair incubates 1–2 white eggs for 43–45 days; pair feeds the young; young remain in the nest until they can fly, often for more than 2 months.
Feeding: swoops on prey from a soaring flight; eats hares, grouse, rodents, foxes and occasionally young ungulates; often eats carrion.
Voice: generally quiet in winter; thin, weak squeal or gull-like cackle: *kleek-kik-kik-kik* or *kah-kah-kah.*
Similar Species: *Bald Eagle* (p. 105): longer neck; shorter tail; immature lacks distinct, white underwing patches and tail base. *Turkey Vulture* (p. 101): naked, pink head; pale flight feathers; dark wing linings.
Best Sites: Crockford-Pigeon Mountain WMA. *Winter:* Okefenokee NWR.

AMERICAN KESTREL

Falco sparverius sparverius

The American Kestrel is the smallest and most common of our cavity-nesting falcons. A helpful identification tip when viewing this bird from afar is that the American Kestrel repeatedly lifts its tail while perched, as it scouts the habitat below for prey. • There are two kestrel subspecies in Georgia. The migratory "northern" subspecies (*F. s. sparverius*) described in this account is a common statewide winter resident in Georgia, most common from October through mid-April. It is thought to breed only in the mountains—recent research indicates a small breeding colony at Carter's Lake in Murray County. • Studies have shown that the Eurasian Kestrel can detect ultraviolet reflections from rodent urine on the ground. It is not known if the American Kestrel has this same ability, but it is frequently seen hovering above the ground while looking for small, ground-dwelling prey. • Old field guides and old-time birders refer to the American Kestrel as "Sparrow Hawk," and its scientific name *sparverius* means "pertaining to a sparrow."

ID: 2 distinctive facial stripes. *Male:* rusty back; blue-gray wings; blue-gray crown with rusty "cap"; lightly spotted underparts; barring on back. *Female:* rusty back, wings and breast streaking. *In flight:* frequently hovers; long, rusty tail; buoyant, indirect flight style.
Size: *L* 9–10½ in; *W* 20–24 in.
Status: permanent breeding resident in the Mountains; common to abundant winter resident statewide, mostly from October to mid-April.
Habitat: open fields, riparian woodlands, woodlots, forest edges, bogs, roadside ditches, grassy highway medians, grasslands and croplands.
Nesting: in a tree cavity (usually in an abandoned woodpecker or flicker cavity); may use a nest box; mostly the female incubates 4–6 white to pale brown eggs,

spotted with brown and gray, for 29–30 days; pair raises the young.
Feeding: swoops from a perch (a tree, post or power line) or from hovering flight; eats mostly insects and some small rodents, birds, reptiles and amphibians.
Voice: loud, often repeated, shrill *killy-killy-killy* when excited; often calls in flight; female's voice is lower pitched.
Similar Species: *Merlin* (p. 115): only 1 facial stripe; less colorful; does not hover; flight is more powerful and direct. *Sharp-shinned Hawk* (p. 107): short, rounded wings; reddish barring on underparts; lacks facial stripes; flap-and-glide flight. *Southeastern Kestrel* (p. 114): smaller; male has reduced rusty "cap," absent or sparse spotting on breast and less barring on upperback; female has light rufous breast streaking.
Best Sites: statewide in winter. *Breeding:* Carters L.

113

SOUTHEASTERN KESTREL

Falco sparverius paulus

This subspecies of the American Kestrel is about one-quarter smaller than its northern counterpart and has some differences in plumage, mostly relating to breast spotting and density of barring on the back of males. It can be difficult to differentiate from the northern migratory subspecies in migration and winter, but only the Southeastern Kestrel is found south of the mountains in summer. • Kestrels hunt largely by sight, and an important component of the open pine woodlands that they prefer is short understory vegetation, which allows these birds to forage more effectively. This habitat also provides snags with natural cavities, in which Southeastern Kestrels make their nests. Loss of open pine woodlands is largely responsible for this species' decline in part of its range. • These adaptive birds readily adopt nest boxes, and they will even nest in the tubular cross-arms of electrical transmission towers. In fact, the largest population in the state nests in these towers from Pierce County westward to Dougherty County. • There is some evidence to suggest that the Southeastern Kestrel may be a separate species rather than a subspecies of the American Kestrel.

ID: 2 distinctive facial stripes. *Male:* rusty back; blue-gray wings; blue-gray crown with small, rusty "cap"; no spots on breast and only a few spots on belly; very little barring on upperback. *Female:* rusty back, wings and breast streaking. *In flight:* frequently hovers; long, rusty tail; buoyant, indirect flight style.

Size: *L* 7–8 in; 16½–18 in.

Status: permanent breeding resident in the Piedmont and the Coastal Plain.

Habitat: open pine woodlands, open fields, riparian woodlands, forest edges, bogs, grasslands and croplands.

Nesting: in a tree cavity (usually an abandoned woodpecker or flicker cavity); commonly use a nest box; mostly the female incubates 4–6 white to pale brown eggs, spotted with brown and gray, for 29–30 days; pair raises the young.

Feeding: swoops from a perch (tree, post or power line) or from hovering flight; eats mostly insects and lizards; also eats small rodents, birds and other reptiles.

Voice: loud, often repeated, shrill *killy-killy-killy* when excited; often calls in flight; female's voice is lower pitched.

Similar Species: *Merlin* (p. 115): only 1 facial stripe; less colorful; does not hover; flight is more powerful and direct. *Sharp-shinned Hawk* (p. 107): short, rounded wings; reddish barring on underparts; lacks facial stripes; flap-and-glide flight. *American Kestrel* (p. 113): larger; male has larger rusty "cap," more heavily spotted underparts and more heavily barred back; female has dark brown breast streaking.

Best Sites: Pierce Co. to Dougherty Co.; Atlanta; Statesboro; Ft. Gordon.

MERLIN
Falco columbarius

Like all its falcon relatives, the Merlin has speed, surprise and sharp, daggerlike talons as its main weapons. This small falcon's sleek body, long, narrow tail and pointed wings increase its aerodynamic efficiency for high-speed songbird pursuits. Horned Larks and Cedar Waxwings are famous for trying to outfly the Merlin, which results in prey and pursuer circling to great heights. • Most Merlins migrate to Central and South America each fall, but a few overwinter in Georgia, capitalizing on the abundance of shorebirds and songbirds. • Medieval falconers termed the Merlin "the lady's hawk," and Catherine the Great and Mary Queen of Scots were among the enthusiasts who would pitch Merlins and Sky Larks (*Alauda arvensis*) into matches of aerial prowess. • The Merlin was formerly known as the "Pigeon Hawk," and its scientific name *columbarius* comes from the Latin for "pigeon," which it somewhat resembles in flight.

prairie morph

taiga morph

ID: banded tail; heavily streaked underparts; 1 indistinct facial stripe; long, narrow wings and tail. *Male:* blue-gray back and crown; rufous leg feathers. *Female:* brown back and crown. *In flight:* very rapid, shallow wingbeats.
Size: *L* 10–12 in; *W* 23–26 in.
Status: uncommon migrant and rare to uncommon winter resident from July to May; more common along the Coast.
Habitat: open fields and shorelines.
Nesting: does not nest in Georgia.
Feeding: overtakes smaller birds in flight; also eats rodents and large insects, such as grasshoppers and dragonflies; may also take bats.

Voice: generally silent in Georgia; loud, noisy, cackling cry: *kek-kek-kek-kek-kek* or *ki-ki-ki-ki* calls in flight.
Similar Species: *American Kestrel* (pp. 113–14): 2 facial stripes; more colorful; less direct flight style; often hovers. *Peregrine Falcon* (p. 116): larger; well-marked, dark "helmet"; pale, unmarked upper breast; black flecking on light under-parts. *Sharp-shinned Hawk* (p. 107) and *Cooper's Hawk* (p. 108): short, rounded wings; reddish barring on breast and belly. *Rock Pigeon* (p. 187): broader wings in flight; shorter tail; often glides with wings held in a "V."
Best Sites: along the coast in fall migration; Harris Neck NWR; St. Catherines I; Jekyll I. (HC: 12); Cumberland I. (HC: 36).

PEREGRINE FALCON

Falco peregrinus

No bird elicits more admiration than a hunting Peregrine Falcon in full flight, and nothing causes more panic in a tightly packed flock of ducks or shorebirds. Every twist and turn the flock makes is matched by the falcon until it finds a weaker or less experienced bird. Diving at speeds of up to 200 miles per hour, the Peregrine clenches its feet and then strikes its prey with a lethal blow that often sends both falcon and prey tumbling. • The Peregrine Falcon's awesome speed and hunting skills were little defense against the pesticide DDT. The chemical caused contaminated birds to lay eggs with thin shells, and the eggs broke when the adults incubated them. This bird was completely eradicated east of the Mississippi River by 1964. DDT was banned in North America in 1972 and, in 1975, the Eastern Peregrine Recovery Program was created and has successfully reintroduced the Peregrine Falcon in the eastern U.S. • Peregrine Falcons are a cosmopolitan species, nesting on every continent except Antarctica.

ID: blue-gray back; prominent, dark "helmet"; light underparts with dark, fine spotting and flecking. *Immature:* brown where adult is blue-gray; heavier breast streaks; gray (rather than yellow) feet and cere. *In flight:* pointed wings; long, narrow, dark-banded tail.

Size: *Male: L* 15–17 in; *W* 3–3½ ft.
Female: L 17–19 in; *W* 3½–4 ft.

Status: uncommon migrant and winter resident; nests in downtown Atlanta; historical nesting at Lookout Mt.

Habitat: coastal areas, lakeshores, river valleys, river mouths, urban areas and open fields.

Nesting: usually on a rocky cliff or cut-bank; may use a skyscraper ledge; no material is added, but nest is littered with prey remains, leaves and grass; nest sites are often reused;

mostly the female incubates 3–4 creamy to buff eggs, heavily blotched with reddish brown, for 32–34 days.

Feeding: high-speed, diving stoops; strikes birds with clenched feet in midair; takes primarily pigeons, waterfowl, shorebirds, flickers and larger songbirds; rarely eats small mammals or carrion; prey is consumed on a nearby perch.

Voice: loud, harsh, continuous *cack-cack-cack-cack-cack* near the nest site.

Similar Species: *Merlin* (p. 115): smaller; lacks prominent, dark "helmet"; heavily streaked breast and belly. *American Kestrel* (pp. 113–14): 2 facial stripes; more colorful; often hovers.

Best Sites: nesting pair at Marriott Marquis Hotel in downtown Atlanta. *Fall:* on the coast; Altamaha WMA (HC: 17); Cumberland I. (HC: 93).

BLACK RAIL

Laterallus jamaicensis

The sparrow-sized Black Rail is one of North America's most elusive marshland birds. Its small size and secretive, partly nocturnal habits have most birders wondering if this bird really exists. Its voice—a repeated *ki-kee-der* for the male and a *who-whoo* for the female—is often the only clue to its presence. • When high tides force this bird to higher, drier areas, you may, if you're lucky, catch a glimpse of a Black Rail scampering rodentlike through saltwater marshes. Another approach is to visit the beach at dawn or dusk during low tide, when it cautiously forages in mudflats or bathes at the water's edge. This rail often inhabits wetland swales in migration; listen for it in these areas near dusk or dawn. • In Georgia, this poorly known rail is thought to breed in the Piedmont at Greene County and also in scattered locations along the coast. It often nests in clumps of cordgrass, saltgrass or bulrushes. The well-concealed nest is often covered by a domed roof and is connected to the ground by an entrance ramp, constructed out of vegetation. • Protection of marshland and critical rethinking of the consequences of draining and ditching fragile marshes will help to ensure the survival of this enigmatic creature.

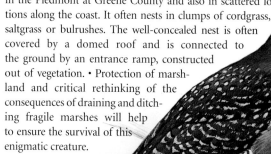

ID: tiny; short, black bill; small, stocky body; large feet; blackish upperparts with white flecking and chestnut nape; dark grayish black underparts with white barring on the flanks; red eyes.
Size: *L* 6 in; *W* 9 in.
Status: poorly known rare to uncommon migrant; possible rare local breeder in the Piedmont and along along the Coast.
Habitat: saltwater or brackish tidal marshes; also freshwater cattail and bulrush marshes at lower elevations.
Nesting: breeds very locally; a cup-shaped nest of vegetation, sometimes with a woven domed canopy, is located among dense vegetation just above the water; ramp of dead vegetation connects nest entrance to the ground; pair incubates 4–10 creamy white eggs for 16–20 days; pair probably raises young together.
Feeding: foraging behavior and diet are poorly understood; eats mostly insects, small crustaceans and seeds.
Voice: male call-note is a repeated *ki-kee-der*; female call-note is a deeper *who-whoo*.
Similar Species: *Yellow Rail* (p. 361): larger; white trailing edge on inner wing is visible in flight. *Virginia Rail* (p. 120): reddish bill; rusty breast; gray "cheek." *Sora* (p. 121): has much lighter coloration; yellow bill; black face "mask."
Best Sites: most often reported at Altamaha WMA; recently seen in Greene Co. (HC: 7) and Phinizy Swamp Nature Park.

CLAPPER RAIL

Rallus longirostris

The Clapper Rail characteristically flicks its tail as it walks and wades through tidal marshes and mangroves in search of crayfish, crabs and other prey. This bird's thin profile and long, spreading toes allow it to move quickly and efficiently through dense, squishy saltwater marshes. The Clapper Rail is more often heard than seen, especially at sunrise and sunset when it vehemently issues loud *kek* calls. • These birds may be fairly common residents in some of Georgia's coastal marshes, but they have been extirpated from many other areas of the United States. For years, Clapper Rail habitat throughout North America has been under siege by humans hoping to convert "inhospitable" marshland into airports, malls and landfills. • Clapper Rails can lay up to a dozen eggs over the course of a few days, resulting in asynchronous hatching. Young rails leave the nest within hours of hatching, so adults often split up—one adult stays on the nest to incubate any remaining eggs, while the other adult moves to a nearby auxiliary nest where the vulnerable new hatchlings are safely brooded.

ID: long, slightly down-curved bill; four recognized subspecies differ in brightness of coloration; generally darker back feathers have lighter, pale surrounding edges; grayish brown to cinnamon breast; gray to brown and white barring on the flanks; grayish face.
Size: *L* 14½ in; *W* 19 in.
Status: common to abundant permanent breeding resident in marshes on the Coast and adjacent to the barrier islands.
Habitat: mangroves; tidal saltwater marshes of pickleweed and cordgrass; often feeds along marshy tidal channels during low tide.
Nesting: pair builds a cup nest of vegetation in dense cover above or near water; nest usually includes a domed canopy and an entrance ramp; pair incubates up to 12 cream to buff eggs with variable markings.
Feeding: aquatic insects, crustaceans and small fish are caught by probing, snatching or gleaning from water, ground or vegetation; seeds, amphibians, worms and other small items may also be eaten.
Voice: call is a series of 10 or more loud, harsh *kek* notes, accelerating at first, then slowing toward the end.
Similar Species: *Virginia Rail* (p. 120): much smaller; brown back feathers, gray face and red bill. *Least Bittern* (p. 85): solid black back feathers lack the lighter edging; buffy orange wing patches and face; not normally in the same habitat. *King Rail* (p. 119): richer colors; bolder black and white barring; breast and foreneck more rufous; buffy lores.
Best Sites: coastal marshes from Tybee I. to Cumberland I.; St. Catherines I. (HC: 263).

KING RAIL

Rallus elegans

The King Rail is the largest rail in North America, even though it is only roughly the size of a farmyard chicken. Unlike some of the more secretive rails, it is often seen wading through shallow water along the edge of a freshwater marsh, stalking its prey within full view of eager onlookers. Crayfish, crabs, small fish, spiders, beetles, snails, frogs and a whole host of aquatic insects keep this formidable hunter occupied and well fed. • King Rail nests, which are commonly built above shallow water, often include a protective dome of woven vegetation and a well-engineered entrance ramp. Despite these deluxe features, young rails and their attending parents desert the nest mere hours after the eggs hatch.

ID: long, slightly down-curved bill; black back feathers have buffy or tawny edges; cinnamon shoulders and under-parts; strongly barred, black and white flanks; grayish brown "cheeks." *Immature:* similar plumage patterning with lighter, washed-out colors.
Size: *L* 15 in; *W* 20 in.
Status: locally common permanent breeding resident of the Coast and Coastal Plain; uncommon to locally common in winter on the Coast and the Coastal Plain; uncommon local breeding resident and rare to uncommon in winter in the Piedmont.
Habitat: freshwater marshes, shrubby swamps, marshy riparian shorelines and flooded fields with shrubby margins.

Nesting: among clumps of grass or sedge just above the water or the ground; male builds most of the platform nest with a canopy and entrance ramp using marsh vegetation; pair shares the incubation of 10–12 pale buff eggs, lightly spotted with brown, for about 21–23 days.
Feeding: aquatic insects, crustaceans and occasionally seeds; small fish and amphibians are caught by foraging in shallow water, often in or near dense plant cover.
Voice: chattering call is 10 or fewer evenly spaced *kek* notes.
Similar Species: *Virginia Rail* (p. 120): much smaller; brown back feathers; gray face; red bill. *Least Bittern* (p. 85): solid black back feathers lack the lighter edging; buff orange face and wing patches; thicker bill. *Clapper Rail* (p. 118): more washed-out colors; buffy, brown-orange breast; gray "cheeks"; white lore.
Best Sites: Eufaula NWR; Laurens Co. marshes; Harris Neck NWR; Okefenokee NWR; Phinizy Swamp Nature Park (HC-winter: 16).

VIRGINIA RAIL

Rallus limicola

The best way to meet a Virginia Rail is to sit alongside a wetland marsh in spring, clap your hands three or four times to imitate this bird's *ki-dick* calls and wait patiently. If you are lucky, a Virginia Rail will reveal itself for a brief instant, but on most occasions you will only hear this elusive bird. • When pursued by an intruder or predator, a rail will almost always attempt to scurry away through dense, concealing vegetation, rather than risk exposure in a getaway flight. Rails are very narrow birds that have modified feather tips and flexible vertebrae, which allow them to squeeze through the narrow confines of their marshy homes. • The Virginia Rail and its relative the Sora are often found living in the same marshes. The secret of their successful coexistence is in their microhabitat preferences and distinct diets. The Virginia Rail typically favors dry shoresides of marshes and feeds on invertebrates, whereas the Sora prefers waterfront property and eats plants and seeds.

ID: long, downcurved, reddish bill; gray face; rusty breast; barred flanks; chestnut brown wing patch; very short tail. *Immature:* much darker overall; light bill. **Size:** *L* 9–11 in; *W* 13 in.

Status: locally common migrant and winter resident of the Coast and the Coastal Plain; uncommon local breeding and winter resident in the Piedmont; nesting not well known, but confirmed records in Atlanta, Kennesaw Mountain Marsh and near Tybee I.
Habitat: wetlands, especially bulrush marshes.
Nesting: concealed in emergent vegetation, usually suspended just over the water; loose basket nest is made of coarse grass, cattail stems or sedges; pair incubates 5–13 spotted, pale buff eggs for up to 20 days.
Feeding: probes into soft substrates and gleans vegetation for invertebrates, such as beetles, snails, spiders, earthworms, insect larvae and nymphs; also eats some pondweeds and seeds.
Voice: call is an often-repeated, telegraph-like *kidick, kidick;* also "oinks" and croaks.
Similar Species: *King Rail* (p. 119): much larger; dark legs; lacks reddish bill and gray face; immature is mostly pale gray. *Sora* (p. 121): short, yellow bill; black face and throat. *Yellow Rail* (p. 361): short, pale yellowish bill; black and tawny stripes on back; white trailing edges of wings are seen in flight.
Best Sites: Phinizy Swamp Nature Park (HC-winter: 22); Greene Co. (HC-winter: 24).

SORA

Porzana carolina

Two ascending whistles followed by a strange, descending whinny abruptly announce the presence of the otherwise undetectable Sora. The Sora is the most common and widespread rail in North America, and like most rails it is seldom seen by birders. Its elusive habits and preference for dense marshlands force most would-be observers to settle for a quick look at this small bird. On occasion, however, it has been known to parade around, unconcerned with onlookers, while it searches the shallows for food. • The Sora has two main calls: a clear, whistled *coo-wee* that is easy to imitate and a strange, descending whinny.
• Even though its feet are not webbed or lobed, the Sora swims quite well over short distances. Though it appears to be a weak and reluctant flier, the Sora migrates hundreds of miles each year between its breeding and wintering wetlands.
• The species name *carolina* means "of Carolina" and this bird is also known as the "Carolina Rail."

nonbreeding

ID: short, yellow bill; gray neck and breast; black and white flank bars; buffy brown crown and nape; brownish back and tail. *Breeding:* black "mask." *Nonbreeding:* faded black "mask."
Immature: generally brown with white markings; dull buff face and breast; barred flanks; dusky bill.
Size: *L* 8–10 in; *W* 14 in.
Status: common migrant and uncommon winter resident in freshwater marshes of the Coast and the Coastal Plain, usually from mid-September to May; uncommon in brackish marshes of the Coast; rare elsewhere in winter.

Habitat: wetlands with abundant emergent cattails, bulrushes, sedges and grasses.
Nesting: does not nest in Georgia.
Feeding: gleans and probes for seeds, plants, aquatic insects and mollusks.
Voice: usual call is a clear, 2-note *coo-wee;* alarm call is a sharp *keek.*
Similar Species: *Virginia Rail* (p. 120) and *King Rail* (p. 119): larger; long, downcurved bill; chestnut brown wing patch; rufous breast. *Yellow Rail* (p. 361): streaked back; tawny upperparts; white throat; white trailing edges of wings are seen in flight.
Best Sites: Altamaha WMA; Eufaula NWR; Savannah NWR; Harris Neck NWR; Phinizy Swamp Nature Park (HC: 167); Greene Co. (HC: 28).

PURPLE GALLINULE

Porphyrio martinica

The Purple Gallinule is closely related to the Common Moorhen and the American Coot. All three species have similar habitat preferences, a similar body shape and a prominent forehead "shield," but the Purple Gallinule's richly colored attire certainly makes it the most attractive bird of the bunch. • This bird's large feet and long toes distribute the bird's weight, allowing it to walk on top of floating lily pads and mats of vegetation. While foraging for snails, insects, spiders and fresh plant matter, the Purple Gallinule may nervously flick its tail. Otherwise, watch for it swimming through the shallows, bobbing its head with great zeal. • Purple Gallinules are awkward fliers and are often seen lamely dangling their long legs and huge feet during short, reluctant flights.

ID: all-white undertail coverts; glossy, purplish blue head and underparts; greenish upperparts; light blue forehead "shield"; red bill with yellow tip; pale yellow legs and feet. *Immature:* tawny brown overall with greenish tinge in wings; darkish bill and crown.

Size: *L* 12–14 in; *W* 22 in.

Status: uncommon local breeding resident of the Coast and the Coastal Plain; more numerous in summer; rare in migration above the Fall Line.

Habitat: freshwater swamps, lagoons, marshes and ponds with a complete cover of floating vegetation and dense camouflage.

Nesting: pair builds a platform of cattails, sedges and grass over water in dense, standing marsh vegetation; pair alternates incubation of 5–10 eggs for 22–25 days.

Feeding: gleans food from vegetation or water by walking or swimming; omnivorous diet includes seeds, fruits, leaves, insects, spiders, worms, small fish and snails.

Voice: noisy henlike clucking sounds; gives cackling *kek kek kek* call in flight.

Similar Species: *Common Moorhen* (p. 123) and *American Coot* (p. 124): have dark gray or gray-brown bodies and lack light blue forehead "shield"; immature moorhen and coot are darker.

Best Sites: Savannah NWR near exit road; Lake Seminole WMA; Eufaula NWR; Grand Bay WMA; Big Cypress Pond, Dougherty Co. (HC: 12 pairs).

COMMON MOORHEN

Gallinula chloropus

The Common Moorhen is a curious-looking creature that appears to have been assembled from bits and pieces left over from other birds: it has the bill of a chicken, the body of a duck and the long legs and large feet of a small heron. As it strolls around a wetland, its head bobs back and forth in synchrony with its legs, producing a comical, chugging stride. • Unlike most other members of the rail family, the Common Moorhen is quite comfortable feeding in open areas. • For moorhens, the responsibilities of parenthood do not end when their eggs have hatched—parents feed and shelter their young until they are capable of feeding themselves and flying on their own. • Although the Common Moorhen looks similar to its close relative, the American Coot, its delicate manner and elusive tendencies easily separate it from the loud and gregarious coot. • The scientific name *chloropus* is Greek for "green foot."

breeding

ID: reddish forehead "shield"; yellow-tipped bill; gray-black body; white streak on sides and flanks; long, greenish yellow legs. *Breeding:* brighter bill and forehead "shield." *Immature:* paler plumage; duller legs and bill; white throat.
Size: *L* 12–15 in; *W* 21 in.
Status: common permanent breeding resident throughout the Coast and the Coastal Plain; rare north of the Fall Line.
Habitat: freshwater marshes, ponds, lakes and sewage lagoons.
Nesting: pair builds a platform nest or a wide, shallow cup of bulrushes, cattails and reeds in shallow water or along a shoreline; often built with a ramp leading to the water; pair incubates 8–11 buff-colored, spotted or blotched eggs for 19–22 days.
Feeding: eats mostly aquatic vegetation, berries, fruits, tadpoles, insects, snails, worms and spiders; may take carrion and eggs.
Voice: various sounds include chickenlike clucks, screams, squeaks and a loud *cup;* courting males give a harsh *ticket-ticket-ticket.*
Similar Species: *American Coot* (p. 124): white bill and forehead "shield"; lacks white streak on flanks. *Purple Gallinule* (p. 122): green back and blue underparts; lacks white streak on flanks.
Best Sites: freshwater lakes or large ponds with thick vegetation near the shoreline; Lake Seminole WMA; Savannah NWR; Harris Neck NWR (HC-winter: 67).

AMERICAN COOT

Fulica americana

The American Coot is truly an all-terrain bird: in its quest for food it dives and dabbles like a duck, grazes confidently on land and swims about skillfully with its lobed feet. • During winter, coots gather amicably together in large groups that sometimes contain thousands of birds. These abundant birds are easy to spot because of their pendulous head movements while swimming. They are also the only birds in Georgia with white bills, which stand out against their dark bodies. • Coots are strong swimmers and can use both their lobed toes and their wings to paddle quickly through the water. They are capable of completely submerging to avoid predators, though the young often fall victim to predatory fish. Young American Coots often hitch a ride on the back of a parent and can even stay aboard when the adult dives under water. • The American Coot is colloquially known as "Mud Hen," and many people mistakenly believe that the American Coot is a species of duck. Other names include "Pond Crow" and "White-bill."

ID: gray-black overall; white, chickenlike bill with dark ring around tip; reddish spot on white forehead "shield"; long, greenish yellow legs; lobed toes; red eyes. *Immature:* lighter body color; darker bill and legs; lacks prominent forehead "shield."

Size: *L* 13–16 in; *W* 24 in.

Status: rare breeding resident of the Coast and the Coastal Plain; has bred in the Piedmont; common to abundant on the Coast and the Coastal Plain in winter; uncommon to common migrant and winter resident of the Piedmont and the mountains.

Habitat: shallow marshes, ponds and wetlands with open water and emergent vegetation; also sewage lagoons.

Nesting: in emergent vegetation; pair builds a floating nest of cattails and grass; pair incubates 6–11 brown-spotted, buffy white eggs for 21–25 days.

Feeding: gleans the water's surface; sometimes dives, tips up or even grazes on land; eats aquatic vegetation, insects, snails, crayfish, worms, tadpoles and fish; may steal food from ducks.

Voice: calls frequently in summer, day and night: *kuk-kuk-kuk-kuk-kuk;* also grunts.

Similar Species: *Ducks* (pp. 39–62): all lack chickenlike, white bill and uniformly black body. *Grebes* (pp. 69–72): lack white forehead "shield" and all-dark plumage. *Common Moorhen* (p. 123): reddish forehead "shield"; yellow-tipped bill; white streak on flanks.

Best Sites: E.L. Huie; Garden Lakes, Rome; Savannah NWR; Eufaula NWR; Harris Neck NWR; Lake Seminole WMA (HC-winter: 300,000+).

SANDHILL CRANE

Grus canadensis

The Sandhill Crane has a coiled trachea, which adds harmonies to the notes in its calls, allowing it to call louder and farther. The deep, resonant, rattling calls announce the approach of a flock of Sandhill Cranes long before they pass overhead. Like geese, cranes often migrate in V-formation, occasionally circling around in swirling groups to gain more altitude. To differentiate this bird in flight from similar long-necked birds, look for the crane's snapping upstroke and slower downstroke. • With a lifespan of more than two decades, Sandhill Cranes are among the longest-living birds. Cranes usually mate for life, reinforcing pair bonds each spring with an elaborate courtship dance that has often been equated with human dancing—a seemingly strange comparison until you see the ritual firsthand. Sandhill Cranes are sensitive nesters, so they prefer to breed and raise their young in areas that are isolated from human disturbance. • The non-migratory Florida subspecies of Sandhill Crane (*G. c. pratensis*) breeds locally in the Okefenokee National Wildlife Refuge and has been introduced at Grand Bay Wildlife Management Area and at St. Catherines Island, where it is found year-round.

ID: very large, gray bird with long neck and legs; naked, red crown; long, straight bill; plumage is often stained rusty red from iron oxides in the water. *Immature:* lacks red crown; reddish brown plumage may appear patchy. *In flight:* extends neck and legs; often glides, soars and circles.
Size: *L* 3½–4 ft; *W* 6–7 ft.
Status: locally uncommon permanent breeding resident in Okefenokee NWR, Grand Bay WMA and St. Catherines I.; northern migratory subspecies is an uncommon to common migrant from February to March and from November to January.
Habitat: *Breeding:* isolated, open marshes. *In migration:* agricultural fields.

Nesting: on a large mound of aquatic vegetation in water or along a shoreline; pair incubates 2 brown-splotched, olive buff eggs for 29–32 days; egg hatching is staggered; young fly at about 50 days.
Feeding: probes and gleans the ground for insects, soft-bodied invertebrates, waste grain, shoots and tubers; frequently eats small vertebrates.
Voice: loud, resonant, rattling *gu-rrroo gu-rrroo gurrroo.*
Similar Species: *Great Blue Heron* (p. 86): lacks red forehead patch; neck is folded back over shoulders in flight. *Whooping Crane* (p. 126): all-white plumage; black flight feathers.
Best Sites: Okefenokee NWR; Grand Bay WMA; Eufaula NWR. *Fall and winter:* mostly from north-central to south-central Georgia; Houston Co. (HC: 8000); Cobb Co. (HC: 7000+)

WHOOPING CRANE

Grus americana

One of the most impressive and rarest birds in North America, the extraordinary Whooping Crane wavered on the brink of extinction in the 1940s, when the world population of wild Whooping Cranes dipped to only 15 birds. By 2005, one of the most intensive conservation programs in history had increased that number to about 400 wild, captive and reintroduced birds. We now face the task of removing this magnificent crane from the endangered species list, a serious challenge because cranes do not reach maturity until five years of age and usually lay only one egg per year. • The only traditional, wild population of Whooping Cranes consists of about 180 birds that breed in a remote and virtually inaccessible area of Wood Buffalo National Park in northwestern Canada. These birds migrate to Aransas National Wildlife Refuge in Texas each winter. • Starting in 2000, a group of Whooping Cranes was led by ultralight aircraft from Wisconsin to Florida, establishing a new migratory population of reintroduced birds. The Whooping Crane was formerly an accidental visitor to Georgia, with no records since the 1800s, but now Georgians can hope to see Whooping Cranes during their annual migrations to and from Florida. • Because the Whooping Crane population is so fragile, the Whooping Crane Eastern Partnership asks that people remain at least 600 feet away from the birds (by foot or by car) and that people remain inconspicuous and in their vehicles, speaking quietly enough that the birds can't hear.

ID: tall, very large bird; mostly white; black primary feathers; bare, red skin on the forehead and "chin"; long, pointed bill; black legs. *Immature:* orange-red head and neck. *In flight:* neck and legs are extended.

Size: *L* 4¼–5 ft; *W* 6½–8 ft.

Status: endangered (federal); rare; accidental visitor from October to December and from late March to early May statewide.

Habitat: lakes, coastal and freshwater marshes; prefers remote areas.

Nesting: does not nest in Georgia.

Feeding: picks food from the water or the ground; eats invertebrates and small animals including fish, amphibians, reptiles and small mammals; also eats plant material such as roots, acorns and berries.

Voice: gravelly rattle: *ker-loo ker-lee-loo.*

Similar Species: *Sandhill Crane* (p. 125): gray, not white and black. *Great Egret* (p. 87): smaller; yellow bill; lacks red on forehead.

Best Sites: open fields or lakes and ponds statewide.

BLACK-BELLIED PLOVER

Pluvialis squatarola

Black-bellied Plovers may be seen along the coast in winter, roosting in tight flocks or running along the mudflats when the tide goes out. These large plovers forage for small invertebrates with a robinlike run-and-stop technique, frequently pausing to lift their heads for a reassuring scan of their surroundings. They are usually found in coastal habitats but are equally comfortable foraging inland near fresh water. In migration they may associate with American Golden-Plovers. • The Black-bellied Plover is the largest North American plover, with several unique characteristics. Most plovers have three toes, but the Black-belly has a fourth toe higher on its leg, a trait more similar to sandpipers. In addition, this plover has large eyes, an adaptation that allows it to search for prey at night.

nonbreeding

nonbreeding

ID: short, black bill; long, black legs. *Breeding:* black face, breast, belly and flanks; white undertail coverts; white stripe leads from crown down "collar," neck and sides of breast; mottled, black and white back. *Nonbreeding:* mottled, gray-brown upperparts; lightly streaked, pale underparts. *In flight:* black "wing pits"; whitish rump; white wing linings.
Size: *L* 10½–13 in; *W* 29 in.
Status: common migrant and winter resident on the Coast from March to May and from July to November; rare migrant inland.

Habitat: coastal regions, including beaches, mudflats and brackish marshes; inland on plowed fields, sod farms, meadows, lakeshores, marshes and sewage lagoons.
Nesting: does not nest in Georgia.
Feeding: run-and-stop foraging technique; eats insects, mollusks and crustaceans.
Voice: rich, plaintive, 3-syllable whistle: *pee-oo-ee.*
Similar Species: *American Golden-Plover* (p. 128): gold-mottled upperparts; black undertail coverts in breeding plumage; lacks black "wing pits."
Best Sites: along coastal beaches of mainland and barrier islands; Savannah NWR; St. Catherines I. (HC: 1000+). *In migration:* Bartow Co. (HC: 5).

AMERICAN GOLDEN-PLOVER

Pluvialis dominica

A mere 150 years ago, the American Golden-Plover population was among the largest of any bird population in the world, but in the late 1800s, market gunners mercilessly culled the great flocks in both spring and fall—a single day's shooting often yielded tens of thousands of birds. Populations have recovered somewhat, but they will likely never return to their former numbers. • Because they migrate through central North America, few golden-plovers are found in the East. In Georgia, these birds are sometimes found among flocks of Upland Sandpipers. • Although this bird is boldly marked, the white stripe down its side disrupts the vision of a predator, confusing the stalker as to where the bird's head or tail is. The cryptic coloration of speckles on the top of the body blends well with the golden, mottled earth of its arctic breeding grounds. • The Eskimo Curlew (*Numenius borealis*), now probably extinct, once migrated with the American Golden-Plover between the Canadian Arctic and South America. If the Eskimo Curlew does still exist, it may be found traveling alongside the American Golden-Plover.

nonbreeding

nonbreeding

Status: uncommon migrant, except rare in the Mountains, from March to April and from August to October.
Habitat: cultivated fields, sod farms, meadows, lakeshores and mudflats along the edges of reservoirs, marshes and sewage lagoons.
Nesting: does not nest in Georgia.
Feeding: run-and-stop foraging technique; snatches insects, mollusks and crustaceans; also takes seeds and berries.
Voice: soft, melodious whistle: *quee, quee-dle.*
Similar Species: *Black-bellied Plover* (p. 127): white undertail coverts; whitish crown; lacks gold speckling on upperparts; conspicuous, black "wing pits" in flight.
Best Sites: sod and turf farms and airport fields.

ID: straight, black bill; long, black legs.
Breeding: black face and underparts, including undertail coverts; S-shaped, white stripe from forehead down to shoulders; dark upperparts are speckled with gold and white.
Nonbreeding: broad, pale "eyebrow"; dark streaking on pale neck and underparts; much less gold on upperparts. *In flight:* gray "wing pits."
Size: *L* 10–11 in; *W* 26 in.

WILSON'S PLOVER

Charadrius wilsonia

Watching the frenzied foraging behavior and synchronous flying stunts of shorebirds can leave observers in a paralyzed state of wonder and bewilderment. Similarly, attempts to identify the running herds and swirling clouds of these look-alike birds can be just as puzzling. Fortunately, the Wilson's Plover affords us the opportunity to easily identify at least one species among the hordes of shore-dwelling species. • Take note of this plover's unusually long, heavy, black bill—most other plovers have a much smaller, bicolored bill. This relatively large bill helps the Wilson's Plover to feed on crayfish, fiddler crabs and small shellfish that its relatives have difficulty handling. Further scrutiny of this uncommon beachcomber will also reveal a broad, dark breast band that in breeding plumage is black on males and brown on females. • This plover was named after the father of American ornithology, Alexander Wilson.

breeding

ID: *Breeding male:* long, thick, black bill; broad black band across breast; black band on forehead; broad, dark eye line; brownish upperparts and white underparts; grayish pink legs. *Breeding female:* brown replaces black bands on breast and head. *Nonbreeding:* brown breast band may be incomplete.
Size: *L* 7¾ in; *W* 19 in.
Status: uncommon summer breeding resident on barrier islands of the Coast from February to November (about 200 breeding pairs); rare winter resident on the Coast.
Habitat: sandy beaches, tidal mudflats, dredge spoil islands and coastal islands.
Nesting: female chooses one of several scrapes in dry sand excavated by the male near some concealing piece of vegetation or debris; nest is sparsely lined with grass,

pebbles, shell fragments or debris; pair incubates 2–4 cream-colored eggs with dark markings for about 25 days; young leave the nest shortly after hatching.
Feeding: forages by sight, running and pausing to snatch prey from the ground or low vegetation; crustaceans, insects, worms and small mollusks form bulk of diet.
Voice: calls include a shrill alarm whistle *wheat!* and a lower *quit*.
Similar Species: *Semipalmated Plover* (p. 130): small, orange bill with black tip; orange legs; male's dark forehead band connects to eye. *Piping Plover* (p. 131): small, orange bill with black tip; orange legs; pale gray upperparts; narrow breast band. *Snowy Plover:* thin bill; lacks broad, connected breast band.
Best Sites: along coasts of most barrier islands; Little Tybee I. (HC: 40+); Jekyll Island South Beach; St. Catherines I.; Cumberland I.

SEMIPALMATED PLOVER

Charadrius semipalmatus

The Semipalmated Plover overwinters along the Atlantic Coast, where it spends much of its time searching for bottom-dwelling invertebrates along damp, coastal mudflats. This adaptable plover uses a variety of habitats and foods and is one of the few plover species with an increasing population. • Long, slender wings make this bird a fast flier, able to reach speeds of 30 miles per hour. With powerful wingbeats, Semipalmated Plovers can even negotiate strong winds with relative ease. • The scientific name *semipalmatus* means "half-webbed" and refers to the slight webbing between the toes of this plover. The webbing is thought to give the bird's feet more surface area when it is walking on soft substrates.

breeding

nonbreeding

ID: dark brown back; white breast with 1 black, horizontal band; long, orange legs; stubby, orange, black-tipped bill; white patch above bill; white throat and "collar"; brown head; black band across forehead; small, white "eyebrow." *Immature:* dark legs and bill; brown banding.

Size: *L* 7 in; *W* 19 in.

Status: common to abundant migrant and winter resident on the Coast; uncommon migrant in the interior from March to May and from July to October; rare nonbreeder on the Coast in summer.

Habitat: mainly coastal; rarely seen inland; mudflats and sandy beaches.

Nesting: does not nest in Georgia.

Feeding: usually on damp shorelines and beaches, including inland ponds; run-and-stop foraging technique; eats crustaceans, worms and insects.

Voice: crisp, high-pitched, 2-part, rising whistle: *tu-wee.*

Similar Species: *Killdeer* (p. 132): larger; 2 black bands across breast. *Piping Plover* (p. 131): lacks dark band through eyes; much lighter upperparts; narrower breast band is incomplete in females and most males.

Best Sites: most barrier islands; St. Catherines I. (HC: 900+); Savannah NWR; Tybee I.; Jekyll I.

PIPING PLOVER

Charadrius melodus

A master of illusion, the Piping Plover is hardly noticeable when it settles on shore-lines and beaches. Its pale, sand-colored plumage is the perfect camouflage against a sandy beach. As well, the dark bands across this bird's forehead and neckline resemble scattered pebbles or strips of washed-up vegetation. Unfortunately, this plover's cryptic plumage has done little to protect it from wetland drainage, increased predation and disturbance by humans. Though the Piping Plover is locally common along undisturbed areas of Georgia's coast in winter, this bird is threatened in many areas of North America. The recreational use of beaches during summer, and an increase in human-tolerant predators, such as gulls, raccoons and skunks, has impeded this plover's ability to reproduce successfully. • On beaches with wave action, these birds often employ a foot-trembling strategy to entice invertebrates to the surface. • If threatened, Piping Plover chicks typically take to the water and swim away, whereas adults rarely swim at all.

breeding

nonbreeding

ID: pale, sandy upper-parts; white underparts; orange legs. *Breeding:* black-tipped, orange bill; black forehead band; black "necklace" (sometimes incomplete, especially on females). *Nonbreeding:* no breast or forehead band; all-black bill.
Size: *L* 7 in; *W* 19 in.
Status: threatened (state and federal); uncommon to locally common migrant and winter resident on the Coast, most commonly from September to April; accidental inland.

Habitat: sandy, undisturbed coastal beaches.
Nesting: does not nest in Georgia.
Feeding: run-and-stop foraging technique; eats worms and insects; almost all its food is taken from the ground.
Voice: clear, whistled melody: *peep peep peep-lo.*
Similar Species: *Semipalmated Plover* (p. 130): dark band over eye; much darker upperparts. *Killdeer* (p. 132): larger; 2 breast bands; much darker upperparts.
Best Sites: Little St. Simons I. (HC: 100+); Tybee I.; St. Catherines I.; Sapelo I.; Jekyll I.; Cumberland I.

KILLDEER

Charadrius vociferus

The ubiquitous Killdeer is often the first shorebird a birder learns to identify. Its boisterous calls rarely fail to catch the attention of people passing through its wide variety of nesting environments. The Killdeer's preference for open fields, gravel driveways, beach edges, golf courses and abandoned industrial areas has allowed it to thrive throughout our rural and suburban landscapes. • If you happen to wander too close to a Killdeer nest, the parent will try to lure you away by issuing loud alarm calls and feigning a broken wing. Most predators take the bait and are led far enough away for the parent to suddenly recover from its injury and fly off, sounding its piercing calls. Similar distraction displays are a widespread phenomena in the bird world, but in our region, the Killdeer's broken wing act is by far the gold medal winner. • The scientific name *vociferus* aptly describes this vocal bird, but double-check the source of all calls in the spring, when the Killdeer is often imitated by frisky European Starlings.

ID: long, dark yellow legs; white upperparts with 2 black breast bands; brown back; white underparts; brown head; white "eyebrow"; white face patch above bill; black forehead band; rufous rump; tail projects beyond wing tips. *Immature:* downy; only 1 breast band.

Size: *L* 9–11 in; *W* 24 in.

Status: common breeding permanent resident statewide, except high Mountains.

Habitat: open ground, fields, lakeshores, sandy beaches, mudflats, gravel streambeds, wet meadows and grasslands.

Nesting: on open ground; in a shallow, usually unlined, depression; pair incubates 4 darkly spotted and blotched, pale buff eggs for 24–28 days; occasionally raises 2 broods.

Feeding: run-and-stop foraging technique; eats mostly insects; also takes spiders, snails, earthworms and crayfish.

Voice: loud, distinctive *kill-dee kill-dee kill-deer* and variations, including *deer-deer*.

Similar Species: *Semipalmated Plover* (p. 130): smaller; only 1 breast band. *Piping Plover* (p. 131): smaller; lighter upperparts; 1 breast band.

Best Sites: extremely widespread; open areas and disturbed sites; Laurens Co. (HC-winter: 2000).

AMERICAN OYSTERCATCHER
Haematopus palliatus

Wouldn't life be great if you could leave the city rat-race behind to spend every day wading in the ocean surf, eating fresh, tasty seafood morsels and sunbathing? And of course there is nothing like rounding out each day with some "wing-surfing" on the salty ocean breeze... if only you were as lucky as those peculiar American Oystercatchers! • These large, stocky shorebirds with long, razor-sharp bills specialize in prying or hammering open shellfish, including oysters, clams and mussels. When the opportunity arises, they will gladly eat a host of other intertidal invertebrates including limpets, crabs, marine worms, sea urchins, chitons and even jellyfish. • During the summer breeding season, watch for mating pairs performing their loud "piping" courtship display, which is often given in flight. American Oystercatchers may form a breeding trio, made up of two females and one male. Together, the group tends one or two nests and takes care of the young for the first two months. • The species name *pallustris* comes from the Latin for "clad in a Greek mantle," referring to the bird's dark upperparts and white shoulders.

ID: long, orange-red bill; black head and neck; brown back; white wing and rump patches; white underparts.
Size: *L* 18½ in; *W* 32 in.
Status: uncommon permanent breeding resident of saline areas of the Coast, with an estimated breeding population of 200+; more numerous in winter, with an estimated population of nearly 1000.
Habitat: coastal marine habitats including saltwater marshes, sandy beaches and tidal mudflats; will nest on dredge spoil islands.
Nesting: pair scrapes out a depression in sand and may line it with shells or pebbles; pair incubates 2–4 dark-spotted, grayish eggs for 27 days; pair cares for precocial young, which leave the nest soon after hatching.
Feeding: intertidal life, including mollusks, crustaceans, marine worms and other invertebrates are caught by sight or by probing while walking in shallow water, on rocks or on mud; shellfish form bulk of diet and are either hammered open or quickly stabbed and cut open.
Voice: call is a loud *wheet!*, often given in series during flight.
Similar Species: none.
Best Sites: barrier islands; Tybee I.; St. Catherines I.; Wolf I. (HC-winter: 200); Sea I.; St. Simons I. (HC-winter: 500+); Jekyll I.; Cumberland I.

BLACK-NECKED STILT

Himantopus mexicanus

This bird has the longest legs, proportionately, of any North American bird and is truly deserving of the name "stilt." It strides daintily around coastal and interior wetlands. Whether wandering along a smelly sewage lagoon or wading along the shorelines of an impoundment, the stilt's dignity adds a sense of subtle glory to the bleak landscape it is most often associated with. This bird may be found along the Coast in summer, but most birds leave Georgia after the breeding season. • On hot summer days, adult Black-necked Stilts routinely take turns sheltering their eggs from the warmth of the hot sun. Adults might even be observed wetting their belly feathers in order to cool off their encased young during their next incubation duty. • Black-necked Stilts are in the family Recurvirostridae, along with the American Avocet, but unlike the Avocet, which has an upcurved bill, the stilt's bill is straight.

Nesting: in a shallow depression on slightly raised ground near water; nest is lined with shells, pebbles or vegetative debris; pair incubates 4 darkly blotched, buff eggs for about 25 days; pair tends the precocial young.

Feeding: picks prey from the water's surface or from the bottom substrate; primarily eats insects, crustaceans and other aquatic invertebrates; rarely eats seeds of aquatic plants.

Voice: not vocal during migration; loud, sharp *yip-yip-yip-yip* in summer; *kek-kek-kek-kek* in flight.

Similar Species: *American Avocet* (p. 135): upturned bill; lacks black on head.

Best Sites: Onslow I.; Ossabaw I.; St. Catherines I.; Blackbeard I.; Little St. Simons I.; Andrews I.; Cumberland I.; Harris Neck NWR; Altamaha WMA.

ID: very long, orange legs; dark upperparts; clean white underparts; long, straight, needlelike bill; small, white "eyebrow"; male is blacker above than female.

Size: *L* 14–15 in; *W* 29 in.

Status: locally common breeding summer resident along several barrier islands and Altamaha WMA from March to November; rare migrant inland.

Habitat: along the margins of freshwater, brackish and saltwater marshes, and on the marshy shorelines of lakes, ponds and tidal mudflats; also forages in flooded agricultural fields, impoundments and salt-evaporation ponds.

AMERICAN AVOCET

Recurvirostra americana

An American Avocet in full breeding plumage is a strikingly elegant bird, with its long, peachy red neck accentuating the length of its slender bill and stiltlike legs. Often by August, its peach-colored "hood" has been replaced by more subdued winter grays, which this bird will wear for the greater part of the year. It is the only avocet in the world that undergoes a yearly color change. • The American Avocet's upcurved bill looks bent out of shape but is actually ideal for efficiently skimming aquatic vegetation and invertebrates off the surface of shallow water. Avocets will walk rapidly or run about in fairly deep water, swinging their bills from side to side along the muddy bottom. At other times, they use their webbed feet to swim and feed by tipping up like dabbling ducks. • If an American Avocet is disturbed while standing in its one-legged resting position, it will take off, switch legs in midair, and land on the rested leg.

nonbreeding

breeding

ID: long, upturned, black bill; long, pale blue legs; black wings with wide, white patches; white underparts; female's bill is more upturned and shorter than male's. *Breeding:* peachy red head, neck and breast. *Nonbreeding:* gray head, neck and breast. *In flight:* a "winged stick"; long, skinny legs and neck; black and white wings.

Size: *L* 17–18 in; *W* 31 in.

Status: uncommon to locally common visitor to the Coast year-round (nonbreeder in summer); rare migrant inland from July to November.

Habitat: tidal mudflats and brackish coastal marshes; inland on marshy lakeshores and flooded fields.

Nesting: does not nest in Georgia.

Feeding: sweeps its bill from side to side along the water's surface, picking up minute crustaceans, aquatic insects and occasionally seeds; male sweeps lower in the water than female; occasionally swims and tips up like a duck.

Voice: harsh, shrill *plee-eek plee-eek*.

Similar Species: *Willet* (p. 139): grayish overall; straight bill.

Best Sites: Savannah NWR; Andrews I. (HC: 350); Jekyll I.

GREATER YELLOWLEGS

Tringa melanoleuca

The Greater Yellowlegs is the more solitary of the two yellowlegs species, but it can be seen in small flocks in migration and winter. It is one of the birds that performs the role of lookout among mixed flocks of shorebirds. At the first sign of danger, this large sandpiper bobs its head and calls incessantly. If forced to, the Greater Yellowlegs will usually retreat into deeper water, becoming airborne only as a last resort. • During migration, many shorebirds, including the Greater Yellowlegs, often stand or hop around beach flats on one leg. These stubborn "one-leggers" may be mistaken for crippled individuals, but this stance may be an adaptation that conserves body heat. Despite its long bill, the Greater Yellowlegs does not probe for its food, but rather picks it off the water's surface or swings its bill from side to side through the water. This side-sweeping behavior may be a clue that you are looking at a Greater Yellowlegs and not its Lesser relative, which uses this technique far less often.

nonbreeding

nonbreeding

ID: long, bright yellow legs; slightly upturned, dark bill is noticeably longer than head width. *Breeding:* brown black back and upperwing; fine, dense, dark streaking on head and neck; dark barring on breast often extends onto belly; subtle, dark eye line; light lores. *Nonbreeding:* gray overall; fine streaks on breast.
Size: *L* 13–15 in; *W* 28 in.
Status: common migrant and uncommon winter resident, but rare in the Mountains; rare nonbreeder in midsummer.
Habitat: almost all wetlands, including lakeshores, marshes, flooded fields and river shorelines; saltwater and freshwater ponds.

Nesting: does not nest in Georgia.
Feeding: usually wades in water over its knees; sometimes sweeps its bill from side to side; primarily eats aquatic invertebrates, but will also eat small fish; occasionally snatches prey from the water's surface.
Voice: quick, whistled *tew-tew-tew* (usually 3 notes).
Similar Species: *Lesser Yellowlegs* (p. 137): smaller; straight bill is shorter than width of head; lacks barring on belly; call is generally a pair of higher notes: *tew-tew*. *Willet* (p. 139): black and white wings; heavier, straighter bill; dark greenish legs.
Best Sites: wet inland areas during migration; E.L. Huie; Eufaula NWR; Altamaha WMA; Savannah NWR; Tybee I.; Harris Neck NWR; St. Simons I.; Jekyll I.

LESSER YELLOWLEGS
Tringa flavipes

With a series of continuous, rapid-fire *tew-tew* calls, Lesser Yellowlegs streak across the surface of wetlands and lakeshores. Visits by yellowlegs are relatively brief in spring, but the fall migration period is lengthy, and these birds can be seen from mid-August to mid-November. • Many birders find it a challenge to separate Lesser Yellowlegs and Greater Yellowlegs in the field. With practice, you will notice that the Lesser's bill is finer, straighter and not noticeably longer than the width of its head. The Lesser appears to have longer legs and wings, making it seem slimmer and taller than the Greater, and is also more commonly seen in flocks. If you are unable to visually distinguish between the two species, listen carefully to the calls of the yellowlegs you are viewing: the Lesser Yellowlegs gives a pair of peeps, whereas the Greater gives three. These characteristics should allow you to readily differentiate between these two species of yellowlegs. If you are still puzzled at the bird's identity, simply write "yellowlegs spp." in your field notes and try again next time. • The scientific name *flavipes* is derived from Latin words meaning "yellow foot."

nonbreeding

nonbreeding

ID: *Breeding:* bright yellow legs; all-dark bill is shorter than width of head; brown-black back and upperwing; fine, dense, dark streaking on head, neck and breast; subtle, dark eye line; light lores. *Nonbreeding:* paler coloring overall.
Size: *L* 10–11 in; *W* 24 in.
Status: common migrant statewide; rare nonbreeder in midsummer; common on the Coast, uncommon on the lower Coastal Plain in winter, but rare in the Mountains.
Habitat: freshwater ponds along the coast; shorelines of lakes, rivers, marshes and ponds; sod farms.

Nesting: does not nest in Georgia.
Feeding: snatches prey from the water's surface; frequently wades in shallow water; primarily eats aquatic invertebrates, but also takes small fish and tadpoles.
Voice: typically a high-pitched pair of *tew* notes.
Similar Species: *Greater Yellowlegs* (p. 136): larger; bill slightly upturned and noticeably longer than width of head; barring extends onto belly; *tew* call is usually given in a series of 3 notes. *Solitary Sandpiper* (p. 138): white eye ring; greenish legs. *Willet* (p. 139): much bulkier; black and white wings; heavier bill; dark greenish legs.
Best Sites: wet inland areas in migration; E.L. Huie; Eufaula NWR; Altamaha WMA; Savannah NWR; Harris Neck NWR; Jekyll I.

SOLITARY SANDPIPER

Tringa solitaria

True to its name, the Solitary Sandpiper is usually seen alone, bobbing its body like a spirited dancer as it forages for insects along our wetlands. Every so often, a lucky observer may happen upon a small group of these birds during spring or fall. • A favorite foraging method of the Solitary Sandpiper is to wade in shallow water, slowly advancing and vibrating the leading foot, thus stirring the mucky bottom sufficiently to flush out prey. In this way it captures aquatic insects and their larvae, including water boatmen and small crustaceans. • Shorebirds lay very large eggs and incubate them for long periods of time compared to many other bird species. Once sandpiper chicks break out of their eggs, they are ready to run, hide and feed on their own. These highly developed hatchlings, known as precocial young, can immediately fend for themselves in a dangerous world.

ID: white eye ring; short, green legs; dark yellowish bill with black tip; spotted, gray-brown back; white lores; fine, white streaks on gray-brown head, neck and breast; dark uppertail feathers with black and white barring on sides. *In flight:* dark underwings.
Size: *L* 7½–9 in; *W* 22 in.
Status: common migrant statewide from February to June, and from June to November.
Habitat: freshwater coastal sites; wet meadows, sewage lagoons, muddy ponds, sedge wetlands and beaver ponds.
Nesting: does not nest in Georgia.

Feeding: stalks shorelines, picking up aquatic invertebrates, such as water boatmen and damselfly nymphs; also gleans for terrestrial invertebrates; occasionally stirs the water with its foot to spook out prey.
Voice: high, thin *peet-wheet* or *wheat wheat wheat.*
Similar Species: *Lesser Yellowlegs* (p. 137): no eye ring; longer, bright yellow legs. *Spotted Sandpiper* (p. 140): incomplete eye ring; spotted breast in breeding plumage; black-tipped, orange bill. *Other sandpipers* (pp. 136–64): black bills and legs; no white eye ring.
Best Sites: inland wetlands and ponds and along the coast; Greene Co. (HC-spring: 29); E.L. Huie (HC-spring: 30+); Savannah NWR.

WILLET

Catoptrophorus semipalmatus

When grounded, the Willet cuts a rather dull figure. In flight or when displaying, the Willet transforms into a striking black and white figure, calling attention to itself with a loud, rhythmic *will-will willet, will-will-willet!* The bright, bold flashes of the Willet's wings may alert other shorebirds to imminent danger. If you look closely, you may notice that the white markings across the Willet's wingspan form a rough "W" as it flies away. • Willets are loud, social, easily identified birds—a nice change when dealing with sandpipers. Willets may be seen in Georgia year-round, and they breed in the salt marshes along our coastlines. These birds are most commonly seen in winter, when nonresident birds return from their northern breeding grounds. • There are two distinct subspecies of Willet, a western (*C. s. inornatus*) and an eastern (*C. s. semipalmatus*). The eastern race rarely ventures far from the Atlantic Coast and is the breeder in Georgia, but departs before winter. In contrast, the western race, which breeds far inland and winters primarily on the Pacific Coast, is a common winter visitor to our state.

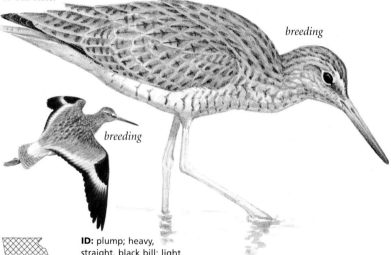

breeding

breeding

ID: plump; heavy, straight, black bill; light throat and belly. *Breeding:* dark streaking and barring overall. *Nonbreeding:* grayer upperparts. *In flight:* black and white wing pattern.

Size: *L* 14–16 in; *W* 26 in.

Status: eastern race is a common breeding resident on the Coast (about 1000 breeding pairs); western race winters on the Coast and is a rare migrant inland from July to September and from March to May.

Habitat: coastal mudflats and beaches; any shallow wetland in migration.

Nesting: on ground; well-hidden among low bushes in fields or bushy pastures;

shallow depression with a lining of leaves and dry grass; pair incubates 4 olive or buff, heavily spotted eggs for 22 days.

Feeding: feeds by probing muddy areas; also gleans the ground for insects; occasionally eats shoots and seeds.

Voice: loud, rolling *will-will willet, will-will-willet.*

Similar Species: *Marbled Godwit* (p. 144) and *Hudsonian Godwit* (p. 362): larger; much longer, pinkish yellow bill with dark, slightly upturned tip; lack black and white wing pattern. *Greater Yellowlegs* (p. 136): long, yellow legs; slightly upturned bill; lacks black and white wing pattern.

Best Sites: along the coast and barrier islands; Ossabaw I. (HC: 1600).

139

SPOTTED SANDPIPER

Actitis macularius

Even though its breast spots are not noticeable from a distance, the Spotted Sandpiper's stiff-winged, quivering flight pattern and tendency to burst from the shore are easily recognizable traits. This bird is also known for its continuous "teetering" behavior as it forages. • It wasn't until 1972 that the unexpected truth about the Spotted Sandpiper's breeding activities were realized. The female Spotted Sandpiper defends a territory and mates with more than one male in a single breeding season, leaving the male to tend the nest and eggs. This unusual nesting behavior, known as polyandry, is found in about one percent of all bird species. • The Spotted Sandpiper doesn't breed in Georgia—its breeding range extends from the central United States to the Arctic. • The scientific name *macularius* is Latin for "spot," referring to the spots on this bird's underparts in breeding plumage. Wintering and immature birds lack the spots and sport a pure white breast in Georgia, but the almost continuous teetering behavior helps separate this shorebird from all others except the Solitary Sandpiper, which is absent in winter.

nonbreeding

nonbreeding

ID: teeters almost continuously. *Breeding:* white underparts heavily spotted with black; yellow-orange legs; black-tipped, yellow-orange bill; white "eyebrow." *Nonbreeding* and *immature:* pure white breast, foreneck and throat; brown bill; dull yellow legs. *In flight:* flies close to the water's surface with very rapid, shallow wingbeats; white upperwing stripe.
Size: *L* 7–8 in; *W* 15 in.
Status: common migrant statewide from March to June and from July to November; uncommon in winter on the Coast and along the Chattahoochee R., south of Columbus; rare summer nesting records near Atlanta in past years.

Habitat: coastal areas; shorelines, gravel beaches, ponds, marshes, alluvial wetlands, rivers, streams, swamps and sewage lagoons; occasionally in cultivated fields.
Nesting: does not usually nest in Georgia.
Feeding: picks and gleans along shorelines for terrestrial and aquatic invertebrates; also snatches flying insects from the air.
Voice: sharp, crisp *eat-wheat, eat-wheat, wheat-wheat-wheat-wheat.*
Similar Species: *Solitary Sandpiper* (p. 138): complete eye ring; lacks spotting on breast; yellowish bill with dark tip. *Other sandpipers* (pp. 136–64): black bills and legs; lack spotting on breast.
Best Sites: inland at ponds and along rivers during migration; Savannah NWR; Tybee I. (HC-spring: 100+); McQueens I. (HC-spring: 100); Harris Neck NWR; Jekyll I.

UPLAND SANDPIPER

Bartramia longicauda

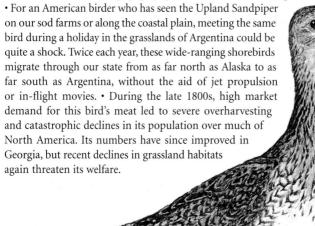

A rare visitor to our region, the Upland Sandpiper is sometimes seen in grassy habitats, moving with a ploverlike stop-and-start run. In spring migration, its soft, distinctive *quip-ip-ip-ip* calls can be heard at night as it flies overhead. • For an American birder who has seen the Upland Sandpiper on our sod farms or along the coastal plain, meeting the same bird during a holiday in the grasslands of Argentina could be quite a shock. Twice each year, these wide-ranging shorebirds migrate through our state from as far north as Alaska to as far south as Argentina, without the aid of jet propulsion or in-flight movies. • During the late 1800s, high market demand for this bird's meat led to severe overharvesting and catastrophic declines in its population over much of North America. Its numbers have since improved in Georgia, but recent declines in grassland habitats again threaten its welfare.

ID: small head; long, streaked neck; large, dark eyes; yellow legs; mottled, brownish upperparts; lightly streaked breast, sides and flanks; white belly and undertail coverts; bill is about same length as head.

Size: *L* 11–12½ in; *W* 26 in.

Status: uncommon migrant statewide from March to May and from July to September.

Habitat: sod farms, pastures, airports, grassy meadows, abandoned fields and natural grasslands.

Nesting: does not nest in Georgia.

Feeding: gleans the ground for insects, especially grasshoppers and beetles.

Voice: nocturnal flight call is a soft *quip-ip-ip-ip;* alarm call is *quip-ip-ip.*

Similar Species: *Willet* (p. 139): longer, heavier bill; dark greenish legs; black and white wings in flight. *Buff-breasted Sandpiper* (p. 157): shorter neck; larger head; daintier bill; lacks streaking on "cheek" and foreneck. *Pectoral Sandpiper* (p. 153): streaking on breast ends abruptly; smaller eyes; shorter neck; usually seen in larger numbers.

Best Sites: Laurens Co. pastures (HC-spring: 29); Macon Co. sod farms (HC-spring: 21); Sod Atlanta Inc.; Bulloch Co. sod farm (HC-spring: 10); Augusta Bush Field Airport.

WHIMBREL

Numenius phaeopus

W himbrels often travel in long lines and "V" formations, calling with four short whistles and sailing for short periods on set wings. East Coast birders are most likely to see Whimbrels during spring migration, as these birds pass along the shorelines. Whimbrels travel in flocks, so expect to see either sizeable groups of them or none at all. • It is impossible to talk about the Whimbrel without mentioning the Eskimo Curlew (*N. borealis*). Both of these birds suffered devastating losses to their populations during the commercial hunts of the late 1800s. Whereas the Whimbrel population slowly recovered, the Eskimo Curlew seemed to vanish into thin air—the last confirmed sighting was in 1963. Encouraging reports from South American wintering grounds in 1993 offer a tiny glimmer of hope that a few Eskimo Curlews still remain. • *Numenius*, from the Greek for "new moon," refers to the curved shape of this bird's bill. *Phaeopus* is Latin for "brown feet."

ID: long, downcurved bill; striped crown; dark eye line; mottled brown body; long legs. *In flight:* dark underwings.
Size: *L* 18 in; *W* 32 in.
Status: common spring migrant on the Coast from March through May; uncommon fall migrant from July to November; rare on the Coast in winter.
Habitat: mudflats, sandy coastal beaches, farmlands, grassy lakeshores, airports and flooded agricultural fields.
Nesting: does not nest in Georgia.
Feeding: probes and pecks for invertebrates in mud or vegetation; also eats berries in fall.

Voice: incoming flocks can be heard uttering a distinctive and easily imitated, rippling *bibibibibibibi* long before they come into sight.
Similar Species: *Upland Sandpiper* (p. 141): smaller; straight bill; lacks head markings; yellowish legs. *Willet* (p. 139): straight bill; plain, unmarked crown; gray color; prominent, white wing stripe along back. *Eskimo Curlew:* unbarred primaries; pale cinnamon wing linings; shorter, slightly straighter bill; darker upperparts; thought to be extinct.
Best Sites: Harris Neck NWR; St. Catherines Island Bar (HC-spring: 2500+); St. Catherines I. (HC: 2000); St. Simons I. (HC-spring: 1400+); Jekyll I.; Cumberland I.

LONG-BILLED CURLEW
Numenius americanus

Armed with a bill that reaches more than 7 inches long, the Long-billed Curlew—North America's largest sandpiper—is a remarkable bird indeed. Its long, downcurved bill is a dexterous tool designed for extracting buried mollusks from soft, penetrable mud or for picking grasshoppers from dense prairie grasslands. • Recent studies indicate that individual Long-billed Curlews return to the same winter foraging territory each year and defend this territory. In Georgia they prefer the quiet, undisturbed beaches of Sapelo Island or Cumberland Island. • Over the years, decimation by gun and by plow have led to a decline over most of the Long-billed Curlew's range. The future of this sandpiper is largely tied to adoption of conservative range and grassland management strategies.

ID: very large, long-necked sandpiper with a very long, downcurved bill (slightly longer for female); buff brown underparts; mottled brown upperparts; unstriped head; long legs; cinnamon orange underwing linings.
Size: *L* 20–26 in; *W* 35 in.
Status: rare migrant and winter visitor on the Coast, mostly from October to January.
Habitat: tidal mudflats, estuaries, saltwater marshes and tidal channels; sometimes farm fields.
Nesting: does not nest in Georgia.

Feeding: probes grasslands for insects, including grasshoppers and beetles; probes shorelines and coastal mudflats for mollusks, crabs, crayfish, marine worms and insects; may eat nestling birds, eggs and some berries.
Voice: most common call is a loud whistle: *cur-lee cur-lee cur-lee;* also a melodious, rolling *cuurrleeeuuu.*
Similar Species: *Marbled Godwit* (p. 144): often found among or near curlews along the coast; shorter, slightly upturned, bicolored bill. *Whimbrel* (p. 142): smaller; much shorter, downcurved bill; dark and pale striping on head; unmarked white belly.
Best Sites: Sapelo I.; Cumberland I.

MARBLED GODWIT

Limosa fedoa

The Marbled Godwit's bill certainly looks long enough to reach buried prey, but this bird doesn't seem content with the length of its bill. It is frequently seen with its head submerged beneath the water or with its face pressed into a mudflat. These deep probings seem to pay off for this large, resourceful shorebird, and a godwit looks genuinely pleased with a freshly extracted meal and a face covered in mud. • Unlike Hudsonian Godwits, which undertake long migrations from the Arctic to South America, Marbled Godwits migrate relatively short distances to coastal wintering areas in the southern U.S. and Central America. These birds are uncommon in Georgia, but in winter a few may turn up at Gould's Inlet, St. Simons Island or Jekyll Island South Beach • The genus name *Limosa*, meaning "muddy," refers to this bird's preference for muddy foraging habitats. • Godwits get their name from the ducklike, squawking *god-wit god-wit* that they issue on their breeding grounds.

nonbreeding

ID: long, yellow-orange bill with dark, slightly upturned tip; long neck and legs; mottled, buff brown plumage is darkest on upperparts; long, black-blue legs. *Breeding:* heavy barring on breast and belly. *Nonbreeding:* buff breast and belly. *In flight:* cinnamon wing linings.
Size: *L* 16–20 in; *W* 30 in.
Status: uncommon migrant and winter resident on the Coast from July through May; rare nonbreeder in summer.
Habitat: coastal beaches, inlets and mudflats.
Nesting: does not nest in Georgia.

Feeding: probes deeply in soft substrates for worms, insect larvae, crustaceans and mollusks; picks insects from grass; may also eat the tubers and seeds of aquatic vegetation.
Voice: usually silent in Georgia.
Similar Species: *Hudsonian Godwit* (p. 362): smaller; chestnut red neck and underparts; white rump. *Greater Yellowlegs* (p. 136): shorter, all-dark bill; bright yellow legs. *Long-billed Dowitcher* (p. 159) and *Short-billed Dowitcher* (p. 158): smaller; straight, all-dark bill; white rump wedge; yellow-green legs.
Best Sites: St. Catherines Island Bar (HC: 130+); Little St. Simons I. (HC: 275); Jekyll I.

RUDDY TURNSTONE

Arenaria interpres

For most of the year, small flocks of boldly patterned Ruddy Turnstones run along our coastal shores, mingling and foraging among the shorebirds. These birds' painted faces and eye-catching, black and red backs set them apart from the multitudes of brown and white sandpipers. • Ruddy Turnstones are truly long-distance migrants. Individuals that nest along the shores of Canada's Arctic routinely fly to South America or western Europe to avoid frosty winters. In Georgia, Ruddy Turnstones are most common from fall to spring when many of these shorebirds stop to refuel or stay to winter along our shorelines. • The name "turnstone" is appropriate for this bird, which uses its bill to flip over pebbles, shells and washed-up vegetation to expose hidden invertebrates. Its short, stubby, slightly upturned bill is an ideal utensil for this unusual foraging style. The Ruddy Turnstone has a varied diet that may occasionally include the eggs of other birds.

nonbreeding

nonbreeding

ID: white belly; black "bib" curves up to shoulder; stout, black, slightly upturned bill; orange-red legs. *Breeding:* ruddy upperparts (female is slightly paler); white face; black "collar"; dark, streaky crown. *Nonbreeding:* brownish upperparts and face.
Size: *L* 9½ in; *W* 21 in.
Status: common migrant and winter resident on the Coast; rare nonbreeder in summer; rare migrant inland.
Habitat: coastal beaches, shores of lakes, reservoirs and sewage lagoons in migration.
Nesting: does not nest in Georgia.

Feeding: probes under and flips rocks, weeds and shells for food items; picks, digs and probes for invertebrates from the soil or from mud; also eats berries, seeds, spiders and carrion.
Voice: low, repeated contact notes; also a sharp *cut-a-cut* alarm call.
Similar Species: *Other sandpipers* (pp. 136–64): lack bold patterning and flashy wing markings in flight. *Plovers* (pp. 127–32): equally bold plumage but in significantly different patterns.
Best Sites: along coastal beaches and barrier island shores in migration or winter; Cumberland I. (HC: 500+); especially on the rocks at Tybee I.

145

RED KNOT

Calidris canutus

Small flocks of migrating Red Knots appear for a brief period in spring, usually beginning in the middle of March. These tubby, red-bellied knots are distinguished from the masses of migrating plovers and sandpipers by their bright rufous breeding plumage. During the breeding season, their red plumage serves to attract mates and camouflage the birds against the sea of grasses and colorful wildflowers on their arctic nesting grounds. • During the slightly longer fall migration period, which lasts from July to October, drab, gray and white Red Knots are difficult to distinguish from other migrating and overwintering shorebirds. They blend in perfectly with the open sandy beaches that they inhabit at this time of year. • The Red Knot is another migratory champion, flying up to 19,000 miles in a single year. Some birds fly from their breeding grounds to winter on the southern tip of South America, whereas others migrate to western Europe.

nonbreeding

nonbreeding

ID: chunky, round body; greenish legs. *Breeding:* rusty face, breast and underparts; brown, black and buff upperparts. *Nonbreeding:* pale gray upperparts; white underparts with some faint streaking on upper breast; faint barring on rump; scaly-looking back. *In flight:* white wing stripe.

Size: *L* 10½ in; *W* 23 in.

Status: common to abundant migrant from April to May and from July to November; less common in winter; rare nonbreeder in summer.

Habitat: coastal beaches, lakeshores, marshes and plowed fields.

Nesting: does not nest in Georgia.

Feeding: gleans shorelines for insects, crustaceans and mollusks; probes soft substrates, creating lines of small holes.

Voice: melodious, soft *ker ek* in flight; usually silent in Georgia.

Similar Species: *Long-billed Dowitcher* (p. 159) and *Short-billed Dowitcher* (p. 158): much longer bill; barring under tail and on flanks; white "V" on rump and tail and on trailing edge of wings. *Buff-breasted Sandpiper* (p. 157): light buff in color; finer, shorter bill; dark flecking on sides. *Other peeps* (pp. 147–56): smaller; most have black legs.

Best Sites: coastal beaches and barrier island shores during migration; Wassaw Island NWR (HC-spring: 12,000+); Gould's Inlet; St. Simons I.; Cumberland I.

SANDERLING
Calidris alba

As the wavefront spills in and out on sandy beaches, lines of lively Sanderlings sprint up and back, running and cavorting in the surf. Their well-known habit of chasing waves has a simple purpose: to snatch washed-up aquatic invertebrates before the next wave rolls into shore. To vary their diet, Sanderlings are also expert tweakers of marine worms and other soft-bodied critters just below the surface of wet mudflats. • When engaged in the rapid sprints of their beach-foraging strategy, Sanderlings move so fast on their dark legs that they appear to be gliding across the sand. When resting, Sanderlings often tuck one leg up to preserve body heat. • Sanderlings, among the world's most cosmopolitan creatures, are found on every continent except Antarctica. They breed across the Arctic in Alaska, Canada and Asia, and spend winters running up and down sandy shorelines in more temperate climes.

nonbreeding

nonbreeding

ID: straight, sturdy, black bill; black legs. *Breeding:* rusty head and breast with dark spotting or mottling. *Nonbreeding:* quite pale; white underparts; pale gray upperparts; black shoulder patch (often concealed). *Immature:* white-edged blackish upperparts; conspicuous buffy wash on upper breast.
Size: *L* 7–8½ in; *W* 17 in.
Status: common nonbreeding permanent resident on the Coast; less common in summer; rare migrant inland.
Habitat: lower waveslope of sandy ocean beaches; also uses rocky shorelines, breakwaters, tidal mudflats and estuaries; occasionally uses inland freshwater shorelines and mudflats.
Nesting: does not nest in Georgia.
Feeding: diet in winter is mainly coastal invertebrates, including sand crabs, marine worms, amphipods, insects and small mollusks; may eat carrion; diet in summer includes mostly insects and some leaves, seeds and algae.
Voice: generally vocal; flocks converse and flush with electric *twik!* notes, sometimes continued in an irregular series.
Similar Species: *Least Sandpiper* (p. 150): smaller and browner. *Dunlin* (p. 155): darker-backed and dark-breasted; slightly down-curved bill. *Red Knot* (p. 146): larger; whitish rump barred with gray; breeding adult has rufous underparts. *Western Sandpiper* (p. 149) and *Semipalmated Sandpiper* (p. 148): smaller; dark shoulder mark; lack uniformly copper-colored head and upper breast in spring and summer; sandy upperparts in winter.
Best Sites: coastal beaches and barrier island shores in migration and winter; St. Catherines Island Bar (HC-fall: 6000+); Little Tybee I. (HC-fall: 1600+).

SEMIPALMATED SANDPIPER

Calidris pusilla

The small, plain Semipalmated Sandpiper can be difficult to identify among the swarms of similar-looking *Calidris* sandpipers that migrate along the coast. The Semipalmated, Western, Least, White-rumped and Baird's sandpipers are known collectively as "peeps" because of the similarity of their high-pitched calls. These strikingly similar "miniatures" can make shorebird identification either a complete nightmare or an uplifting challenge. • Each spring and fall, large numbers of Semipalmated Sandpipers touch down on our coastal shorelines, pecking and probing in mechanized fury to replenish their body fat for the remainder of their long journey. Semipalmated Sandpipers fly almost the entire length of the Americas during migration, so their staging sites must provide ample food sources. Highly efficient, these birds raise up to four young in just a few weeks of arctic summer, then fly 2000 nonstop miles, over water, back to their wintering grounds in Central and South America. • *Pusilla* is Latin for "very small," which aptly describes this, and most other, sandpipers.

nonbreeding

nonbreeding

ID: short, straight, black bill; black legs. *Breeding:* mottled upperparts; slight tinge of rufous on ear patch, crown and scapulars; faint streaks on upper breast and flanks. *Nonbreeding:* white "eyebrow"; gray-brown upperparts; white underparts with light brown wash on sides of upper breast. *In flight:* narrow, white wing stripe; black line through white rump.

Size: *L* 5½–7 in; *W* 14 in.

Status: abundant migrant on the Coast from April to June and from July to November; uncommon migrant inland.

Habitat: coastal mudflats and the shores of ponds and lakes.

Nesting: does not nest in Georgia.

Feeding: probes soft substrates and gleans for aquatic insects and crustaceans.

Voice: flight call is a harsh *cherk;* sometimes a longer *chirrup* or a chittering alarm call.

Similar Species: *Least Sandpiper* (p. 150): yellowish legs; darker upperparts. *Western Sandpiper* (p. 149): longer, slightly down-curved bill; bright rufous wash on crown and ear patch in spring. *Sanderling* (p. 147): larger; pale gray upperparts and blackish trailing edge on flight feathers in nonbreeding plumage. *White-rumped Sandpiper* (p. 151): larger; white rump; folded wings extend beyond tail. *Baird's Sandpiper* (p. 152): larger; longer bill; folded wings extend beyond tail.

Best Sites: coastal beaches and barrier island shores; inland at small ponds and marshy edges.

WESTERN SANDPIPER

Calidris mauri

Most Western Sandpipers are seen along the Pacific Coast, but many adventurous individuals traverse the continent and winter along Atlantic shores. In spring, large flocks of these birds migrate northward to Alaskan breeding grounds. It is estimated that up to 6.5 million Western Sandpipers converge on the Copper River Delta in Alaska. • Many identification guides will tell you to look for this bird's downcurved bill, and on paper this seems like a sensible plan. In the field, however, as angles and lighting change, the bills of peeps can look downcurved one moment, straight the next, and anything in between when double-checked. It is a good idea to spend some time getting to know the peeps before trying to identity them. The Western Sandpiper can be easily confused with other peeps, in particular the Semipalmated Sandpiper. • Though Western Sandpipers are common to abundant along the coast from August to May, they are rare inland migrants in the state.

nonbreeding

nonbreeding

ID: black, slightly down-curved bill; black legs. *Breeding:* rufous crown, ear patch and scapulars; V-shaped streaking on upper breast and flanks; light underparts. *Nonbreeding:* white "eyebrow"; gray-brown upperparts; white underparts; streaky, light brown wash on upper breast. *In flight:* narrow, white wing stripe; black line through white rump.
Size: *L* 6–7 in; *W* 14 in.
Status: common to abundant nonbreeding resident on the Coast, except rare in mid-summer; uncommon inland migrant from March to May and from July to October; accidental inland in winter at Augusta and Albany.
Habitat: pond edges, lakeshores and mudflats.
Nesting: does not nest in Georgia.
Feeding: gleans and probes mud and shallow water; occasionally submerges

its head; primarily eats aquatic insects, worms and crustaceans.
Voice: flight call is a high-pitched *cheep*.
Similar Species: *Semipalmated Sandpiper* (p. 148): shorter, straight bill, thicker at base; less rufous on crown, ear patch and scapulars. *Least Sandpiper* (p. 150): smaller; yellowish legs; darker breast wash in all plumages; lacks rufous patches. *White-rumped Sandpiper* (p. 151): larger; white rump; folded wings extend beyond tail; lacks rufous wing patches. *Baird's Sandpiper* (p. 152): larger; folded wings extend beyond tail; lacks rufous patches. *Dunlin* (p. 155): larger; black belly in breeding plumage; longer bill is thicker at base and droops at tip; grayer, unstreaked back in nonbreeding plumage. *Sanderling* (p. 147): nonbreeding plumage shows pale gray upperparts, black-ish trailing edge on flight feathers and bold, white upperwing stripe in flight.
Best Sites: coastal beaches and barrier island shores in migration; Jekyll I. (HC-fall: 5000+); E.L. Huie.

149

LEAST SANDPIPER

Calidris minutilla

Least Sandpipers are the smallest North American shorebirds, but their small size does not deter them from performing huge migratory feats. Like most other "peeps," Least Sandpipers migrate almost the entire length of the globe twice each year, from the Arctic to the southern tip of South America and back. • Arctic summers are incredibly short, so shorebirds must maximize their breeding efforts. Least Sandpipers lay large eggs relative to those of other sandpipers, and the entire clutch might weigh over half the weight of the female! The young hatch in an advanced state of development, getting an early start on preparations for the fall migration. These tiny shorebirds begin moving south as early as the first week of July, so they are some of the first sandpipers to arrive back in Georgia during fall migration. · Although light-colored legs are a good field mark for this species, bad lighting or mud can confuse matters. Dark mud can make the legs look dark, whereas light-colored mud can make other species' dark legs look light. • The scientific name *minutilla* is Latin for "very small"—apt for this, the littlest of the sandpipers.

nonbreeding

nonbreeding

ID: black bill; yellowish legs; dark, mottled back. *Breeding:* buff brown breast, head and nape; light breast streaking; prominent white "V" on back. *Nonbreeding:* more gray-brown overall. *Immature:* similar to adult, but with faintly streaked breast; warmer brown than the other two small peeps.
Size: *L* 5–6½ in; *W* 13 in.
Status: common to abundant nonbreeding resident on the Coast, except rare in midsummer; common migrant inland from March to June and from early July to November; uncommon in the Coastal Plain and the Piedmont, and accidental in the Mountains in winter; uncommon winter resident inland, mostly south of the Fall Line.

Habitat: tidal pools, sewage lagoons, mudflats, lakeshores, ditches and wetland edges.
Nesting: does not nest in Georgia.
Feeding: probes or pecks for insects, crustaceans, small mollusks and occasionally seeds.
Voice: high-pitched *kree.*
Similar Species: *Semipalmated Sandpiper* (p. 148): black legs; lighter upperparts; rufous tinge on crown, ear patch and scapulars. *Western Sandpiper* (p. 149): slightly larger; black legs; lighter breast wash in all plumages; rufous patches on crown, ear and scapulars in breeding plumage. *Other peeps* (pp. 146–56): larger; dark legs.
Best Sites: coastal beaches and barrier island shores during migration; Baker Co. (HC: 100+); E.L. Huie; Bulloch Co. sod farms.

WHITE-RUMPED SANDPIPER
Calidris fuscicollis

Just as a die-hard shorebird-watcher is about to go into a peep-induced stupor, small brownish heads emerge from hiding. Back feathers are ruffled, wings are stretched and, almost without warning, the birds take flight and flash pure white rumps. There is no doubt that the beautiful White-rumped Sandpiper has been identified. • This sandpiper's white rump may serve the same purpose as the tail of a white-tailed deer—to alert other birds when danger threatens. • When flocks of White-rumps and other sandpipers take to the air, they often defecate in unison. This spontaneous evacuation might benefit the birds by reducing their weight for takeoff. Flocks of White-rumped Sandpipers have also been known to collectively rush at a predator and then suddenly scatter in its face. • Like many sandpipers, White-rumps are accomplished long-distance migrants, often flying for stretches of 60 hours nonstop. • The scientific name *fuscicollis* means "brown neck," a characteristic this bird shares with many of its close relatives.

nonbreeding

nonbreeding

ID: black legs; black bill, about as long as head width; folded wings extend beyond tail. *Breeding:* brown-mottled upperparts; dark streaking on breast, sides and flanks. *Nonbreeding:* gray upperparts and breast. *In flight:* white rump; dark tail; indistinct wing bar.
Size: *L* 7–8 in; *W* 17 in.
Status: uncommon migrant from April to June; rare migrant from July to November.
Habitat: coastal tidal pools and mudflats; inland on lakeshores, marshes, sewage lagoons and reservoirs; flooded and cultivated fields.

Nesting: does not nest in Georgia.
Feeding: gleans the ground and shorelines for insects, crustaceans and mollusks.
Voice: flight call is a characteristic, squeal-like *tzeet*, higher-pitched than any other peep.
Similar Species: *Other peeps* (pp. 146–56): all have dark line through rump. *Baird's Sandpiper* (p. 152): lacks clean white rump; breast streaking does not extend onto flanks. *Stilt Sandpiper* (p. 156) and *Curlew Sandpiper:* much longer legs trail beyond tail in flight.
Best Sites: coastal and barrier island shores during migration; Onslow I.; Altamaha WMA; inland ponds and lagoons; E.L. Huie (HC: 20).

BAIRD'S SANDPIPER

Calidris bairdii

The Baird's Sandpiper is one of the most difficult sandpipers to identify correctly. One clue to its identification is that while it often migrates with other sandpipers, upon landing it leaves them and feeds alone. • Baird's Sandpipers remain on their northern breeding grounds for only a short time. Soon after the chicks hatch and are able to fend for themselves, the adults flock together to begin their southward migration. After a few weeks of accumulating fat reserves, the young gather in a second wave of southbound migrants. • Spencer Fullerton Baird, an early director of the Smithsonian Institute, organized several natural history expeditions across North America. In the 19th century, Elliott Coues named this bird in recognition of Baird's efforts.

nonbreeding

nonbreeding

ID: black legs and bill; faint, buff brown breast speckling; folded wings extend beyond tail. *Breeding:* large, black, diamondlike patterns on back and wing coverts. *Nonbreeding:* gray-brown upperparts, head and breast.
Size: *L* 7–7½ in; *W* 17 in.
Status: rare migrant from April to May; rare to uncommon migrant from July to October.
Habitat: tidal pools, sandy beaches, mudflats and wetland edges; inland on dry pastures and lakeshores; often found in slightly drier areas than other peeps.

Nesting: does not nest in Georgia.
Feeding: gleans aquatic invertebrates, especially larval flies; also eats beetles and grasshoppers; rarely probes.
Voice: soft, rolling *kriit kriit.*
Similar Species: "scaly" back is distinctive. *White-rumped Sandpiper* (p. 151): clean white rump; breast streaking extends onto flanks. *Pectoral Sandpiper* (p. 153): dark breast ends abruptly at edge of white belly. *Least Sandpiper* (p. 150): smaller; yellowish legs. *Western Sandpiper* (p. 149) and *Sanderling* (p. 147): lack streaked, gray buff breast. *Semipalmated Sandpiper* (p. 148): smaller; shorter bill; lacks streaked breast in nonbreeding plumage.
Best Sites: sod farms in Laurens Co. and Bulloch Co.; E.L. Huie; Peach Co. (HC: 6).

PECTORAL SANDPIPER

Calidris melanotos

The Pectoral Sandpiper is sometimes referred to as the "Grass Snipe" because of its preference for wet meadows and grassy marshes. This widespread traveler has been observed in every state and province in North America during its epic annual migrations. In spring and fall, Pectoral Sandpipers are conspicuous along our coastlines and in wet, grassy fields, often in large flocks of over 1000 birds. Peak numbers occur from mid-April to the end of May, and from early August to late September. • Unlike most sandpipers, the Pectoral exhibits sexual dimorphism—the female is only two-thirds the size of the male. • The name "pectoral" refers to the location of the male's prominent air sacs. When displaying on his arctic breeding grounds, the male will inflate these air sacs, causing his feathers to rise. During displays, a male will also emit a hollow hooting sound, which has been likened to the sound of a foghorn. • If threatened, flocks of Pectorals suddenly launch into the air and converge into a single, swirling mass.

ID: brown breast streaks end abruptly at edge of white belly; white undertail coverts; black bill has slightly downcurved tip; long, yellow legs; mottled upperparts; may have faintly rusty, dark crown and back; folded wings extend beyond tail. *Immature:* less spotting on breast; broader, white feather edges on back form 2 white "V"s.
Size: *L* 9 in; *W* 18 in (female is noticeably smaller).
Status: common migrant from April to May and from July to August.

Habitat: lakeshores, marshes, mudflats and flooded fields or pastures; at sod farms and ponds inland.
Nesting: does not nest in Georgia.
Feeding: probes and pecks for small insects; eats mainly flies, but also takes beetles and some grasshoppers; may eat small mollusks, amphipods, berries, seeds, moss, algae and some plant material.
Voice: sharp, short, low *krrick krrick*.
Similar Species: *Other peeps* (pp. 146–56): all lack well-defined, dark "bib" and yellow legs.
Best Sites: all sod farms and virtually any shallow puddle; Bartow Co.; E.L. Huie; Bulloch Co. sod farm (HC: 250+).

PURPLE SANDPIPER
Calidris maritima

Unlike most shorebirds, which prefer shallow marshy areas, sand beaches or mudflats, Purple Sandpipers forage perilously close to crashing waves along rocky headlands, piers and breakwaters. These birds expertly navigate their way across rugged, slippery rocks while foraging for crustaceans, mollusks and insect larvae. In fact, they are rarely seen associated with any beach that is not near a rocky area. • Purple Sandpipers breed in high arctic coastal regions and winter along the Atlantic Coast from maritime Canada south to northeast Florida. No other shorebird winters as far north along the Atlantic Coast as the Purple Sandpiper. • The name "purple" was given to this sandpiper for the purplish iridescence that is occasionally observed on its shoulders. *Calidris* is Greek for "sandpiper," whereas *maritima* is Latin for "belonging to the sea."

nonbreeding

nonbreeding

ID: long, slightly drooping, black-tipped bill with yellow-orange base; yellow-orange legs; dull streaking on breast and flanks. *Breeding:* streaked neck; buff crown with dark streaks; dark back feathers with tawny to rusty brown edges. *Nonbreeding:* unstreaked, gray head, neck and upper breast form a "hood"; gray-spotted white belly.
Size: *L* 9 in; *W* 17 in.
Status: uncommon and local winter resident on the Coast along barrier island rocky jetties from October to March.

Habitat: rocky shorelines, piers and breakwaters; occasionally roosting along high-tide line on sandy beaches.
Nesting: does not nest in Georgia.
Feeding: food is found visually and is snatched while moving over rocks and sand; eats mostly mollusks, insects, crustaceans and other invertebrates; also eats a variety of plant material.
Voice: call is a soft *prrt-prrt*, but usually silent in Georgia.
Similar Species: *Other peeps* (pp. 146–56): all lack bicolored bill, yellow-orange legs and unstreaked, gray "hood" in nonbreeding plumage.
Best Sites: rocky jetty on north end of Tybee I. (HC: 30); Cumberland I. jetty.

DUNLIN

Calidris alpina

Outside the breeding season, Dunlins form dynamic, synchronous flocks. These tight flocks are generally more exclusive than other shorebird troops and rarely include other species. Sometimes hundreds of these birds are seen flying wing tip to wing tip. Unlike many of their shorebird relatives, Dunlins overwinter in North America, mostly in coastal areas—few ever cross the equator. They gather in flocks that can number in the tens of thousands. • Dunlins are fairly distinctive in their breeding attire: their black bellies and legs make them look as though they have been wading belly-deep in puddles of ink. • This bird was originally called "Dunling," meaning "little dark one," but with the passage of time, the "g" was dropped. It was also known as "Red-backed Sandpiper" because of its rufous back in breeding plumage.

nonbreeding

nonbreeding

ID: slightly downcurved, black bill; black legs. *Breeding:* black belly; streaked, white neck and underparts; rufous wings, back and crown. *Nonbreeding:* pale gray underparts; brownish gray upperparts; light brown streaking on breast and nape. *In flight:* white wing stripe.
Size: *L* 7½–9 in; *W* 17 in.
Status: common to abundant migrant and winter visitor on the Coast from September to June; rare nonbreeder in summer; rare migrant and winter visitor inland in small numbers from March to May and from October to November.
Habitat: mudflats and the shores of ponds, marshes and lakes.

Nesting: does not nest in Georgia.
Feeding: gleans and probes mudflats for aquatic crustaceans, worms, mollusks and insects.
Voice: flight call is a grating *cheezp* or *treezp.*
Similar Species: black belly in breeding plumage is distinctive. *Western Sandpiper* (p. 149) and *Semipalmated Sandpiper* (p. 148): smaller; nonbreeding plumage is browner overall; bill tips are less downcurved. *Least Sandpiper* (p. 150): smaller; darker upperparts; yellowish legs. *Sanderling* (p. 147): paler; straight bill; usually seen running in the surf.
Best Sites: coastal and barrier island shores in migration and winter; Ossabaw I. (HC: 6000+); Cumberland I. (HC: 3000+); St. Catherines I. (HC: 8000+); Gainesville Airport (HC: 21).

STILT SANDPIPER

Calidris himantopus

With the silhouette of a small Lesser Yellowlegs and the foraging behavior of a dowitcher, both of which this bird often associates, the Stilt Sandpiper is easily overlooked by most birders. Named for its relatively long legs, this shorebird prefers to feed in shallow water, where it digs like a dowitcher, often dunking its head completely under water. Because its bill is shorter than a dowitcher's, however, it has to lean farther forward than its larger cousin—a characteristic that can aid in identification. Moving on tall, stiltlike legs, this sandpiper will also wade into deep water up to its breast in search of a meal. • The omnivorous Stilt Sandpiper eats everything from insects to roots and seeds. To snag freshwater shrimp, insect larvae or tiny minnows from just below the water's surface, the Stilt Sandpiper may occasionally sweep its bill from side to side like an American Avocet. • Unlike many of its

nonbreeding

Calidris relatives, the Stilt Sandpiper never gathers in large flocks. At most, you may see a gathering of 50 or so Stilts between mid-August and the end of September.

nonbreeding

ID: long, greenish legs; long bill droops slightly at tip. *Breeding:* chestnut red ear patch; white "eyebrow"; striped crown; streaked neck; barred underparts. *Nonbreeding:* less conspicuous white "eyebrow"; dirty white neck and breast; white belly; dark brownish gray upperparts. *In flight:* white rump; legs trail behind tail; no wing stripe.
Size: *L* 8–9 in; *W* 18 in.
Status: uncommon to common migrant, more numerous on the Coast from March to May and from July to November; accidental in the Mountains; rare on the Coast in winter.
Habitat: shores of lakes, reservoirs and marshes.
Nesting: does not nest in Georgia.

Feeding: probes deeply in shallow water; eats mostly invertebrates; occasionally picks insects from the water's surface or the ground; also eats seeds, roots and leaves.
Voice: simple, sharp *querp* or *kirr* in flight; clearer *whu*.
Similar Species: *Greater Yellowlegs* (p. 136) and *Lesser Yellowlegs* (p. 137): yellow legs; straight bills; lack red ear patch. *Curlew Sandpiper:* bill has more obvious curve; black legs; paler gray upperparts in nonbreeding plumage. *Dunlin* (p. 155): shorter, black legs; longer, downcurved bill; dark rump; whitish wing bar.
Best Sites: coastal beaches and barrier island shores during migration; rare in winter at Onslow, Tybee, Sapelo, Jekyll and St. Catherines islands; Altamaha WMA; Kings Bay Submarine Base in Camden Co. (HC: 200+); inland at E.L. Huie (HC: 29).

BUFF-BREASTED SANDPIPER

Tryngites subruficollis

Shy in behavior and humble in appearance, the Buff-breasted Sandpiper is an uncommon migrant to Georgia. Most Buff-breasted Sandpipers migrate through the center of the continent, so the individuals that we see here are mainly dispersing juveniles heading south in fall. These sandpipers regularly mingle with flocks of foraging Black-bellied Plovers and American Golden-Plovers. • The Buff-breast prefers drier habitats than most other sandpipers. When feeding, this subtly colored bird stands motionless, blending beautifully into a backdrop of cultivated fields, mudflats or managed sod farms. Only when it catches sight of moving prey does it become visible, making a short, forward sprint to snatch a fresh meal. • Buff-breasted Sandpipers are the only North American shorebirds to use a lek for mating purposes, similar to the prairie-chickens of the Great Plains. The males display for the females on the lek (mating arena), with the females often mating with more than one male before they lay their egg clutches.

adult

immature

ID: buffy, unpatterned face and foreneck; large, dark eyes; very thin, straight, black bill; buff underparts; small spots on crown, nape, breast, sides and flanks; "scaly" look to back and upper-wings; yellow legs. *Immature:* "scaly" feather pattern on back. *In flight:* pure white underwings; no wing stripe.
Size: *L* 7½–8 in; *W* 18 in.
Status: rare spring migrant inland; uncommon fall migrant on the Coast; uncommon migrant inland from July to October.
Habitat: shores of lakes, reservoirs and marshes; also sod farms, airports, highway ditches and both cultivated and flooded fields.
Nesting: does not nest in Georgia.
Feeding: gleans the ground and shorelines for insects, spiders and small crustaceans; may eat seeds.
Voice: usually silent; calls include *chup* or *tick* notes; *preet* flight call.
Similar Species: *Upland Sandpiper* (p. 141): bolder streaking on breast; longer neck; smaller head; larger bill; streaking on "cheek" and foreneck.
Best Sites: sod farms, especially Peach Co. sod farm (HC-fall: 36); shorebird pond habitat.

157

SHORT-BILLED DOWITCHER

Limnodromus griseus

Dowitchers tend to be stockier than most shorebirds, and they generally avoid venturing into deep water. While foraging along shorelines, these birds use their bills to "stitch" up and down into the mud with a rhythm like a sewing machine. The drilling motion liquefies the mud or sand, allowing the dowitchers to reach their hidden prey. This behavior is fascinating to watch and it is also helpful for long-range field identification. • These plump shorebirds are seen in good numbers on most of our coastal mudflats, marshes and beaches, though numbers can fluctuate from year to year. Winter reports of Short-billed Dowitchers inland are unusual, though a few may turn up during migration. • The best way to distinguish between Short-billed Dowitchers and the very similar Long-billed Dowitchers is by their flight calls or by listening to them while they feed—Short-bills feed silently, whereas Long-bills chatter softly while feeding.

nonbreeding

nonbreeding

ID: straight, long, dark bill; white "eyebrow"; chunky body; yellow-green legs. *Breeding:* white belly; dark spots or bars on reddish buff neck and upper breast; prominent dark barring on white sides and flanks. *Nonbreeding:* dirty gray upperparts; dirty white underparts. *In flight:* white wedge on rump and lower back.

Size: *L* 11–12 in; *W* 19 in.

Status: common migrant and winter resident on the Coast from July to May; rare nonbreeder in summer; uncommon migrant inland from March to May and more common from July to October; accidental in winter in Laurens Co. and Macon.

Habitat: coastal mudflats, salt marshes, shores of lakes, reservoirs and marshes.

Nesting: does not nest in Georgia.

Feeding: wades in shallow water or on mud, probing deeply into the substrate with a rapid up-down bill motion; eats aquatic invertebrates, including insects, mollusks, crustaceans and worms; may feed on seeds, aquatic plants and grasses.

Voice: generally silent; flight call is a mellow, repeated *tututu, toodulu* or *toodu.*

Similar Species: *Long-billed Dowitcher* (p. 159): black and white barring on red flanks in breeding plumage; very little white on belly; dark spotting on neck and upper breast; alarm call is a high-pitched *keek. Red Knot* (p. 146): much shorter bill; unmarked, red breast in breeding plumage; nonbreeding birds lack barring on tail and white wedge on back in flight. *Wilson's Snipe* (p. 160): heavy streaking on neck and breast; bicolored bill; pale median stripe on crown; shorter legs. *American Woodcock* (p. 161): unmarked, buff underparts; yellow bill; light-colored bars on black crown and nape.

Best Sites: coastal and barrier island shores during migration; Glynn Co. (HC-winter: 900+).

LONG-BILLED DOWITCHER

Limnodromus scolopaceus

Each winter, mudflats and marshes host small numbers of enthusiastic Long-billed Dowitchers. These chunky, sword-billed shorebirds diligently forage up and down through shallow water and mud in a quest for invertebrate sustenance. A diet of insects, freshwater shrimp, mussels, clams and snails provides migrating and over-wintering Long-bills with plenty of fuel for flight and essential calcium for bone and egg development. • Dowitchers have shorter wings than most shorebirds that migrate long distances. This feature makes it more practical for dowitchers to take flight from shallow water, where a series of hops helps them to become airborne. • Mixed flocks of shorebirds demonstrate a variety of foraging styles: some species probe deeply, whereas others pick at the water's surface or glean the shorelines. It is thought that large numbers of shorebird species are able to coexist because of their different foraging styles and specialized diets.

nonbreeding

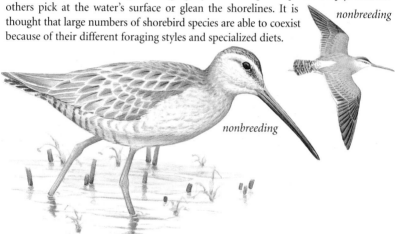

nonbreeding

ID: very long, straight, dark bill; dark eye line; white "eyebrow"; chunky body; yellow-green legs. *Breeding:* black and white barring on reddish underparts; some white on belly; dark, mottled upperparts. *Nonbreeding:* gray overall; dirty white underparts. *In flight:* white wedge on rump and lower back.

Size: *L* 11–12½ in; *W* 19 in.

Status: rare to uncommon migrant and winter visitor on the Coast from late July to May; rare fall migrant inland from August to December; accidental spring visitor inland in Baker Co., Pendergrass, Macon and E.L. Huie.

Habitat: mudflats, salt marshes, lakeshores and shallow marshes; prefers fresh water.

Nesting: does not nest in Georgia.

Feeding: probes in shallow water and mudflats with a repeated up-down bill

motion; frequently plunges its head under water; eats shrimps, snails, worms, larval flies and other soft-bodied invertebrates.

Voice: alarm call, usually given in flight, is a loud, high-pitched *keek*, occasionally given in series.

Similar Species: *Short-billed Dowitcher* (p. 158): white sides, flanks and belly; more spots than bars on reddish sides and flanks; brighter feather edges on upperparts; call is a lower-pitched *toodu* or *tututu*. *Red Knot* (p. 146): much shorter bill; unmarked, red breast in breeding plumage; nonbreeding birds lack barring on tail and white wedge on back in flight. *Wilson's Snipe* (p. 160): shorter legs; heavy streaking on neck and breast; bicolored bill; pale median stripe on crown. *American Woodcock* (p. 161): unmarked, buff underparts; yellow bill; light-colored bars on black crown and nape.

Best Sites: coastal and barrier island shores during migration; Jekyll I. (HC: 50); Altamaha WMA (HC: 50); Onslow I.

159

WILSON'S SNIPE

Gallinago delicata

While in Georgia, the well-camouflaged Wilson's Snipe is shy and secretive, often remaining concealed in vegetation. Only when an intruder approaches too closely will the snipe flush from cover, performing a series of aerial zigzags—an evasive maneuver designed to confuse predators. Because of this habit, hunters who were skilled enough to shoot a snipe came to be known as "snipers," a term later adopted by the military. • The snipe's eyes are placed far back on its head, allowing the bird to see both forward and backward. This bird is also equipped with a unique, flexible bill tip that is useful for snatching up earthworms and other underground prey. • Each spring, the eerie, hollow, winnowing sound of a courting male Wilson's Snipe is heard above almost every wetland on breeding grounds in the northern United States and Canada. The sound is produced when the snipe's specialized outer tail feathers vibrate rapidly through the air during daring, headfirst dives high above the marshland. • This bird was previously known as "Common Snipe," but was recently split into two separate species: the Wilson's Snipe of North America, and the Common Snipe of Eurasia.

ID: long, sturdy, bicolored bill; relatively short legs; heavily striped head, back, neck and breast; dark eye stripe; dark barring on sides and flanks; unmarked white belly.
In flight: quick zigzags on take off.
Size: *L* 10½–11½ in; *W* 18 in.
Status: common migrant and winter resident from August to April.
Habitat: cattail and bulrush marshes, poorly drained floodplains or soggy fields, pastures, sod farms, roadside ditches and muddy lakeshores.
Nesting: does not nest in Georgia.
Feeding: probes soft substrates for larvae, earthworms and other soft-bodied invertebrates; also eats mollusks, crustaceans, spiders, small amphibians and some seeds.
Voice: alarm call is a nasal *scaip*.
Similar Species: *Short-billed Dowitcher* (p. 158) and *Long-billed Dowitcher* (p. 159): lack heavy striping on head, back, neck and breast; longer legs; all-dark bills; usually seen in flocks. *Marbled Godwit* (p. 144): much larger; slightly upturned bill; much longer legs. *American Woodcock* (p. 161): unmarked, buff underparts; yellowish bill; light-colored bars on black crown and nape.
Best Sites: E.L. Huie; Eufaula NWR; Harris Neck NWR; Altamaha WMA; Bulloch Co. and other sod farms; Augusta and Greene Co. (HC: 200+).

AMERICAN WOODCOCK

Scolopax minor

The American Woodcock's behavior usually suits its cryptic and inconspicuous attire—this denizen of moist woodlands and damp thickets normally goes about its business in a quiet and reclusive manner. But during courtship the male woodcock reveals his true character. Just before dawn or just after sunset, he struts provocatively in an open woodland clearing or a brushy, abandoned field while calling out a series of loud *peeent* notes. He then launches into the air, twittering upward in a circular flight display until, with wings partly folded, he plummets to the ground in the zigzag pattern of a falling leaf, producing chirping sounds with the primary flight feathers of his wings. At the end of this stunning "sky dance," he lands precisely where he started. • The secretive American Woodcock has endured many changes to its traditional nesting grounds. The clearing of forests and draining of woodland swamps has degraded and eliminated large tracts of woodcock habitat, resulting in a decline in this bird's populations.

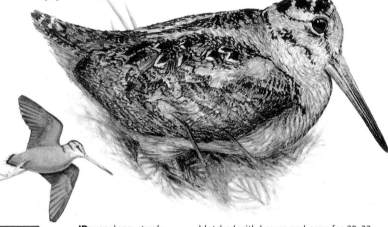

ID: very long, sturdy bill; very short legs; large head; short neck; chunky body; large, dark eyes; unmarked, buff underparts; light-colored bars on black crown and nape.
In flight: rounded wings.
Size: *L* 11 in; *W* 18 in.
Status: rare and local permanent breeding resident in the Piedmont and the Coastal Plain; more numerous in winter, but migrants depart by the end of February.
Habitat: moist woodlands and brushy thickets adjacent to grassy clearings or abandoned fields.
Nesting: on the ground in woods or in an overgrown field; female digs a scrape and lines it with dead leaves and other debris; female incubates 4 pinkish buff eggs,

blotched with brown and gray, for 20–22 days; female tends the young.
Feeding: probes in soft, moist or wet soil for earthworms and insect larvae; also takes spiders, snails, millipedes and some plant material, including seeds, sedges and grasses.
Voice: nasal *peent;* makes a twittering sound when flushed from cover; during courtship dance male produces high-pitched, twittering, whistling sounds.
Similar Species: *Wilson's Snipe* (p. 160): heavily striped head, back, neck and breast; dark barring on sides and flanks. *Long-billed Dowitcher* (p. 159) and *Short-billed Dowitcher* (p. 158): all-dark bill; longer legs; lack light-colored barring on dark crown and nape; usually seen in flocks.
Best Sites: mostly at dusk or dawn in February at Chattahoochee River National RA; Rum Creek WMA/Piedmont NWR (HC: 16).

WILSON'S PHALAROPE

Phalaropus tricolor

Of the three North American phalarope species, the Wilson's Phalarope is the only one that migrates mainly over land instead of over the sea. As individuals or small flocks pass through Georgia, they stop to forage in flooded agricultural fields, along muddy shorelines or in tidal pools. • Phalaropes are among the most colorful and unusual shorebirds. They practice an uncommon mating strategy known as polyandry: each female mates with several males and often produces a clutch of eggs with each mate. After laying a clutch, the female usually abandons her mate, leaving him to incubate the eggs and tend the precocial young. This reversal of gender roles includes a reversal of plumage characteristics as well—the female is more brightly colored than her male counterpart. Even John James Audubon was fooled by these reversals: he mislabeled the male and female birds in all of his phalarope illustrations. • Most phalaropes have lobed, or individually webbed, feet for swimming in the shallows of wetlands, but the Wilson's Phalarope is more terrestrial than its relatives and lacks this characteristic.

nonbreeding

nonbreeding

ID: dark, needlelike bill; white "eyebrow," throat and nape; light underparts; black legs. *Breeding female:* very sharp colors; gray "cap"; chestnut brown sides of neck; black eye line extends down side of neck and onto back. *Breeding male:* duller overall; dark "cap." *Nonbreeding:* all-gray upperparts; white "eyebrow" and gray eye line; white underparts; dark yellowish or greenish legs.
Size: *L* 9–9½ in; *W* 17 in.
Status: rare to uncommon migrant on the Coast from July to October; accidental on the Coast in spring; rare migrant inland from April to June and from July to November.
Habitat: coastal mudflats; lakeshores, marshes, flooded fields and sewage lagoons.

Nesting: does not nest in Georgia.
Feeding: whirls in tight circles in shallow or deep water to stir up prey, then picks aquatic insects, worms and small crustaceans from the water's surface or just below it; on land, makes short jabs to pick up invertebrates.
Voice: generally silent.
Similar Species: *Red-necked Phalarope* (p. 163): rufous stripe down side of neck in breeding plumage; dark nape and line behind eye in nonbreeding plumage. *Red Phalarope* (p. 164): reddish neck, breast and underparts in breeding plumage; dark nape and broad, dark line behind eye in nonbreeding plumage; rarely seen inland. *Lesser Yellowlegs* (p. 137): larger; yellow legs; streaked neck; mottled upperparts.
Best Sites: Savannah NWR; E.L. Huie; Augusta ponds (HC: 60).

RED-NECKED PHALAROPE

Phalaropus lobatus

Most Red-necked Phalaropes migrate to and from their arctic wintering grounds via the Atlantic Coast, passing over the open ocean alongside the Florida coastline in spring and fall. Occasionally Red-necks join Wilson's Phalaropes inland to forage on the shores of muddy wetlands or sewage lagoons. • When foraging on the water with other shorebirds, phalaropes can usually be singled out by their unusual behavior—they spin and whirl about in tight circles, stirring up tiny crustaceans, mollusks and other aquatic invertebrates. As prey funnels toward the water's surface, these birds daintily pluck at them with their needlelike bills. • "Phalarope" is the Greek word for "coot's foot." Like coots and grebes, Red-necked Phalaropes have individually webbed, or "lobed," toes, a feature that makes them proficient swimmers.

breeding

♀ ♂

nonbreeding

ID: thin, black bill; long, dark gray legs. *Breeding female:* chestnut brown stripe on neck and throat; white "chin"; blue-black head; incomplete, white eye ring; white belly; 2 rusty buff stripes on each upperwing. *Breeding male:* white "eyebrow"; less intense colors than female. *Nonbreeding:* white underparts; black "cap"; broad, dark band from eye to ear; whitish stripes on blue-gray upperparts.
Size: *L* 7 in; *W* 15 in.
Status: uncommon to common migrant and rare winter visitor far Offshore from August to May; rare migrant on the Coast and inland from May to June and from July to October.
Habitat: open ocean on drifting mats of *Sargassum* spp.; coastal mudflats; occasionally

on open water bodies, including ponds, lakes, marshes and sewage lagoons.
Nesting: does not nest in Georgia.
Feeding: whirls in tight circles in shallow or deep water to stir up prey, then picks insects, mollusks and small crustaceans from the water's surface; on land, makes short jabs to pick up invertebrates.
Voice: often noisy in migration; soft *krit krit krit*.
Similar Species: *Wilson's Phalarope* (p. 162): female has gray "cap" and black eye line extending down side of neck and onto back in breeding plumage. *Red Phalarope* (p. 164): all-red neck, breast and underparts in breeding plumage; lacks white stripes on upperwing in nonbreeding plumage.
Best Sites: boating far offshore (HC: 240); Hutchinson I. (HC-fall: 11 over one month); accidental at E.L. Huie.

RED PHALAROPE

Phalaropus fulicarius

In winter, Red Phalaropes are entirely pelagic, following zooplankton blooms for most of the year. Many of these birds overwinter in the Pacific Ocean, off the coast of Chile or Peru, though some are also found in our temperate Atlantic waters. The Red Phalaropes that nest in the eastern Canadian Arctic may migrate across the Atlantic to wintering grounds near west Africa, but thousands may also spend winter well off the shores of South Carolina, Georgia and Florida, foraging along the Gulf Stream. The bulk of the Red Phalarope migration takes place miles out to sea. • Whalers in the Arctic Ocean once used Red Phalarope flocks to find nearby whales, because these pelagic birds feed on crustaceans stirred up by the pod. Red Phalaropes have also been observed tending surfaced whales, quickly snatching parasites living on their backs.

nonbreeding

ID: *Breeding female:* odd and striking; chestnut red neck and underparts; white face; black on crown and around base of bill; stout yellow bill tipped with black. *Breeding male:* similar to female, but has a mottled brown crown and generally duller colors. *Nonbreeding:* white head, neck and underparts; gray upperparts; black bill, nape and "phalarope mark" extending from eye to ear. *Immature:* duller, buffy version of breeding male.
Size: *L* 8–9 in; *W* 14–16 in.
Status: uncommon to common migrant and common winter resident far offshore from August to May; accidental migrant on the Coast and inland.
Habitat: birds inhabit open ocean waters well away from shore, preferring upwellings and current edges; associate with drifting mats of *Sargassum* spp.; occasionally seen at more inshore locations such as bays, lagoons, estuaries, tide-rips and salt evaporation ponds; rarely seen well inland.
Nesting: does not nest in Georgia.
Feeding: gleans from the water's surface, usually while swimming in tight, spinning circles; winter diet is poorly known; summer diet includes small crustaceans, mollusks, insects and other invertebrates; rarely takes vegetation or small fish.
Voice: calls include a shrill, high-pitched *wit* and a low *clink clink*, rarely heard in Georgia.
Similar Species: *Red-necked Phalarope* (p. 163): more petite; nonbreeding adult has a darker back and thinner bill; dark nape extends over crown; white "V" on upper back in flight. *Sanderling* (p. 147): lacks wide, dark eye patch extending to ear; sprints back and forth at edge of surf.
Best Sites: boating far offshore; offshore of Sapelo I. (HC: 1250); St. Simons I.; accidental inland at Atlanta, Macon, Dublin, Thomaston, Laurens Co., Eufaula NWR and E.L. Huie.

POMARINE JAEGER

Stercorarius pomarinus

Pomarine Jaegers are powerful, swift predators and notorious "pirates" of the vast, open oceans. Jaegers spend most of their lives in the air, occasionally resting on the ocean's surface, seeking the solid footing of land only during the nesting season. A small number of Pomarine Jaegers regularly patrol Georgia's pelagic waters in winter, gliding with unhurried wingbeats over the swells. • Most novice birders differentiate the three jaeger species based on the shape and length of their central tail feathers. This task would seem to be easy, but the comparison applies only to adult jaegers. Knowing the subtleties of plumage, wingbeat rhythm and wing breadth is most important in making an accurate identification. It may take many years of detailed field observation and the study of museum specimens to accurately identify these birds in the field, only to find that many fall migrants cannot be reliably identified at all!

immature light morph

immature intermediate morph

ID: long, twisted, central tail feathers; black "cap." *Dark morph:* dark body except for white in wing. *Light morph:* dark, mottled breast band, sides and flanks; dark vent. *Immature:* central tail feathers extend just past tail; white at base of upperwing primaries; variable, dark barring on underwings and underparts; lacks black "cap." *In flight:* wings are wide at base of body; white flash at base of underwing primaries; powerful, steady wingbeats.
Size: *L* 20–23 in; *W* 4 ft.
Status: uncommon spring and fall visitor to the Offshore, and rare in winter near the Coast from September to June; accidental in summer Offshore and onshore at Jekyll I.
Habitat: birds inhabit open ocean waters well away from shore.

Nesting: does not nest in Georgia.
Feeding: snatches fish from the water's surface while in flight; chases down small birds; pirates food from gulls; may scavenge at landfills.
Voice: generally silent; may give a sharp *which-yew,* a squealing *weak-weak* or a squeaky, whistled note during migration.
Similar Species: *Parasitic Jaeger* (p. 166): long, thin, pointed tail; lacks mottled sides and flanks; very little white on upperwing primaries; short, sharp tail streamers; immature and subadult have barred underparts. *Long-tailed Jaeger:* very long, thin, pointed tail; very little white on upperwing primaries; lacks white on base of underwing primaries, very dark vent and dark, mottled breast band, sides and flanks; juvenile has stubby, spoon-shaped tail streamers and solid, dark markings on throat and upper breast.
Best Sites: boating near to far Offshore; offshore of St. Simons I. (HC: 6).

PARASITIC JAEGER

Stercorarius parasiticus

Although "jaeger" means "hunter" in German, "parasitic" more aptly describes this bird's foraging tactics. "Kleptoparasitism" is the scientific term for this jaeger's pirating ways, and these birds can be truly relentless. Parasitic Jaegers will harass and intimidate terns and gulls until the victims regurgitate their partially digested meals. As soon as the food is ejected, these aerial pirates snatch it out of midair or pick it from the water's surface in a swooping dive. Less than 25 percent of these encounters are successful, and many Parasitic Jaegers are content to find their own food. • Jaegers, the most numerous predatory birds in the Arctic, fill the same niche over ocean waters and arctic tundra as hawks do over land. • On their arctic breeding grounds, adults defend their eggs and young aggressively. They will attack approaching danger in stooping, parabolic dives or aggressive, blazing pursuits. In such scenarios, the intruders are forced into a rapid retreat, often assessing how many feathers or how much hair has been lost! • The Parasitic Jaeger is the most abundant jaeger in the world and is the most commonly seen jaeger in Georgia.

*breeding
light morph*

*immature
light morph*

ID: long, dark, pointed wings; slightly longer, pointed central tail feathers; brown upper-parts; dark "cap"; light underwing tips. *Dark morph:* all-brown underparts and "collar." *Light morph:* white underparts; white to cream-colored "collar"; light brown neck band. *Immature:* barred underparts; central tail feather extends just past tail.
Size: *L* 15–20 in; *W* 3 ft.
Status: uncommon visitor to near Offshore and the immediate Coast from August to May; accidental in summer at St. Simons I., and inland at Lake Chatuge, along the Oconee R., Augusta and Lake Walter F. George.

Habitat: shorelines.
Nesting: does not nest in Georgia.
Feeding: pirates, scavenges and hunts for food; eats fish, eggs, large insects and small birds and mammals; often pirates food from other birds; may scavenge at landfills.
Voice: generally silent; may make shrill calls in migration.
Similar Species: *Pomarine Jaeger* (p. 165): shorter, blunt, twisted, central tail feathers; dark, mottled sides and flanks; white on upperwing primaries. *Long-tailed Jaeger:* much smaller; much longer, pointed central tail feathers; lacks dark neck band.
Best Sites: possibly among gull groups flying around shrimping boats offshore of Tybee I., Sapelo I. (HC: 10), St. Catherines I. and Jekyll I.

LAUGHING GULL

Larus atricilla

The black-hooded Laughing Gull's beautiful plumage and lilting laugh are readily accepted by humans today, but life has not always been so easy for this bird. In the late 19th century, high commercial demand for egg collections and for feathers used in women's headdresses resulted in the extirpation of the Laughing Gull from most of its Atlantic Coast breeding range. Today, East Coast populations are gradually assuming their former abundance, and Laughing Gulls are once again commonly seen throughout the year along much of Georgia's coastline. • Colonies often nest on small offshore islands, where they are somewhat protected from human disturbance but are still vulnerable to weather conditions. Occasionally, spring storms cause high tides to submerge entire islands or flood shoreline nests. • Whereas the laughing call explains this bird's common name, the Latin name *atricilla* refers to a black band present only on the tails of immature birds.

breeding

nonbreeding

ID: *Breeding:* black head; broken, white eye ring; red bill. *Nonbreeding:* white head with some pale gray bands; black bill. *3rd year:* white neck and underparts; dark gray back; black-tipped wings; black legs. *Immature:* variable plumage; brown to gray and white overall; broad, black subterminal tail band.
Size: *L* 15–17 in; *W* 3 ft.
Status: abundant breeding resident on the Coast, less common in midwinter; rare inland visitor, except accidental in the Mountains, from March to January; only recently breeding (1500 pairs) at Little Egg Island Bar.
Habitat: primarily coastal in bays and estuaries; salt marshes and sandy beaches; occasionally inland shores, streams or landfills.
Nesting: colonial nester; nests on dry islands, sandy, coastal beaches or salt marshes; cup-shaped nest of marsh vegetation is constructed on the ground; nest may be attached to vegetation and float on water during storm tides; pair

incubates 3 buff to dark brown eggs with dark splotches for 22–27 days.
Feeding: omnivorous; gleans insects, small mollusks, crustaceans, spiders and small fish while flying, wading, walking or swimming; may steal food from other birds; may eat the eggs and nestlings of other birds; often scavenges at landfills.
Voice: loud, high-pitched, laughing call: *ha-ha-ha-ha-ha-ha.*
Similar Species: *Franklin's Gull* (p. 168): smaller overall; red legs; shorter, slimmer bill; nonbreeding adult has black "mask." *Bonaparte's Gull* (p. 169) and *Black-headed Gull:* orange or reddish legs; slimmer bill (Bonaparte's has black bill); lighter mantle; white wedge on upper leading edge of wing; black "hood" on breeding adult does not extend over nape; white head with black head spot in nonbreeding plumage.
Best Sites: coast and barrier islands from Savannah NWR to Kings Bay Submarine Base; Jekyll I. (HC: 5000+); Tybee I. (HC: 5000); Columbus (HC: 31); Lake Oconee (HC: 17).

FRANKLIN'S GULL

Larus pipixcan

Franklin's Gulls drift into the east from their prairie stronghold on a rare but regular basis. While making semi-annual tours through our area, individuals or small flocks are usually seen intermingled with large groups of Bonaparte's Gulls and other gull relatives. Most Franklin's Gulls are seen along the coast in spring and fall, although keen birders occasionally detect a few strays inland as well. • Franklin's Gulls are not typical "seagulls"—they spend a large part of their lives inland, and they nest on the northern U.S. prairies. These gulls often forage by following tractors on agricultural fields, snatching up grasshoppers and insects from the tractor's path in much the same way other gulls follow fishing boats. • The Franklin's Gull is one of only two gull species that migrate long distances between breeding and wintering grounds—the majority of Franklin's Gulls winter along the Pacific coast of Peru and Chile. • This gull was named for Sir John Franklin, the British navigator and explorer who led four expeditions to the Arctic in the 19th century.

nonbreeding

nonbreeding

ID: dark gray mantle; broken, white eye ring; white underparts. *Breeding:* black head; orange-red bill and legs; breast might have pinkish tinge. *Nonbreeding:* white head; dark patch on side of head. *In flight:* black crescent on white wing tips.

Size: *L* 13–15 in; *W* 3 ft.

Status: rare migrant on the Coast and the Coastal Plain from March to May and from October to December; accidental north of the Fall Line at Lake Lanier, Lake Chatuge, Lake Hartwell and Atlanta.

Habitat: coastal areas, below river dams, marshlands and landfills.

Nesting: does not nest in Georgia.

Feeding: very opportunistic; often catches insects in midair; also eats small fish and some crustaceans.

Voice: usually silent in Georgia; soft *crick* or "mewing," shrill *weeeh-ah weeeh-ah* while feeding and in migration.

Similar Species: *Bonaparte's Gull* (p. 169): black bill; conspicuous white wedge on forewing. *Little Gull:* much smaller; paler mantle; lacks black crescent on wing tips; breeding adult lacks broken, white eye ring and white nape; nonbreeding adult lacks black "mask." *Black-headed Gull:* paler mantle; conspicuous, white wedge on forewing; breeding adult has much more white on back of head; nonbreeding adult lacks black face "mask." *Sabine's Gull:* large, black, white and gray triangles on upperwing; dark, yellow-tipped bill. *Laughing Gull* (p. 167): larger; black legs; longer, heavier bill; nonbreeding adult lacks black "mask."

Best Sites: many reports from the Coast; also found along dams of Chattahoochee R., such as Walter F. George Dam (HC: 11).

BONAPARTE'S GULL

Larus philadelphia

Many people feel great disdain for gulls, but they might feel differently when they meet the Bonaparte's Gull. This graceful, reserved gull is nothing like its contentious, aggressive relatives. Delicate in plumage and behavior, this small gull avoids landfills, preferring to dine on insects caught in midair or plucked from the water's surface. It sometimes tips up like a dabbling duck to catch small invertebrates in the shallows. Only when flocks of Bonaparte's spy a school of fish or an intruder do these birds raise their soft, scratchy voices in excitement. • In winter, these gulls are seen flying about for hours on end, wheeling and flashing their pale wings. Flocks are fairly common along the coast and are occasionally spotted at large, inland lakes such as West Point Dam. • This gull was named after Charles-Lucien Bonaparte, a nephew of Napoleon and a naturalist who made significant contributions to the study of ornithology in the 1800s.

nonbreeding

nonbreeding

ID: black bill; gray mantle; white under-parts. *Breeding:* black head; white eye ring; orange legs. *Nonbreeding:* white head; dark ear patch. *In flight:* white forewing wedge; black wing tips.
Size: *L* 11½–14 in; *W* 33 in.
Status: common but erratic visitor to the Coast and Offshore from August to May; uncommon migrant and winter resident inland from August to May.
Habitat: coastal areas; occasionally along the Coastal Plain or near large lakes and reservoirs, rivers and marshes.
Nesting: does not nest in Georgia.
Feeding: dabbles and tips up for aquatic invertebrates, small fish and tadpoles; gleans the ground for terrestrial invertebrates; also captures insects in the air.

Voice: scratchy, soft *ear ear* while feeding.
Similar Species: *Franklin's Gull* (p. 168): larger; lacks white upper forewing wedge; breeding adult has orange bill; nonbreeding adult has black "mask." *Little Gull:* smaller; daintier bill; adult has white wing tips; black "hood" of breeding adult lacks white eye ring and extends over nape; nonbreeding adult has white "cap." *Black-headed Gull:* larger; larger, red bill; dark underwing primaries; more red than orange on legs; breeding adult has brownish "hood." *Sabine's Gull:* large black, white and gray triangles on upperwings; dark, yellow-tipped bill.
Best Sites: Eufaula NWR; Rum Creek WMA; Lake Lanier; West Point L. (HC-winter: 250); Savannah NWR; Harris Neck NWR; Jekyll I. (HC: 250+ offshore).

RING-BILLED GULL

Larus delawarensis

The Ring-billed Gull's numbers have greatly increased in recent years, and its tolerance for humans has made it a part of our everyday lives—an association that often involves Ring-bills scavenging our litter or fouling the windshields of our automobiles! • In winter, Ring-bills are our most common gull. They can be found along the coast, at landfills, shopping centers or on nearly all of our inland lakes. Many Ring-billed Gulls remain on the coast of Georgia year-round, but they do not breed here. • Some people feel that Ring-billed Gulls have become pests—many parks, beaches, golf courses and even fast-food and mall parking lots are inundated with marauding gulls looking for food handouts. Few species, however, have fared as well as the Ring-billed Gull in the face of human development, which in itself is something to appreciate.

nonbreeding

nonbreeding

ID: *Breeding:* white head; yellow bill and legs; black ring around bill tip; pale gray mantle; yellow eyes; white underparts. *Nonbreeding:* pale brown markings on head and nape. *Immature:* gray back; brown wings and breast. *In flight:* black wing tips with a few white spots.
Size: *L* 18–20 in; *W* 4 ft.
Status: abundant on the Coast year-round; less common as a nonbreeder on the Coast in summer and most abundant on the Coast from October to April; common to uncommon migrant and winter visitor inland, especially on large reservoirs during colder winters from July to June, with most arriving inland after September.
Habitat: coastal areas; lakes, rivers, landfills, golf courses, fields and parks.
Nesting: does not nest in Georgia.
Feeding: gleans the ground for human food waste, spiders, insects, rodents, earthworms, grubs and some waste grain; scavenges for carrion; surface-tips for aquatic invertebrates and fish.
Voice: high-pitched *kakakaka-akakaka;* also a low, laughing *yook-yook-yook.*
Similar Species: *Herring* (p. 171), *Glaucous* (p. 173) and *Iceland* (p. 362) *gulls:* larger; pinkish legs; red spot near tip of lower mandible; lack bill ring. *Lesser Black-backed Gull* (p. 172): larger; much darker mantle; much less white on wing tips; lacks bill ring.
Best Sites: coast and barrier island shores; Cumberland I. (HC-winter: 4000+); Lake Lanier (HC-winter: 12,000).

HERRING GULL

Larus argentatus

Although Herring Gulls are as adept as their smaller Ring-billed relatives at scrounging handouts on the beach, they are more likely to be found in wilderness areas than urban settings. Watch for Herring Gulls along coastal shorelines or near large lakes and rivers. • Herring Gulls are skilled hunters and enjoy a variety of food sources. In some areas, increasing Herring Gull populations have meant decreasing tern numbers owing to this gull's fondness for tern eggs and nestlings. Resourceful Herring Gulls have learned that dropping shellfish on rocks or pavement will break open the hard shell, exposing the tasty meat inside. • Like many gulls, Herring Gulls have a small red spot on the lower mandible that serves as a target for nestling young. When a downy chick pecks at the lower mandible, the parent recognizes the cue and regurgitates its meal.

nonbreeding

nonbreeding

ID: large gull; yellow bill; red spot on lower mandible; light eyes; light gray mantle; pink legs. *Breeding:* white head and underparts. *Nonbreeding:* white head and nape are washed with brown. *Immature:* mottled brown overall. *In flight:* white-spotted, black wing tips.
Size: *L* 23–26 in; *W* 4 ft.
Status: abundant resident on the Coast and near Offshore, less common non-breeder in summer; uncommon migrant inland, especially on large reservoirs, from September to June; rare nonbreeder inland in summer.
Habitat: along the coast; occasionally near large lakes, wetlands, rivers, landfills and urban areas.

Nesting: does not nest in Georgia.
Feeding: surface-tips for aquatic inverte-brates and fish; gleans the ground for insects and worms; scavenges dead fish and human food waste; eats other birds' eggs and young.
Voice: loud, buglelike *kleew-kleew;* also an alarmed *kak-kak-kak.*
Similar Species: *Ring-billed Gull* (p. 170): smaller; black bill ring; yellow legs. *Glaucous Gull* (p. 173) and *Iceland Gull* (p. 362): paler mantle; lack black on wings. *Lesser Black-backed Gull* (p. 172): much darker mantle.
Best Sites: coast and barrier island shores; Cumberland I. (HC-winter: 1500+); Lake Lanier (HC-winter: 73); Columbus (HC-winter: 70).

LESSER BLACK-BACKED GULL

Larus fuscus

Equipped with long wings for long-distance flights, small numbers of Lesser Black-backed Gulls leave their familiar European and Icelandic surroundings each fall to make their way to North America. Most of these gulls settle along the Atlantic Coast in winter. In recent years, Lesser Black-backed sightings have increased in North America, so it is possible that this Eurasian species will soon colonize North America. Birders are advised to keep a close eye on coastal shores and landfills—the most likely locations to find Lesser Black-backed Gulls. • The Lesser Black-backed Gull is most similar to the Herring Gull and the Great Black-backed Gull, but the Herring Gull lacks the Lesser's dark wings, the Great Black-backed is considerably larger, and neither sports the yellow legs of the Lesser. Some Lesser Black-backed Gulls have already been found paired with Herring Gulls, which indicates that we may see even more puzzling hybrids in the future.

nonbreeding

nonbreeding

ID: *Breeding:* dark gray mantle; mostly black wing tips; yellow bill has red spot on lower mandible; yellow eyes and legs; white head and underparts. *Nonbreeding:* brown-streaked head and neck. *Immature:* eyes may be dark or light; black bill, or pale bill with black tip; various plumages with varying amounts of gray on upperparts and brown flecking over entire body.
Size: *L* 21 in; *W* 4½ ft.

Status: uncommon nonbreeding late summer through spring visitor on the Coast and near Offshore from July through May (most records from August to November); accidental inland in Macon, Lake Lanier, Lake Walter F. George and West Point L.
Habitat: coastal beaches; landfills and open water on large lakes and rivers.
Nesting: does not nest in Georgia.
Feeding: eats mostly fish, aquatic invertebrates, small rodents, seeds, carrion and human food waste; scavenges at landfills.
Voice: screechy call.
Similar Species: *Herring Gull* (p. 171): lighter mantle; pink legs. *Glaucous Gull* (p. 173) and *Iceland Gull* (p. 362): pale gray mantle; white or gray wing tips; pink legs. *Ring-billed Gull* (p. 170): smaller; dark ring on yellow bill; paler mantle. *Great Black-backed Gull* (p. 174): much larger; black mantle; pale pinkish legs.
Best Sites: coast and barrier island shores; first records from Jekyll I.; Wassaw I. (HC: 44).

GLAUCOUS GULL
Larus hyperboreus

White underparts and a pale gray mantle camouflage the Glaucous Gull against the cloud-filled winter skies. The Glaucous Gull's pale plumage can help birders to distinguish its ghostly figure from other, more numerous, overwintering gull species. • Glaucous Gulls feed farther off-shore than other gulls. They have traditionally fished for their meals or stolen food from smaller gulls. More recently, many wintering birds have traded the rigors of hunting for the job of defending plots of garbage at various landfills. • Like many marine birds, Glaucous Gulls can drink salt water. Excess salt is removed from their bloodstream by tiny, specialized salt glands located above their eyes. The salty fluid, nearly twice the concentration of the seawater, then dribbles out of the gull's nostrils. • In summer, while other gulls are strolling along local beaches or hanging out in fast-food restaurant parking lots, the Glaucous Gull is far away, on breeding grounds in the arctic wilderness. The scientific name *hyperboreus* means "of the Far North." • There are only about 16 records of this bird for the state, so this is one of the rarest gulls in Georgia.

nonbreeding

1st winter

ID: *Breeding:* relatively long, heavy, yellow bill has red spot on lower mandible; pure white wing tips; flattened crown profile; yellow eyes; pink legs; white underparts; very pale gray mantle. *Nonbreeding:* brown-streaked head, neck and breast. *Immature:* dark eyes; pale, black-tipped bill; various plumages have varying amounts of brown flecking on body.
Size: *L* 27 in; *W* 5 ft.
Status: rare winter and spring visitor on the Coast and near Offshore from December through May; accidental inland in Dekalb Co., Lake Lanier and West Point L.
Habitat: coastal areas; landfills; open water on large lakes and rivers.
Nesting: does not nest in Georgia.
Feeding: predator, pirate and scavenger; eats mostly fish, crustaceans, mollusks and some seeds; feeds on carrion and at landfills.
Voice: high, screechy *kak-kak-kak* calls.
Similar Species: *Herring Gull* (p. 171): slightly smaller; black wing tips; much darker mantle. *Great Black-backed Gull* (p. 174): darker in all plumages. *Iceland Gull* (p. 362): smaller; slightly darker mantle; gray on wing tips.
Best Sites: most reports are from along the Coast.

GREAT BLACK-BACKED GULL

Larus marinus

The Great Black-backed Gull's commanding size and bold, aggressive disposition enable it to dominate other gulls, ensuring that it has first dibs at food, whether it is fresh fish or a meal from a landfill. No other gull species, with the exception of the Glaucous Gull, is equipped to dispute ownership with this domineering gull. • In the 1800s, egg collectors and plume hunters nearly extirpated Great Black-backed Gulls from North America. Fortunately, once protective measures were put in place the species recovered. Populations have thrived in recent years, and today good numbers of Great Black-backs overwinter along the Georgia coast. In other areas, both the breeding and wintering ranges of Greater Black-backed Gulls are expanding, possibly because human refuse supplies a plentiful food source. • Like many other North American gulls, the Great Black-backed Gull is a "four-year gull," which means it goes through various plumage stages until its fourth winter, when it develops its refined adult plumage. Most immature gulls have dark streaking, spotting or mottling, which allows them to blend into their surroundings and avoid detection by predators.

nonbreeding

nonbreeding

ID: very large gull. *Breeding:* all white except for gray underwings and dark gray mantle; pale pinkish legs; light-colored eyes; large, yellow bill has red spot on lower mandible. *Nonbreeding:* gray-brown wash on head and nape. *Immature:* variable plumage; mottled gray-brown, white and black; black bill or pale, black-tipped bill. **Size:** *L* 30 in; *W* 5½ ft.

Status: uncommon visitor on the Coast, except rare nonbreeder in summer; accidental inland at West Point L.
Habitat: coastal areas, near docks, ports and estuaries; landfills.
Nesting: does not nest in Georgia.
Feeding: opportunistic feeder; finds food by flying, swimming or walking; eats fish, eggs, birds, small mammals, berries, carrion, mollusks, crustaceans, insects and other invertebrates, as well as human food waste; scavenges at landfills.
Voice: a harsh *kyow*.
Similar Species: *All other gulls* (pp. 167–75): smaller; most lack very dark mantle.
Best Sites: Tybee I.; St Simons I.; Jekyll I. (HC-winter: 60); Cumberland I.

BLACK-LEGGED KITTIWAKE

Rissa tridactyla

The Black-legged Kittiwake is more closely associated with the marine environment than any other North American gull. For this reason, few birders watching from the comfort of our shores will ever see this small, graceful gull. Even during the most violent storms, these birds remain on open water, floating among massive freshwater swells that are likely reminiscent of their saltwater homes. Because they spend most of their lives in saltwater environments, Black-legged Kittiwakes have evolved salt glands above their eyes that enable them to extract and secrete excess salt from the seawater that they drink. • Unlike the majority of gulls in Georgia, the Black-legged Kittiwake makes its living by fishing rather than by foraging in landfills or near fast-food restaurants.

1st winter

breeding

nonbreeding

ID: *Breeding:* black legs; gray mantle; white underparts and head; yellow bill. *Nonbreeding:* gray nape; dark gray smudge behind eye. *Immature:* black bill and "half collar"; dark ear patch. *In flight:* solid black, triangular wing tips; immature has black "M" on upper forewing from wing tip to wing tip and black terminal tail band.

Size: *L* 16–18 in; *W* 3 ft.

Status: far Offshore visitor; accidental on the Coast and inland.

Habitat: open water on large lakes and rivers; open ocean far Offshore.

Nesting: does not nest in Georgia.

Feeding: dips to the water's surface to snatch prey; gleans the water's surface or plunges under water while swimming; prefers small fish; also takes crustaceans, insects and mollusks.

Voice: usually silent in Georgia, calls are *kittewake* and *kekekek*.

Similar Species: *Franklin's* (p. 168), *Laughing* (p. 167), *Bonaparte's* (p. 169), *Black-headed* and *Little gulls:* all lack combination of black legs, yellow bill, gray nape and solid black, triangular wing tips. *Sabine's Gull:* immature has gray brown wash on sides and head and lacks dark "M" on wings and mantle.

Best Sites: most likely Offshore or more rarely along the Chattahoochee R. dams in fall; accidental at Savannah R., Tybee I., Jekyll I., near Columbus, Lake Walter F. George and West Point L.

GULL-BILLED TERN
Sterna nilotica

Rather than adhering to the tern family habit of plunging into water in pursuit of fish, the large Gull-billed Tern typically flies into the wind, scooping up airborne insects in its path. Its thickened, gull-like bill (for which it is named) also allows for the occasional meal of various nontraditional tern foods such as lizards, frogs and mice. • Young Gull-billed Terns leave their nest within days of hatching and find shelter under nearby vegetation or debris, where they receive regular feedings from their hard-working parents. Young terns can't fly for the first five weeks after hatching, and they may have a hard time eluding the many predators and other dangers lurking in their midst. Those that survive until fledging stay with their parents for three months or more to learn the new joys of flying and foraging. • *Sterna* is Latin for tern. These small, graceful terns were called "sea swallows" until the 18th century when the Swedish name "*tarna*" was adopted for this group of birds. • The Gull-billed Tern is an uncommon breeding resident on the coast, nesting only at Little Egg Island Bar (40+ pairs), with previous nesting records on Oysterbed, Ossabaw, Cumberland and Crab islands and Pelican Split.

breeding

ID: *Breeding:* black legs, "cap," nape and thickened bill; pale gray upperparts and white underparts. *Nonbreeding:* black ear patch and darkish nape patch. *Immature:* like nonbreeding adult but with dark mottling on head and mantle.

Size: *L* 14 in; *W* 34 in.

Status: threatened (state); local and uncommon breeding resident on the Coast; most depart at the end of September; accidental in winter at Jekyll I. and St. Catherines I.

Habitat: pelagic, saltwater marshes, coastal bays, farmlands and open country close to the Coast.

Nesting: colony nester; pair lines a shallow depression in soil, sand or gravel with vegetation or debris; pair incubates 3 light buff eggs, lightly marked with brown, for 22–23 days.

Feeding: insects caught on the wing, on the ground and on the water's surface form bulk of diet; may also eat crustaceans, mollusks, other invertebrates and small amphibians, reptiles and mammals.

Voice: call is a raspy *kay-weck* or *zah zah zah;* immatures give a high, faint *peep peep.*

Similar Species: *Sandwich Tern* (p. 179): slightly larger but more slender; usually has yellow tip on long, thin, black bill. *Common Tern* (p.180) and *Forster's Tern* (p. 181): slightly smaller, with more slender, black bills (only in winter); Forster's eye patch is similar in winter.

Best Sites: McIntosh Co. beach areas; Savannah NWR; Altamaha WMA; Jekyll I. (HC-away from breeding area: 20).

CASPIAN TERN

Sterna caspia

In size and habits, the mighty Caspian Tern bridges the gulf between the smaller terns and the larger, raucous gulls. It is the largest tern in North America, and its wingbeats are slower and more gull-like than those of most other terns—a trait that can lead birders to confuse it with a gull. But this tern's distinctive, heavy, red-orange bill and forked tail usually give away its identity. • Caspian Terns are often seen together with gulls on shoreline sandbars and mudflats during migration. • The sight of a Caspian Tern foraging for small, schooling fish is impressive. Flying high over open waters, this tern hovers, then suddenly folds its wings and plunges headfirst toward its target. • This species was first collected from the Caspian Sea, hence its name. Caspian Terns are found nesting the world over, in Eurasia, Africa and even Australia.

breeding

ID: *Breeding:* black "cap" and legs; heavy, red-orange bill has faint black tip; light gray mantle; shallowly forked tail; white underparts; long, frosty, pointed wings; dark gray on underside of outer primaries. *Nonbreeding:* black "cap" is streaked with white.
Size: *L* 19–23 in; *W* 4–4½ ft.
Status: uncommon nonbreeding resident on the Coast year-round, more common from September to mid-October; rare inland from April to July and from July to November.

Habitat: coastal areas; wetlands and shorelines of large lakes and rivers.
Nesting: does not nest in Georgia.
Feeding: hovers over water and plunges headfirst after small fish, tadpoles and aquatic invertebrates; also feeds by swimming and gleaning at the water's surface.
Voice: low, harsh *ca-arr;* loud *kraa-uh.*
Similar Species: *Common Tern* (p. 180) and *Forster's Tern* (p. 181): much smaller; daintier bills; lack dark underwing patch. *Royal Tern* (p. 178): more slender; orange bill; longer tail.
Best Sites: Tybee I.; Jekyll I.; Savannah NWR; Harris Neck NWR; St Simons I. (HC-fall: 200); Cumberland I. (HC-fall: 200+); Augusta (HC-spring: 7).

177

ROYAL TERN

Sterna maxima

The breeding behavior of the regal-looking Royal Tern is rather unique among North American birds. Elegant courtship displays include spiraling aerial flights, stylish strutting, respectful bowing and offerings of delicious fish. Female Royal Terns lay a single egg (or occasionally two) amidst a tightly-packed colony of up to 10,000 or more nests. Both adults take responsibility for incubating their treasure through hot, sun-drenched days, cool coastal nights and brutal summer storms. Most of the eggs in the colony hatch within a period of a few days, instantly turning the beach colony into a raucous muddle of commotion. Fortunately, these civilized birds have a special plan for ordering the prevailing chaos: parenting terns quickly shepherd their semiprecocial young into a massive herd of fluffy, hungry newborns known as a "creche." Constantly supervised by incoming squadrons of food-carrying adults, the creche remains well protected while allowing adult males and females to continuously hunt for food. Adults returning to the creche with food can recognize their own young by voice. • Royal Terns currently nest only on Little Egg Island Bar (8000+ pairs), but have previously nested on Pelican Split and St. Catherines Island Bar.

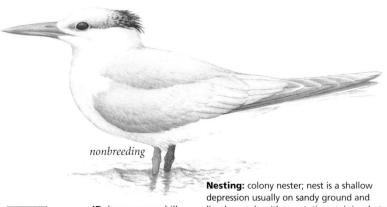

nonbreeding

ID: long, orange bill; thick, dark wedge on tips of upperwing; narrow dark edging on outer underwing primaries; deeply forked tail; legs usually black but can be orange; white underparts; pale gray upperparts. *Breeding:* black "cap" is frayed at back of head. *Nonbreeding:* frayed, black fringe at back of head. *Immature:* dusky version of nonbreeding adult with dusky tip on tail.
Size: *L* 20 in; *W* 3¼ ft.
Status: common permanent breeding resident on the Coast; also common far Offshore; accidental inland.
Habitat: coastal habitats including sandy beaches, estuaries, saltwater marshes, islands, bays and lagoons.

Nesting: colony nester; nest is a shallow depression usually on sandy ground and lined sparsely with vegetation; pair incubates 1–2 whitish, heavily spotted eggs for 20–25 days.
Feeding: typically forages by hovering over, then plunging into, water; may snatch items from the ground or from the water's surface; small fish and crabs form bulk of diet; may also eat shrimp, squid and other crustaceans.
Voice: bleating call is a high-pitched *kee-er;* also gives a whistling *turreee.*
Similar Species: *Caspian Tern* (p. 177): thick, reddish bill; lacks frayed crest and deeply forked tail; dark, faded "cap" in nonbreeding plumage. *Sandwich Tern* (p. 179) smaller; slender, black bill. *Common Tern* (p. 180) and *Forster's Tern* (p. 181): much smaller; daintier bills.
Best Sites: coastal and barrier island beaches from Savannah NWR to Cumberland I.; Jekyll I. (HC-away from breeding area in fall: 2000+).

SANDWICH TERN

Sterna sandvicensis

The increasingly scarce and strictly coastal Sandwich Tern frequently shares the company of the orange-billed Royal Tern. The close relationship between these two species often includes the formation of mixed nesting colonies on undisturbed sandy beaches, islands, lagoons and offshore sandbars. Unfortunately, these vital nesting habitats are often in high demand by humans and are slowly being claimed for housing development and recreation. In Georgia, Sandwich Terns nest only at Little Egg Island Bar, and only since 1994. This colony consists of over 600 breeding pairs. • Watching Sandwich Terns forage and frolic over the open water is an exciting spectacle. They will dive nearly straight down into deep water, and sometimes a bird will emerge with several fish lined up in its bill. Occasionally these terns dive immediately after Brown Pelicans to capture escaped fish. Terns of all ages entertain themselves by repeatedly dropping a piece of seaweed into the water from high above, then diving down to retrieve their makeshift toy. • The first ever specimen of this bird came from Sandwich in Kent, England. Dr. Samuel Cabot collected the first North American specimen on the coast of Yucatan. Hence, earlier names for this tern included Kentish Tern and Cabot's Tern.

breeding

ID: black bill with yellow tip; black legs; deeply forked tail; dark wedge on upperwing primaries; dark border on lower-wing primaries. *Breeding:* black "cap" with shaggy crest. *Nonbreeding:* white forehead. *Immature:* shorter crest; less deeply forked tail; mottled upperparts.

Size: *L* 14–16 in; *W* 34 in.

Status: uncommon breeding resident on the Coast and near Offshore from March to December; most depart by end of October; accidental inland after Hurricane Hugo at Augusta in 1989.

Habitat: pelagic; coastal waters, beaches, lagoons, estuaries and islands.

Nesting: tightly packed colonies nest on undisturbed beaches or islands; shallow scrape in sand may be lined with debris; pair incubates 1–2 eggs for 21–25 days; pair feeds young, which leave nest within days of hatching.

Feeding: hovers, then plunges headfirst into water; eats mostly fish; will eat shrimp, squid and marine worms; may take flying insects on the wing.

Voice: calls include a grating *kee-rick* and a quick *gwit gwit*.

Similar Species: black bill with yellow tip is unique. *Gull-billed Tern* (p. 176): thicker, all-black bill. *Common Tern* (p. 180) and *Forster's Tern* (p. 181): smaller; shorter bills of variable color but without yellow tip. *Royal Tern* (p. 178) and *Caspian Tern* (p. 177): decidedly larger.

Best Sites: Tybee I.; Wassaw I. (HC-fall: 350+); St. Simons I.; Jekyll I.; Cumberland I.

COMMON TERN

Sterna hirundo

The sleek appearance and graceful flight of the Common Tern is a familiar sight around much of North America. This tern patrols Georgia's offshore waters during spring and fall but migrates to large nesting colonies north of our state in summer. • During the late 19th century, ladies hats with feathers or sometimes whole stuffed terns were popular fashionable items. The hat trade nearly extirpated Common Terns from the Atlantic Coast. Populations quickly recovered after laws were enacted to protect nesting colonies, and the Common Tern became a symbol of the successful conservation. • Terns are effortless fliers, as well as some of the most impressive long-distance migrants. Once, a Common Tern banded in Great Britain was recovered in Australia.

nonbreeding

nonbreeding

Feeding: hovers over the water and plunges headfirst after small fish and aquatic invertebrates.

Voice: high-pitched, drawn-out *keee-are;* mostly silent in Georgia.

Similar Species: *Forster's Tern* (p. 181): gray tail with white outer edges; upper primaries have silvery look; broad, black eye band in nonbreeding plumage. *Arctic Tern* (p. 363): all-red bill; deeply forked tail; upper primaries lack dark gray wedge; grayer underparts; very rare in migration. *Sandwich Tern* (p. 179): larger; longer black bill with yellow tip. *Gull-billed Tern* (p. 176): slightly larger; thicker all-black bill.

Best Sites: boating offshore (HC-fall: 125); Tybee I.; Little Egg Island Bar (HC-fall: 700); St. Simons I.; Jekyll I.; Cumberland I.

ID: *Nonbreeding:* black nape; lacks black "cap." *In flight:* shallowly forked tail; long, pointed wings; dark gray wedge near lighter gray upper-wing tips.

Size: *L* 13–16 in; *W* 30 in.

Status: common migrant on the Coast and near Offshore; rare in winter; rare nonbreeder in midsummer; rare migrant inland from March to May and from July to November.

Habitat: pelagic; coastal areas; rare inland.

Nesting: does not nest in Georgia.

FORSTER'S TERN

Sterna forsteri

The Forster's Tern so closely resembles the Common Tern that the two often seem indistinguishable to the eyes of many observers. It is usually not until these terns acquire their distinct fall plumages that birders begin to note the Forster's presence. • Most terns are known for their extraordinary ability to catch fish in dramatic headfirst dives, but the Forster's excels at gracefully snatching flying insects in midair. • The Forster's Tern has an exclusively North American breeding distribution, but it bears the name of a man who never visited this continent: German naturalist Johann Reinhold Forster. Forster, who lived and worked in England, and who accompanied Captain Cook on his 1772 voyage around the world, examined tern specimens sent from Hudson Bay, Canada. He was the first to recognize this bird as a distinct species. Taxonomist Thomas Nuttall agreed, and in 1832, he named the species "Forster's Tern" in his *Manual of Ornithology*.

nonbreeding

breeding

ID: *Breeding:* black "cap" and nape; thin, orange, black-tipped bill; orange legs; light gray mantle; pure white underparts; white rump; gray tail with white outer edges. *Nonbreeding:* lacks black "cap"; black band through eyes; bill becomes all black. *In flight:* forked, gray tail; long, pointed wings.
Size: *L* 14–16 in; *W* 31 in.
Status: permanent resident on the Coast, common in winter, rare nonbreeder in summer; rare migrant inland from April to July; uncommon migrant inland from July to November; rare inland in winter, but more common along Chattahoochee R. lakes as far north as West Point L.
Habitat: coastal beaches; brackish wetlands; freshwater lakes, rivers and marshes.

Nesting: does not nest in Georgia.
Feeding: hovers above the water and plunges headfirst after small fish and aquatic invertebrates; catches flying insects and snatches prey from the water's surface.
Voice: flight call is a nasal, short *keer keer;* also a grating *tzaap.*
Similar Species: *Common Tern* (p. 180): darker red bill and legs; mostly white tail; gray wash on underparts; dark wedge near tip of primaries. *Arctic Tern* (p. 363): lacks black-tipped bill; short, red legs; gray underparts; white tail with gray outer edges. *Sandwich Tern* (p. 179): larger; longer black bill with yellow tip. *Gull-billed Tern* (p. 176): slightly larger; thicker all-black bill.
Best Sites: Savannah NWR; St. Catherines I.; Harris Neck NWR; Jekyll I.; Cumberland I. (HC-winter: 1700+); Eufaula NWR; West Point L. (HC-winter: 150).

LEAST TERN

Sterna antillarum

Though Least Terns can be fairly common along Georgia's coastline, much of their North American breeding habitat has been lost to development and disturbance. With only a few colonies persisting today, the plight of Least Terns dramatizes the impact that human activities can have upon birds of the estuarine beaches. As is true for many colonial waterbirds, breeding success also varies annually in response to food supply, weather, predation and disturbance. • Adult terns shelter their eggs from the elements in very practical ways. During heavy rains, Least Terns have been known to roll their eggs to drier areas. In hot weather, adults use their bodies to provide shade, or they wet their undersides, then drip the cool water onto the eggs or chicks. The best places to observe these breeding behaviors are at Oyster Bed Island (up to 1000 pairs), Andrews Island (more than 200 pairs) and Cumberland Island (100 pairs).

breeding

ID: *Breeding:* black "cap" and nape; white forehead; black-tipped, orange-yellow bill; orange-yellow legs; gray upperparts; white underparts; black wedge on upper side of the outer primaries. *1st summer:* black bill, legs and eye line extending into nape; grayish "cap" and white forehead. *In flight:* flies with dashing, rapid wing strokes.

Size: *L* 9 in; *W* 20 in.

Status: endangered (federal; state); uncommon breeding summer resident on the Coast and the Coastal Plain from March to September (most depart by late August); rare migrant inland, mostly along the Chattahoochee R. and Savannah R., from April to June and from July to October.

Habitat: coastal beaches; inland near large lakes.

Nesting: colonial; on undisturbed flat ground or flat rooftops (especially those with small pebbles) near water; nest is a shallow scraped-out depression often lined with pebbles, grass or debris; pair incubates 1–3 beige eggs with dark spots or splotches for 20–22 days and raises the young together; chicks leave the nest shortly after hatching.

Feeding: hovers above water and then plunges; eats mostly fish, crustaceans and insects; may eat mollusks and other invertebrates; will take insects on the wing or snatch prey from the ground or the water's surface.

Voice: call is a loud, high-pitched *chirreek!* and *kip kip kip.*

Similar Species: *Black* (p. 185), *Common* (p. 180) and *Forster's* (p. 181) *terns:* larger; breeding birds lack white forehead and yellow, black-tipped bill.

Best Sites: *Breeding:* Sea (50 pairs), Ossabaw (25 pairs), and Little Tybee (25 pairs) Islands; flat rooftops near Savannah, Ft. Stewart, Brunswick, Kings Bay and Vidalia. *Fall:* Jekyll I. (HC: 350); Columbus (HC: 20); Augusta (HC: 20+).

BRIDLED TERN

Sterna anaethetus

The only time you will see this dainty tern on land is when it has been blown off course by a hurricane. The Bridled Tern lives most of its life in flight, dipping and bobbing its light little body along the winds of the Gulf Stream. This bird even feeds in flight, picking at crustaceans and insects on the water's surface. It doesn't feed in congregations, but if a school of small fish is chased to the surface by predators, more than one Bridled Tern may show up. When it does land, a Bridled Tern prefers not to get its feet wet and rests on floating debris, usually along the weed line of the Gulf Stream. • *Anaethetus* is a misspelling of a Greek word meaning "senseless" or "dumb," because nesting birds will not raise any alarm when approached (though approaching occupied nests is, of course, not accepted among ethical birders). Only a few nests a year are recorded in the United States, in the Florida Keys among congregations of Roseate Terns.

breeding

ID: *Breeding:* dark gray upperparts; white underparts; white tail with gray stripe down center; black "cap," eye line, bill and feet.
Size: *L* 15 in; *W* 30 in.
Status: uncommon far Offshore from April to December; accidental on barrier islands and inland after storms.

Habitat: far Offshore; tends to stay away from completely open ocean.
Nesting: does not nest in Georgia.
Feeding: hovers over the water's surface and picks up squid, small fish, crustaceans.
Voice: high-pitched, ascending, quiet whistle; usually silent in Georgia.
Similar Species: *Sooty Tern* (p. 184): larger; black upperparts; flight is more direct.
Best Sites: boating far offshore (HC-fall: 50+).

SOOTY TERN

Sterna fuscata

High oceanic wind speeds help this bird stay aloft, and its long, narrow wings allow it to glide efficiently. Perhaps the most aerial seabird alive, the Sooty Tern can remain at sea for up to a decade, landing only occasionally on the back of a sea turtle or on floating debris. With poor waterproofed feathers, this tern would become waterlogged if it alighted for too long. • At six to ten years of age, shortly before they first breed, Sooty Terns return to their nesting grounds. Colonies are extremely large; some say that the Sooty Tern is the most plentiful pelagic bird in the world. • Spending years following schools of fish around the ocean would disorientate most, but not the Sooty Tern. Researchers in Florida tested the bird's homing ability by marking terns from the Dry Tortugas breeding colony with dye, then releasing them along the coasts of Texas and North Carolina. Within a week, all of the birds had returned to their breeding grounds.

breeding

ID: *Breeding:* sooty black crown and back; white underparts and throat; black eye line; thin bill; deeply forked black tail with narrow, white outer edges. *Nonbreeding:* mottled black on forehead and nape. *Immature:* dark brown; white blotches on back and wings; head, throat and breast are dark sooty brown.
Size: *L* 16 in; *W* 30 in.
Status: rare to uncommon far Offshore visitor in the Gulf Stream from May to September; accidental on the Coast and inland after severe tropical storms.

Habitat: open ocean; breeds on coastal or oceanic islands.
Nesting: does not nest in Georgia.
Feeding: snatches fish or small invertebrates from the water's surface; follows large schools of predatory fish that flush smaller fish to the surface; feeds mainly at night.
Voice: harsh screeches or nasal croaks resembling *wide-a-wake* or *ka weedy weedy*.
Similar Species: *Bridled Tern* (p. 183): smaller; slimmer; longer tail; white "collar"; pale upperparts. *Brown Noddy:* wedged tail, dark belly.
Best Sites: boating far offshore in the Gulf Stream (HC: 200+).

BLACK TERN

Chlidonias niger

Wheeling about in foraging flights, Black Terns pick small minnows from the water's surface or catch flying insects in midair. Black Terns have dominion over the winds, and these acrobats slice through the sky with grace, even in a stiff wind. • Black Terns are finicky nesters and refuse to return to nesting areas that show even slight changes in water level or in the density of emergent vegetation. This selectiveness, coupled with the degradation of marshes across North America, has contributed to a significant decline in populations of the Black Tern in recent decades. Commitment to restoring and protecting valuable wetland habitats will eventually help this bird to reclaim its once prominent place in the bird kingdom. • In order to spell this tern's genus name correctly, one must misspell *chelidonias*, the Greek word for "swallow." This bird is named for its swallowlike, darting flight as it pursues insects.

nonbreeding

nonbreeding

ID: *Breeding:* black head, bill and underparts; gray back, tail and wings; white undertail coverts; reddish black legs. *Nonbreeding:* white underparts and forehead; molting fall birds may be mottled with brown. *In flight:* long, pointed wings; shallowly forked tail.
Size: *L* 9–10 in; *W* 24 in.
Status: common migrant far Offshore and on the Coast from June to October; accidental far Offshore and on the Coast in spring; rare migrant from April to June and uncommon migrant from July to October inland, especially near large reservoirs and rivers.

Habitat: shallow, freshwater cattail marshes, wetlands, lake edges and sewage ponds with emergent vegetation, coastal beaches and mudflats.
Nesting: does not nest in Georgia.
Feeding: snatches insects from the air, tall grass and the water's surface; also eats small fish.
Voice: normally silent in Georgia; greeting call is a shrill, metallic *kik-kik-kik-kik-kik;* typical alarm call is *kreea.*
Similar Species: *Other terns* (pp. 176–84): all are light in color, not dark.
Best Sites: boating far offshore (HC-late spring: 60); offshore of Wassaw I. (HC-fall: 300+). *Fall:* Wolf I. NWR (HC: 250); Little Egg Island Bar (HC: 1500); Lake Lanier (HC: 20+); McRae (HC: 51); Columbus (HC: 50).

185

BLACK SKIMMER

Rynchops niger

The Black Skimmer is the only bird in North America with a lower mandible that is longer than its upper mandible. Uniquely designed for scooping fish, the skimmer forages by plowing its lower mandible just below the water's surface. When the lower mandible makes contact with a fish, the upper mandible slams down on the slippery body, clamping the meal securely. • The amazing Black Skimmer is a unique and wonderful bird to observe as it propels through the air on long, swept-back wings. The Black Skimmer's vertical pupils, similar to a cat's or rattlesnake's eyes, are designed to reduce the blinding glare of sun-drenched sandy beaches and reflective ocean water. • Young squawking skimmers contribute to the loud, chaotic atmosphere of typical breeding colonies. When impatient young wander too far from the nest, they will attempt to lie flat or even burrow underneath the hot sand to elude predatory gulls and crows. • Skimmers are currently nesting in Georgia only on Little Egg Island Bar (300 pairs) and Little Tybee Island (three pairs), with nesting also suspected on Little St. Simons Island. Nesting has also occurred previously on St. Catherines Island Bar, Cumberland Island, Pelican Split and Ossabaw Island.

nonbreeding

ID: *Breeding:* black upperparts and white underparts; long, thick, red bill with black tip (lower mandible longer than upper mandible). *Nonbreeding:* white "collar" and duller upperparts. *Immature:* dull, mottled brown upperparts.
Size: *L* 18 in; *W* 3½ ft.
Status: common permanent breeding resident on the Coast; accidental inland at Okefenokee NWR and other sites after severe tropical storms.

Habitat: coastal marine habitats including estuaries, lagoons, sheltered bays and inlets.
Nesting: colony nester; on beaches, sandy islands, and rarely on gravel roofs; nest is a shallow scrape in sand; pair incubates 4 pale eggs with intricate dark markings for 21–25 days; pair feeds young by regurgitation.
Feeding: small fish are caught by flying close to the water's surface and skimming the water with lower mandible; may eat some crustaceans.
Voice: call is a series of yapping notes.
Similar Species: none.
Best Sites: all coast and barrier island shores.

ROCK PIGEON

Columba livia

Introduced to North America in the early 17th century, Rock Pigeons have settled wherever cities, towns and farms are found. Most birds seem content to nest on buildings or farmhouses, but "wilder" members of this species can occasionally be seen nesting on tall cliffs, usually along lakeshores. • It is believed that Rock Pigeons were domesticated from Eurasian birds as a source of meat in about 4500 BC. Since their domestication, Rock Pigeons have been used as message couriers (both Caesar and Napoleon used them), scientific subjects and even as pets. Much of our understanding of bird migration, endocrinology and sensory perception derives from experiments involving Rock Pigeons. In fact, the ability of many birds to see ultraviolet light, which is important for mate selection, feeding and migration, was first demonstrated in these pigeons. • No other "wild" bird varies as much in coloration—a result of semidomestication and extensive inbreeding over time. Contrary to the fame of "Darwin's finches" on the Galapagos Island, most of Darwin's proof for natural selection was derived from his knowledge of the selective breeding biology of these domestic birds by European "pigeon fanciers."

ID: color is highly variable (iridescent blue-gray, red, white or tan); usually has white rump and orange feet; dark bill with white cere; dark-tipped tail. *In flight:* holds wings in deep "V" while gliding.

Size: *L* 12–13 in; *W* 28 in.

Status: common permanent breeding resident throughout Georgia in urban areas, as well as rural areas near buildings (barns and silos), under bridges and on larger dams.

Habitat: urban areas, railroad yards and agricultural areas; high cliffs provide a more natural habitat for some.

Nesting: on a ledge in a barn or on a cliff, bridge, building or tower; flimsy nest is built from sticks, grass and assorted vegetation;

pair incubates 2 white eggs for 16–19 days; pair feeds the young "pigeon milk"; may raise broods year-round.

Feeding: gleans the ground for waste grain, seeds and fruits; occasionally eats insects.

Voice: soft, cooing *coorrr-coorrr-coorrr.*

Similar Species: *Mourning Dove* (p. 190) and *White-winged Dove* (p. 189): smaller; slimmer; pale brown plumage; Mourning Dove has long tail and wings. *Common Ground-Dove* (p. 191): much smaller; pale brown plumage; pink or orange bill with black tip; dark spots on wings. *Eurasian Collared-Dove* (p. 188): black "collar" with white edges on hindneck. *Merlin* (p. 115): not as heavy bodied; longer tail; does not hold wings in a "V"; wings do not clap on takeoff.

Best Sites: statewide in urban and rural areas.

EURASIAN COLLARED-DOVE

Streptopelia decaocto

Originally from the Middle East, the Eurasian Collared-Dove expanded through Europe along with the human population in the 20th century. The species spread to the Western Hemisphere when 50 individuals were released in the Bahamas in 1974. After a few years, some birds had made their way to mainland Florida and soon after spilled over into neighboring states. The first record of this dove in Georgia was in 1988, and it has been reported in more than 100 Georgia counties, to date. • In warmer climates, the Eurasian Collared-Dove can breed up to six times a year. The young will disperse long distances, which helps the population spread. At ease around humans and with a love of suburban areas, this bird will likely soon expand its range to include much of North America. • All members of the pigeon family, including doves, feed "milk" to their young. Because birds lack mammary glands, it is not true milk but rather a nutritious liquid produced by glands in the bird's crop. A chick will insert its bill down the adult's throat to eat the thick, protein-rich fluid.

ID: pale gray overall; white outer tail; gray band across wing coverts; dark "collar" across back of neck is outlined in white.
Size: *L* 12–13 in; *W* 18–20 in.

Status: common permanent breeding resident along the Coast and the Coastal Plain, mostly near towns and rapidly increasing; rare, but increasing in the Piedmont as far north as Rome.
Habitat: coastal areas; suburbs and farmland; parks with both open ground and tree cover.

Nesting: in a tree, bush, or in house "holes"; nest is a thin platform of twigs and sticks; pair incubates 2 glossy, white eggs for 14–18 days.
Feeding: mostly seeds, grains, vegetation and berries; occasionally eats invertebrates; often forages on the ground below feeders and in agricultural areas.
Voice: a soft, repeated *coo-COO-coo*.
Similar Species: *Mourning Dove* (p. 190), *Common Ground-Dove* (p. 191) and *White-winged Dove* (p. 189): lack black "collar." *Rock Pigeon* (p. 187): stockier; white rump; black tail band.
Best Sites: cities and parks in the Coast and Coastal Plain regions; Glynn Co. (HC: 200+); Houston Co. (HC: 90+).

WHITE-WINGED DOVE

Zenaida asiatica

The pre-dawn light of early morning is sometimes punctuated by the soothing cooing calls of the White-winged Dove. The piercing glance of hot red eyes, surrounded by "spectacles" of azure blue skin, make this a captivating bird to observe at close range. • In the fall, White-winged Doves migrate eastward, rather than southward, from their breeding grounds in Texas, where more than 500,000 of these doves are found in the city of San Antonio alone. It is also possible that strays from the small resident populations in the southern half of Florida may wander northward, as well. • The White-winged Dove is one of few birds that has been able to recover from the destruction of much of its native brushland habitat. In recent decades it has adapted well to human-altered environments, including croplands, citrus groves, suburbs and townsites. • In the southwestern states, the White-winged Dove often feeds on the seeds and fruit of cactus, acting as one of many important pollinators for the *Saguaro* cactus and other spiny succulents of the region.

ID: large white patch across center of wing; blunt, rounded tail with white corners; bold blue patch around red eye; light brownish gray plumage.
Size: *L* 11–12 in; *W* 19 in.

Status: rare visitor to the Coastal Plain and along the Coast (more than 20 records) from November to June; accidental in summer and early fall on Sea I. and Jekyll I.; recent increase in numbers with most records from November to January and from March to May.
Habitat: variety of semi-open habitats including farmland, townsites and suburbs, brushlands, tree groves, riparian woodlands and chaparral.
Nesting: does not nest in Georgia.
Feeding: eats mostly seeds with some berries and fruits; forages on the ground and occasionally in trees, shrubs and on cactus flowers; young are fed "pigeon milk."
Voice: cooing call is a variable *who-cooks-for-you?*
Similar Species: *Mourning Dove* (p. 190) and *Common Ground-Dove* (p. 191): lack white patches in wings. *Rock Pigeon* (p. 187): stockier; white rump; black tail band. *Eurasian Collared-Dove* (p. 188): black "collar" with white edges on hindneck.
Best Sites: Sea I.; Jekyll I. (HC-spring: 4).

189

MOURNING DOVE

Zenaida macroura

The soft cooing of the Mourning Dove filters through our broken woodlands, farmlands and suburban parks and gardens, and is often confused with the muted sounds of a hooting owl. Birders are often surprised to track the source of these calls to one or two doves perched upon a fence, tree branch or utility wire. • The Mourning Dove is one of the most abundant and widespread native birds in North America and one of the most popular game birds. This species has benefited from human-induced changes to the landscape, and its numbers and distribution have increased since the continent was settled. It is encountered in both rural and urban habitats but avoids heavily forested areas. • When this bird bursts into flight, its wings clap above and below its body. The Mourning Dove's wings whistle as it cuts through the air at high speed, flying swiftly and directly over woodlands and open areas. • This bird's common name reflects its sad, cooing song. The scientific name *Zenaida* honors Zenaïde, Princess of Naples and the wife of Charles-Lucien Bonaparte, a naturalist and the nephew of the French emperor.

ID: buffy, gray-brown plumage; small head; long, white-trimmed, tapering tail; sleek body; dark, shiny patch below ear; dull red legs; dark bill; pale rosy underparts; black spots on upperwing.

Size: *L* 11–13 in; *W* 18 in.

Status: common to abundant permanent breeding resident statewide; more numerous in winter, especially from October to March.

Habitat: open and riparian woodlands, woodlots, forest edges, agricultural and suburban areas and open parks; has benefited from human-induced habitat change.

Nesting: in the fork of a shrub or tree, occasionally on the ground; female builds a fragile, shallow platform nest from twigs supplied by the male; pair incubates 2 white eggs for 14 days; young are fed "pigeon milk."

Feeding: gleans the ground and vegetation for seeds; visits feeders.

Voice: mournful, soft, slow *oh-woe-woe-woe*.

Similar Species: *Rock Pigeon* (p. 187): stockier; white rump; shorter tail; iridescent neck. *Eurasian Collared-Dove* (p. 188): black "collar" with white edges on hindneck. *Yellow-billed Cuckoo* (p. 193) and *Black-billed Cuckoo* (p. 192): curved bill; long tail with white spots and broad, rounded tip; brown upperparts; white underparts.

Best Sites: ubiquitous statewide year-round; abundant around agricultural areas in fall.

COMMON GROUND-DOVE

Columbina passerina

The Common Ground-Dove may be found trotting briskly through coastal agricultural areas, rhythmically bobbing its head to an unheard beat. This small dove is very tame but unlike many other doves, it is seldom found in urban environments. True to its name, the Common Ground-Dove favors the terrestrial, preferring to walk along roadsides or grainfields in search of food. • Common Ground-Doves will flock in winter, then pair up when the weather allows. To charm the lady of his choice, the male will prance around with his feathers puffed out, tail up and head bowed, while emitting an enticing *coo*. • These doves are marathon "cooers," perching for hours on end, all the while calling their inquisitive *cooOOO?* Their call is so soothing and soft that Common Ground-Doves often go unnoticed. • *Columbina passerina* is Latin for "sparrowlike dove," pertaining to its diminutive stature compared to other doves.

ID: "scaly" head and breast; brown upperparts; pink-brown underparts; black spots on side; pink legs; pink bill with black tip; iridescent blue and gray head. *In flight:* rufous primaries and wing linings.

Size: *L* 6–7 in; *W* 10½ in.

Status: uncommon to locally common permanent breeding resident south of the Fall Line; rare in the southern Piedmont to Athens and Atlanta.

Habitat: quiet areas such as fields, suburbs, woodland edges.

Nesting: may nest on or off the ground; shallow, ground nest is underneath bushes; off-ground nest is 1–20 ft from the ground and is a flat, simple platform of sticks; pair incubates 2–3 white eggs for about 2 weeks.

Feeding: walks along the ground; eats seeds, grains, insects and sometimes berries.

Voice: soft, repeated, 2-noted, ascending *coo-up, coo-up, coo-up, coo-up*

Similar Species: other doves or pigeons are larger. *Mourning Dove* (p. 190): long tail and wings. *Eurasian Collared-Dove* (p. 188): black "collar" with white edges on hindneck. *White-winged Dove* (p. 189): large, white patch across center of wing; white tail tip; bold blue patch around red eye.

Best Sites: around quiet agricultural areas in the Coastal Plain; Albany (HC: 71); Laurens Co.; Bulloch Co. sod farms; declining on the barrier islands, such as Andrews I., Onslow I. and Cumberland I.

BLACK-BILLED CUCKOO
Coccyzus erythropthalmus

Shrubby field edges, hedgerows, tangled riparian thickets and abandoned, over-grown fields provide preferred nesting haunts for the elusive Black-billed Cuckoo. Arriving in mid- to late April, this casual migrant quietly hops, flits and skulks through low, dense, deciduous vegetation in its ultra-secret search for sustenance. Only when vegetation is in full bloom on its breeding grounds will a male issue his loud, long, irregular calls, advertising to females that it is time to nest. After a brief courtship, a newly joined Black-billed Cuckoo pair will construct a makeshift nest, incubate the eggs and raise the young, then the pair promptly returns to their covert lives. • This cuckoo is one of few birds that thrive on hairy caterpillars, particularly tent caterpillars. There is even evidence to suggest that populations of Black-billed Cuckoo increase when a caterpillar infestation occurs. • The Black-billed Cuckoo is reluctant to fly more than a short distance during nesting, but it will migrate as far as northwestern South America to avoid the North American winter.

ID: brown upperparts; white underparts; long, white-spotted undertail; dark, downcurved bill; reddish eye ring. *Immature:* buff eye ring; may have buff tinge on throat and undertail coverts.

Size: *L* 11–13 in; *W* 18 in.

Status: rare migrant from April to June and from August to November; extremely rare and local summer breeding resident in the upper Piedmont and the Mountains, with historical breeding records from Fulton, Fannin and Rabun counties, but few recent records.

Habitat: dense second-growth woodlands, shrubby areas and thickets; often in tangled riparian areas and abandoned farmlands with low deciduous vegetation and adjacent open areas.

Nesting: in a shrub or small deciduous tree; flimsy nest of twigs is lined with grass and other vegetation; occasionally lays eggs in other birds' nests; pair incubates 2–5 blue-green, occasionally mottled, eggs for 10–14 days.

Feeding: gleans hairy caterpillars from leaves, branches and trunks; also eats other insects and berries.

Voice: fast, repeated *cu-cu-cu* or *cu-cu-cu-cu-cu;* also a series of *ca, cow* and *coo* notes; rarely heard in migration.

Similar Species: *Yellow-billed Cuckoo* (p. 193): yellow bill; rufous tinge to primaries; larger, more prominent, white undertail spots; lacks red eye ring. *Mourning Dove* (p. 190): short, straight bill; pointed, triangular tail; buffy, gray-brown plumage; black spots on upperwing.

Best Sites: small numbers often found at Kennesaw Mt. and Cochran Shoals during migration.

YELLOW-BILLED CUCKOO

Coccyzus americanus

Most of the time, the Yellow-billed Cuckoo skillfully negotiates its tangled home within impenetrable, deciduous undergrowth in silence, relying on obscurity for survival. Then, for a short period during nesting, the male cuckoo tempts fate by issuing a barrage of loud, rhythmic courtship calls. Some people have suggested that the cuckoo has a propensity for calling on dark, cloudy days in late spring and early summer. It is even called "Rain Crow" in some parts of its North American range. • In addition to consuming large quantities of hairy caterpillars, Yellow-billed Cuckoos feast on wild berries, young frogs and newts, small bird eggs and a variety of insects, including beetles, grasshoppers and cicadas. • Though some Yellow-billed Cuckoos may lay eggs in the unattended nests of neighboring Black-billed Cuckoos, neither of these cuckoos is considered to be a "brood parasite." • Some Yellow-billed Cuckoos migrate as far south as Argentina for winter.

ID: olive brown upperparts; white underparts; downcurved bill with black upper mandible and yellow lower mandible; yellow eye ring; long tail with large, white spots on underside; rufous tinge on primaries.
Size: *L* 11–13 in; *W* 18 in.
Status: common summer resident statewide from March to November; more common south of the Fall Line.
Habitat: semi-open deciduous habitats; dense tangles and thickets at the edges of orchards, urban parks, agricultural fields and roadways; sometimes dense second-growth woodlots; south of the Fall Line, often in tangled riparian and wetland areas.
Nesting: on a horizontal branch in a deciduous shrub or small tree, within 7 ft of the ground; builds a flimsy platform of twigs lined with roots and grass; pair

incubates 3–4 pale bluish green eggs for 9–11 days.
Feeding: gleans insect larvae, especially hairy caterpillars, from deciduous vegetation; also eats berries, small fruits, small amphibians and occasionally the eggs of small birds.
Voice: long series of deep, hollow *kuks*, slowing near the end: *kuk-kuk-kuk-kuk kuk kop kow kowlp kowlp.*
Similar Species: *Black-billed Cuckoo* (p. 192): all-black bill; lacks rufous tinge on primaries; less prominent, white undertail spots; red rather than yellow eye ring; juveniles have buff eye ring and may have buff wash on throat and undertail coverts. *Mourning Dove* (p. 190): short, straight bill; pointed, triangular tail; buffy gray brown plumage; black spots on upperwing.
Best Sites: thickly overgrown field and woodland edges statewide; Laurens Co.; Big Hammock WMA; Eufaula NWR; Kennesaw Mt. (HC-fall: 24); Glynn Co. (HC-spring: 39).

BARN OWL

Tyto alba

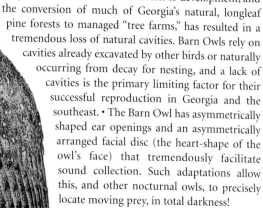

The haunting look of this night hunter has inspired superstitions among many people. Naked faces and black, piercing eyes give downy nestling Barn Owls an eerie look. In truth, however, the dedicated hunting efforts of these rare residents helps to keep farmlands and even city yards free from undesirable rodents. • Unfortunately, the loss of many bottom-land hardwood forests to development, and the conversion of much of Georgia's natural, longleaf pine forests to managed "tree farms," has resulted in a tremendous loss of natural cavities. Barn Owls rely on cavities already excavated by other birds or naturally occurring from decay for nesting, and a lack of cavities is the primary limiting factor for their successful reproduction in Georgia and the southeast. • The Barn Owl has asymmetrically shaped ear openings and an asymmetrically arranged facial disc (the heart-shape of the owl's face) that tremendously facilitate sound collection. Such adaptations allow this, and other nocturnal owls, to precisely locate moving prey, in total darkness!

ID: heart-shaped, white facial disc; dark eyes; pale bill; golden brown upperparts spotted with black and gray; creamy white, black-spotted underparts; long legs; white undertail and underwings.

Size: *L* 12½–18 in; *W* 3¾ ft.

Status: very local, rare to uncommon permanent breeding resident.

Habitat: roosts and nests in cliffs, hollow trees, barns, other unoccupied buildings, mine shafts, caves, bridges, tree groves and riverbanks; requires open areas, including agricultural fields, pastures, lawns, marshy meadows, open beach edges or open streamside areas for hunting.

Nesting: in a large, natural or artificial cavity, often in a sheltered, secluded hollow of an abandoned farm building or silo; may dig a hole in a dirt bank or use an artificial nest box; no actual nest is built; female incubates 3–8 whitish eggs over 29–34 days; male feeds incubating female.

Feeding: eats mostly small mammals, especially rodents; also takes small numbers of snakes, lizards, birds and large insects; rarely takes frogs and fish.

Voice: calls include harsh, raspy screeches and hisses; also makes metallic clicking sounds; often heard flying high over cities and residential areas late at night.

Similar Species: *Short-eared Owl* (p. 198): yellow eyes set in black sockets; vertical streaks on breast and belly; black "wrist" patches; erratic flight pattern. *Barred Owl* (p. 197): barred chest; streaking on belly; darker facial disc.

Best Sites: near prime feeding areas such as agricultural fields; Rome (HC-winter: 7); Eufaula NWR in winter.

EASTERN SCREECH-OWL

Megascops asio

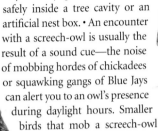

The diminutive Eastern Screech-Owl is a year-round resident of deciduous woodlands, but its presence is rarely detected. Most screech-owls sleep away the daylight hours snuggled safely inside a tree cavity or an artificial nest box. • An encounter with a screech-owl is usually the result of a sound cue—the noise of mobbing hordes of chickadees or squawking gangs of Blue Jays can alert you to an owl's presence during daylight hours. Smaller birds that mob a screech-owl

gray morph

during the day often do so after losing a family member during the night. More commonly, you will find this owl by listening for the male's eerie, "horse-whinny" courtship calls and loud, spooky trills at night. • Despite its small size, the Eastern Screech-Owl is an adaptable hunter. It has a varied diet that ranges from insects, small rodents, earthworms and fish to birds larger than itself. • Unique among the owls found in our region, Eastern Screech-Owls are polychromatic: they show red or gray color morphs. The red (rufous) birds are more common in Georgia and the southern United States. Mixed-color pairs may produce young that are an intermediate, buffy brown.

red morph

ID: short "ear" tufts; reddish or grayish overall; dark breast streaking; yellow eyes; pale grayish bill.
Size: L 8–9 in; W 20–22 in.
Status: locally common permanent breeding resident statewide.
Habitat: mature deciduous forests, open deciduous and riparian woodlands, orchards and shade trees with natural cavities.
Nesting: in a natural cavity or artificial nest box; no lining is added; female incubates 4–5 white eggs for about 26 days; male brings food to the female during incubation.

Feeding: feeds at dusk and at night; takes small mammals, earthworms, fish, birds and insects, including moths in flight.
Voice: horselike "whinny" that rises and falls; long whistled trill on same pitch.
Similar Species: *Great Horned Owl* (p. 196): much larger; lacks vertical breast streaks. *Short-eared Owl* (p. 198) and *Barred Owl* (p. 197): no "ear" tufts. *Long-eared Owl* (p. 363): much longer, slimmer body; longer, closer-set "ear" tufts; rusty facial disc; grayish, brown and white body.
Best Sites: Wood Duck, kestrel and backyard boxes, and natural tree cavities throughout the state; located easily by imitating their whistled call.

GREAT HORNED OWL

Bubo virginianus

The familiar *hoo-hoo-hoooo hoo-hoo* that resounds through campgrounds, suburban parks and farmyards is the call of the adaptable and superbly camouflaged Great Horned Owl. This formidable, primarily nocturnal hunter uses its acute hearing and powerful vision to hunt a wide variety of prey. It has a poorly developed sense of smell, which might explain why it is the only consistent predator of skunks. • Great Horned Owls often begin their courtship as early as January, at which time their hooting calls make them quite conspicuous. By January and February, females are already incubating eggs, and by the time other birds are beginning to fledge, Great Horned owlets are learning to hunt. • The large eyes of an owl are fixed in place, so for an owl to look up, down or to the side, the bird must move its entire head. As an adaptation to this situation, an owl can swivel its neck more than 180 degrees to either side, and 90 degrees up and down! • The leading edges of the flight feathers of nocturnal owls are "fringed" to reduce air turbulence noises, making these birds incredibly stealthy predators.

ID: yellow eyes; tall "ear" tufts set wide apart on head; fine, horizontal barring on breast; facial disc is outlined in black and is often rusty orange in color; white "chin"; heavily mottled gray, brown and black upperparts; overall plumage varies from light gray to dark brown.
Size: *L* 18–25 in; *W* 3–5 ft.
Status: uncommon to locally common permanent breeding resident statewide.
Habitat: fragmented forests, agricultural areas, woodlots, meadows, riparian woodlands, wooded suburban parks and the wooded edges of landfills and town dumps.
Nesting: in the abandoned stick nest of another bird; may also nest on a cliff; adds little or no material to the nest; mostly the female incubates 2–3 dull whitish eggs for 28–35 days.

Feeding: mostly nocturnal, but also hunts at dusk or by day in winter; usually swoops from a perch; eats small mammals, birds, snakes, amphibians and even fish.
Voice: call during the breeding season is 4–6 deep hoots: *hoo-hoo-hoooo hoo-hoo* or *Who's awake? Me too;* male also gives higher-pitched hoots.
Similar Species: *Eastern Screech-Owl* (p. 195): much smaller; vertical breast streaks. *Short-eared Owl* (p. 197): no "ear" tufts. *Barred Owl* (p. 198) and *Long-eared Owl* (p. 363): smaller; thinner; vertical breast streaks; "ear" tufts are close together.
Best Sites: in urban areas, especially parks and cemeteries, and in rural areas statewide; Savannah NWR; Jekyll I. causeway; on Osprey platforms at Altamaha WMA; Thomasville (HC-winter: 31).

BARRED OWL

Strix varia

Each spring, the memorable sound of courting Barred Owls echoes through our forests: *Who cooks for you? Who cooks for you-all?* The escalating laughs, hoots and gargling howls reinforce the bond between pairs. At the height of courtship and when raising young, a pair of Barred Owls may continue their calls well into daylight hours, and they may hunt actively day and night. They also tend to be more vocal during early evening or early morning when the moon is full and the air is calm. • Barred Owls are usually most active between midnight and 4 AM, when the forest floor rustles with the movements of mice, cotton rats and shrews. These owls have relatively weak talons, so they prey on smaller animals, such as deer mice and cotton mice. They may also take flying squirrels, small birds and even smaller owls. • Barred Owls were once inhabitants of the moist, deciduous woodlands and swamps that covered our region, but their numbers have declined with the destruction of these habitats. In the absence of suitable tree hollows— their preferred nesting sites—Barred Owls may resort to abandoned stick nests or may even nest on the ground.

ID: dark eyes; horizontal barring around neck and upper breast; vertical streaking on belly; pale bill; no "ear" tufts; mottled, dark gray-brown plumage.

Size: *L* 17–24 in; *W* 3½–4 ft.

Status: uncommon permanent breeding resident statewide; common in swamps and wetlands of creeks and rivers of the Coastal Plain.

Habitat: mature deciduous and mixed-wood forests, especially in dense stands near swamps, streams and lakes.

Nesting: in a natural tree cavity, broken treetop or abandoned stick nest; adds very little material to the nest; female incubates 2–3 white eggs for 28–33 days; male feeds the female during incubation.

Feeding: nocturnal; swoops down on prey from a perch; eats mostly mice, cotton rats and squirrels; also takes muskrats, amphibians and small birds.

Voice: most characteristic of all the owls; loud, hooting, rhythmic, laughing call is heard mostly in spring but also throughout the year: *Who cooks for you? Who cooks for you-all?;* frequently called "Old Eight-Hooter."

Similar Species: *Great Horned Owl* (p. 196) and *Eastern Screech-Owl* (p. 195): "ear" tufts; light-colored eyes. *Short-eared Owl* (p. 198): yellow eyes; lacks horizontal barring on upper breast.

Best Sites: wetlands along creeks and rivers with large trees for nesting; Okefenokee NWR; Big Hammock WMA; Rum Creek WMA; Chattahoochee NRA; Lake Lanier; Thomasville (HC-winter: 15).

SHORT-EARED OWL

Asio flammeus

Like the Snowy Owl of the Arctic, the Short-eared Owl lacks conspicuous "ear" tufts and fills a niche in open country that has been left unoccupied by forest-dwelling owls. The Short-eared Owl occupies habitats such as wet meadows, marshes, fields and bogs. This owl can be difficult to locate, because it remains well hidden during the day, roosting in grassy meadows, sand dunes and ditches. It is usually solitary, but may form colonial winter roosts on the ground. • Short-eared Owl populations grow and decline over many years in response to dramatic fluctuations in prey availability. Cold weather and decreases in small mammal populations occasionally force large numbers of these owls, especially immature birds, to become temporary nomads, often sending them to areas well outside their usual breeding range. • At dusk and dawn, check for the Short-eared Owl in open areas, especially fields where Northern Harriers are commonly seen during the day. It flies so characteristically that you can learn to identify it from far away. Like a big butterfly, the Short-eared Owl beats its long wings slowly and deeply as it courses erratically, low over meadows and fields. • All owls, as well as many other birds, such as herons, gulls, crows and hawks, cough up "pellets"—the indigestible parts of their prey, such as bones, feathers and fur.

ID: yellow eyes set in black sockets; heavy, vertical streaking on buff belly; straw-colored upperparts; short, inconspicuous "ear" tufts. *In flight:* dark "wrist" crescents; deep wingbeats; long wings.

Size: *L* 13–17 in; *W* 3–4 ft.

Status: rare to uncommon winter resident; more common on the Coast and the Coastal Plain from October to March.

Habitat: open areas, including grasslands, wet meadows, marshes, fields and airports and forest clearings.

Nesting: does not nest in Georgia.

Feeding: forages while flying low over marshes, wet meadows and tall vegetation; pounces on prey from the air; eats mostly voles and other small rodents; also takes insects, small birds and amphibians.

Voice: generally quiet; squeals and barks like a small dog.

Similar Species: *Great Horned Owl* (p. 196) and *Long-eared Owl* (p. 363): long "ear" tufts; rarely hunt during the day. *Barred Owl* (p. 197): dark eyes; horizontal barring on upper breast; nocturnal hunter.

Best Sites: Cobb Owl Fields; also casual on sand near beaches; Crisp Co. (HC: 12).

COMMON NIGHTHAWK

Chordeiles minor

Each May and June, the male Common Nighthawk flies high above forest clearings and lakeshores, gaining elevation in preparation for the climax of his noisy aerial dance. From a great height, he dives swiftly, thrusting his wings forward in a final braking action as he strains to pull out of the steep dive. This quick thrust of the wings produces a deep, hollow *vroom* that attracts female nighthawks. • Like other members of the nightjar family, the Common Nighthawk is adapted for catching insects in midair: its gaping mouth is surrounded by feather shafts that funnel insects into its mouth. • Nighthawks are generally less nocturnal than other nightjars, but they still spend most of the daylight hours resting on a tree limb or on the ground. These birds have very short legs and small feet, and they sit along the length of a tree branch or wire rather than across it, as do most perched birds.

ID: cryptic, mottled plumage; barred underparts. *Male:* white throat. *Female:* buff throat. *In flight:* bold, white "wrist" patches on long, pointed wings; shallowly forked, barred tail; erratic flight.
Size: *L* 8½–10 in; *W* 24 in.
Status: uncommon to common summer resident statewide, except the high Mountains, from March to November; common fall migrant in the northern half of the state from August to October.
Habitat: *Breeding:* in forest openings as well as burns, bogs, rocky outcroppings, gravel rooftops and sometimes fields with sparse cover or bare patches. *In migration:* anywhere large numbers of flying insects can be found; usually roosts in trees, often near water.

Nesting: on bare ground or on flat-topped roofs; no nest is built; female incubates 2 well-camouflaged eggs for about 19 days; pair feeds the young.
Feeding: primarily at dawn and dusk, but also at other times; catches insects in flight, often high in the air; may fly around street lights at night to catch prey attracted to the light; eats mosquitoes, blackflies, midges, beetles, flying ants, moths and other flying insects.
Voice: frequently repeated, nasal *peent peent*; also makes a deep, hollow *vroom* with its wings during courtship flight.
Similar Species: *Whip-poor-will* (p. 201) and *Chuck-will's-widow* (p. 200): less common; found in forests; lack white "wrist" patches; shorter, rounder wings; rounded tails.
Best Sites: readily seen around or above parking lots, ball parks, stadiums or other areas with bright lights at night.

CHUCK-WILL'S-WIDOW

Caprimulgus carolinensis

During the day, you would be lucky to see this perfectly camouflaged bird roosting on the furrowed bark of a horizontal tree limb or sitting among scattered leaves on the forest floor. Even during nesting it is virtually undetectable: this bird incubates its eggs and raises its young on the forest floor. At dusk, however, the Chuck-will's-widow is easily detected as it calls its own name while patrolling the evening skies for flying insects. • If bugs are not your favorite critters, you may learn to value the nightjar family, because

these birds can eat thousands of insects a day. Tiny, stiff feathers with only a few barbs, called "semibristles," encircle this bird's bill to help funnel prey into its mouth. This nightjar's yawning gape allows it to capture flying insects of all sizes. Occasionally, the Chuck-will's-widow will even take a small bird, such as a hummingbird!

ID: mottled brown and buff body with an overall reddish tinge; pale brown to buff throat; whitish "necklace" and dark breast; long, rounded tail. *Male:* inner edges of the outer tail feathers are white.

Size: *L* 12 in; *W* 26 in.

Status: common summer breeding resident statewide at elevations of up to 1700 ft from March to September; less common in the Mountains; accidental in winter in Charlton Co. and Valdosta.

Habitat: riparian woodlands, swamp edges and deciduous and pine woodlands.

Nesting: on bare ground; no nest is built; female incubates 2 heavily blotched, creamy white eggs for about 21 days and raises the young alone.

Feeding: catches insects on the wing or by hawking; eats beetles, moths and other large, flying insects.

Voice: 3 loud whistling notes often paraphrased as *chuck-will's-widow*.

Similar Species: *Whip-poor-will* (p. 201): smaller; "necklace" contrasts with black throat; grayer coloration overall; male shows much more white in tail feathers; female's dark tail feathers are bordered with buff on outer tips. *Common Nighthawk* (p. 199): forked tail; white patches on wings; male has white throat; female has buff throat.

Best Sites: along roads at Paulks Pasture WMA and Pine Log WMA, in the early evening when they begin to call.

WHIP-POOR-WILL

Caprimulgus vociferus

This nocturnal hunter fills the late evening with calls of its own name: *whip-poor-will*. Although the Whip-poor-will is heard throughout many of the open woodlands, this cryptic bird is rarely seen. Because of its camouflaged plumage, sleepy daytime habits and secretive nesting behavior, a hopeful observer must literally stumble upon a Whip-poor-will to see it. Only occasionally is this bird seen roosting on an exposed tree branch or alongside a quiet road. • The Whip-poor-will is one of three members of the nightjar, or "goatsucker," family found in the state. Birds in this family were named "Goatsuckers" during the days of Aristotle, because there was a widely believed superstition that they would suck milk from the udders of female goats, causing the goats to go blind! • Within days of hatching, young Whip-poor-wills scurry away from their nest in search of protective cover. For the first 20 days after hatching, the parents feed them regurgitated insects.

ID: mottled, brown-gray overall with black flecking; reddish tinge on rounded wings; black throat; long, rounded tail. *Male:* white "necklace" and outer tail feathers. *Female:* buff "necklace."
Size: *L* 9–10 in; *W* 16–20 in.
Status: common summer breeding resident in the northern part of state, but also farther south; accidental to rare winter resident in the Coastal Plain; rare to uncommon winter resident along the Coast and barrier islands.
Habitat: open deciduous and pine woodlands; often along forest edges.
Nesting: often along the edge of a clearing under herbaceous plant growth; on the ground in leaf or pine needle litter; no

nest is built; female incubates 2 whitish eggs, blotched with brown and gray, for 19–20 days; pair raises the young.
Feeding: catches large, night-flying insects in flight; eats mostly moths, beetles and mosquitoes; some grasshoppers are taken and swallowed whole.
Voice: loud, whistled *whip-poor-will*, with emphasis on the *will*.
Similar Species: *Chuck-will's-widow* (p. 200): larger; pale brown to buff throat; whitish "necklace"; darker breast; more reddish overall; much less white on male's tail; different call. *Common Nighthawk* (p. 199): shallowly forked, barred tail; white patches on wings; male has white throat; female has buff throat; much more conspicuous behavior.
Best Sites: Pine Log WMA; Beaverdam WMA; Haralson Co.; Burrell's Ford; Cumberland I. (HC-winter: 12).

CHIMNEY SWIFT

Chaetura pelagica

Chimney Swifts are the "frequent fliers" of the bird world—they feed, drink, bathe, collect nest material and even mate while in flight! They spend much of their time scooping up flying insects high above urban neighborhoods, and only the business of nesting or resting keeps these birds off their wings. Chimney Swifts are most conspicuous as they forage on warm summer evenings and during fall migration, when huge flocks migrate south alongside large numbers of Common Nighthawks. • Declining Chimney Swift populations may be the result of a decrease in available tree cavities for nesting. Chimney Swifts got their name from their second choice for nest sites—brick chimneys. • The legs of Chimney Swifts are so weak and small that if one of these birds lands on the ground it may not be able to gain flight again. Swifts do have strong claws, though, which allow them to cling to vertical surfaces. • A Chimney Swift that was banded in Macon in 1939 was later recovered in Peru in 1943, a fact that helped confirm the wintering range of this species in South America.

ID: brown overall; slim body and long, thin, pointed, crescent-shaped wings; squared tail. *In flight:* rapid wing-beats; boomerang-shaped profile; erratic flight pattern.

Size: L 4½–5½ in; W 12–13 in.

Status: common summer breeding resident statewide from March to November.

Habitat: forages over cities and towns; roosts and nests in chimneys; may nest in tree cavities in more remote areas.

Nesting: often colonial; nests deep in the interior of a chimney or tree cavity, or in the attic of an abandoned building; pair uses saliva to attach a half-saucer nest of short, dead twigs to a vertical wall; pair incubates 4–5 white eggs for 19–21 days; pair feeds the young.

Feeding: flying insects are swallowed whole during continuous flight.

Voice: rapid, chattering call is given in flight: *chitter-chitter-chitter;* also gives a rapid series of *chip* notes.

Similar Species: *Swallows* (pp. 241–46): broader, shorter wings; smoother flight pattern; most have forked or notched tail.

Best Sites: urban areas statewide; large fall migration flocks of 500 over Kennesaw Mt.; Duluth (HC-fall: 5000); Macon (HC-fall: 4000).

RUBY-THROATED HUMMINGBIRD

Archilochus colubris

Ruby-throated Hummingbirds are the only breeding hummingbirds in Georgia. They span the ecological gap between birds and bees, feeding on the sweet, energy-rich nectar that flowers provide and pollinating the flowers in the process. • Weighing about as much as a nickel, a hummingbird is capable of briefly achieving speeds of up to 60 miles per hour. It is also among the few birds that can fly vertically and in reverse. In straight-ahead flight, hummingbirds beat their wings up to 80 times per second, and their hearts can beat up to 1200 times per minute! • Each year, Ruby-throated Hummingbirds migrate across the Gulf of Mexico—an incredible, nonstop journey of more than 500 miles. In order to accomplish this, these little birds double their body mass by fattening up on insects and nectar before departing. • Another incredible hummer trick is to conserve up to 75 percent of their daily energy needs by going into a state of torpor each night—they reset their body temperature thermostat down from 104°F to about 68°F! Then in the morning it takes about an hour for them to raise their temperature back up to normal.

ID: tiny; long bill; iridescent, green back; light underparts; dark tail. *Male:* ruby red throat; black "chin." *Female and immature:* fine, dark throat streaking. **Size:** *L* 3½–4 in; *W* 4½ in.

Status: common summer breeding resident statewide from April to November (mostly from early April to early October); uncommon to rare in winter along the Coast, and rare inland in winter south of the Mountains.

Habitat: open, mixed woodlands, wetlands, orchards, tree-lined meadows, flower gardens and backyards with trees and feeders.

Nesting: on a horizontal tree limb; tiny, deep cup nest of plant down and fibers is held together with spider silk; lichens and leaves are pasted on the exterior wall of the nest; female incubates 2 white eggs for 13–16 days; female feeds the young.

Feeding: uses its long bill and tongue to probe blooming flowers and sugar water from feeders; also eats small insects and spiders.

Voice: most noticeable is the soft buzzing of the wings while in flight; also produces a loud *chick* and other high squeaks.

Similar Species: *Rufous Hummingbird* (p. 205): male has bright, reddish orange on flanks and back; female has red-spotted throat and reddish flanks. *Black-chinned Hummingbird* (p. 204): longer bill; usually duller green back; dark purple throat patch.

Best Sites: gardens, nature centers and parks with sugarwater feeders or with good patches of nectar-producing flowers such as honeysuckle or creeper vines.

BLACK-CHINNED HUMMINGBIRD

Archilochus alexandri

The Black-chinned Hummingbird is the western counterpart of the Ruby-throated Hummingbird of the East—the females of these two species are virtually indistinguishable in the field. Black-chinned Hummingbirds consistently stray into Georgia in winter and have been recorded from Cartersville south to Valdosta. The remarkably adaptable hummingbirds may be found in many different habitats, from deserts to lush gardens, and anywhere between sea level and elevations of 6000 feet. • Naturalist and hummingbird taxonomist H.G.L. Reichenbach was deeply influenced by Greek mythology. He named several hummingbird genera after Greeks—*Archilochus* was a notable Greek poet. The species name *alexandri* honors a doctor who collected specimens in Mexico. • It is a myth that hummers will not migrate if you don't take down your feeders in the fall. In fact, if you keep feeders refilled through winter, it often allows western hummers, such as Black-chins, an opportunity to survive should they venture into Georgia, which they often do. Also, there is no reason to add red food coloring to the sugar water in the feeder at any time of year—in fact, it is harmful to hummingbirds to do so.

ID: iridescent, green upperparts; long, thin bill; small, white crescent behind eye. *Male:* black throat with iridescent, violet band; white underparts with green "vest." *Female* and *immature:* black eye line; white throat is usually immaculate but may have faint gray or greenish streaks; immature males may show violet spots on throat; white underparts often with pale grayish sides and a tinge of buff on flanks.
Size: *L* 3–3½ in; *W* 4¾ in.
Status: rare winter visitor to the entire state from October to April; more than 15 records since the first record in 1990–1991.
Habitat: little information available on winter range; deciduous and mixed forests; riparian areas.

Nesting: does not nest in Georgia.
Feeding: hovers in the air and probes flowers for nectar; eats small insects and takes sugar water from feeders.
Voice: buzz and chip alarm calls; males' wings buzz in flight.
Similar Species: *Rufous Hummingbird* (p. 205): females and immatures have rufous or peach color on sides and flanks. *Ruby-throated Hummingbird* (p. 203): shorter bill; brighter green above; red throat.
Best Sites: no best sites; keep sugarwater feeders active all winter; report activity to Georgia Ornithological Society (GOS) Rare Bird Alert hotline at (770) 493-8862 or the GOS web site at http://www.gos.org.

RUFOUS HUMMINGBIRD

Selasphorus rufus

Reports of this western species are increasingly common in our area, possibly because the numbers of bird feeders and birders are increasing. From 20 to 30 vagrant Rufous Hummingbirds are reported each winter in Georgia. The tiny Rufous Hummingbird is, like the Summer Tanager and Townsend's Solitaire (*Myadestes townsendi*), the northernmost representative of a family with mostly tropical affiliations. This hummingbird's breeding range extends from southern Alaska throughout most of the Pacific Northwest, and it overwinters in the southernmost states and Mexico. • The tiny Rufous Hummingbird is a delicate avian jewel, but its beauty hides a relentless mean streak. Male hummers are aggressively territorial. This behavior underlies the remarkable feistiness so evident wherever hummingbirds gather about a concentrated food source. Although it must seem like life and death situations to these birds, to our eyes, the scale of the conflicts between these mini-mites is cute. • To attract pollinators (insects and hummingbirds), plants produce colorful flowers with sweet, energy-rich nectar.

ID: long, thin, black bill; mostly rufous tail. *Male:* orange-brown back, tail and flanks; iridescent, orange-red throat; green crown; white breast and belly. *Female:* green back; red-spotted throat; rufous sides and flanks contrast with the white underparts.

Size: *L* 3¼–3½ in; *W* 4½ in.

Status: uncommon winter visitor to the entire state from August to May, with most records from mid-November to mid-February; up to 50 reports per winter since the first state record in 1978; the highest count is 3 hummers in one yard in Early Co.

Habitat: hummingbird feeders; nearly any habitat offering abundant flowers, especially hibiscus and salvia; mixedwood forests.

Nesting: does not nest in Georgia.

Feeding: probes mostly red flowers for nectar while hovering; also eats small insects, sap and sugar water.

Voice: call is a low *chewp chewp;* also utters a rapid and exuberant confrontation call, *ZEE-chuppity-chup!*

Similar Species: *Ruby-throated Hummingbird* (p. 203) and *Black-chinned Hummingbird* (p. 204): body and tail lack rufous or orange color.

Best Sites: no best sites; keep sugarwater feeders active all winter; report activity to Georgia Ornithological Society (GOS) Rare Bird Alert hotline at (770) 493-8862 or the GOS web site at http://www.gos.org.

BELTED KINGFISHER

Ceryle alcyon

The boisterous Belted Kingfisher closely monitors many of our lakes, rivers, streams, marshes and beaver ponds. Never far from water, this bird is often found uttering its distinctive, rattling call while perched on a bare branch that extends out over a productive pool. With a precise headfirst dive, the Kingfisher can catch fish at depths of up to 23 inches, or snag a frog immersed in only a few inches of water. The Kingfisher has even been observed diving into water to elude avian predators. • During the breeding season, a pair of kingfishers typically takes turns excavating the nest burrow. The birds use their bills to chip away at an exposed sandbank and then kick loose material out of the tunnel with their feet. The female kingfisher has the traditional female reproductive role for birds but is more colorful than her mate—she has an extra red band across her belly. • In Greek mythology, Alcyon (Halcyone), the daughter of the wind god, grieved so deeply for her drowned husband that the gods transformed them both into kingfishers.

ID: bluish upperparts; shaggy crest; blue-gray breast band; white "collar" and under-wings; long, straight bill; short legs; small, white patch near eye. *Male:* no "belt." *Female:* rust-colored "belt" (may be incomplete).

Size: *L* 11–14 in; *W* 20 in.

Status: common permanent breeding resident statewide; less common in summer and more common in winter near the Coast.

Habitat: rivers, large streams, lakes, marshes and beaver ponds, especially near exposed soil banks, gravel pits or bluffs.

Nesting: in a cavity at the end of an earth burrow, often up to 6 ft long, dug by the pair with their bills and claws; pair incubates 6–7 white eggs for 22–24 days; pair feeds the young.

Feeding: dives headfirst into water, either from a perch or from hovering flight; eats mostly small fish, aquatic invertebrates and tadpoles.

Voice: fast, repetitive, cackling rattle, a little like a teacup shaking on a saucer.

Similar Species: *Blue Jay* (p. 236): more intense blue color; smaller bill and head; behaves in a completely different fashion.

Best Sites: along rivers, creeks and streams; check ponds and lakes, as well; Savannah-Ogeechee Canal; Newman Wetlands Center; Glynn Co. (HC-winter: 17).

RED-HEADED WOODPECKER

Melanerpes erythrocephalus

Closely related to the western Acorn Woodpecker *(M. formicivorus)*, the Red-headed Woodpecker is a bird of the East that lives mostly in deciduous woodlands, in urban parks and in fields with open groves of large trees. Red-headed Woodpeckers were once common throughout their range, but their numbers have declined dramatically over the past century. Since the introduction of the European Starling, Red-headed Woodpeckers have been largely outcompeted for nesting cavities. As well, these birds are frequent traffic fatalities, often struck by vehicles when they dart from their perches and over roadways to catch flying insects. • Like other members of the *Melanerpes* genus, Red-headed Woodpeckers will, during the breeding season, hawk for flying insects and store them, as well as acorns and other nuts, in cracks and bark crevices. • Interestingly, contrary to other bird species, most male woodpeckers, including the Red-headed, incubate the eggs at night.

juvenile

ID: bright red head, "chin," throat and "bib" with black border; black back, wings and tail; white breast, belly, rump, lower back and inner wing patches. *Juvenile:* brown head, back, wings and tail; slight brown streaking on white underparts.

Size: *L* 9–9½ in; *W* 17 in.

Status: uncommon to locally common permanent breeding resident statewide, but less numerous in the Mountains.

Habitat: open deciduous woodlands (especially oak woodlands), urban parks, river edges and roadsides with groves of scattered trees.

Nesting: male excavates a nest cavity in a dead tree or limb; pair incubates 4–5 white eggs for 12–13 days; pair feeds the young.

Feeding: flycatches for insects; hammers dead and decaying wood for grubs; eats mostly insects, earthworms, spiders, nuts, berries, seeds and fruit; may also eat some young birds and eggs.

Voice: loud series of *kweer* or *kwrring* notes; occasionally a chattering *kerr-r-ruck;* also drums softly in short bursts.

Similar Species: adult is distinctive. *Red-bellied Woodpecker* (p. 208): whitish face and underparts; black and white barred back. *Yellow-bellied Sapsucker* (p. 209): large, white wing patch.

Best Sites: regularly found in old swampy ponds with dead trees; wildlife management areas and national wildlife refuges statewide, especially Rum Creek WMA/Piedmont NWR (HC: 138).

RED-BELLIED WOODPECKER

Melanerpes carolinus

The familiar Red-bellied Woodpecker is no stranger to suburban backyards and will sometimes nest in birdhouses. This widespread bird is found year-round in woodlands throughout the southeastern states but numbers fluctuate depending on habitat availability and on weather conditions. In recent years, mild winters have enabled this woodpecker to increase its numbers in the northern parts of its range. • These birds often issue noisy, rolling *churr* calls as they poke around wooded landscapes in search of seeds, fruit and a variety of insects.

Unlike most woodpeckers, Red-bellies consume large amounts of plant material, seldom excavating wood for insects. When occupying an area together with Red-headed Woodpeckers, Red-bellies will nest in the trunk, below the foliage, and the Red-heads will nest in dead branches among the foliage. • The Red-bellied Woodpecker's namesake, its red belly, is only a small reddish area that is difficult to see in the field, but is more visible on breeding males in summer. • Studies of banded Red-bellied Woodpeckers have shown that these birds have a lifespan in the wild of more than 20 years.

ID: black-and-white-barred back; white patches on rump and topside base of primaries; reddish tinge on belly. *Female:* red nape. *Male:* red nape extends to forehead. *Immature:* dark gray crown; streaked breast.

Size: L 9–10½ in; W 16 in.

Status: common permanent breeding resident statewide, except rare to uncommon in the Mountains (does not nest above 1800 ft).

Habitat: mature deciduous woodlands; occasionally in wooded residential areas.

Nesting: in a cavity; female selects one of several nest sites excavated by the male; pair may use a natural cavity or the abandoned cavity of another woodpecker; pair incubates 4–5 white eggs for 12–14 days; pair raises the young.

Feeding: forages in trees, on the ground or occasionally on the wing; eats mostly insects, seeds, nuts and fruit; may also eat tree sap, small amphibians, bird eggs or small fish.

Voice: call is a soft, rolling *churr*; drums in second-long bursts.

Similar Species: *Northern Flicker* (p. 213): yellow underwings; gray crown; brown back with dark barring; black "bib"; large, dark spots on underparts. *Red-headed Woodpecker* (p. 207): all-red head; unbarred, black back and wings; white patch on trailing edge of wing.

Best Sites: any forest, good-sized woodland or backyard feeder; Atlanta (HC-winter: 200+).

YELLOW-BELLIED SAPSUCKER

Sphyrapicus varius

Yellow-bellied Sapsuckers visit Georgia in winter, occasionally uttering their quiet *keer* call. The drumming of sapsuckers—with a slow, irregular rhythm reminiscent of Morse code—differs from that of other local woodpeckers. • Lines of parallel, freshly drilled "sap-wells" in tree bark are a sure sign that sapsuckers are nearby. A pair of sapsuckers might drill a number of sites within their forest territory. The wells fill with sweet, sticky sap that attracts insects; the sapsuckers then make their rounds, eating both the trapped bugs and the pooled sap. Sapsuckers do not actually suck sap—they lap it up with a tongue that resembles a paintbrush. • Other species such as hummingbirds, kinglets, warblers, Baltimore Orioles and Cedar Waxwings feed from the wells made by Yellow-bellied Sapsuckers, especially in winters when insects, fruits and nectar are not as readily available.

ID: black "bib"; red forecrown; black and white face, back, wings and tail; large, white wing patch; yellow wash on lower breast and belly. *Male:* red "chin." *Female:* white "chin." *Immature:* brownish overall, but with large, clearly defined wing patches.

Size: *L* 7–9 in; *W* 16 in.

Status: common winter resident statewide from September to May (mostly from October to mid-April); accidental in summer with historical nesting, but none recently.

Habitat: deciduous and mixed forests, especially dry, second-growth woodlands.

Nesting: does not nest in Georgia.

Feeding: hammers trees for insects; drills "wells" in live trees to collect sap and trap insects; also flycatches for insects.

Voice: nasal, catlike meow, *meeur*, is given occasionally in winter; territorial hammering has a quality and rhythm similar to Morse code.

Similar Species: *Red-headed Woodpecker* (p. 207): juvenile lacks white patch on wing. *Downy Woodpecker* (p. 210) and *Hairy Woodpecker* (p. 211): red nape; white back; lack large, white wing patches and red forecrown.

Best Sites: in the north at Kennesaw Mt. and along the Chattahoochee R. basin; in the south, shows preference for productive pecan orchards (look for old and fresh drill-wells).

DOWNY WOODPECKER

Picoides pubescens

A regular patron of backyard feeders, the small and widely common Downy Woodpecker is often the first woodpecker a novice birder will identify with confidence. It is generally more approachable and tolerant of human activities than are most birds, and once you become familiar with its dainty appearance, it won't be long before you recognize it by its soft taps and brisk staccato calls. These encounters are not all free of confusion, however, because the closely related Hairy Woodpecker looks remarkably similar. • The Downy Woodpecker's small bill is extremely effective for poking into tiny crevices and extracting invertebrates and wood-boring grubs. • Like other members of the woodpecker family, the Downy has evolved a number of features that help to cushion the repeated shocks of a lifetime of hammering. These characteristics include a strong bill, strong neck muscles, a flexible, reinforced skull, and a brain that is tightly packed in its protective cranium. Another feature that Downies share with other woodpeckers is feathered nostrils, which serve to filter out the sawdust it produces when hammering.

ID: clear white belly and back; black wings have white bars; black eye line and crown; short, stubby bill; mostly black tail; black-spotted, white outer tail feathers. *Male:* small, red patch on back of head. *Female:* no red patch.

Size: *L* 6–7 in; *W* 12 in.

Status: common permanent breeding resident statewide.

Habitat: all wooded environments, especially deciduous and mixed forests and areas with tall, deciduous shrubs.

Nesting: pair excavates a cavity in a dying or decaying tree trunk or limb and lines it with wood chips; excavation takes more than 2 weeks; pair incubates 4–5 white eggs for 11–13 days; pair feeds the young.

Feeding: forages on trunks and branches, often in saplings and shrubs; attracted to suet feeders; chips and probes for insect eggs, cocoons, larvae and adults; also eats nuts and seeds.

Voice: long, unbroken trill; calls are a sharp *pik* or *ki-ki-ki* or whiny *queek queek;* drums

more than the Hairy Woodpecker and at a higher pitch, usually on smaller trees and dead branches.

Similar Species: *Hairy Woodpecker* (p. 211): larger; bill is as long as head is wide; no spots on white outer tail feathers. *Yellow-bellied Sapsucker* (p. 209): large, white wing patch; red forecrown; lacks red nape and clean white back.

Best Sites: all types of woodlands statewide; common backyard-feeder bird, especially to winter suet feeders.

HAIRY WOODPECKER

Picoides villosus

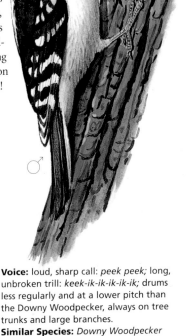

A second look is often required to confirm the identity of this woodpecker, because it is so similar in appearance to its smaller cousin, the Downy Woodpecker. The most convenient way to see woodpeckers, and to distinguish one bird from the other, is to attract these birds to a backyard feeder by offering suet. The Hairy Woodpecker is noticeably larger and more aggressive, and it often thrashes seeds around with its sturdy bill. • The secret to woodpeckers' feeding success is hidden in their skulls. Most woodpeckers have very long tongues—in some cases more than four times the length of the bill—made possible by twin structures that wrap around the perimeter of the skull. These structures store the tongue in much the same way that a measuring tape is stored in its case. Besides being long and maneuverable, the tip of the tongue is sticky with saliva and is finely barbed to help seize reluctant wood-boring insects. • Rather than singing during courtship, woodpeckers drum rhythmically on trees, or sometimes on the side of your house!

ID: white-spotted, black wings; pure white belly; black "cheek" and crown; bill is about as long as head is wide; black tail with unspotted, white outer feathers. *Male:* small, red patch on back of head. *Female:* no red patch.

Size: *L* 8–9½ in; *W* 15 in.

Status: uncommon to locally common permanent breeding resident north of the Fall Line; rare to uncommon in the Coastal Plain; rare in southeastern Georgia and on the Coast.

Habitat: deciduous and mixed forests.

Nesting: pair excavates a nest site in a live or decaying tree trunk or limb; excavation takes more than 2 weeks; cavity is lined with wood chips; pair incubates 4–5 white eggs for 12–14 days; pair feeds the young.

Feeding: forages on tree trunks and branches; chips, hammers and probes bark for insects and their eggs, cocoons and larvae; also eats nuts, fruit and seeds; attracted to feeders with suet, especially in winter.

Voice: loud, sharp call: *peek peek;* long, unbroken trill: *keek-ik-ik-ik-ik-ik;* drums less regularly and at a lower pitch than the Downy Woodpecker, always on tree trunks and large branches.

Similar Species: *Downy Woodpecker* (p. 210): smaller; shorter bill; dark spots on white outer tail feathers. *Yellow-bellied Sapsucker* (p. 209): large, white wing patch; red forecrown; lacks red nape and clean white back.

Best Sites: found in most mountain and Piedmont forests; sometimes backyard suet feeders north of the Fall Line.

RED-COCKADED WOODPECKER

Picoides borealis

The rare Red-cockaded Woodpecker is a highly social bird with intricate nesting requirements. Family groups called "clans" include the breeding pair and up to eight helpers. The group drills a cluster of cavities into live trees, often choosing large, longleaf pines that are infected with red heart fungus. The average cavity takes two years to excavate but may be reused for two decades. • Nest cavities are protected by rows of tiny holes or resin wells that the birds drill above and below the entrance. Gum seeping from these wells forms a barrier against climbing predators such as rat snakes. Wildfire, an important part of these ecosystems, suppresses understory vegetation that could grow above the sap barrier and allow predators access to the nests. • Once common throughout their range, few Red-cockaded Woodpeckers now remain, scattered through isolated islands of old-growth forest. • The common name refers to the red patches of feathers on the head that are often difficult to see in the field. A cockade is "a knot of ribbon on a hat," which resembles a cock's comb. • Three military bases in Georgia have active Red-cockaded Woodpecker reintroduction programs, with the largest number of colonies at Fort Stewart and Fort Benning (both with 200+ pairs), and smaller numbers at Fort Gordon (about 10 pairs). There are also some remaining clusters (180+) in the private land holdings of the Red Hills area in southwestern Georgia.

ID: small; black and white ladder pattern on back and wings; distinctive white "cheeks"; black spots on white belly; broad, black mustache extends from bill to neck. *Male:* red patch behind eye may be difficult to see.
Size: *L* 8½ in; *W* 14 in.
Status: endangered (federal; state); rare to locally common permanent breeding resident in the Coastal Plain; rare in lower Piedmont.
Habitat: stands of open, old-growth (80 years old or more) pine forest with little understory; most common in fire-resistant longleaf pines.
Nesting: a cluster of cavities, commonly 30–50 ft from ground, are constructed in live pines; both parents and sometimes helpers incubate 2–5 shiny white eggs for 10–15 days.
Feeding: flakes off bark on pine trees to expose insects and arthropods; sometimes eats seeds and berries.
Voice: most common call is a *sklit* or *szrek*, given every few seconds; grating and clicking rattle call ends with a hoarse snarl.
Similar Species: *Downy Woodpecker* (p. 210) and *Hairy Woodpecker* (p. 211): lack white barring on back; broad black eye stripe; lack white "cheeks" and hindneck.
Best Public Sites: Piedmont NWR (30+ pairs); Okefenokee NWR (30+ pairs).

NORTHERN FLICKER

Colaptes auratus

Unlike most woodpeckers, this species spends much of its time on the ground, feeding on ants. It appears almost robinlike as it hops about on anthills and in grassy meadows, fields and along forest clearings. • Flickers are often seen bathing in dusty depressions. The dust particles absorb oils and bacteria that are harmful to the birds' feathers. To clean even more thoroughly, flickers will squish captured ants and then preen themselves with the remains: ants contain formic acid, which can kill small parasites on the flickers' skin and feathers. • Like many woodpeckers, the Northern Flicker has zygodactyl feet—each foot has two toes facing forward and two toes pointing backward—which allow the bird to move vertically up and down tree trunks. As well, stiff tail feathers help to prop up woodpeckers' bodies while they scale trees and excavate cavities. • Georgia has the "yellow-shafted" subspecies of flicker, with only one report of the western U.S. "red-shafted" flicker in the state.

"Yellow-shafted Flicker"

ID: brown, barred back and wings; spotted, buff to whitish underparts; black "bib"; yellow underwings and undertail; white rump; long bill; brownish to buff face; gray crown; red on nape. *Male:* black "mustache" stripe; red nape crescent. *Female:* no "mustache."
Size: *L* 12½–13 in; *W* 20 in.
Status: common permanent breeding resident statewide; more numerous in winter.
Habitat: open deciduous, mixed and coniferous woodlands and forest edges, fields, meadows, beaver ponds and other wetlands.
Nesting: pair excavates a cavity in a dead or dying deciduous tree; either sex chooses the nest site; excavation takes about 2 weeks; may also use a nest box; cavity is lined with wood chips; pair incubates 5–8 white eggs for 11–16 days; pair feeds the young.
Feeding: forages on the ground for ants and other terrestrial insects; probes bark; also eats berries and nuts; occasionally flycatches.
Voice: loud, laughing, rapid *kick-kick-kick-kick-kick-kick*; *woika-woika-woika* issued during courtship.
Similar Species: *Red-bellied Woodpecker* (p. 208): black and white pattern on back; more red on head; dark underwings.
Best Sites: forested areas including urban and rural areas; parks, wildlife management areas, and national wildlife refuges; Atlanta (HC-winter: 140+).

PILEATED WOODPECKER

Dryocopus pileatus

With its flaming red crest, swooping flight and maniacal call, this impressive, deep-forest dweller can stop hikers in their tracks. Using its powerful, dagger-shaped bill and stubborn determination, the Pileated Woodpecker chisels out uniquely shaped rectangular cavities in its unending search for grubs and ants. These cavities are often the first indication that a breeding pair is resident in an area. • Because they require large home territories, these magnificent birds are not encountered with much frequency. A pair of breeding Pileated Woodpeckers generally needs more than 100 acres of mature forest in which to settle. • As a primary cavity nester, the Pileated Woodpecker plays an important role in forest ecosystems. Other birds and even mammals depend on the activities of this woodpecker—Wood Ducks, American Kestrels, screech-owls and even flying squirrels are frequent nesters in abandoned Pileated Woodpecker cavities in Georgia. • There is no real consensus on whether this bird's name is pronounced "pie-lee-ated" or "pill-ee-ated"—it's a matter of preference and good-natured debate. • Once thought to be extinct, the Ivory-billed Woodpecker, a close relative, and Pileated look-alike, was recently rediscovered in Arkansas, but there is no evidence that it might still exist in Georgia.

ID: predominantly black; white wing linings; flaming red crest; yellow eyes; stout, dark bill; white stripe runs from bill to shoulder; white "chin." *Male:* red "mustache"; red crest (red extends from bill to nape). *Female:* no red "mustache"; red crest; gray brown forehead.

Size: *L* 16–19 in; *W* 29 in.

Status: common local permanent breeding resident statewide.

Habitat: extensive tracts of mature deciduous, mixed or coniferous forests; some occur in riparian woodlands or wood-lots in suburban and agricultural areas.

Nesting: pair excavates a cavity in a dead or dying tree trunk; excavation takes 3–6 weeks; cavity is lined with wood chips; pair incubates 4 white eggs for 15–18 days; pair feeds the young.

Feeding: often hammers the base of rotting trees, creating fist-sized or larger, rectangular holes; eats carpenter ants, wood-boring beetle larvae, berries and nuts.

Voice: loud, fast, laughing, rolling *woika-woika-woika-woika;* long series of *kuk* notes; loud, resonant drumming.

Similar Species: *Other woodpeckers* (p. 207–14): much smaller. *American Crow* (p. 237) and *Common Raven* (p. 239): lack white underwings and flaming red crest.

Best Sites: Cloudland Canyon SP; Pine Log WMA; Oconee River RA; Rum Creek WMA; Big Hammock WMA; mature pecan groves.

PASSERINES

Flycatchers

Shrikes & Vireos

Jays & Crows

Larks & Swallows

Chickadees,
Nuthatches & Wrens

Kinglets, Gnatcatchers
& Thrushes

Mimics, Starlings
& Waxwings

Wood-warblers
& Tanagers

Sparrows, Grosbeaks
& Buntings

Blackbirds
& Allies

Finchlike Birds

asserines are also commonly known as "songbirds" or "perching birds." Although these terms are easier to comprehend, they are not as strictly accurate, because some passerines neither sing nor perch, and many nonpasserines do sing and perch. In a general sense, however, these terms represent passerines adequately: they are among the best singers, and they are typically seen perched on a branch or wire.

It is believed that passerines, which all belong to the order Passeriformes, make up the most recent evolutionary group of birds. Theirs is the most numerous of all orders, representing about 42 percent of the bird species in Georgia, and nearly three-fifths of all living birds worldwide.

Passerines are grouped together based on the sum total of many morphological and molecular similarities, including such things as reproductive characteristics and the number of tail and flight feathers. All passerines share the same foot shape: three toes face forward and one faces backward, and no passerines have webbed toes. Also, all passerines have a tendon that runs along the back side of the bird's knee and tightens when the bird perches, giving it a firm grip.

Some of our most common and easily identified birds are passerines, such as the Black-capped Chickadee, American Robin and House Sparrow, but the passerines also include some birds that are the most challenging and frustrating to identify until their distinct songs and calls are learned.

OLIVE-SIDED FLYCATCHER

Contopus cooperi

Olive-sided Flycatchers forage high in the forest canopy, far above the daily hubbub of the forest floor. There, they have easy access to an abundance of flying insects, especially the honeybees and wasps that inhabit the sunny forest heights. These feisty birds are difficult to spot, so look for a big-headed silhouette perched at the tip of a mature conifer or dead branch. They are often seen near lakes, wetlands or riparian areas. • These solitary birds are usually silent during spring and fall migration, so they often slip through Georgia unnoticed. On their northern breeding grounds, however, male Olive-sided Flycatchers utter a most curious and incessant wild call: *Quick, three-beers! Quick, three-beers!* This interpretation of the courtship song may be rendered as *quick-three-cheers!* in some social circles. • Like all flycatchers, this olive-vested songbird perches with a distinctive, upright, attentive profile. Its ready-and-waiting stance allows it to quickly launch out and snatch flying insects in midair.

ID: dark, olive gray "vest"; light throat and belly; olive gray to olive brown upperparts; white tufts on sides of rump; dark upper mandible; dull yellow-orange base to lower mandible; inconspicuous eye ring.
Size: *L* 7–8 in; *W* 13 in.
Status: rare migrant from April to June and from July to October, primarily north of the Fall Line; twice as many records in fall as in spring.
Habitat: semi-open mixed and coniferous forests near water; mountainous regions; riparian areas.

Nesting: does not nest in Georgia.
Feeding: flycatches insects from a perch.
Voice: usually silent in Georgia; song is a chipper and lively *quick, three-beers!*, with the 2nd note highest in pitch; descending *pip-pip-pip* when excited.
Similar Species: *Eastern Wood-Pewee* (p. 217): smaller; gray breast; 2 faint wing bars; lacks white rump tufts. *Eastern Phoebe* (p. 222): all-dark bill; often wags tail; lacks white rump tufts. *Eastern Kingbird* (p. 226): all-dark bill; white-tipped tail; lacks white rump tufts.
Best Sites: Eufaula NWR; Kennesaw Mt. (10 records); Newman Wetlands Center.

EASTERN WOOD-PEWEE

Contopus virens

Perched on an exposed tree branch in a suburban park, woodlot edge or neighborhood yard, the male Eastern Wood-Pewee whistles his plaintive *pee-ah-wee, pee-oh* all day long throughout summer. Its song can be readily heard in mesic wooded areas statewide. Some of the keenest suitors will even sing their charms late into the evening, long after most birds have silenced their courtship songs. • Like other flycatchers, the Eastern Wood-Pewee loops out from exposed perches to snatch flying insects in midair, a technique often referred to as "flycatching" or "hawking." • Many insects have evolved defense mechanisms to avert potential predators, such as the Eastern Wood-Pewee and its flycatching relatives. Some flying insects are camouflaged, whereas others are distasteful or poisonous and flaunt their foul nature with vivid colors. Interestingly, some insects even mimic their poisonous allies, displaying warning colors even though they are perfectly tasty.

ID: olive gray to olive brown upperparts; 2 narrow, white wing bars; whitish throat; gray breast and sides; whitish or pale yellow belly, flanks and undertail coverts; dark upper mandible; dull yellow-orange base to lower mandible; no eye ring.

Size: *L* 6–6½ in; *W* 10 in.

Status: common breeding resident statewide from March to November; no confirmed winter sightings.

Habitat: open mixed and deciduous woodlands with a sparse understory, especially woodland openings and edges; rarely in open coniferous woodlands.

Nesting: probably nests in every county in Georgia; on the fork of a horizontal deciduous branch, well away from the trunk; open cup of grass, plant fibers and lichen is bound with spider silk; female incubates 3 whitish eggs, with dark blotches concentrated at the larger end, for 12–13 days.

Feeding: flycatches insects from a perch; may also glean insects from foliage, especially while hovering.

Voice: *chip* call; song is a clear, slow, plaintive *pee-ah-wee*, with the 2nd note lower and third note highest, followed by a down-slurred *pee-oh*, with or without intermittent pauses.

Similar Species: *Olive-sided Flycatcher* (p. 216): larger; white rump tufts; olive gray "vest"; lacks conspicuous, white wing bars. *Eastern Phoebe* (p. 222): lacks conspicuous, white wing bars; all-dark bill; often pumps its tail. *Eastern Kingbird* (p. 226): larger; white-tipped tail; brighter white underparts; all-dark bill. *Empidonax flycatchers* (pp. 218–21): smaller; more conspicuous wing bars; eye rings.

Best Sites: most national wildlife refuges, wildlife management areas and lake sites; Fernbank Forest (HC-fall: 27); Columbus (HC-fall: 25).

YELLOW-BELLIED FLYCATCHER

Empidonax flaviventris

You will have to spend some time in riparian woodlands during migration if you want to find the reclusive Yellow-bellied Flycatcher in Georgia. These flycatchers are difficult to spot unless they give away their whereabouts by zipping out from inconspicuous perches to snatch an unsuspecting insect. Yellow-bellied Flycatchers are uncommon migrants in Georgia, with most sightings occurring in the Piedmont region in fall. These birds are generally silent as they pass through Georgia, which makes positive identification a challenge. • Our region offers fine opportunities for birders to develop their *Empidonax* flycatcher identification skills—it boasts a large assemblage of these nearly indistinguishable flycatchers. • The Yellow-bellied Flycatcher is one of the most elusive and secretive of this confusing genus. It does not habitually perch in the open but distinguishes itself from other flycatchers with its distinctive song and by frequently foraging close to the ground.

ID: olive green upperparts; 2 whitish wing bars; yellowish eye ring; yellow throat; yellow underparts; pale olive breast; very short primary projection. **Size:** *L* 5–6 in; *W* 8 in.

Status: rare migrant north of the Fall Line from August to October (especially early to mid-September); accidental to rare north of the Fall Line from April to May (only about 10 records); very rare in the Coastal Plain during migration; accidental and nonbreeding in summer in Rome.

Habitat: can be found in almost any forested habitat, especially riparian, during migration.

Nesting: does not nest in Georgia.

Feeding: flycatches for insects at low to middle levels of the forest; also gleans vegetation for larval and adult invertebrates while hovering.

Voice: generally silent in Georgia; calls include a chipper *pe-wheep, preee, pur-wee* or *killik;* song is a soft *che-luck,* or *che-lek* (2nd syllable is lower pitched), with each song separated by long pauses.

Similar Species: *Acadian* (p. 219), *Willow* (p. 220) and *Alder* (p. 364) *flycatchers:* all lack extensive yellow wash from throat to belly, except rarely in fall immatures; white eye rings; different songs; all but the Acadian have browner upperparts; all have longer primary projection. *Least Flycatcher* (p. 221): larger head; short primary projection, but much grayer above.

Best Sites: Ocmulgee NM; West Point L.; Lake Walter F. George; Eufaula NWR; Lake Seminole; Kennesaw Mt.; Newman Wetlands Center; Bibb Co. (HC-fall: 5).

ACADIAN FLYCATCHER

Empidonax virescens

Most experienced birders will tell you that one of the keys to identifying a flycatcher is to listen for its distinctive song. The Acadian Flycatcher's singing can be heard throughout Georgia on its breeding grounds; listen for its *peet-sa* song at wooded wetlands on the Coastal Plain and on the coast. Many other flycatchers are silent as they pass through our state. • Learning to identify this bird is only half the fun. Its speedy, aerial courtship chases and the male's hovering flight displays are sights to behold—that is if you can survive the swarming hordes of bloodsucking mosquitoes deep within the swampy woodlands where this flycatcher is primarily found. • Cypress-tupelo swamps, riparian woodlands and river edges are the preferred nest sites of the Acadian Flycatcher. The nest, which is built on a horizontal branch up to 20 feet above the ground, can be quite conspicuous because loose material (especially Spanish moss in south Georgia) often dangles from the nest, giving it a sloppy appearance.

ID: narrow, yellowish eye ring; 2 buff to yellowish wing bars; large bill has dark upper mandible and pinkish yellow lower mandible; white throat; faint olive yellow breast; yellow belly and under-tail coverts; olive green upperparts; very long primary projection.
Size: *L* 5½–6 in; *W* 9 in.
Status: common breeding resident state-wide from March to October; more common south of Fall Line.
Habitat: fairly mature deciduous woodlands, riparian woodlands and wooded swamps.
Nesting: low in a beech or maple tree, usually 6–13 ft high; female builds a loose, sloppy-looking cup nest from bark strips, catkins, fine twigs, or Spanish moss and grasses held together with spider silk; female incubates 3 creamy white eggs, lightly spotted with brown, for 13–15 days.
Feeding: hawks or gleans from foliage while hovering; takes insects and insect larvae, including wasps, bees, spiders and ants; may also eat berries and small fruits.
Voice: song is a forceful *peet-sa;* sometimes accent is on the 2nd syllable, like *peet-seek!;* call is a softer *peet;* may issue a loud, flicker-like *ti-ti-ti-ti-ti* during the breeding season.
Similar Species: *Alder Flycatcher* (p. 364): song is *fee-bee-o;* narrower, white eye ring is often inconspicuous; browner overall; smaller head relative to its body. *Willow Flycatcher* (p. 220): song is an explosive *fitz-bew;* browner overall; smaller head; very faint eye ring. *Least Flycatcher* (p. 221): song is a clear *che-bek;* prominent, white eye ring; rounded head; shorter wings. *Yellow-bellied Flycatcher* (p. 218): song is a liquid *che-lek;* yellow wash from throat to belly; shorter wings.
Best Sites: Grand Bay WMA; Okefenokee NWR; Big Hammock WMA; Savannah-Ogeechee Canal; Beaverdam WMA; Laurens Co. (HC: 35); Hancock Co. (HC:19).

WILLOW FLYCATCHER

Empidonax traillii

As its name suggests, the Willow Flycatcher inhabits the dense willows and thickets that surround swamps and river edges. It often perches low to the ground, skulking in the shadows until a tasty insect happens by. This bird commonly captures flying insects in midair or snatches unsuspecting spiders that dangle from silky threads. • The Willow Flycatcher was once grouped together with the closely related Alder Flycatcher, which shares the same plumage and haunts. The only sure way of identifying these two birds in the field is to listen for their calls: the Willow Flycatcher gives a characteristic, sneezy *fitz-bew* call, whereas the Alder Flycatcher's song is a distinct *fee-bee-o*. Because these birds rarely sing while migrating through our state, Georgia birders often settle for marking "*Empidonax* sp." on their checklists. Birders willing to take a trip to the mountains may be fortunate enough to glimpse Willow Flycatchers during the breeding season. • John James Audubon named this species after Thomas Stewart Traill, an Englishman who helped him find a British publisher for his book *Ornithological Biography*.

ID: olive brown upperparts; 2 whitish wing bars; no eye ring; white throat; yellowish belly; pale olive breast.
Size: *L* 5½–6 in; *W* 8½ in.
Status: rare migrant over most of state from April to October; rare summer breeding resident in the Mountains but has nested in upper Piedmont.
Habitat: shrubby successional areas in old fields, but especially riparian corridors and willows along small creeks.
Nesting: in a fork or on a branch of a dense shrub, usually 3–7 ft high; female builds an open cup nest with grass, bark strips and plant fibers and lines it with down; female incubates 3–4 whitish to pale buff eggs, with brown spots concentrated toward the larger end, for 12–15 days.

Feeding: flycatches insects and gleans them from vegetation, usually while hovering.
Voice: call is a quick *whit;* song is a quick, sneezy *fitz-bew* that drops off at the end (repeated up to 30 times a minute).
Similar Species: *Eastern Wood-Pewee* (p. 217): larger; lacks eye ring and conspicuous wing bars. *Least Flycatcher* (p. 221): song is a clear *che-bek;* bolder white eye ring; grayer upperparts; pale, gray-white underparts; short primary projection. *Acadian Flycatcher* (p. 219): song is a forceful *peet-sa;* yellowish eye ring; greener upperparts; yellower underparts. *Yellow-bellied Flycatcher* (p. 218): song is a liquid *che-lek;* yellowish eye ring; greener upperparts; yellower underparts; shorter primary projection. *Alder Flycatcher* (p. 364): song is *fee-bee-o;* otherwise very similar.
Best Sites: recent nesting at Dillard, Nottely L./Blairsville, Dawsonville, Sand Mt. and Greene Co. (HC: 4).

LEAST FLYCATCHER

Empidonax minimus

This bird might not look like a bully, but the Least Flycatcher is one of the boldest and most pugnacious songbirds of our deciduous woodlands. During the nesting season, it is noisy and conspicuous, forcefully repeating its simple, two-part *che-bek* call throughout much of the day. Intense song battles normally eliminate the need for physical aggression, but feathers fly in fights that are occasionally required to settle disputes over territory and courtship privileges. • These birds often fall victim to nest parasitism by the Brown-headed Cowbird, whose hatched young often smother the much smaller Least Flycatcher nestlings. • *Empidonax* flycatchers are aptly named: the literal translation, "mosquito king," refers to their insect-hunting prowess.

ID: grayish olive-brown upperparts; 2 white wing bars; bold, white eye ring; fairly long, narrow tail in comparison to short primary projection; mostly dark bill has yellow-orange lower mandible; white throat; gray breast; gray-white to yellowish belly and undertail coverts.

Size: *L* 4½–6 in; *W* 7¾ in.

Status: rare migrant over most of the state from April to October; rare, local breeding resident in the northeast Mountains (Suches and Sky Valley) from May to September.

Habitat: open deciduous or mixed woodlands; forest openings and edges; often in second-growth woodlands and occasionally near human habitation.

Nesting: in the crotch or fork of a small tree or shrub, often against the trunk; female builds a small cup nest of plant fibers and bark and lines it with fine grass, plant down and feathers; female incubates 4 creamy white eggs for 13–15 days; both adults feed the young.

Feeding: flycatches insects; gleans trees and shrubs for insects while hovering; may also eat some fruit and seeds.

Voice: soft *whit* call; song is a constantly repeated, dry *che-bek che-bek*.

Similar Species: all of the following flycatchers, except Yellow-bellied, have longer primary projections. *Eastern Wood-Pewee* (p. 217): larger; lacks eye ring and conspicuous wing bars. *Willow Flycatcher* (p. 220): song is an explosive *fitz-bew;* lacks eye ring; greener upperparts; yellower underparts. *Acadian Flycatcher* (p. 219): song is a forceful *peet-sa;* yellowish eye ring; greener upperparts; yellower underparts. *Yellow-bellied Flycatcher* (p. 218): song is a liquid *che-lek;* yellowish eye ring; greener upperparts; yellower underparts. *Ruby-crowned Kinglet* (p. 259): broken eye ring; much daintier bill; shorter tail; occurs in opposite seasons. *Alder Flycatcher* (p. 364): song is *fee-bee-o;* faint eye ring; usually found in wetter areas.

Best Sites: Rabun Bald, along Hale Ridge Rd. or Sky Valley; Athens (HC: 5).

221

EASTERN PHOEBE

Sayornis phoebe

Whether you are poking around Lake Lanier or wandering through a park in Atlanta, there is a fairly good chance that you will stumble upon an Eastern Phoebe. This drab bird can be found statewide in winter and breeds in northern Georgia. It is often seen perched on a fence post or on top of a tall bush overlooking a local watering hole. Watch for the Eastern Phoebe's characteristic tail pumping, exhibited with a zest and frequency that few species can match. • Most Eastern Phoebes leave southern Georgia in April and travel farther north to their breeding grounds starting just below the Fall Line, where they construct marvelous mud nests on any available platform. Once limited to nesting on natural cliffs and fallen riparian trees, this adaptive flycatcher has gradually found success in nesting on buildings and bridges, though it prefers sites near water. • Eastern Phoebes sometimes reuse their nest sites for many years and, too often, people unnecessarily destroy the phoebe's mud nests. Other people have caught on to the benefits of having phoebe tenants—these birds can be effective at controlling pesky insects.

ID: gray-brown upperparts; white underparts with gray wash on breast and sides; belly may be washed with yellow in fall; no eye ring; no obvious wing bars; all-black bill; dark legs; frequently pumps its tail.
Size: L 6½–7 in; W 10½ in.
Status: common migrant and winter resident in the Coastal Plain from August to April, with the highest numbers from October to March; uncommon north of the Fall Line in winter; summer breeding resident north of the Fall Line, or rarely, the upper Coastal Plain.
Habitat: open deciduous woodlands, forest edges and clearings; usually near water.
Nesting: under the ledge of a building, picnic shelter, culvert, bridge, cliff or well; cup-shaped mud nest is lined with moss, grass, fur and feathers; female incubates 4–5 white eggs, often with a few reddish brown spots, for about 16 days; both adults feed the young.
Feeding: flycatches beetles, flies, wasps, grasshoppers, mayflies and other insects; occasionally plucks aquatic invertebrates and small fish from the water's surface; eats small berries and fruit in cold snaps.
Voice: call is a sharp *chip;* song is a hearty, snappy *fee-bee,* delivered frequently.
Similar Species: *Eastern Wood-Pewee* (p. 217): smaller; pale wing bars; bicolored bill; does not pump its tail. *Olive-sided Flycatcher* (p. 216): dark "vest"; white, fluffy patches border rump. *Empidonax flycatchers* (pp. 218–21): most have eye ring and conspicuous wing bars. *Eastern Kingbird* (p. 226): white-tipped tail; black upperparts.
Best Sites: mesic areas in summer and winter; Athens (HC-winter: 86); Jekyll I. (HC-fall: 75).

VERMILION FLYCATCHER

Pyrocephalus rubinus

Your next winter hike through a riparian woodland or near a shallow pond with "stick-ups" may include a startling glimpse of a brilliant, flaming bird with plumage that somehow seems redder than red. Indeed, the generic name *Pyrocephalus,* meaning "firehead," accurately describes the stunning appearance of the male Vermilion Flycatcher. • Equally sublime in a more subtle fashion is the female, who secretly evaluates her courtier for style, grace and vocal appeal. The male's ability to provide for her future young is very important, because her chosen mate must care for two full broods during the summer nesting season. • Foraging Vermilion Flycatchers acrobatically chase grasshoppers, beetles and butterflies through the woodlands, boomeranging back to their perch. After crunching down large insects, these flycatchers cough up owl-like pellets to eliminate the indigestible parts. • There are now over 25 records of this visitor to Georgia, all in fall and winter and almost all in southern Georgia. They prefer open clearings and bushy areas near water in winter.

ID: *Male:* bright red head and underparts; black "mask" and upperparts; immature male has streaked breast, reddish lower underparts and may have red blotches on head and breast. *Female:* grayish brown upperparts; white throat and breast with dark streaking; pinkish lower underparts; dark "mask"; immature female may have yellowish lower underparts. *Immature:* similar to female but with spotted rather than streaked breast and white underparts.

Size: *L* 6 in; *W* 10 in.

Status: rare winter visitor on the Coastal Plain from November to March; accidental on the Coast at Harris Neck NWR and Jekyll I.

Habitat: riparian woodlands; grasslands with scattered trees and shrubs; most common near water.

Nesting: does not nest in Georgia.

Feeding: insects are usually caught by hawking or by dropping to the ground after hovering above prey; may eat large numbers of bees and wasps; pellets consisting of indigestible insect parts are coughed up.

Voice: courtship flight is a soft *pit-a-see pit-a-see;* call is a sharp *pitsk;* usually silent in our area.

Similar Species: *Say's Phoebe:* rarer than the Vermilion; lacks streaking on pale gray throat and upper breast or on tawny-orange lower underparts.

Best Sites: open clearings and bushy areas near water; Okefenokee Swamp; Grand Bay WMA; Brooks Co. (HC: 3).

223

GREAT CRESTED FLYCATCHER

Myiarchus crinitus

The Great Crested Flycatcher's nesting habits are unusual for a flycatcher. Instead of building a traditional cup nest, this flycatcher uses a natural tree cavity, an abandoned woodpecker hole or, occasionally, a nest box intended for a bluebird or kestrel. Then, with great ingenuity, the Great Crested Flycatcher decorates the nest entrance with a shed snakeskin or, if genuine reptilian skin is hard to come by, a piece of translucent plastic wrap. The purpose of this practice is not fully understood, though it might make any would-be predators think twice! • The males announce their spring arrival by calling loudly as they invade open or semi-open mixed forests, wooded backyards, parks, cemeteries and campuses. • Great Crested Flycatchers are fairly common statewide wherever suitable nesting cavities, including nest boxes, are available.

ID: bright yellow belly and undertail coverts; gray throat and upper breast; reddish brown tail; peaked, "crested" head; dark olive brown upperparts; heavy black bill.

Size: *L* 8–9 in; *W* 13 in.

Status: common summer breeding resident statewide from March to October.

Habitat: deciduous and mixed woodlands and forests, usually near openings or edges.

Nesting: in a tree cavity, nest box or other artificial cavity; nest is lined with grass, bark strips and feathers; may hang a shed snakeskin or plastic wrap from the entrance hole; female incubates 5 creamy white to pale buff eggs, marked with lavender, olive and brown, for 13–15 days.

Feeding: often in the upper branches of deciduous trees, where it flycatches for insects; may also glean caterpillars and occasionally fruit.

Voice: loud, whistled *wheep!* and a rolling *prrrrreet!*

Similar Species: *Yellow-bellied Flycatcher* (p. 218): much smaller; yellow throat; lacks reddish brown tail and large, all-black bill. *Eastern Kingbird* (p. 226): dark gray "cap" and back; darker tail with white outer margins; lacks head crest.

Best Sites: woodlots, treed parklands and forest edges; Glynn Co. (HC: 178).

WESTERN KINGBIRD

Tyrannus verticalis

More typical of the prairies, the Western Kingbird is a rare visitor to the east. Very few are reported here each year, most often in winter and along the coast. • Western Kingbirds can be observed watching for prey from fence posts, power lines or utility poles. When a kingbird spots an insect, it may chase it for up to 50 feet before a capture is made. • Once you have witnessed the kingbird's brave attacks against much larger birds, such as crows and hawks, it is easy to understand why this brawler was awarded the name "kingbird." Its scientific name *verticalis* refers to the bird's hidden, red crown patch, which is flared during courtship displays and while in combat with rivals. This red patch, however, is not a good identification mark because it is rarely visible outside the breeding season. • On several occasions, Western Kingbirds have hybridized with Eastern Kingbirds. • This kingbird has been a more common recent winter visitor to the coast and barrier islands in Georgia, with accidental summer reports in Washington and Fayette counties.

ID: gray head and breast; yellow belly and undertail coverts; black tail; white edge on outer tail feathers; white "chin"; black bill; ashy gray upperparts; faint, dark gray "mask"; thin, orange-red crown (rarely seen).
Size: *L* 8–9 in; *W* 15½ in.
Status: rare migrant and winter visitor statewide from September to May; more common on the Coast and barrier islands.

Habitat: open scrubland areas with scattered patches of brush or hedgerows; along the edges of open fields.
Nesting: does not nest in Georgia.
Feeding: flycatches aerial insects, including bees, wasps, butterflies, moths, grasshoppers and flies; occasionally eats berries.
Voice: chatty, twittering *whit-ker-whit;* also a short *kit* or extended *kit-kit-keetle-dot;* usually silent in Georgia.
Similar Species: *Eastern Kingbird* (p. 226): black upperparts; white underparts; white-tipped tail. *Great Crested Flycatcher* (p. 224): slightly crested head; brownish upperparts; reddish brown tail; yellowish wing bars; lacks white edges to outer tail feathers.
Best Sites: barrier islands from Tybee I. (HC: 5) to Cumberland I.

225

EASTERN KINGBIRD

Tyrannus tyrannus

When you think of a tyrant, images of an oppressive dictator or a large carnivorous dinosaur are much more likely to come to mind than images of a little bird. True as that might be, no one familiar with the pugnacity of the Eastern Kingbird is likely to refute its scientific name, *Tyrannus tyrannus*. This bird is a brawler that will fearlessly attack crows, hawks and even humans that pass through its territory. Intruders are often vigorously pursued, pecked and plucked for some distance until the kingbird is satisfied that there is no further threat. In contrast, its butterfly-like courtship flight, which is characterized by short, quivering wingbeats, reveals a gentler side of this bird. • Eastern Kingbirds are quite common throughout Georgia, and during a summer drive through the country, you will likely spot at least one kingbird sitting on a fenceline or utility wire. These birds are normally found in pairs, but in late summer and fall, Eastern Kingbirds gather together in conspicuous flocks that may contain over a thousand birds. • Eastern Kingbirds rarely walk or hop on the ground—they prefer to fly, even for very short distances.

ID: dark gray to black upperparts; white underparts; white-tipped tail; black bill; small head crest; thin, orange-red crown (rarely seen); no eye ring; black legs.

Size: *L* 8½ in; *W* 15 in.

Status: common summer breeding resident statewide from March to October; no confirmed winter records in North America for this species.

Habitat: rural fields with scattered trees or hedgerows, clearings in fragmented forests, open roadsides, burned areas and near human settlements; very common near ponds and lakes.

Nesting: on a horizontal tree or shrub limb; also on a standing stump or an upturned tree root; pair builds a cup nest of weeds, twigs and grass and lines it with root fibers, fine grass and fur; female incubates 3–4 darkly blotched, white to pinkish white eggs for 14–18 days.

Feeding: flycatches aerial insects; infrequently eats berries.

Voice: call is a quick, loud, chattering *kit-kit-kitter-kitter;* also a buzzy *dzee-dzee-dzee.*

Similar Species: *Tree Swallow* (p. 242): iridescent, dark blue back; lacks white-tipped tail; more streamlined body; smaller bill. *Olive-sided Flycatcher* (p. 216): 2 white tufts border rump; lacks white-tipped tail and all-white underparts. *Eastern Wood-Pewee* (p. 217): smaller; bicolored bill; lacks white-tipped tail and all-white underparts. *Western Kingbird* (p. 225): gray head and breast; yellow belly and undertail coverts; black tail; white edge on outer tail feathers.

Best Sites: rural fields with scattered trees or hedgerows.

GRAY KINGBIRD

Tyrannus dominicensis

Noisy and fearless, the black-masked Gray Kingbird haunts south Georgia's barrier islands, usually in areas with large, live oaks. This ever-vigilant bird often perches on a protruding branch or telephone wire before darting out to snatch a bee or dragonfly in midair. With an audible snap of its sturdy bill, the Gray Kingbird nabs the prey and then returns to the same perch. • Do not be surprised if you see a Gray Kingbird chasing a hawk or crow. Aggressive behavior is typical of all members of the *Tyrannus* species, as their name reveals. *Dominicensis* translates to "of Hispaniola," referring to the origin of the first specimen. • Gray Kingbirds tolerate humans and have even expanded their range with increased forest clearing and agricultural development. However, instances of death following pesticide spraying have been observed.

ID: gray overall; stocky, with large head; dark strike through eye and "cheeks"; long, sturdy bill; notched tail; red crown feathers usually concealed, brighter on male. *Immature:* brownish upperparts.
Size: *L* 9 in; *W* 14 in.
Status: rare migrant and very local summer breeding resident on the southern Coast from April to November; accidental inland at Okefenokee NWR.
Habitat: coastal; mangroves and palm groves; pine and hardwood forests.

Nesting: canopy nester; female builds an open stick nest; female incubates 2–4 pinkish eggs, with brown blotches, for 14–15 days.
Feeding: catches flying insects in midair and then returns to same perch; may also take some berries and fruits.
Voice: high, sharp *preeerr-krr.*
Similar Species: *Eastern Kingbird* (p. 226): white-tipped tail; square tail (not forked); black head. *Western Kingbird* (p. 225): gray head and breast; yellow belly and undertail coverts; black tail; white edge on outer tail feathers.
Best Sites: southern coast and barrier islands, with (sporadic nesting on St. Simon I., Sea I. (HC: 12), Jekyll I., at Brunswick and in Camden Co.

SCISSOR-TAILED FLYCATCHER
Tyrannus forficatus

Endowed with the refined, long tail feathers of a tropical bird of paradise, the Scissor-tailed Flycatcher tops many birders' "must-see" lists. As if acknowledging its enduring popularity, this lovely bird often perches on roadside fences or utility wires, allowing observers to marvel at its beauty and grace. • The name "Scissor-tailed" is derived from the male's habit of opening and closing the gap between his long tail feathers during courtship flight. The rollercoaster-like courtship ritual often includes dazzling backward somersaults that enhance the beauty of the male's streaming tail. • Flycatchers, and closely related kingbirds, aggressively defend their nests, giving shrill, piercing calls and attacking much larger birds such as jays, magpies, crows and hawks. • Stray Scissor-tailed Flycatchers wander nationwide and may turn up in any of the lower 48 states, including Georgia, where they are rare breeders in the Piedmont.

ID: dark wings; extremely long outer tail feathers give forked appearance in flight; whitish to grayish head, back and breast; salmon pink underwing linings, flanks and lower underparts; bright pink "wing pits." *Immature:* duller, shorter-tailed version of adult; brownish back.

Size: *L* 10 in (adult male up to 15 in, including tail); *W* 15 in.

Status: rare year-round visitor statewide, but mostly from April to August, September to November and January to February; accidental in the Mountains in Floyd and Whitfield counties.

Habitat: grasslands, pastures, roadsides and semi-open country with scattered groves of trees and shrubs or utility poles for nesting.

Nesting: rare breeder; female builds a messy nest cup of twigs, vegetation and animal hair placed in a tree or shrub or on a utility pole or other suitable structure; female incubates 4–5 whitish eggs, blotched with red or purple, for 14–15 days; pair raises the young.

Feeding: typically catches insects by hawking; may catch insects on the ground, while flying or by gleaning them from foliage while hovering.

Voice: calls include a repeated *ka-leap* and a sharp, harsh *kek*.

Similar Species: long tail is distinctive. *Western Kingbird* (p. 225): similar to immature; bright yellow underparts; square, black tail. *Northern Mockingbird* (p. 269): similar to immature; stockier overall; longer legs with larger feet; two white wing bars; light gray underparts.

Best Sites: *In migration:* the Mountains (Floyd and Whitfield counties). *Breeding:* rare records near McDonough (HC: 5), Cartersville and Comer.

LOGGERHEAD SHRIKE

Lanius ludovicianus

Sometimes called the "French Mockingbird," the Loggerhead Shrike resembles a Northern Mockingbird in body shape and color. However, the Loggerhead's method of hunting is very different: it often perches atop trees and on wires to scan for small prey, which is caught in fast, direct flight or a swooping dive. • Loggerhead Shrike populations have severely declined in many parts of North America, earning this bird endangered species status in parts of its northern range. Habitat destruction and encounters with motor vehicles are the main reasons for its decline. On their wintering grounds in the southern U.S., shrikes often become traffic fatalities when they fly low across roads to prey on insects attracted to the warm pavement. Because of the precipitous decline in the northern subspecies *(L. l. migrans)*, few birds currently migrate to Georgia for winter. • Males display their hunting prowess by impaling prey on thorns or barbed wire. This behavior may also serve as a means of storing excess food during times of plenty. In spring, you may see a variety of skewered creatures baking in the sun. The family name Laniidae and genus name *Lanius* are both derived from the Latin for "butcher," and, with good reason, the shrike is often called the "Butcher Bird."

ID: black tail and wings; gray crown and back; white underparts; black "mask" extends above hooked bill onto forehead. *Immature:* brownish gray, barred upperparts. *In flight:* white wing patches; white-edged tail.
Size: *L* 9 in; *W* 12 in.
Status: permanent breeding resident statewide; uncommon to common below the Fall Line; uncommon in the Piedmont; rare in the Mountains.
Habitat: grazed pastures and marginal and abandoned farmlands with scattered hawthorn shrubs, fence posts, barbed wire and nearby wetlands.
Nesting: low in the crotch of a shrub or small tree; thorny hawthorn shrubs are often preferred; bulky cup nest of twigs and grass is lined with animal hair, feathers, plant down and rootlets; female incubates 5–6 pale buff to grayish white eggs, with dark spots concentrated at the larger end, for 15–17 days.
Feeding: swoops down on prey from a perch or attacks in pursuit; takes mostly large insects; regularly eats small birds, rodents and shrews; also eats carrion, small snakes and amphibians.
Voice: high-pitched, hiccupy *bird-ee bird-ee* in summer; infrequently a harsh *shack-shack* year-round.
Similar Species: *Northern Mockingbird* (p. 269): slim bill; no "mask"; obvious white patches on wings; slimmer overall; wingbeats much slower (shrike's wingbeats too fast to count).
Best Sites: on wires or fences in the Coastal Plain and the Coast, especially along I-16; Dublin (HC-winter: 44); Altamaha WMA; Harris Neck NWR; Lake Seminole.

WHITE-EYED VIREO

Vireo griseus

Like most vireos, the White-eyed Vireo keeps out of sight as it sneaks through dense tangles of branches and foliage in search of insects. Though several vireo species share the same winter range, each forages in a specific niche to avoid competition. The White-eyed Vireo feeds at the middle heights of trees, whereas other vireos may stick to food sources found higher in the canopy or closer to the ground. • This cryptic vireo can be a challenge to spot but is renowned for its complex vocalizations. A single bird may have a repertoire of a dozen or more songs. It is also an excellent vocal mimic and may incorporate the calls of other birds into its own songs. • Vireos construct intricate hanging nests, weaving together plant material and the fibrous paper from wasp nests. The nests of vireos are even more cryptic than the birds themselves and are a challenge to find. The best time to locate nests is in winter, when nestlings will not be disturbed and the swinging nests are revealed among bare deciduous branches.

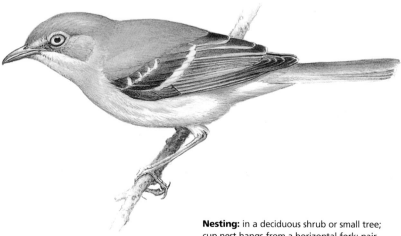

ID: yellow "spectacles"; olive gray upperparts; white underparts with yellow sides and flanks; 2 whitish wing bars; dark wings and tail; white eyes, dark in juveniles.
Size: *L* 5 in; *W* 7½ in.

Status: common migrant and summer breeding resident from March to November, statewide and below 2300 ft in Mountains; uncommon winter resident below the Fall Line; rare in the Piedmont in winter.

Habitat: dense, shrubby undergrowth and thickets in open, swampy, deciduous woodlands, overgrown fields, young second-growth woodlands, woodland clearings and along woodlot edges.

Nesting: in a deciduous shrub or small tree; cup nest hangs from a horizontal fork; pair incubates 4 lightly speckled, white eggs for 13–15 days; both adults feed the young.

Feeding: gleans insects from branches and foliage during very active foraging; often hovers while gleaning.

Voice: loud, snappy, 3–9 note song, usually beginning and ending with *chick: chick-ticha-wheeyou, chick-ticha-wheeyou-chick!*

Similar Species: *Pine Warbler* (p. 289) and *Yellow-throated Vireo* (p. 231): yellow throat. *Blue-headed Vireo* (p. 232): white "spectacles"; dark eyes; yellow highlights on wings and tail.

Best Sites: Pine Log WMA; Kennesaw Mt.; Ocmulgee NM; almost any WMA below the Fall Line; Savannah-Ogeechee Canal; Cumberland I. (HC-spring: 40); McIntosh Co. (HC-spring: 130); Glynn Co. (HC-winter: 20).

YELLOW-THROATED VIREO

Vireo flavifrons

The Yellow-throated Vireo is usually found in mature, deciduous woodlands with little or no understory, particularly tall oak or maple groves. This bird forages high above the forest floor, making observation difficult. • An unmated male will sing tirelessly as he searches for nest sites, often placing a few pieces of nest material in several locations. When a female appears, the male dazzles her with his displays and leads her on a tour of potential nest sites within his large territory. If a bond is established, they will mate and build an intricately woven, hanging nest in the forking branches of a deciduous tree. The male is a devoted partner, helping the female build the nest, incubate the eggs and rear the young.
• The Yellow-throated is North America's most colorful vireo, and it is the only vireo with a bright yellow throat and breast and a white belly. • The scientific name *flavifrons* means "yellow front."

ID: bright yellow "spectacles," "chin," throat and breast; yellow ends in a clean line; olive upperparts, except for gray rump and dark wings and tail; 2 white wing bars; gleaming white belly and undertail coverts; bluish gray legs.

Size: *L* 5½ in; *W* 9½ in.

Status: uncommon summer breeding resident statewide from February to November; no documented winter sightings.

Habitat: mature, deciduous woodlands with minimal understory.

Nesting: pair builds a hanging cup nest in the fork of a horizontal, deciduous tree branch; pair incubates 4 creamy white to pinkish eggs, with dark spots toward the larger end, for 14–15 days; each parent takes on guardianship of half the fledged young.

Feeding: forages by inspecting branches and foliage in the upper canopy; eats mostly insects; also feeds on seasonally available berries.

Voice: song is a slowly repeated series of hoarse phrases with long pauses in between: *ahweeo, eeoway, away;* calls include a throaty *heh heh heh.*

Similar Species: *Pine Warbler* (p. 289): olive yellow rump; thinner bill; faint, darkish streaking along sides; yellow belly; faint "spectacles." *White-eyed Vireo* (p. 230): white "chin" and throat; grayer head and back; white eyes. *Blue-headed Vireo* (p. 232): white "spectacles" and throat; yellow highlights on wings and tail.

Best Sites: Pine Log WMA; Newman Wetlands Center; Ocmulgee NM; Beaverdam WMA; Okefenokee NWR; Savannah-Ogeechee Canal; McIntosh Co. (HC: 32); Piedmont NWR (HC: 14).

BLUE-HEADED VIREO

Vireo solitarius

From the canopies of shady woodlands, the purposeful, liquid notes of the Blue-headed Vireo penetrate the dense foliage. This vireo prefers different habitat than many of its relatives—it is the only vireo to commonly occupy coniferous forests. It breeds throughout Canada's boreal forests and southward along the Appalachian Mountains to northern Georgia. • During courtship, male Blue-headed Vireos fluff out their yellowish flanks and bob ceremoniously to their prospective mates. When mating is complete and the eggs are in the nest, the parents become extremely quiet. Once the young hatch, however, Blue-headed parents will readily scold an intruder long before it gets close to the nest. Even so, Brown-headed Cowbirds manage to find temporarily vacated vireo nests in which to lay their eggs. As human development continues to fragment our forests, cowbirds pose an increasing threat to their Blue-headed hosts.

• The distinctive "spectacles" that frame this bird's eyes provide a good field mark. They are among the boldest of the eye rings seen on our songbirds. • Until 1997, the now newly named Blue-headed, Cassin's (*V. cassinii*) and Plumbeous (*V. plumbeus*) vireos were lumped together as one species, the Solitary Vireo. Thus, the species name, *solitarius*, for the Blue-headed Vireo.

ID: white "spectacles"; blue-gray head; 2 white wing bars; olive green upperparts; white under-parts; yellow sides and flanks; yellow highlights on dark wings and tail; stout bill; dark legs.

Size: *L* 5–6 in; *W* 9½ in.

Status: common summer breeding resident in the Mountains; uncommon breeder in the northern Piedmont but locally common in the southern Piedmont to the Fall Line; common migrant, except on the Coast; uncommon winter resident from September to May; 1 summer record from Jekyll I.

Habitat: remote, mixed coniferous-deciduous forests; also pure coniferous forests and pine plantations.

Nesting: in a horizontal fork in a coniferous tree or tall shrub; hanging, basketlike cup

nest is made of grass, roots, plant down, spider silk and cocoons; pair incubates 3–5 whitish eggs, lightly spotted with black and brown, for 12–14 days.

Feeding: gleans branches for insects; frequently hovers to pluck insects from vegetation.

Voice: *churr* call; slow, purposeful, slurred, robinlike notes with moderate pauses in between: *chu-wee, taweeto, toowip, cheerio, teeyay*; similar to Red-eyed Vireo but "thinner" notes.

Similar Species: *White-eyed Vireo* (p. 230): yellow "spectacles"; light-colored eyes. *Yellow-throated Vireo* (p. 231): yellow "spectacles" and throat.

Best Sites: Cohutta WMA; Cloudland Canyon SP; Brasstown Bald; Rabun Bald; Kennesaw Mt. (HC-fall: 22); Thomasville (HC-winter: 29).

WARBLING VIREO
Vireo gilvus

Though Warbling Vireos are common throughout most of North America, only a few have been reported during migration in Georgia. These pale-colored birds occasionally grace our forest canopies during spring and fall migration, and may turn up in any forested area, including orchards, neighborhoods and urban parks. • The Warbling Vireo lacks splashy field marks and is only readily observed when it moves from one leaf-hidden area to another. Searching treetops for this generally inconspicuous vireo may literally be a "pain in the neck," but the satisfaction of visually confirming its identity is exceptionally rewarding. • Warbling Vireos are often mistaken for other vireos that share similar, drab plumage. Even their song is easily confused with that of the female Orchard Oriole.

ID: partial, dark eye line borders white "eyebrow"; no wing bars; olive gray upperparts; greenish or yellowish flanks; white to pale gray underparts; gray crown; bluish gray legs; if there is yellow in the underparts, it is always restricted to the flanks.
Size: *L* 5–5½ in; *W* 8½ in.
Status: rare migrant statewide from April to May and from August to October, except very rare on the Coast.
Habitat: open deciduous woodlands; parks and gardens with deciduous trees.
Nesting: not known to nest in Georgia.

Feeding: gleans foliage for insects; occasionally hovers to glean insects from vegetation.
Voice: usually silent; call is a harsh nasal *eeah;* song is a long, musical warble of slurred whistles.
Similar Species: *Philadelphia Vireo* (p. 234): yellow breast, sides and flanks (yellow is strongest in throat and weakest in flanks); full, dark eye line borders white "eyebrow." *Red-eyed Vireo* (p. 235): black eye line extends to bill; blue-gray crown; red eyes. *Tennessee Warbler* (p. 276): blue-gray "cap" and nape; olive green back; slimmer bill. *Orange-crowned Warbler* (p. 277): yellow overall; slimmer bill.
Best Sites: Kennesaw Mt. (14 records); typically in scrub or thinner sections of forest.

PHILADELPHIA VIREO

Vireo philadelphicus

Although many similar-looking birds sound quite different, the Philadelphia Vireo and Red-eyed Vireo are two species that sound very similar but are somewhat easy to tell apart if you find them with your binoculars. However, managing to track down bluish green vireos among Georgia's rich green foliage is never easy. Most forest songbirds are initially identified by voice, so the Philadelphia Vireo is often overlooked because its song is almost identical to that of the more abundant Red-eyed Vireo. • This bird bears the name of the city in which this species' first scientific specimen was collected. Philadelphia was the center of America's budding scientific community in the early 1800s, and much of the study of birds and other natural sciences originated in Pennsylvania.

ID: gray "cap"; full, dark eye line borders bold, white "eyebrow"; dark olive green upperparts; pale yellow breast, sides and flanks; white belly (underparts may be completely yellow in fall); yellow color strongest on throat; robust bill.

Size: *L* 4½–5 in; *W* 8 in.

Status: variably uncommon fall migrant, mostly above the Fall Line from August to October; rare below the Fall Line in fall; rare spring migrant mostly above the Fall Line from April to May.

Habitat: open, deciduous woodlands, including urban areas and parks.

Nesting: does not nest in Georgia.

Feeding: gleans vegetation for insects; frequently hovers to glean food from foliage.

Voice: song (rarely heard in migration) is similar to that of the Red-eyed Vireo, but is usually slower, slightly higher pitched and not as variable: *Look-up way-up tree-top see-me.*

Similar Species: *Red-eyed Vireo* (p. 235): black-bordered, blue-gray "cap"; red eyes; lacks yellow breast; song is very similar. *Warbling Vireo* (p. 233): partial, dark eye line (mostly behind eye); lacks yellow breast; any yellow present strongest in flanks. *Tennessee Warbler* (p. 276): blue-gray "cap" and nape; olive green back; slimmer bill; lacks yellow breast.

Best Sites: upper half of Kennesaw Mt. (HC-fall: 3); Lake Conasauga (HC-fall: 12); Cobb Co. (HC-fall: 10).

RED-EYED VIREO

Vireo olivaceus

The Red-eyed Vireo is the undisputed champion of vocal endurance in Georgia: in spring and early summer, males sing continuously through the day. One particularly vigorous Red-eyed Vireo male holds the record for most songs delivered in a single day: approximately 21,000! This propensity for nonstop vocalizations has led to the dubious name "Preacher Bird."
• The Red-eyed Vireo adopts a particular stance when it hops up and along branches. It tends to be more hunched over than other songbirds and hops with its body diagonal to the direction of travel. • This vireo is the most common and widespread vireo in our area, and its adaptive nature has enabled it to become part of many of our communities. Red-eyed Vireos sound a lot like American Robins; beginning birders are often delighted to discover these shy birds hiding behind a familiar song. • As evidence of the widespread abundance of Red-eyeds in Georgia, more than 180 were counted in a single day in Bartow County.

ID: dark eye line; white "eyebrow"; black-bordered, blue-gray crown; olive "cheek"; olive green upperparts; white to pale gray underparts; may have yellow wash on sides, flanks and undertail coverts, especially in fall; no wing bars; red eyes (seen only at close range).
Size: *L* 6 in; *W* 10 in.
Status: common migrant and summer breeding resident statewide from March to October, less common in the extreme south.
Habitat: deciduous or mixed woodlands with a shrubby understory.

Nesting: in a horizontal fork in a deciduous tree or shrub; hanging, basketlike cup nest is made of grass, roots, spider silk and cocoons; female incubates 4 white eggs, darkly spotted at the larger end, for 11–14 days.
Feeding: gleans foliage for insects, especially caterpillars; often hovers; also eats berries.
Voice: oft-heard call is a short, scolding *neeah*; song is a continuous, variable, robinlike run of quick, short phrases with distinct pauses in between: *Look-up, way-up, tree-top, see-me, here-I-am!*
Similar Species: *Philadelphia Vireo* (p. 234): yellow breast; lacks black border on blue-gray "cap"; song is very similar but slightly higher pitched. *Warbling Vireo* (p. 233): dusky eye line does not extend to bill; lacks black border on gray "cap." *Tennessee Warbler* (p. 276): blue-gray "cap" and nape; olive green back; slimmer bill.
Best Sites: Pine Log WMA; Lake Conasauga; Rabun Bald; Lake Lanier; Piedmont NWR; Savannah-Ogeechee Canal.

BLUE JAY

Cyanocitta cristata

The large trees and bushy ornamental shrubs of our suburban neighborhoods are perfect habitat for the adaptable Blue Jay. Common wherever there are fruit-bearing plants and backyard feeding stations that are maintained with a generous supply of sunflower seeds and peanuts, this jay is one of the most recognizable songbirds. Blue Jays can appear a bit "piggish" at the feeder but they are often only storing the food in caches strategically placed around the neighborhood. • Many of the cached acorns from oaks, and other seeds, are not eaten by the jay, and thus these birds may be an important tree dispersal agent. • The Blue Jay embodies all the admirable traits and aggressive qualities of the corvid family, which also includes the magpie, crow and raven. Beautiful, resourceful and vocally diverse, the Blue Jay occasionally raids nests and bullies other feeder occupants. • Whether on its own or gathered in a mob, the Blue Jay will rarely hesitate to drive away smaller birds, squirrels or even cats when threatened. It seems there is no predator, not even the Great Horned Owl, that is too formidable for this bird to cajole or harass.

ID: blue crest; black "necklace"; black eye line; blue upperparts; white underparts; white bar and flecking on wings; dark bars and white corners on blue tail; black bill.

Size: *L* 11–12½ in; *W* 16 in.

Status: common permanent breeding resident statewide; lower numbers on barrier islands; sometimes seen in large migratory flocks from September to October.

Habitat: mixed deciduous forests, agricultural areas, scrubby fields and townsites.

Nesting: in the crotch of a tree or tall shrub; pair builds a bulky stick nest and incubates 4–5 greenish, buff or pale blue eggs, spotted with gray and brown, for 16–18 days.

Feeding: forages on the ground and among vegetation for nuts, berries, eggs, nestlings and seeds; also eats insects and carrion.

Voice: noisy, screaming *jay-jay-jay;* nasal *queedle queedle queedle-queedle* sounds a little like a muted trumpet; often imitates sounds, including calls of Red-tailed, Broad-winged and Red-shouldered Hawks.

Similar Species: none.

Best Sites: almost anywhere; Atlanta (HC-fall: 1500+); Oconee R. (HC-fall: 100+).

AMERICAN CROW

Corvus brachyrhynchos

American Crows are wary and intelligent birds that have flourished despite considerable human effort, over many generations, to reduce their numbers. As ecological generalists, crows can survive in a wide variety of habitats and conditions. In January, when crows in Georgia are busy capturing frogs and lizards in thriving wetlands, crows in southern Canada are searching the snow-covered fields for mice or carrion. • The American Crow is an impressive mimic, able to whine like a dog, cry like a child, squawk like a hen and even laugh like a human. In captivity, some crows can even repeat simple spoken words. • Many hundreds of crows may roost together on any given fall night. These aggregations of crows are known as "murders." • The American Crow's cumbersome-sounding scientific name *Corvus brachyrhynchos* is Latin for "raven with the small nose."

ID: all-black body; square-shaped tail; black bill and legs; slim, sleek head and throat; broad wings. **Size:** *L* 17–21 in; *W* 3 ft. **Status:** common permanent breeding resident statewide. **Habitat:** urban areas, agricultural fields and other open areas with scattered woodlands; also among clearings, marshes, lakes and rivers in densely forested areas. **Nesting:** in a coniferous or deciduous tree or on a utility pole; large stick-and-branch nest is lined with fur and soft plant materials; female incubates 4–6 gray-green to blue-green eggs, blotched with brown and gray, for about 18 days.

Feeding: very opportunistic; feeds on carrion, small vertebrates, other birds' eggs and nestlings, berries, seeds, invertebrates and human food waste; also visits bird feeders.

Voice: distinctive, far-carrying, repetitive *caw-caw-caw*.

Similar Species: *Fish Crow* (p. 238): small head; smaller bill; more pointed, swept back wing tips; shorter legs; relatively long tail; almost impossible to tell apart without hearing calls. *Common Raven* (p. 239): larger; wedge-shaped tail; shaggy throat; heavier bill.

Best Sites: almost anywhere; Atlanta (HC-winter: 1300+).

FISH CROW

Corvus ossifragus

Most people who come across this ebony bird quickly dismiss it as another one of those seemingly omnipresent American Crows, not realizing that it possesses a unique identity separate from that of its larger relative. Best identified by its more nasal, two-note call, *uh-oh*, the Fish Crow has adapted to survive in association with aquatic environments and seems to be expanding its range inland along large rivers and their tributaries. • A large part of the Fish Crow's continuing success is owed to its ability to eat a diverse array of foods, including carrion, insects, crustaceans, fish, seeds and fruits. Other food sources, such as the carefully guarded eggs and young of other birds, or the odorous food waste left behind by humans in awkward, concealing containers, often require this crafty bird to employ more intelligent strategies characteristic of the corvid clan. Its effective combination of problem-solving abilities, strong, dextrous feet and a nimble bill allow this bird to solve most foraging problems.

ID: all black; virtually identical to American Crow except smaller head and bill and more pointed; swept back wing tips; relatively long, square-shaped tail; best identified by voice.

Size: *L* 15½ in; *W* 3 ft.

Status: common permanent breeding resident on the Coast; locally common and increasing in the Coastal Plain and into the Piedmont; accidental in the Mountains; less common inland in winter.

Habitat: river valleys and coastal habitats, including tidal saltwater marshes, swamps, beaches, estuaries, riparian woodlands, fields and dumps near water.

Nesting: both adults probably help to build a bulky stick nest in the fork of a tree or large shrub; often nests in small, loose colonies; female incubates eggs; both adults probably help raise young.

Feeding: omnivorous scavenger; feeds on a wide variety of foods, including carrion, fish, shellfish, crayfish, crabs, insects, shrimp, eggs, seeds, nestling birds and human food waste; typically forages by walking along shorelines, in shallow water and on fields in small flocks.

Voice: calls are a nasal *carr-carr-carr* or a hoarse, double call-note *uh-oh*.

Similar Species: *American Crow* (p. 237): slightly larger; larger head and bill; slightly shorter tail; broad wings; call note is a single *cah* note. *Common Raven* (p. 239): larger; wedge-shaped tail; shaggy throat; heavier bill.

Best Sites: along the Coast or south of the Fall Line.

COMMON RAVEN

Corvus corax

Whether stealing food from a flock of gulls, harassing a soaring hawk in midair, dining from a roadside carcass or confidently strutting among campers at a park, the Common Raven is worthy of its reputation as a bold and clever bird. It is glorified in native cultures across the Northern Hemisphere as the avian embodiment of humankind. From its complex vocalizations to its occasional playful bouts of sliding down snowbanks, this raucous bird exhibits behaviors, such as playfulness, that many people once thought of as exclusively human. • Common Ravens are the largest of the passerines, or perching birds. They maintain loyal, life-long pair bonds, raising the young together and enduring everything from food scarcity to harsh weather. • Few birds occupy as large a natural range as the Common Raven. Distributed throughout the Northern Hemisphere, it is found along coastlines, in deserts, on mountaintops and even on the arctic tundra.
In Georgia it is found only in the northern mountains, breeding in Union, Towns and Rabun counties.

ID: all-black plumage; heavy, black bill; wedge-shaped tail; shaggy throat; rounded wings.
Size: *L* 17–21 in; *W* 4 ft.
Status: rare permanent breeding resident of the Mountains above 3200 ft; accidental to rare in adjacent areas.
Habitat: coniferous and mixed forests and woodlands; also townsites, campgrounds and landfills.
Nesting: on a ledge, bluff or utility pole or in a tall coniferous tree; large stick-and-branch nest is lined with fur and soft plant materials; female incubates 4–6 greenish eggs, blotched with brown or olive, for 18–21 days.
Feeding: very opportunistic; some birds forage along roadways; feeds on carrion, small vertebrates, other birds' eggs and nestlings, berries, invertebrates and human food waste.
Voice: deep, guttural, far-carrying, repetitive *craww-craww* or *quork quork;* also many other vocalizations.
Similar Species: *American Crow* (p. 237) and *Fish Crow* (p. 238): smaller; square-shaped tail; slim throat; slimmer bill; call is higher pitched.
Best Sites: near Brasstown, Hightower and Rabun balds; Chattahoochee NF (HC-winter: 5).

239

HORNED LARK

Eremophila alpestris

Horned Larks are uniquely patterned, small ground birds nearly always encountered in treeless, open country. Widespread across the plains and steppes of the Northern Hemisphere, they live throughout North America outside regions of extensive forest. They may be found in a spectrum of habitats ranging from ocean beaches and dunelands, to plowed fields, croplands, rangelands and alpine tundra. • Many Horned Larks spend their winters north of the Fall Line in Georgia, and occasionally breed in grassy pastures. They are also rare breeders and winter residents south of the Fall Line. • To escape the eye of predators, Horned Larks rely upon their disruptive light-and-dark coloring, their creeping or "strolling" foraging technique, and a low profile among the scattered grass tufts. They may not be detected until closely approached, whereupon the entire flock flushes and scatters on the breeze, to reassemble elsewhere in the vicinity. • Horned Larks are easy to see but difficult to identify because they fly off into the brush or distant fields at the approach of a vehicle. • Males perform an elaborate flight-song courtship display to attract a mate, flying high in circles before plummeting dramatically toward the Earth.

ID: *Male:* small black "horns" (rarely raised); black line under eye extends from bill to "cheek"; light yellow to white face; dull brown upperparts; black breast band; dark tail with white outer tail feathers; pale throat. *Female:* less distinctively patterned; duller plumage overall.

Size: *L* 7 in; *W* 12 in.

Status: rare summer breeding resident; uncommon to common from October to April south to Wilcox and Bulloch Co.

Habitat: extensive barren-ground and short-grass habitats from sea level to over 12,000 ft.

Nesting: a well-concealed cup nest in a shallow, often next to a rock or dried manure; nest is lined with grass, plant fibers and roots; female chooses the nest site and incubates 3–4 brown-blotched, pale gray to greenish white eggs for up to 12 days.

Feeding: gleans the ground for seeds; feeds insects to its young during the breeding season.

Voice: call is a tinkling *tsee-titi* or *zoot;* flight song is a long series of tinkling, twittered whistles.

Similar Species: *Sparrows* (pp. 313–33), *Lapland Longspur* (p. 367) and *American Pipit* (p. 272): all lack distinctive facial pattern, "horns" and solid black breast band.

Best Sites: Sod Atlanta Inc.; Atlanta Motor Speedway; Perry Super-Sod Farm; Titan Turf Farm (Bulloch Co.).

PURPLE MARTIN

Progne subis

Purple Martins once nested in natural tree hollows and cliff crevices, but with today's modern martin "condo" complexes, these birds have all but abandoned natural nest sites. To be successful in attracting these large swallows to your backyard, make sure the cavity openings are the right size for Purple Martins and place the martin condo high on a pole in a large, open area, preferably within 100 feet of your house. Sites near water, such as ponds and lakes, usually enjoy greater success in attracting martins. Remove any aggressive House Sparrows and European Starlings that may lay claim to the "martin house." The condo must be cleaned out and closed up each winter. If all goes well, a Purple Martin colony will return to your martin complex each spring, usually by mid-February. The result will be an endlessly entertaining summer spectacle as the adults spiral around the house in pursuit of flying insects and the young birds perch clumsily at the opening of their apartment cavity. • The scientific name *Progne* refers to Procne, the daughter of the king of Athens who, according to Greek mythology, was transformed into a swallow.

ID: glossy, dark blue body; slightly forked tail; pointed wings; small bill. *Male:* dark underparts. *Female:* sooty gray underparts. **Size:** *L* 7–8 in; *W* 18 in. **Status:** common breeding resident statewide from March to September.
Habitat: semi-open areas, often near water.
Nesting: communal; usually in a human-made, apartment-style birdhouse; also in a hollowed-out gourd; rarely in a tree cavity or cliff crevice; nest materials include feathers, grass, mud and vegetation; female incubates 4–5 white eggs for 15–18 days.
Feeding: mostly while in flight; usually eats flies, ants, bugs, dragonflies and mosquitoes; may also walk on the ground, taking insects and rarely berries.
Voice: rich, fluty, robinlike *pew-pew,* often heard in flight.
Similar Species: *European Starling* (p. 271): longer bill (yellow in summer); lacks forked tail. *Barn Swallow* (p. 246): deeply forked tail; buff orange to reddish brown throat; whitish to cinnamon underparts. *Tree Swallow* (p. 242): white underparts.
Best Sites: Cohutta WMA; Chattahoochee River NRA; Ocmulgee NM; Dyar Pasture WMA; Grand Bay WMA; backyard martin houses.

TREE SWALLOW

Tachycineta bicolor

Tree Swallows are our most common winter swallows, often seen frolicking over wetlands or open fields in southeast Georgia, as well as along the coastal and barrier island shores. Swarms of insects can attract dense clouds of foraging Tree Swallows, which can become hazardous if flocks form over highways. During the cool nights, huge flocks of these litle birds gather at roosts that can contain several hundred thousand birds. • Sleek Tree Swallows are expanding their breeding range into Georgia. When conditions are favorable, these busy birds are known to return to their young 10 to 20 times per hour, providing observers with numerous opportunities to watch and photograph the birds in action. • In bright spring sunshine, the iridescent back of the Tree Swallow appears dark blue, but in fall, it appears green. Unlike other North American swallows, female Tree Swallows do not acquire their full adult plumage until their second or third year.

ID: iridescent, dark blue or green head and upperparts; white underparts; no white on "cheek"; dark rump; small bill; long, pointed wings; shallowly forked tail. *Female:* slightly duller. *Immature:* brown above; white below.

Size: *L* 5½ in; *W* 14½ in.

Status: rare breeder in the Mountains and the Piedmont; abundant migrant and winter resident on the Coast from July to May.

Habitat: open areas, such as beaver ponds, marshes, lakeshores, field fencelines, townsites and open woodlands.

Nesting: in a tree cavity or nest box lined with weeds, grass and feathers; female incubates 4–7 pale pink to white eggs for up to 19 days.

Feeding: often feeds in loose flocks; catches insects on the wing, often over water; occasionally picks insects and spiders off the ground; in winter eats seeds and berries, especially wax myrtle fruit.

Voice: alarm call is a metallic, buzzy *klweet;* song is a liquid, chattering twitter.

Similar Species: *Bank Swallow* (p. 244): brown upperparts and band across chest. *Northern Rough-winged Swallow* (p. 243): brown upperparts and dingy underparts, females difficult to distinguish. *Purple Martin* (p. 241): female has sooty gray underparts; male is dark blue overall. *Eastern Kingbird* (p. 226): larger; white-tipped tail; longer bill; dark gray to blackish upperparts. *Barn Swallow* (p. 246): buff orange to reddish brown throat; deeply forked tail.

Best Sites: rare breeders at Arrowhead Wildlife Education Center, E.L. Huie, Lake Chatuge and Carters, Folly, Hartwell, Russell and Juliette lakes; coast and barrier island shores in winter; Sapelo I. (HC-winter: 500,000).

NORTHERN ROUGH-WINGED SWALLOW

Stelgidopteryx serripennis

The inconspicuous Northern Rough-winged Swallow typically nests in sandy banks along rivers and streams, enjoying its own private piece of waterfront. At Lake Lanier, it nests in the crevices of the rocky cliffs below Buford Dam. In the Coastal Plain, it will use vertical cuts on back roads, often far from water, to dig out nesting burrows. • This swallow is usually seen in single pairs, but it doesn't mind joining a crowd of other swallow species while gulping down insects when feeding on the wing. In the wheeling flocks of feeding birds, the Northern Rough-winged Swallow is often completely overlooked among its similar-looking cousins. The Rough-wing is most likely to be feeding over water, picking off insects on or near the water's surface. • Unlike other swallows, male Northern Rough-wings have curved barbs along the outer edge of their primary wing feathers. The purpose of this saw-toothed edge remains a mystery, but it may be used to produce sound during courtship displays. The ornithologist who initially named this bird must have been very impressed with its wings: *Stelgidopteryx* means "scraper wing" and *serripennis* means "saw feather."

ID: brown upperparts; light, brownish gray underparts; small bill; dark "cheek"; pale throat; dark rump. *In flight:* long, pointed wings; notched tail. **Size:** *L* 5½ in; *W* 14 in.

Status: uncommon to locally common breeding resident statewide from February to November; breeds to southwestern Georgia, Sapelo I. and Cumberland I.; rare in southeastern Georgia.

Habitat: open and semi-open areas, including fields and open woodlands, usually near water; also gravel pits.

Nesting: occasionally in small colonies; pair excavates a long burrow in a steep, earthen bank; sometimes reuses a kingfisher burrow, rodent burrow or other land crevice; the end of the burrow is lined with leaves and dry grass; mostly the female incubates 4–8 white eggs for 12–16 days.

Feeding: catches flying insects on the wing; occasionally eats insects from the ground; drinks while flying.

Voice: generally quiet; occasionally a quick, short, squeaky *brrrtt*.

Similar Species: *Bank Swallow* (p. 244): dark breast band. *Tree Swallow* (p. 242): dark, iridescent, bluish to greenish upperparts; clean, white underparts. *Cliff Swallow* (p. 245): brown and blue upperparts; buff forehead and rump patch.

Best Sites: Lake Lanier; Carters L.; Brasstown Bald; Dyar Pasture WMA; Titan Turf Farm (Bulloch Co.); Macon (HC-fall: 400).

BANK SWALLOW

Riparia riparia

The highly social Bank Swallow is one of the most broadly distributed members of the swallow family and is found throughout North America and northern Eurasia. Even so, this bird is uncommon in our region. Check sod farms and coastal lowlands for this swift, colorful bird in late summer and during its lengthy fall migration. • Small flocks of migrating Bank Swallows will sometimes gather along our sandy shores to preen each other in a communal dust bath. They will also squat on the ground and spread out their wings while resting and sunbathing. • In medieval Europe, it was believed that swallows spent winter in the mud at the bottom of swamps because they were not seen at that time of year. In those days, it was beyond imagination that these birds might fly south for the winter. • *Riparia* is from the Latin for "riverbank," which is a common nest site for this bird.

ID: brown upperparts; light underparts; brown breast band; long, pointed wings; shallowly forked tail; gray-brown crown; dark "cheek"; small legs.
Size: *L* 5½ in; *W* 13 in.
Status: statewide migrant, uncommon from March to June and locally common from July to October; few Mountain records.
Habitat: steep banks, lakeshore bluffs and gravel pits.
Nesting: does not nest in Georgia.

Feeding: catches flying insects; drinks on the wing.
Voice: twittering chatter: *speed-zeet speed-zeet.*
Similar Species: *Northern Rough-winged Swallow* (p. 243): lacks dark, defined breast band. *Tree Swallow* (p. 242): dark, iridescent, bluish to greenish upperparts; lacks dark breast band. *Cliff Swallow* (p. 245): brown and blue upperparts; buff forehead and rump; lacks dark breast band.
Best Sites: Arrowhead Wildlife Education Center; E.L. Huie; Altamaha NWR; Lake Oconee; Harris Neck NWR (HC-fall: 1000s).

CLIFF SWALLOW

Petrochelidon pyrrhonota

If the Cliff Swallow were to be renamed in the 20th century, it would probably be called "Bridge Swallow," because so many bridges over rivers and lakes have a colony living under them. In recent decades, Cliff Swallows have expanded their range across eastern North America, taking advantage of nest sites provided by highway culverts and bridges. Although most Cliff Swallows in Georgia are seen during migration, they currently nest at more than 30 sites and are expanding their range to the south and east. • Master mud masons, Cliff Swallows roll mud into balls with their bills and press the pellets together to form their characteristic gourd-shaped nests. Brooding parents peer out of the circular neck of the nest, their gleaming eyes watching the world go by. Their buff forehead patch warns intruders that somebody is home. • Agricultural fields and marshes are favorite foraging sites for Cliff Swallows, which catch insects on the wing. Watch for their square tail, cinnamon-colored rump patch, cinnamon to blackish throat, and distinctive flight pattern: they ascend with rapid wing strokes, then glide gracefully down. • In winter, be on the lookout for the Cave Swallow, a close relative of the Cliff Swallow. This "buffy throated" swallow has recently been seen in south Georgia, possibly as a vagrant from Mexico and Texas.

ID: orangy rump; buff forehead; blue-gray head and wings; rusty nape, "cheek" and throat; buff breast; white belly; spotted undertail coverts; nearly square tail.

Size: *L* 5½ in; *W* 13½ in.

Status: uncommon migrant north of the Fall Line from March to May and from June to November; rare in the Coastal Plain and on the Coast; breeds to the Fall Line and into Crisp Co. and Sumter Co.

Habitat: steep banks, cliffs, bridges and buildings, often near watercourses.

Nesting: colonial; under a bridge or on a cliff or building; often under the eaves of a barn; pair builds a gourd-shaped mud nest with a small opening near the bottom; pair incubates 4–5 brown-spotted, white to pinkish eggs for 14–16 days.

Feeding: forages over water, fields and marshes; catches flying insects on the wing; occasionally eats berries; drinks on the wing.

Voice: twittering chatter: *churrr-churrr;* also an alarm call: *nyew.*

Similar Species: *Barn Swallow* (p. 246): deeply forked tail; dark rump; usually has rust-colored underparts and forehead. *Other swallows* (pp. 241–46): lack buff forehead and rump patch.

Best Sites: bridges over Etowah and Ocmulgee Rivers, West Point L., Oconee and Jackson lakes; Troup Co. (HC-colony: 150); Greene Co. (HC-fall: 200+).

BARN SWALLOW

Hirundo rustica

Barn Swallows are the most abundant and wide-ranging swallows on the globe. They are very familiar birds to most of us because they usually build their nests on human-made structures. Barn Swallows once nested on cliffs and in entrances to caves, but their cup-shaped mud nests are now found under house eaves, in barns and boathouses, under bridges or on any other structure that provides shelter. • Unfortunately, not everyone appreciates nesting Barn Swallows—the young can be very messy—and people often scrape Barn Swallow nests off buildings just as the nesting season begins. However, these graceful birds are natural pest controllers, and their close association with urban areas and tolerance for human activity affords us the wonderful opportunity to observe and study the normally secretive reproductive cycle of birds. • Barn Swallows are the only swallows with deeply forked "swallow tails" found in Georgia. • *Hirundo* is Latin for "swallow," and *rustica* refers to this bird's preference for rural habitats.

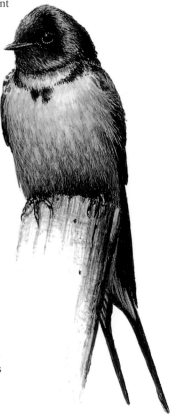

ID: long, deeply forked tail; rufous throat and forehead; blue-black upperparts; rust- to buff-colored underparts; long, pointed wings.
Size: *L* 7 in; *W* 15 in.
Status: summer breeding resident and migrant from March to November (common north of Fall Line, locally common south of the Fall Line to Okefenokee NWR and Cumberland I.); absent in southeastern Georgia in droughts; accidental in winter.
Habitat: open rural and urban areas where bridges, culverts and buildings are found near rivers, lakes, marshes or ponds.
Nesting: singly or in small, loose colonies; on a vertical or horizontal building structure under a suitable overhang, on a bridge or in a culvert; half or full cup nest is made of mud and grass or straw; pair incubates 4–7 white eggs, spotted with brown, for 13–17 days.
Feeding: catches flying insects on the wing.
Voice: continuous, twittering chatter: *zip-zip-zip;* also *kvick-kvick.*
Similar Species: *Cliff Swallow* (p. 245): squared tail; buff rump and forehead; pale underparts. *Purple Martin* (p. 241): shallowly forked tail; male is completely blue-black; female has sooty gray underparts. *Tree Swallow* (p. 242): clean, white underparts; notched tail.
Best Sites: open country and around farms; Jekyll I. (HC-fall: 5800).

CAROLINA CHICKADEE

Poecile carolinensis

The Carolina Chickadee is a friendly little bird that frequently bustles into backyard feeding stations. When watching this busy bird pluck up a sunflower seed with its tiny bill, it's hard to imagine that this same bill is used to excavate a nesting cavity. But sure enough, come breeding season, the Carolina Chickadee can be found hammering out a hollow in a rotting tree. Occasionally chickadees also nest in abandoned woodpecker holes or nest boxes. • Outside of the breeding season, family groups of chickadees often join the company of foraging mixed-species flocks that consist of titmice, warblers, vireos, kinglets, nuthatches, creepers and small woodpeckers. • Like some woodpeckers and nuthatches, the Carolina Chickadee hoards food for later seasons when food may become scarce. Keeping a bird feeder consistently stocked with sunflower seeds and peanut butter may not only provide you with hours of great birding, but may also help these endearing birds survive unexpected food shortages.

ID: black "cap" and "bib"; white "cheeks" and underparts; gray upperparts; buffy flanks. **Size:** *L* 4¾ in; *W* 7½ in. **Status:** common year-round resident statewide.
Habitat: deciduous and mixed woods, riparian woodlands, groves and isolated shade trees; frequents urban areas.
Nesting: adults excavate or enlarge the interior of a natural tree cavity; may also use a nest box or woodpecker cavity; cavity is lined with soft plant material and animal hair; female incubates 5–8 finely speckled white eggs for 11–14 days; pair raises the young.

Feeding: a variety of insects, seeds and berries are gleaned from vegetation; may hawk for insects, hang upside down on branches to glean items or glean while hovering; may visit seed and suet feeders. **Voice:** whistling song has 4 clear notes sounding like *fee-bee fee-bay.*
Similar Species: *White-breasted Nuthatch* (p. 250): slightly larger; all-white face; longer, pointed bill; often climbs down trees head first. *Blackpoll Warbler* (p. 293): breeding male has a black throat stripe (instead of "bib") and black streaks on underparts.
Best Sites: suburban and rural areas and backyard feeders statewide; Atlanta (HC-winter: 782).

TUFTED TITMOUSE

Baeolophus bicolor

This bird's amusing feeding antics and its insatiable appetite keep curious observers entertained at bird feeders. Grasping an acorn or sunflower seed with its tiny feet, the dexterous Tufted Titmouse strikes its dainty bill repeatedly against the hard outer coating, exposing the inner seed. • A breeding pair of Tufted Titmice will maintain their bond throughout the year, even when joining small, multispecies flocks for the cold winter months. The titmouse family bond is so strong that the young from one breeding season will often stay with their parents long enough to help them with nesting and feeding duties the following year. In late winter, mating pairs break from their flocks to search for nesting cavities and soft lining material. • If you are fortunate enough to have titmice living in your area, you might attract nesting pairs by setting out your own hair that has accumulated in a hairbrush. There is a good chance that these curious birds will gladly incorporate your offering into the construction of their nest, allowing you the pleasure of knowing you are helping to keep titmice eggs and young as snug as can be.

ID: gray crest and upperparts; black forehead; white underparts; buffy flanks.
Size: *L* 6–6½ in; *W* 10 in.
Status: common year-round resident statewide.
Habitat: deciduous and coniferous woodlands, groves and suburban parks with large, mature trees.
Nesting: in a natural cavity or woodpecker cavity lined with soft vegetation and animal hair; female may be fed by the male from courtship to time of hatching; female incubates 5–6 finely dotted, white eggs for 12–14 days; both adults and occasionally a "helper" raise the young.
Feeding: forages on the ground and in trees, often hanging upside down like a chickadee; eats insects, supplemented with seeds, nuts and fruits; will eat seeds and suet from feeders.
Voice: noisy, scolding call, like that of a chickadee; song is a whistled *peter peter* or *peter peter peter*.
Similar Species: none.
Best Sites: woodlands; backyard feeders.

RED-BREASTED NUTHATCH

Sitta canadensis

The Red-breasted Nuthatch looks a lot like a red rocket as it streaks toward a neighborhood bird feeder from the cover of a coniferous tree. The nuthatch ejects empty shells left behind by other birds and then selects its own meal before speeding off, never lingering longer than it takes to pick up a seed. • Red-breasted Nuthatches occasionally join in on bird waves—groups of warblers, chickadees, kinglets, titmice and small woodpeckers that often forage together through woodlands in winter or during migration. Nuthatches stand out from other songbirds because of their unusual body form and their habit of moving headfirst down tree trunks. Their loud, nasal *yank-yank-yank* calls, which are frequently heard in spring, are also distinctive. • These long-distance migrants are no strangers to travel. Vagrant Red-breasted Nuthatches occasionally show up in Europe, making them the only members of the nuthatch family known to have crossed the Atlantic Ocean. • *Sitta* means "nuthatch" in Greek, and *canadensis* refers to this bird's partially Canadian distribution. • In recent years the Red-breasted Nuthatch has nested in Rabun, Union and Fannin counties in Georgia.

ID: rusty underparts; gray-blue upperparts; white "eyebrow"; black eye line and "cap"; straight bill; short tail; white "cheek." *Male:* deeper rust on breast; black crown. *Female:* light red wash on breast; dark gray crown.
Size: *L* 4½ in; *W* 8½ in.
Status: irregular migrant and winter resident north of the Fall Line from September to May; uncommon in the Coastal Plain and the Coast in "irruption" years; rare breeder in the Mountains.
Habitat: *Breeding:* old-growth pine-hemlock forests. *In migration* and *winter:* around conifers and mixed woodlands, especially near bird feeders.

Nesting: excavates a cavity or uses an abandoned woodpecker nest; usually smears the entrance with pitch; nest is made of bark shreds, grass and fur; female incubates 5–6 brown-spotted, white eggs for about 12 days.
Feeding: forages down trees while probing under loose bark for larval and adult invertebrates; eats pine and spruce seeds in winter; often seen at feeders.
Voice: call is a slow, continually repeated, nasal *eenk eenk eenk,* higher than the White-breasted Nuthatch; also a short *tsip.*
Similar Species: *White-breasted Nuthatch* (p. 250) and *Brown-headed Nuthatch* (p. 251): lack black eye line and red underparts; White-breasted Nuthatch is larger.
Best Sites: Rabun Bald; Cohutta WMA; Burrell's Ford Rd.; old-growth pine-hemlock forests in Rabun Co. and Union Co.; Rabun Co. (HC-winter: 18); Sapelo I. (HC-winter: 36); Glynn Co. (HC-winter: 34).

WHITE-BREASTED NUTHATCH

Sitta carolinensis

Seeing a White-breasted Nuthatch calling repeatedly while clinging to the underside of a branch is an odd sight to a novice birder. Moving headfirst down a tree trunk, the White-breasted Nuthatch forages for invertebrates, sometimes pausing to survey its surroundings and occasionally issuing a noisy call. Unlike woodpeckers and creepers, nuthatches do not use their tails to brace themselves against tree trunks—nuthatches grasp the tree through foot power alone.
• Nuthatches are presumably named for their habit of wedging seeds and nuts into crevices and hacking them open with their bills. • Although the White-breasted Nuthatch is a regular visitor to most backyard feeders, it stays around just long enough to grab a seed and then dash off. Only an offering of suet can persuade this tiny bird to remain in a single spot for any length of time.
• The scientific name *carolinensis* means "of Carolina"—the first specimen was collected in South Carolina.

ID: white underparts and face; gray-blue back; rusty undertail coverts; short tail; straight bill; short legs. *Male:* black "cap." *Female:* dark gray "cap." **Size:** *L* 5½–6 in; *W* 11 in.

Status: locally common year-round resident, except rare in the southeast and on the Coast.
Habitat: mixedwood forests, woodlots and backyards.
Nesting: in a natural cavity or an abandoned woodpecker nest in a large deciduous tree; female lines the cavity with bark, grass, fur and feathers; female incubates 5–8 white eggs, spotted with reddish brown, for 12–14 days.
Feeding: forages down trees headfirst in search of larval and adult invertebrates; also eats nuts and seeds; regularly visits feeders.

Voice: calls include *ha-ha-ha ha-ha-ha, ank ank* and *ip;* song is a fast, nasal *yank-hank yank-hank,* lower than the Red-breasted Nuthatch.
Similar Species: *Brown-headed Nuthatch* (p. 251): brown "cap"; white spot on nape. *Red-breasted Nuthatch* (p. 249): black eye line; rusty underparts. *Carolina Chickadee* (p. 247): black "bib"; smaller bill.
Best Sites: Lake Winfield Scott RA; Cloudland Canyon SP; any mountain with hardwoods; Kennesaw Mt.; Blairsville (HC-winter: 77).

BROWN-HEADED NUTHATCH

Sitta pusilla

These birds spend most of their lives flitting about in pine woodlands, foraging upside down and exchanging contact calls in small family groups. During the breeding season, when adult pairs break away from larger groups to establish small breeding territories, a nonbreeding male may join the pair. This "helper" aids in excavating the nest cavity, gathering the soft nest lining or feeding the nestlings. • Like other nuthatches, this species is commonly seen foraging in larger, multispecies flocks that may include chickadees, Pine Warblers, titmice or woodpeckers. • Close observation of Brown-headed Nuthatches reveals a remarkable mechanical advantage—they will often hold a loose slab of bark in their bills for use as a prying tool. These ingenious birds then use the tool to lift fastened bark from the tree, revealing the tasty spiders or the juicy larva of a wood-boring beetle hiding underneath.

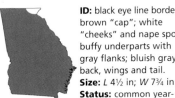

ID: black eye line borders brown "cap"; white "cheeks" and nape spot; buffy underparts with gray flanks; bluish gray back, wings and tail.
Size: *L* 4½ in; *W* 7¾ in.
Status: common year-round resident statewide, except absent from most of the Blue Ridge Mountains.
Habitat: open and mixed mature pine woodlands.
Nesting: doesn't nest above 2200 ft; pair excavates a nest cavity in a dead pine tree; may use existing cavities; cavity is lined with softer materials; male feeds female as she incubates 4–7 creamy white eggs with purple-red markings for 13–15 days; both parents, and often an additional helping male, help to raise young; may raise two broods.
Feeding: pine seeds and insects are found by foraging along tree branches and trunks;

commonly seen walking head first down tree trunks; males may forage lower on tree; seeds often stored under pine bark for later retrieval.
Voice: repeated double call note has a squeaky quality, sounds like a bathtub rubber duckie; nasal, twittering *bit bit bit* call often given by foraging flocks.
Similar Species: *Red-breasted Nuthatch* (p. 249): has black crown and eye line with white "eyebrow" and "cheeks"; rusty red to orange underparts. *White-breasted Nuthatch* (p. 250): larger; white face; male has dark stripe on crown. *Carolina Chickadee* (p. 247): black "bib"; smaller bill.
Best Sites: mature pine forests in the Piedmont and the Coastal Plain; Newman Wetlands Center; Piedmont NWR/Rum Creek WMA (HC-winter: 360); Lake Lanier; Savannah-Ogeechee Canal.

BROWN CREEPER
Certhia americana

The cryptic Brown Creeper is never easy to find. Inhabiting coniferous and mixed forests in winter, it often goes unnoticed until a flake of bark suddenly takes the shape of a bird. If a creeper is frightened, it will freeze and flatten itself against a tree trunk, becoming even more difficult to see. • Unlike nuthatches, the Brown Creeper feeds by slowly spiraling up a tree trunk, searching for hidden invertebrates. When it reaches the upper branches, the creeper floats down to the base of a neighboring tree to begin another foraging ascent. Its long, stiff tail feathers prop it up against vertical tree trunks as it hitches its way skyward. • Like the call of the Golden-crowned Kinglet, the thin whistle of the Brown Creeper is so high pitched that many birders often fail to hear it. To increase the confusion, the creeper's song often takes on the boisterous quality of a warbler's song. • There are many species of creepers in Europe and Asia, but the Brown Creeper is the only member of its family found in North America. • Not surprisingly, *Certhia* is Greek for "tree creeper."

ID: brown back with buffy white streaks; white "eyebrow" and underparts; downcurved bill; long, pointed tail feathers; rusty rump.
Size: L 5–5½ in; W 7½ in.
Status: uncommon migrant and winter resident statewide from September to May; rare in the extreme south.
Habitat: mature deciduous, coniferous and mixed forests and woodlands, especially in wet areas with large, dead trees; also found near bogs.
Nesting: not known to nest in Georgia, but potentially could nest in old-growth, white pine–hemlock forest in Rabun Co.
Feeding: hops up tree trunks and large limbs, probing loose bark for adult and larval invertebrates.
Voice: call is a high *tseee:* song is a faint, high-pitched *trees-trees-trees see the trees.*
Similar Species: *Nuthatches* (pp. 249–51): gray-blue back; straight or slightly upturned bill; white nape patch on Brown-headed. *Woodpeckers* (pp. 207–14): straight bills; lack brown back streaking.
Best Sites: riparian hardwood areas; Kennesaw Mt.; Lake Lanier; Atlanta (HC: 34).

CAROLINA WREN

Thryothorus ludovicianus

The energetic and cheerful Carolina Wren can be shy and retiring, often hiding deep inside dense shrubbery. The best way to view this large wren is to wait until it sits on a conspicuous perch and unleashes its impressive song. Pairs perform lively "duets" at any time of day and in any season. The duet often begins with introductory chatter by the female, followed by innumerable ringing variations of *tea-kettle tea-kettle tea-kettle tea* from her mate. • Watch for Carolina Wrens creeping along tree trunks similar to creepers and nuthatches or flitting near the ground in search of food. These birds seem to appear everywhere, in both urban gardens and remote woodlands. They readily nest in the brushy thickets of an overgrown backyard or in an obscure nook or crevice in a house or barn. Carolina Wrens can make do with just about any nesting cavity, including tin cans, forgotten boots and empty plant pots! • If conditions are favorable, two or three broods may be raised in a single season. • Backyard birders can provide mealworms as a "treat" for nesting wrens.

ID: long, prominent, white "eyebrow"; rusty brown upperparts; rich, buff-colored underparts; white throat; slightly downcurved bill.
Size: *L* 5½ in; *W* 7½ in.
Status: common year-round resident statewide.
Habitat: dense forest undergrowth, especially shrubby tangles and thickets.
Nesting: pair builds a dome nest, either in open cavities or unused garden nooks; female incubates 4–5 creamy white eggs, flecked with rusty brown, for 12–16 days; pair raises the young.
Feeding: usually forages in pairs on the ground and among vegetation; eats mostly insects and other invertebrates; also takes berries, fruits and seeds; will visit bird feeders for peanuts and suet.
Voice: loud, repetitious *tea-kettle tea-kettle tea-kettle tea* may be heard at any time of day or year; female often chatters while male sings.
Similar Species: *House Wren* (p. 254) and *Winter Wren* (p. 255): lack prominent, white "eyebrow." *Marsh Wren* (p. 257): black, triangular back patch is streaked with white; prefers marsh habitat. *Sedge Wren* (p. 256): dark crown and back are streaked with white; pale, indistinct "eyebrow."
Best Sites: urban or rural sites.

253

HOUSE WREN

Troglodytes aedon

The House Wren will undoubtedly give away its presence with a loud, distinctive chatter if you pass close by. Hearing a House Wren is one thing, but getting a good look at this energetic little bird is quite another. It often hides among tangled bushes and brush piles, moving rapidly from one location to another, sending birders crashing through the brambles in pursuit. • These joyful little birds spend the winter in Georgia, but most move on to nest farther north. A few House Wrens breed in the mountainous regions of northern Georgia, choosing small cavities in standing dead trees or custom-made nest boxes in backyard gardens. Sometimes even empty flowerpots or vacant drainpipes are deemed suitable as nest sites, provided insect prey is abundant. Occasionally, you may find a nest site packed full of twigs and then abandoned. Male wrens often build numerous nests, which later serve as decoys or "dummy" nests. • In Greek mythology, Zeus transformed Aedon, the queen of Thebes, into a nightingale. The wonderfully warbled song of the House Wren is somewhat similar to a nightingale's.

ID: brown upperparts; fine, dark barring on upperwings and lower back; faint, pale "eyebrow" and eye ring; short, upraised tail is finely barred with black; whitish throat; whitish to buff underparts; faintly barred flanks.

Size: *L* 4½–5 in; *W* 6 in.

Status: uncommon year-round resident, breeding south to Fall Line; uncommon migrant and winter resident statewide from September to May.

Habitat: thickets and shrubby openings in or at the edge of deciduous or mixed woodlands; often in shrubs and thickets near buildings.

Nesting: in a natural cavity or abandoned woodpecker nest; also in a nest box or other artificial cavity; nest of sticks and grass is lined with feathers, fur and other soft materials; female incubates 6–8 white eggs, heavily dotted with reddish brown, for 12–15 days.

Feeding: gleans the ground and vegetation for insects, especially beetles, caterpillars, grasshoppers and spiders.

Voice: song is a smooth, running, bubbly warble: *tsi-tsi-tsi-tsi oodle-oodle-oodle-oodle*, lasting about 2–3 seconds.

Similar Species: *Winter Wren* (p. 255): smaller; darker overall; much shorter, stubby tail; prominent, dark barring on flanks. *Sedge Wren* (p. 256): faint white streaking on dark crown and back.

Best Sites: *Winter:* often observed when "pishing" shrubby habitats in the Coastal Plain.

WINTER WREN

Troglodytes troglodytes

Winter Wrens boldly announce their claims to patches of moist coniferous woodland in winter and early spring; here, they often make their homes in the green moss and gnarled, upturned roots of decomposing tree trunks. • The song of the Winter Wren is distinguished by its explosive delivery, melodious, bubbly tone and extended duration. Few other singers can sustain their songs for up to 10 music-packed seconds. When the Winter Wren is not singing or nesting, it skulks through the forest understory, quietly probing the myriad nooks and crannies for spiders and invertebrates. • While the female raises the young, the male wren brings food to the nest and defends the territory through song. At night, he sleeps away from his family in an unfinished nest. • *Troglodytes* is Greek for "creeping in holes" or "cave dweller." • The Winter Wren is the only North American wren that is also found across Europe and Asia, where it is a common garden bird known simply as a "Wren."

ID: very short, stubby, upraised tail; fine, pale buff "eyebrow"; dark brown upperparts; lighter brown underparts; prominent, dark barring on flanks.
Size: *L* 4 in; *W* 5½ in.
Status: rare and local summer breeder in the Blue Ridge Mountains, particularly on Brasstown Bald; uncommon winter resident from September to May (less common in the south).
Habitat: tangled brush piles and woodland thickets, often near lakes or riparian areas.
Nesting: rare breeder in Georgia; nests in a natural cavity, under bark or under upturned tree roots; bulky nest of twigs, moss, grass and fur; male frequently builds up to 4 "dummy" nests prior to egg laying;

female incubates 6–7 sparsely speckled, white eggs for up to 16 days.
Feeding: forages on the ground and on trees for beetles, wood-boring insects and other invertebrates.
Voice: call is a sharp *chip-chip;* song is a warbled, tinkling series of quick trills and twitters, often more than 8 seconds long.
Similar Species: *House Wren* (p. 254): tail is longer than legs; paler overall; less conspicuous barring on flanks. *Carolina Wren* (p. 253): much larger; long, bold, white "eyebrow"; long tail. *Marsh Wren* (p. 257): white streaking on black back; bold, white "eyebrow." *Sedge Wren* (p. 256): white streaking on black back and crown; longer tail; paler underparts.
Best Sites: *Breeding:* Rabun Bald; Brasstown Bald; Cooper Creek; Tray Mt. *Winter:* Kennesaw Mt.; Chattahoochee NRA; Newman Wetlands Center; Atlanta (HC-winter: 42).

255

SEDGE WREN

Cistothorus platensis

Like most wrens, Sedge Wrens are secretive and difficult to observe. They are the least familiar of all our wrens because they keep themselves well concealed in dense stands of sedges and tall, wet grass. Sedge Wrens are also less loyal to specific sites than other wrens and may totally disappear from an area after a few years. Their transient nature may have to do with their unstable habitat, which changes annually with natural flooding and drying cycles. • Though Sedge Wrens breed northwest of Kentucky and Virginia, they are known for spending summers outside of their breeding range. Occasionally, these wrens are heard in early spring or summer, belting out a courtship song under the Georgian sun, but they are more regularly found as winter residents in our state, mostly along the Coast and in the Coastal Plain. • The scientific name *platensis* refers to the Rio de la Plata in Argentina, where another isolated population of this wren is found. • This bird used to be known as "Short-billed Marsh Wren" until the name was changed to emphasize habitat differences between it and the similar Marsh Wren.

ID: short, narrow tail (often upraised); faint, pale "eyebrow"; dark crown and back are faintly streaked with white; barring on wing coverts; whitish underparts with buff orange sides, flanks and undertail coverts.

Size: L 4–4½ in; W 5½ in.

Status: uncommon migrant and winter resident inland from August to May; rare north of the Fall Line; uncommon in winter on the Coast.

Habitat: brackish or freshwater sedge meadows; wet, grassy fields; marshes, bogs and beaver ponds; abandoned, wet fields with dense weeds or grass; power line cuts; pine savannahs.

Nesting: does not nest in Georgia.

Feeding: forages low in dense vegetation, where it picks and probes for adult and larval insects and spiders; occasionally catches flying insects.

Voice: call is a sharp *chat* or *chep;* song is a few short, staccato notes followed by a rattling trill: *chap-chap-chap-chap, chap, churr-r-r-r-r.*

Similar Species: *Marsh Wren* (p. 257): broad, conspicuous white "eyebrow"; prominent white streaking on black back; unstreaked crown; prefers cattail marshes. *Winter Wren* (p. 255): darker overall; shorter, stubby tail; unstreaked crown. *House Wren* (p. 254): unstreaked, dark brown crown and back.

Best Sites: Eufaula NWR (HC: 33); Grand Bay WMA; Paulks Pasture WMA; Altamaha NWR; salt marshes along the Coast; Sapelo I. (HC: 36).

MARSH WREN

Cistothorus palustris

Fueled by newly emerged aquatic insects, the Marsh Wren zips about in short bursts through the tall grasses and cattails that surround wetlands. This expert hunter catches flying insects with lightning speed, but don't expect to see the Marsh Wren in action—it is a reclusive bird that prefers to remain hidden deep within its dense marshland habitat. A patient observer might be rewarded with a brief glimpse of a Marsh Wren, but it is more likely that this bird's distinctive song, reminiscent of an old-fashioned treadle sewing machine, will inform you of its presence. • The Marsh Wren occasionally destroys the nests and eggs of other Marsh Wrens and other marsh-nesting songbirds such as the Red-winged Blackbird. Other birds are usually prevented from doing the same, because the Marsh Wren's globe nest keeps the eggs well hidden, and several decoy nests help to divert predators from the real nest. • The scientific name *palustris* is Latin for "marsh." This bird was formerly known as "Long-billed Marsh Wren." • The gray subspecies (*C. p. griseus*) breeds in the salt marshes of the Coast. The browner northern subspecies (*C. p. palustris*) is an uncommon migrant and winter resident inland and a common winter resident on the Coast.

ID: white "chin" and belly; white to light brown upperparts; black triangle on upper back is streaked with white; bold, white "eyebrow"; unstreaked brown crown; long, thin, downcurved bill.

Size: *L* 5 in; *W* 6 in.

Status: common year-round resident, breeding in salt marshes of the Coast; northern subspecies is an uncommon migrant inland but common winter resident on the Coast from August to May.

Habitat: freshwater, saltwater and brackish wetlands surrounded by tall grass, bulrushes or cattails interspersed with open water; occasionally in tall grass-sedge marshes.

Nesting: in brackish or salt marshes among cattails or tall emergent vegetation; globe-like nest is woven from cattails, bulrushes, weeds and grass and lined with cattail down; female incubates 4–6 white to pale brown eggs, heavily dotted with dark brown, for 12–16 days.

Feeding: gleans vegetation and flycatches for adult aquatic invertebrates, especially dragonflies and damselflies.

Voice: rapid, rattling, staccato warble sounds like an old-fashioned treadle sewing machine; call is a harsh *chek*.

Similar Species: *Sedge Wren* (p. 256): smaller; streaked crown. *House Wren* (p. 254): faint "eyebrow"; black back lacks white streaking. *Carolina Wren* (p. 253): larger; buff underparts; black back lacks white streaking.

Best Sites: salt marshes from Ft. Pulaski NM to Cumberland I.; Sapelo I. (HC-winter: 93); Phinizy Swamp Nature Park (HC-winter: 40).

GOLDEN-CROWNED KINGLET

Regulus satrapa

While they refuel on insects and berries, Golden-crowned Kinglets use tree branches as swings and trapezes, flashing their regal crowns and constantly flicking their tiny wings. Not much larger than hummingbirds, Golden-crowned Kinglets can be difficult to spot as they flit and hover among coniferous treetops. • Binoculars are a must to distinguish tiny Golden-crowned Kinglets from similar-sized Ruby-crowned Kinglets. If the orange crown of the male, or the yellow crown of the female, is not readily seen, look to the eyes: Golden-crowned Kinglets have a prominent white eye-stripe whereas Ruby-crowned Kinglets sport a white eye ring. • In the northern part of their range, Golden-crowned Kinglets manage to survive cold winter weather by roosting together in groups or in empty squirrel nests. Like chickadees, these birds can lower their body temperatures at night to conserve energy. • The Golden-crowned Kinglet's extremely high-pitched call is a very faint *tsee-tsee-tsee* and is often lost in the slightest woodland breeze. • Recent summer sightings in the northeastern Mountains suggests possible breeding in the mature coniferous forests of Rabun Bald, Burrell's Ford and Cooper Creek, but this has yet to be confirmed.

ID: olive back; darker wings and tail; light underparts; dark "cheek"; 2 white wing bars; black eye line; white "eyebrow"; crown has black border. *Male:* reddish orange crown. *Female:* yellow crown.
Size: *L* 4 in; *W* 7 in.
Status: common winter resident statewide from September to May; more irruptive in the southern Coastal Plain and the Coast.
Habitat: coniferous, deciduous and mixed forests and woodlands.
Nesting: not known to nest in Georgia.

Feeding: gleans and hovers among the forest canopy for insects, berries and occasionally sap.
Voice: call is a very high-pitched *tsee-tsee-tsee*; song is a faint, high-pitched, accelerating *tsee-tsee-tsee-tsee, why do you shilly-shally?*
Similar Species: *Ruby-crowned Kinglet* (p. 259): bold, broken, white eye ring; crown lacks black border. *Brown Creeper* (p. 252): song is extremely similar.
Best Sites: Atlanta (HC: 600); Kennesaw Mt. (HC: 41); St. Catherines I. (HC: 71).

258

RUBY-CROWNED KINGLET

Regulus calendula

The Ruby-crowned Kinglet's rolling, three-part song, reminiscent of a car starting up, echoes through the coniferous woodlands in winter and early spring. The male kinglet erects his brilliant, red crown and sings to impress prospective mates during courtship. Throughout most of winter, though, his red crown remains hidden among dull gray feathers on his head and is impossible to see, even through binoculars. • While in Georgia, Ruby-crowned Kinglets are seen flitting among the branches, intermingling with a colorful assortment of warblers and vireos. This bird might easily be mistaken for an *Empidonax* flycatcher, but the kinglet's frequent hovering and energetic wing-flicking behavior set it apart from look-alikes. The wing flicking is thought to startle insects into movement, allowing the kinglet to spot them and pounce.

ID: bold, broken white eye ring; 2 bold, white wing bars; olive green upperparts; dark wings and tail; whitish to yellowish underparts; short tail; flicks its wings. *Male:* small, red crown (usually hidden). *Female:* lacks red crown.
Size: *L* 4 in; *W* 7½ in.
Status: abundant winter resident statewide from August to May.
Habitat: mixed woodlands and pure coniferous forests, especially those dominated by spruce; often found near wet forest openings and edges.
Nesting: does not nest in Georgia.

Feeding: gleans and hovers for insects and spiders; also eats seeds and berries.
Voice: call is a husky *ji-dit;* song is an accelerating and rising *tea-tea-tea-tew-tew-tew look-at-Me, look-at-Me, look-at-Me.*
Similar Species: *Golden-crowned Kinglet* (p. 258): dark "cheek"; black border around crown; male has orange crown with yellow border; female has yellow crown. *Orange-crowned Warbler* (p. 277): no eye ring or wing bars. Empidonax *flycatchers* (pp. 218–21): complete eye ring or no eye ring at all; larger bill; longer tail; all lack red crown.
Best Sites: woodlands and wet forest edges statewide; Atlanta (HC-winter: 572); Kings Bay Submarine Base (HC-migration: 100+).

BLUE-GRAY GNATCATCHER

Polioptila caerulea

The fidgety Blue-gray Gnatcatcher is constantly on the move. This woodland inhabitant holds its tail upward like a wren and issues a quiet, banjolike twang as it flits restlessly from shrub to shrub, gleaning insects from branches and leaves. • Gnatcatcher pairs remain close once a bond is established, and both parents share the responsibilities of nest-building, incubation and raising the young. As soon as the young gnatcatchers are ready to fly, they leave the nest for the cover of dense shrubby tangles along woodland edges. Like most songbirds, Blue-gray Gnatcatchers mature quickly and will fly as far as South America within months of hatching. • Although this bird undoubtedly eats gnats, this food item is only a small part of its insectivorous diet. • The scientific name *Polioptila* means "gray feather," whereas *caerulea* means "blue."

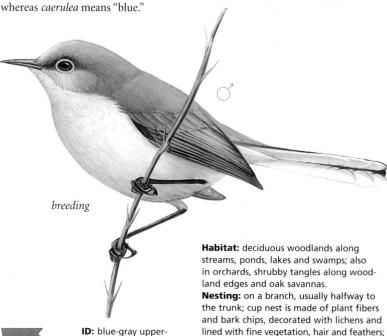

breeding

ID: blue-gray upperparts; long tail; white eye ring; pale gray underparts; no wing bars; black uppertail with white outer tail feathers. *Breeding male:* darker upperparts; black border on side of forecrown.
Size: *L* 4½ in; *W* 6 in.
Status: common breeding resident over most of the state, except the Mountains above 2300 ft, from February to October; rare winter resident in the Piedmont and uncommon on the Coastal Plain and the Coast.

Habitat: deciduous woodlands along streams, ponds, lakes and swamps; also in orchards, shrubby tangles along woodland edges and oak savannas.
Nesting: on a branch, usually halfway to the trunk; cup nest is made of plant fibers and bark chips, decorated with lichens and lined with fine vegetation, hair and feathers; female incubates 3–5 pale bluish white eggs, dotted with reddish brown, for 11–15 days; male feeds female and young.
Feeding: gleans vegetation and flycatches for insects, spiders and other invertebrates.
Voice: calls are thin, high *see* notes or a short series of "mewing" or chattering notes; song is a faint, airy *puree*.
Similar Species: *Golden-crowned Kinglet* (p. 258) and *Ruby-crowned Kinglet* (p. 259): olive green overall; short tail; wing bars.
Best Sites: mature woodlands and scrubby areas in winter; McIntosh Co. (HC-summer: 142); Atlanta (HC-spring: 45); Cumberland I. (HC-winter: 23).

EASTERN BLUEBIRD

Sialia sialis

Perhaps no other bird is as cherished and admired in rural areas as the lovely Eastern Bluebird. With the colors of the cool sky on his back and the warm setting sun on his breast, the male Eastern Bluebird looks like a piece of pure sky come to life. • When House Sparrows and European Starlings were introduced to North America, Eastern Bluebirds were forced to compete with them for nest sites, and bluebird numbers began to decline. The creation of bluebird nest boxes has helped matters—these boxes exclude competing European Starlings because the entrances are too small for them, but are perfect for bluebirds. The development of "bluebird trails" has allowed bluebird populations to recover gradually throughout our region. Nest boxes are mounted on fence posts along highways and rural roads, providing bluebirds with convenient nesting places. • Eastern Bluebirds are fond of fields, uncultivated farmlands and mature wood edges, but an elevated perch is necessary as a base from which to hunt insects. • They often eat berries and fruits when insect populations are low in winter.

ID: chestnut red "chin," throat, breast and sides; white belly and undertail coverts; dark bill and legs. *Male:* deep blue upperparts. *Female:* thin, white eye ring; gray-brown head and back are tinged with blue; blue wings and tail; paler chestnut on underparts.
Size: *L* 7 in; *W* 13 in.
Status: common permanent breeding resident statewide.
Habitat: cropland fencelines, meadows, fallow and abandoned fields, pastures, forest clearings and edges; also golf courses, large lawns and cemeteries.

Nesting: in an abandoned woodpecker cavity, natural cavity or nest box; female builds a cup nest of grass, weed stems and small twigs and lines it with finer materials; mostly the female incubates 4–5 pale blue eggs for 13–16 days.
Feeding: swoops from a perch to pursue flying insects; also forages on the ground for invertebrates.
Voice: call is a chittering *pew*: song is a rich, warbling *turr, turr-lee, turr-lee.*
Similar Species: *Indigo Bunting* (p. 337): blue throat, breast and sides; nonbreeding female is brown with bluish wash on tail.
Best Sites: open country, farmlands and nest boxes statewide; Atlanta (HC-winter: 400+).

VEERY

Catharus fuscescens

Navigating the forest floor in short, springy hops, the Veery flips leaves and scatters leaf litter in search of worms and grubs. This shy, well-camouflaged bird is always attuned to the sounds of wiggling prey or approaching danger. The Veery is the most terrestrial of the North American thrushes and is often difficult to find. Listen for the Veery's fluty, cascading song in spring as the birds travel northward. • These birds migrate to South America each winter, so there's a very good chance that the Veery you see flying overhead in fall may be heading to the rainforests of the Amazon! • This bird's common name is an imitation of its down-slurred call note. The scientific name *fuscescens* is from the Latin word for "dusky," in reference to the Veery's color. • Veeries breed in Georgia above 3500 feet in the northeastern mountains at Rabun Bald, Brasstown Bald and Blood, Cowpen, and Tray mountains, from late April to early October. Recent nocturnal flight-call surveys showed more than 100 Veeries migrating over Kennesaw Mountain and 150 near Cumming.

ID: reddish brown or tawny upperparts; very thin, grayish eye ring; faintly streaked, buff throat and upper breast; light underparts; gray flanks and face patch.
Size: L 6½–7½ in; W 12 in.
Status: uncommon summer resident in the northeastern Mountains; uncommon migrant from April to May statewide; uncommon to common migrant from August to October statewide.
Habitat: cool, moist deciduous and mixed forests and woodlands with a dense understory of shrubs and ferns; often in disturbed woodlands, including parks and backyards.

Nesting: on the ground or in a shrub; female builds a bulky nest of leaves, weeds, bark strips and rootlets; female incubates 3–4 pale greenish blue eggs for 10–15 days.
Feeding: gleans the ground and lower vegetation for invertebrates and berries.
Voice: call is a high, whistled *feeyou; veer* flight call; song is a fluty, descending *da-vee-ur, vee-ur, vee-ur, veer, veer, veer.*
Similar Species: *Wood Thrush* (p 266): larger; large, dark spots on breast and sides; dark streaks on face; white eye ring; reddish head. *Swainson's Thrush* (p. 264): bold eye ring; olive brown upperparts; darker spotting on throat and upper breast. *Hermit Thrush* (p. 265): reddish rump and tail; brownish back; bold eye ring; buff brown flanks; large, dark spots on throat and breast. *Gray-cheeked Thrush* (p. 263): gray-brown upperparts; dark breast spots; brownish gray flanks.
Best Sites: as mentioned above.

GRAY-CHEEKED THRUSH

Catharus minimus

Few people have ever heard of the Gray-cheeked Thrush, but keen birders find this inconspicuous bird a source of great interest. A champion migrant, this thrush winters as far south as Peru and regularly summers in the Arctic, farther north than any other North American thrush. Each spring the Gray-cheeked Thrush migrates through Florida to the Hudson Bay Lowlands in Canada, where it nests among willows and stunted black spruce. Unfortunately, the inaccessibility of this remote northern region has prevented most birders and ornithologists from documenting more than a few nesting records for this elusive bird. • In migration, the Gray-cheeked Thrush travels primarily at night, so it is most often seen or heard rustling through shrub-covered leaf litter early in the morning. This bird will settle in almost any habitat while migrating but does not stay for long and rarely utters more than a simple warning note, a loud nasal *jeeer*, during its brief refueling stops.

ID: gray-brown upper-parts; gray face; inconspicuous eye ring may not be visible; heavily spotted breast; pale underparts; brownish gray flanks; pink legs.
Size: *L* 7–8 in; *W* 13 in.

Status: rare migrant from April to May statewide; uncommon migrant from August to November statewide; more common above the Fall Line.

Habitat: a variety of forested areas, parks and backyards.

Nesting: does not nest in Georgia.

Feeding: hops along the ground, picking up insects and other invertebrates; may also feed on berries during migration.

Voice: call is a down-slurred *wee-o;* flight call is a high *queer;* song is typically thrush-like, ending with a clear, 3-part whistle, higher in the middle: *wee-a, wee-o, titi wheeee.*

Similar Species: *Swainson's Thrush* (p. 264): prominent eye ring; buff "cheek" and upper breast. *Hermit Thrush* (p. 265): reddish tail; olive brown upperparts; lacks gray "cheek." *Veery* (p. 262): reddish brown upperparts; very light breast streaking.

Best Sites: woodlands, parks and cemeteries; Kennesaw Mt. (HC-fall: 84).

SWAINSON'S THRUSH

Catharus ustulatus

The upward spiralling song of the Swainson's Thrush lifts the soul of any listener with each rising note. Though spring migrants occasionally add their inspiring song to the morning chorus, pre-dawn Georgia birders are likely to hear the Swainson's Thrush's distinct, nocturnal *eep!* call, which is likened to the sound made by spring peeper frogs. • Most thrushes feed on the ground, but the Swainson's Thrush is also adept at gleaning food from the airy heights of trees, sometimes briefly hover-gleaning like a warbler or vireo. Search for this thrush in large, mixed-species flocks that gather where berries are numerous. • In migration, the Swainson's Thrush skulks low on the ground under shrubs and tangles, occasionally finding itself in backyards and neighborhood parks. A wary bird, this thrush does not allow many viewing opportunities, often giving a sharp warning call from some distance. • William Swainson was an English zoologist and illustrator in the early 19th century. His name also graces the Swainson's Hawk. • Swainson's Thrush is our most abundant, spot-breasted, migrant thrush, with fall pre-dawn flight counts at Kennesaw Mountain near 800 thrushes.

ID: gray-brown upperparts; noticeable buff eye ring; buff wash on "cheek" and upper breast; spots arranged in streaks on throat and breast; white belly and undertail coverts; brownish gray flanks.
Size: *L* 7 in; *W* 12 in.
Status: common migrant from March to June and from August to November statewide.
Habitat: a variety of forested areas, parks and backyards.
Nesting: does not nest in Georgia.

Feeding: gleans vegetation and forages on the ground for invertebrates; also eats berries.
Voice: call is a sharp *wick;* migrating birds utter a distinct *eep!;* occasionally heard in spring, song is a slow, rolling, rising spiral: *Oh, Aurelia will-ya, will-ya will-yeee.*
Similar Species: *Gray-cheeked Thrush* (p. 263): gray "cheek"; less or no buff wash on breast; lacks conspicuous eye ring. *Hermit Thrush* (p. 265): reddish tail and rump; grayish brown upperparts; darker breast spotting on whiter breast. *Veery* (p. 262): lacks bold eye ring; upperparts are more reddish; faint breast streaking.
Best Sites: woodlands, parks and cemeteries; listen for overhead flight calls on quiet spring and fall evenings; Kennesaw Mt. (HC-fall: 790).

HERMIT THRUSH

Catharus guttatus

There is no doubt the Hermit Thrush would be deemed one of the most beautiful birds in the world if the beauty of forest birds were gauged by sound rather than by appearance. On its nesting grounds in the western U.S. and Canada, its song is very familiar, as much a part of the forest ecosystem as are the trees and wildflowers. • In some winters, the Hermit Thrush can be fairly common in Georgia, but it is the only member of the *Catharus* group that stays in North America for winter. During the cooler months, the Hermit Thrush feeds on berries and fruit, but it switches to a diet of insects during the breeding season. It is often seen flicking its tail up and down and spends much of its time foraging in the tangled understory of our floodplain forests. • Though a rufous-colored tail is this bird's trademark, the Hermit Thrush is otherwise extremely variable in size, color and structure. The plumage of eastern populations is often tinged with reddish brown, whereas western birds are grayer. • The scientific name *guttatus* is Latin for "spotted" or "speckled," in reference to this bird's breast.

ID: reddish brown tail, rump and upperparts; black-spotted throat and breast; pale underparts; gray flanks; thin, whitish eye ring; thin bill; pink legs.
Size: *L* 7 in; *W* 11½ in.

Status: common winter resident from September to April statewide.
Habitat: deciduous, mixed or coniferous woodlands; wooded urban parks.
Nesting: does not nest in Georgia.
Feeding: forages on the ground and gleans vegetation for insects and other invertebrates; also eats berries.

Voice: calls include a faint *chuck* and a fluty *treee;* song is a series of beautiful flutelike notes, both rising and falling in pitch; a small questioning note may precede the song.
Similar Species: *Swainson's Thrush* (p. 264): buff "cheek" and wash on breast; grayish brown back and tail. *Veery* (p. 262): lightly streaked upper breast; reddish brown upperparts and tail. *Gray-cheeked Thrush* (p. 263): gray "cheek"; lacks conspicuous eye ring. *Fox Sparrow* (p. 327): stockier build; conical bill; brown breast spots.
Best Sites: woodlands, parks, cemeteries and backyards; Sweetwater Creek SP; Kennesaw Mt.; Dublin (HC: 100+).

WOOD THRUSH

Hylocichla mustelina

Though the loud, warbled notes of the Wood Thrush resound through many of our woodlands in spring, forest fragmentation and urban sprawl have eliminated much of this bird's traditional nesting habitat. Broken forests and diminutive woodlots have allowed for the invasion of common, open-area predators and parasites, such as raccoons, skunks, crows, jays and cowbirds, which traditionally had little access to nests that were insulated deep within vast stands of hardwood forest. Many tracts of forest that have been urbanized or developed for agriculture now host families of American Robins rather than the once-prominent Wood Thrushes. Unfortunately, those Wood Thrushes that do nest in populated areas often fall victim to house cats. • Naturalist and author Henry David Thoreau considered the Wood Thrush's song to be the most beautiful of avian sounds. The male Wood Thrush, like most other songbirds, can sing two notes at once!

ID: plump body; large, black spots on white breast, sides and flanks; bold white eye ring; streaked "cheeks"; rusty head and back; brown wings, rump and tail.
Size: *L* 8 in; *W* 13 in.

Status: common summer breeding resident from March to November statewide; rare in the southeast, the Coast and the barrier islands.

Habitat: moist, mature and preferably undisturbed deciduous woodlands and mixed forests.

Nesting: low in a fork of a deciduous tree; female builds a bulky cup nest of grass, twigs, moss, weeds, bark strips and mud and lines it with softer materials; female

incubates 3–4 pale, greenish blue eggs for 13–14 days.

Feeding: forages on the ground and gleans vegetation for insects and other invertebrates; also eats berries.

Voice: calls include a *pit pit* and *bweebee-beep*; bell-like phrases of 3–5 notes, with each note at a different pitch and followed by a trill: *Will you live with me? Way up high in a tree, I'll come right down and...seeee!*

Similar Species: *Other thrushes* (pp. 262–67): smaller spots on underparts; most have colored wash on sides and flanks; all lack bold white eye ring and rusty "cap" and back.

Best Sites: wildlife management areas and national wildlife refuges statewide; Kennesaw Mt. (HC-migration: 100+); Callaway Gardens (HC-fall: 50).

AMERICAN ROBIN

Turdus migratorius

American Robins are widespread and abundant in many of our natural habitats, but they are familiar to most of us because they commonly inhabit residential lawns, gardens and parks. • A hunting robin may appear to be listening for prey, but it is actually looking for movements in the soil—it tilts its head because its eyes are placed on the sides of its head. • Robins are occasionally seen hunting with their bills stuffed full of earthworms and grubs, a sign that hungry young robins are somewhere close at hand. Young robins are easily distinguished from their parents by their disheveled appearance and heavily spotted underparts. • The American Robin was named by English colonists after the European Robin (*Erithacus rubecula*) of their native land. Both birds look and behave similarly, even though they are only distantly related.

ID: gray-brown back; dark head; white throat streaked with black; white undertail coverts; incomplete, white eye ring; black-tipped, yellow bill. *Male:* deep brick red breast; black head. *Female:* dark gray head; light red-orange breast. *Immature:* heavily spotted breast.
Size: *L* 10 in; *W* 17 in.
Status: common permanent breeding resident statewide; uncommon in the Coastal Plain, but increasing; rare on the Coast.
Habitat: residential lawns and gardens, pastures, urban parks, broken forests, bogs and river shorelines.

Nesting: in a coniferous or deciduous tree or shrub; sturdy cup nest is built of grass, moss and loose bark and cemented with mud; female incubates 4 light blue eggs for 11–16 days; may raise up to 3 broods each year in some areas.
Feeding: forages on the ground and among vegetation for larval and adult insects, earthworms, other invertebrates and berries.
Voice: call is a rapid *tut-tut-tut;* song is an evenly spaced warble: *cheerily cheer-up cheerio.*
Similar Species: *Varied Thrush:* very rare in the southeast; black breast band; 2 orange wing bars.
Best Sites: rural woodlands and urban lawns and gardens; Piedmont NWR/Rum Creek WMA (HC-winter: 2,000,000).

267

GRAY CATBIRD

Dumetella carolinensis

What could be more amusing than a bird that meows like a cat! The Gray Catbird is a member of the mimic family and issues an assortment of boisterous, mimicked phrases in addition to its characteristic "meow" call. • Most Gray Catbirds in Georgia build their loose cup nest deep within the impenetrable tangles of shrubs, brambles and thorny thickets. The Gray Catbird vigorously defends its nesting territory with such effective defense tactics that the nesting success of neighboring warblers and sparrows may increase as a result of this catbird's constant vigilance. Gray Catbirds are less prone to parasitism by Brown-headed Cowbirds because female catbirds are very loyal to their nests. Even if a cowbird sneaks past the watchful female catbird to deposit an egg in the nest, the mother catbird often recognizes the foreign egg and immediately ejects it. • Catbirds and other back-yard birds are among the estimated more than 1 billion birds killed by approximately 100 million feral and "house" cats present in the U.S.

ID: dark gray overall; long tail may be dark gray to black; chestnut undertail coverts; black eyes, bill, legs and "cap."
Size: *L* 8½–9 in; *W* 11 in.
Status: common summer breeding resident statewide from March to November, but rare on the Coast; in winter it is common on the Coast, uncommon in the Coastal Plain and rare north of the Fall Line.
Habitat: dense thickets, brambles, shrubby or brushy areas and hedgerows, often near water.

Nesting: in a dense shrub or thicket; bulky cup nest is loosely built with twigs, leaves and grass and is lined with fine material; female incubates 4 greenish blue eggs for 12–15 days.
Feeding: forages on the ground and in vegetation for a wide variety of ants, beetles, grasshoppers, caterpillars, moths and spiders; also eats berries and visits feeders.
Voice: calls include a catlike *meoow* and a harsh *check-check;* song is a variety of warbles, squeaks and mimicked phrases repeated only once and often interspersed with a *mew* call.
Similar Species: *Northern Mockingbird* (p. 269): lacks black "cap" and chestnut undertail coverts. *Brown Thrasher* (p. 270): rusty brown upperparts; streaked under-parts; wing bars; repeats each song phrase twice.
Best Sites: widespread; Richmond Co. (HC-breeding: 81); Jekyll I. (HC-fall: 150); Okefenokee NWR (HC-winter: 85).

NORTHERN MOCKINGBIRD

Mimus polyglottos

The Northern Mockingbird is a common, charismatic bird and has been designated the state bird in five states. It thrives in a variety of habitats ranging from lush gardens to arid deserts and is currently expanding its range northward. • The Northern Mockingbird's vocal repertoire is amazing—over 200 different song types have been attributed to this bird. It can imitate almost anything, from the vocalizations of other birds and animals to musical instruments and even car alarms! In fact, it replicates sounds so accurately that even computerized auditory analysis may be unable to detect the differences between the original source and the mockingbird's imitation. • The Northern Mockingbird's nighttime singing is most likely from a male still seeking a mate. The female mockingbird is known to give calls that decrease the singing of "her male," which functions to decrease extramarital copulations by her mate. • The scientific name *polyglottos* is Greek for "many tongues" and refers to this bird's ability to mimic a wide variety of sounds.

ID: gray upperparts; dark wings; 2 thin, white wing bars; long, dark tail with white outer tail feathers; light gray underparts. *Immature:* paler overall; spotted breast. *In flight:* large white patch at base of black primaries.
Size: *L* 10 in; *W* 14 in.
Status: common to abundant permanent breeding resident statewide, except in the Mountains above 2300 ft.
Habitat: hedges, suburban gardens and orchard margins with an abundance of available fruit; hedgerows of multiflora roses are especially important in winter.
Nesting: often in a small shrub or small tree; cup nest is built with twigs, grass, fur and leaves; female incubates 3–4 brown-blotched, bluish gray to greenish eggs for 12–13 days.

Feeding: gleans vegetation and forages on the ground for beetles, ants, wasps and grasshoppers; also eats berries and wild fruit; visits feeders for suet and raisins.
Voice: calls include a harsh *chair* and *chewk;* song is a medley of mimicked phrases, with the phrases often repeated 3 times or more.
Similar Species: *Loggerhead Shrike* (p. 229): thicker, hooked bill; black "mask"; juveniles are stockier and less vocal; much faster wingbeats. *Gray Catbird* (p. 268): gray overall; black "cap"; chestnut under-tail coverts; lacks white outer tail feathers.
Best Sites: roadsides and urban sites; Atlanta (HC-winter: 294); Tybee I. (HC-winter: 69).

BROWN THRASHER

Toxostoma rufum

Amid the various chirps and warbles that rise from woodland and lakefront edges in spring and early summer, the song of the male Brown Thrasher stands alone—its lengthy, complex chorus of twice-repeated phrases is truly unique. This thrasher has the most extensive vocal repertoire of any North American bird, and estimates indicate it is capable of more than 2000 distinctive combinations of various phrases. • Because the Brown Thrasher nests on or close to the ground, its eggs and nestlings are particularly vulnerable to predation by snakes, weasels, skunks and other animals. Even though Brown Thrashers are aggressive, vigilant nest defenders, the parents' spirited defense is not always enough to protect their progeny. • In a campaign inaugurated in 1928 by the Fifth District of the State Federation of Women's Club, and sponsored by the Atlanta Bird Club and other state bird clubs, the school children of Georgia selected the Brown Thrasher as the state bird. The passage of Joint Resolution No. 128, on March 20, 1970, made this official and also designated the Northern Bobwhite as the state game bird.

ID: reddish brown upperparts; pale underparts with heavy, brown spotting and streaking; long, slender, downcurved bill; yellow-orange eyes; long, rufous tail; yellow legs; 2 white wing bars.

Size: *L* 11½ in; *W* 13 in.

Status: common permanent breeding resident statewide; less numerous north of the Fall Line in winter.

Habitat: dense shrubs and thickets, overgrown pastures (especially those with hawthorns), woodland edges and brushy areas; rarely close to human habitation, except in the Coastal Plain and the Coast.

Nesting: usually in a low shrub; often on the ground; cup nest of grass, twigs and leaves is lined with fine vegetation; pair incubates 4 bluish white to pale blue eggs, dotted with reddish brown, for 11–14 days.

Feeding: gleans the ground and vegetation for larval and adult invertebrates; occasionally tosses leaves aside with its bill; also eats seeds and berries.

Voice: sings a large variety of phrases, with each phrase usually repeated twice: *dig-it dig-it, hoe-it hoe-it, pull-it-up pull-it-up*; calls include a loud crackling note, a harsh *shuck*, a soft *churr* and a whistled, 3-note *pit-cher-ee*.

Similar Species: *Hermit Thrush* (p. 265): shorter tail; gray-brown back and crown; dark brown eyes; much shorter bill; lacks wing bars.

Best Sites: dense thickets; often in backyards in the south; Atlanta (HC-winter: 130).

EUROPEAN STARLING

Sturnus vulgaris

The European Starling was introduced to North America in 1890 and 1891, when about 100 birds were released into New York's Central Park as part of the local Shakespeare society's plan to introduce all the birds mentioned in their favorite author's writings. The European Starling quickly established itself in the New York landscape, then spread rapidly across the continent, often at the expense of many native cavity-nesting birds, such as the Tree Swallow, Eastern Bluebird and Red-headed Woodpecker. Despite many concerted efforts to control or even eradicate this species, the European Starling will no doubt continue to assert its claim in the New World. The more than 200 million individuals in North America today are believed to have sprung from these first 100 birds. • Courting European Starlings are infamous for their ability to reproduce the sounds of other birds such as Killdeers, Red-tailed Hawks, Soras and meadowlarks, as well as mechanical sounds, and even human speech!

breeding

ID: short, squared tail; dark eyes. *Breeding:* blackish, iridescent plumage; yellow bill. *Nonbreeding:* blackish wings; feather tips are heavily spotted with white and buff. *Immature:* gray-brown plumage; brown bill. *In flight:* pointed, triangular wings.
Size: *L* 8½ in; *W* 16 in.
Status: abundant permanent breeding resident statewide; more numerous in winter.
Habitat: agricultural areas, townsites, woodland and forest edges, landfills and roadsides.
Nesting: in an abandoned woodpecker cavity, natural cavity, nest box or other artificial cavity; nest is made of grass, twigs and straw; mostly the female incubates 4–6 bluish to greenish white eggs for 12–14 days.
Feeding: forages mostly on the ground; diverse diet includes many invertebrates, berries, seeds and human food waste.
Voice: variety of whistles, squeaks and gurgles; imitates other birds.
Similar Species: *Rusty Blackbird* (p. 344): longer tail; black bill; lacks spotting; yellow eyes; rusty tinge on upperparts in fall. *Brewer's Blackbird* (p. 345): longer tail; black bill; lacks spotting; male has yellow eyes; female is brown overall. *Brown-headed Cowbird* (p. 349): lacks spotting; adult male has longer tail, shorter, dark bill and brown head; juvenile has streaked underparts, stout bill and longer tail.
Best Sites: widespread; fast-food parking lots; Milledgeville (HC-winter: 2,000,000+).

AMERICAN PIPIT

Anthus rubescens

Each winter, sod farms, grassy fields and even mudflats become foraging grounds for American Pipits. Flocks of pipits fluctuate annually and may go unnoticed because their dull brown-and-buff plumage blends into the landscape. But to keen observers, their plain attire, slender bill, white outer tail feathers and habit of continuous tail wagging make them readily identifiable. The best indicator that pipits are near is their telltale, two-syllable call, *pip-it pip-it*, which is usually given in flight. • American Pipits may resemble sparrows, but they move very differently. Pipits typically stride along the ground, whereas sparrows and most other passerines hop. The reason for these distinct movement styles may be simply that long-legged birds move a greater distance with one long stride, whereas a single hop takes short-legged birds farther. • This bird was formerly known as the "Water Pipit" (*A. spinoletta*). • Pipits are found worldwide and occupy every continent except Antarctica.

nonbreeding

ID: gray "cheek," crown and upperparts; 2 white wing bars; white outer tail feathers. *Breeding:* dark streaking on buff-colored breast and flanks; buff "eyebrow" and lore. *Nonbreeding:* faint, dark streaking on back; dark streaking on white breast and buff flanks; white "eyebrow" and lore.
Size: *L* 6–7 in; *W* 10½ in.
Status: common migrant and winter resident statewide, except uncommon in the Mountains, from September to May.

Habitat: agricultural fields, pastures and shores of wetlands, lakes and rivers.
Nesting: does not nest in Georgia.
Feeding: gleans the ground and vegetation for seeds and insects; eats agricultural pests, including grasshoppers and weevils; also takes aquatic invertebrates and mollusks.
Voice: familiar flight call is *pip-it pip-it*; song is a harsh, sharp *tsip-tsip* or *chiwee*.
Similar Species: *Horned Lark* (p. 240): black "horns"; facial markings. *Sprague's Pipit* (p. 365): lighter back with strong streaking; paler buff breast.
Best Sites: E.L. Huie; Sod Atlanta Inc.; Perry Super-Sod Farm; Titan Turf Farm.

CEDAR WAXWING

Bombycilla cedrorum

Cedar Waxwings are named for their bright red wing tips, which look like they have been dipped in red candle wax, and for their fondness of cedar "berries" in winter. Waxwings can digest a wide variety of berries, some of which are inedible or even poisonous to humans. If the fruits have fermented, these birds will sometimes be found on the ground in a state of alcoholic stupor (unfortunately, alcohol intoxication can sometimes have lethal consequences for Cedar Waxwings). Native berry-producing trees and shrubs planted in your backyard can attract Cedar Waxwings and provide an opportunity to observe the striking plumage of these birds up close. • On their north Georgia breeding grounds in riparian habitats, Cedar Waxwing pairs perform a wonderful courtship dance: the male first lands slightly away from the female, then tentatively hops toward her and offers her a berry. The female accepts the berry and hops away from the male, then she stops, hops back, and offers him the berry in a gentle ritual that can last for several minutes.

Habitat: wooded residential parks and gardens, overgrown fields, forest edges, second-growth, riparian and open woodlands.

Nesting: in a coniferous or deciduous tree or shrub; cup nest is made of twigs, grass, moss and lichens, often lined with fine grass; female incubates 3–5 pale gray to bluish eggs for 12–16 days.

Feeding: catches flying insects on the wing or gleans vegetation; also eats large amounts of berries and wild fruit, especially in fall and winter.

Voice: faint, high-pitched, trilled whistle: *tseee-tseee-tseee.*

Similar Species: none.

Best Sites: *Breeding:* Cloudland Canyon SP; Lake Conasauga. *Winter:* near junipers, holly or other fruit-bearing plants, though visits may be brief.

ID: cinnamon crest; brown upperparts; black "mask"; yellow wash on belly; gray rump; yellow terminal tail band; white undertail coverts; small red "drops" on wings. *Immature:* no "mask"; streaked underparts; gray-brown body.

Size: *L* 7 in; *W* 12 in.

Status: common but erratic winter resident statewide; rare breeder in the upper Piedmont and the Mountains.

273

BLUE-WINGED WARBLER

Vermivora pinus

During the mid-1800s, the Blue-winged Warbler began expanding its range eastward and northward from its home in the central midwestern U.S., finding new breeding territories among overgrown fields and pastures near abandoned human settlements. Eventually it came into contact with the Golden-winged Warbler, a bird with completely different looks but practically identical habitat requirements and breeding biology. Where both species share the same habitat, a distinctive, fertile hybrid known as the Brewster's Warbler may be produced. This hybrid tends to be more grayish overall, like the Golden-winged Warbler, but it retains the thin, black eye line and the touch of yellow on the breast from its Blue-winged parent. In rare instances when two of these hybrids are able to reproduce successfully, a second-generation hybrid known as the Lawrence's Warbler is produced. It is more yellowish overall, like the Blue-winged Warbler, but has the black "mask," "chin" and throat of the Golden-winged Warbler. • Because both Blue-winged Warblers and Golden-winged Warblers are found in the mountains, both Brewster's and Lawrence's Warblers have been reported in Georgia, but both are quite rare.

ID: bright yellow head and underparts, except for white to yellowish undertail coverts; olive yellow upperparts; bluish gray wings and tail; black eye line; thin, dark bill; 2 white wing bars; bold white tail spots on underside of tail.

Size: L 4½–5 in; W 7½ in.

Status: rare to uncommon summer breeding resident in the northeastern Mountains and eastern upper Piedmont to 2200 ft from April to September; uncommon migrant north of the Fall Line and rare migrant on the Coastal Plain and Coast from March to June and from July to October.

Habitat: second-growth woodlands, willow swamps, shrubby, overgrown fields, pastures, woodland edges and woodland openings.

Nesting: on or near the ground, concealed by vegetation; female builds a narrow, inverted, cone-shaped nest of grass, leaves and bark strips and lines it with soft materials; female incubates 5 white eggs, with fine brown spots toward the larger end, for about 11 days.

Feeding: gleans insects and spiders from the lower branches of trees and shrubs.

Voice: soft *tzip* call; buzzy, 2-note song: *beee-bzzz.*

Similar Species: *Prothonotary Warbler* (p. 297): lacks black eye line and white wing bars. *Pine Warbler* (p. 289): darker; white belly; faint streaking on sides and breast. *Yellow Warbler* (p. 280): yellow wings; lacks black eye line. *Prairie Warbler* (p. 290): black streaking on sides and flanks; darker wings.

Best Sites: *Breeding:* Dawson Forest WMA; Pine Log WMA. *In migration:* Kennesaw Mt.; Ocmulgee NM; Bartow Co. (HC: 8).

GOLDEN-WINGED WARBLER

Vermivora chrysoptera

The Golden-winged Warbler is a tiny bird facing big issues and population declines. Battles to maintain breeding territory are not confined within the species—the Golden-winged Warbler is losing ground to its colonizing relative the Blue-winged Warbler, through competition and hybridization. Habitat loss and Brown-headed Cowbird parasitism are additional hardships threatening the Golden-winged Warbler. • Both Golden-winged Warblers and Blue-winged Warblers prefer scrub and brush habitat, but the Golden-winged favors 1- to 3-year-old clearings. These clearings have become rare because of fire suppression above 2500 feet, and as a result there has been a decrease in breeding records in Georgia in recent years. • Blue-winged Warblers and Golden-winged Warblers have very similar songs. The Blue-winged Warbler will even sometimes sing the Golden-winged Warbler's primary song, which can make identification based on song very difficult.

ID: yellow forecrown and wing patch; dark "chin," throat and "mask" over eye are bordered by white; bluish gray upperparts and flanks; white underparts; white tail spots on underside of tail. *Female* and *immature:* duller overall with gray throat and "mask."
Size: *L* 4½–5 in; *W* 7½ in.
Status: very rare breeder (declining) in the Mountains above 2500 ft, from April to October; uncommon migrant north of the Fall Line and rare migrant south of the Fall Line from April to May and from July to October.
Habitat: moist, shrubby fields, woodland edges and early-succession forest clearings.

Nesting: rarely nests in Georgia; on the ground, concealed by vegetation; open cup nest of grass, leaves and grapevine bark, lined with softer materials; female incubates 5 pinkish to pale cream eggs, marked with brown and lilac, for about 11 days.
Feeding: gleans insects and spiders from tree and shrub canopies; unrolls curled leaves to find insects.
Voice: call is a sweet *chip;* buzzy song begins with a higher note: *zee-bz-bz-bz.*
Similar Species: *Yellow-rumped Warbler* (p. 285): white throat; dark breast patches; yellow sides. *Yellow-throated Warbler* (p. 288): lacks yellow crown; 2 white wing bars; yellow throat. *Black-throated Green Warbler* (p. 286): lacks dark "mask"; 2 white wing bars; black streaking on sides.
Best Sites: Kennesaw Mt. in migration (HC-fall: 6).

TENNESSEE WARBLER

Vermivora peregrina

Migrating Tennessee Warblers often sing their tunes and forage for insects high in the forest canopy, but inclement weather and the need for food after a long flight can force these birds to lower levels in the forest. • Tennessee Warblers lack the bold, bright features found on other warblers—without their loud, twittering song, these birds would easily pass through Georgia unnoticed. • Tennessee Warblers thrive during spruce budworm outbreaks. During times of plenty, these birds may produce more than seven young in a single brood. • Alexander Wilson discovered this bird along the Cumberland River in Tennessee and named it after that state. This warbler only migrates through Tennessee, though, breeding in only Canada, northern Michigan and northeastern Minnesota. • Tennessee Warblers are easily confused with Warbling Vireos and Philadelphia Vireos in spring, and with Orange-crowned Warblers in fall, when they are much more drab in appearance. • This warbler is uncommon to fairly common during its migration through Georgia, but there is also a slim chance of seeing it in winter, with accidental winter reports in Cobb County, Social Circle, Valdosta and St. Catherines Island.

breeding

ID: *Breeding male:* blue gray "cap"; olive green back, wings and tail edgings; white "eyebrow"; black eye line; clean white underparts; thin bill. *Breeding female:* yellow wash on breast and "eyebrow"; olive gray "cap." *Nonbreeding:* olive yellow upperparts; yellow "eyebrow"; yellow underparts except for white undertail coverts; male may have white belly.
Size: *L* 4½–5 in; *W* 8 in.

Status: uncommon migrant from April to May and common migrant from August to November north of the Fall Line; rare and uncommon migrant south of the Fall Line.
Habitat: woodlands or areas with tall shrubs.
Nesting: does not nest in Georgia.
Feeding: gleans foliage and buds for small insects, caterpillars and other invertebrates; also eats berries; occasionally visits suet feeders.
Voice: call is a sweet *chip;* song is a loud, sharp, accelerating *ticka-ticka-ticka swit-swit-swit-swit chew-chew-chew-chew-chew.*
Similar Species: *Warbling Vireo* (p. 233): stouter overall; thicker bill; much less green on upperparts. *Philadelphia Vireo* (p. 234): stouter overall; thicker bill; yellow breast and sides. *Orange-crowned Warbler* (p. 277): yellowish undertail coverts; lacks white "eyebrow" and blue-gray head.
Best Sites: Chattahoochee River NRA; Kennesaw Mt. (HC-spring: 14; HC-fall: 70).

ORANGE-CROWNED WARBLER

Vermivora celata

D on't be disappointed if you can't see the Orange-crowned Warbler's orange crown, because this bird's most distinguishing characteristic is its lack of field marks: wing bars, eye rings and color patches are all conspicuously absent. When encountered, the Orange-crowned Warbler usually appears as a blurred, olive yellow bundle flitting nervously among the leaves and branches of low shrubs. Its drab, olive yellow appearance makes it frustratingly similar to females of other warbler species. • The Orange-crowned Warbler is often the most common species to capitalize on the sap-wells drilled by Yellow-bellied Sapsuckers. • *Vermivora* is Latin for "worm eating," whereas *celata* is derived from the Latin word for "hidden," a reference to this bird's inconspicuous crown.

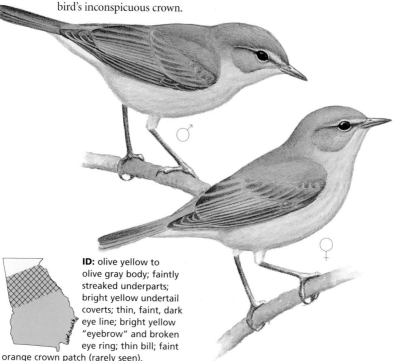

ID: olive yellow to olive gray body; faintly streaked underparts; bright yellow undertail coverts; thin, faint, dark eye line; bright yellow "eyebrow" and broken eye ring; thin bill; faint orange crown patch (rarely seen).

Size: *L* 5 in; *W* 7 in.

Status: uncommon migrant and winter resident north of the Fall Line from September to May; uncommon to common in winter south of the Fall Line.

Habitat: woodlands or areas with tall shrubs.

Nesting: does not nest in Georgia.

Feeding: gleans foliage for invertebrates, berries, nectar and sap; often hover-gleans.

Voice: call is a clear, sharp *chip;* faint trill that breaks downward halfway through.

Similar Species: *Tennessee Warbler* (p. 276): blue-gray head; dark eye line; bold white "eyebrow"; white underparts including undertail coverts. *Ruby-crowned Kinglet* (p. 259): broken white eye ring; white wing bars. *Wilson's Warbler* (p. 308): complete, bright yellow eye ring; brighter yellow underparts; pale legs; lacks breast streaks. *Yellow Warbler* (p. 280): brighter head and underparts; reddish breast streaks (faint or absent on female). *Common Yellowthroat* (p. 306): female has darker face and upperparts; lacks breast streaks.

Best Sites: Kennesaw Mt.; Merry Brothers Brickyard Ponds; Atlanta (HC-spring: 20); Glynn Co. (HC-winter: 15).

277

NASHVILLE WARBLER
Vermivora ruficapilla

Nashville Warblers have an unusual distribution, with two widely separated summer populations: one eastern and the other western. Scientists believe that these populations were created thousands of years ago when a single core population was split apart during continental glaciation. • Nashville Warblers are uncommon migrants here. They are best found in overgrown farmlands and second-growth forests as they forage low in trees and thickets, often at the edge of a dry forest or burn area. • This warbler was first described near Nashville, Tennessee, but it does not breed in that state. This misnomer is not an isolated incident: the Tennessee, Cape May and Connecticut warblers all bear names that misrepresent their breeding distributions.

ID: bold white eye ring; yellow-green upperparts; yellow underparts; white between legs. *Male:* blue-gray head; may show a small, chestnut red crown. *Female and immature:* duller overall; light eye ring; olive gray head; blue-gray nape.
Size: *L* 4½–5 in; *W* 7½ in.
Status: rare to uncommon northern migrant from August to November and from March to May; rare migrant from August to November on the Coast.
Habitat: second-growth mixed woodlands are preferred; also wet coniferous forests,

riparian woodlands, cedar-spruce swamps and moist, shrubby, abandoned fields.
Nesting: does not nest in Georgia.
Feeding: gleans foliage for insects, such as caterpillars, flies and aphids.
Voice: call is a metallic *chink;* song begins with a thin, high-pitched *see-it see-it see-it see-it,* followed by a trilling.
Similar Species: *Common Yellowthroat* (p. 306) and *Wilson's Warbler* (p. 308): all-yellow underparts; females lack grayish head and bold white eye ring. *Connecticut Warbler* (p. 304) and *Mourning Warbler* (p. 305): yellow between legs; females have grayish to brownish "hood."
Best Sites: Chattahoochee River NRA; Kennesaw Mt. (HC-spring: 6).

NORTHERN PARULA

Parula americana

Young Northern Parulas spend the first few weeks of their lives enclosed in a fragile, socklike nest suspended from a tree branch. Once they have grown too large for the nest and their wing feathers are strong enough to allow for a short, awkward flight, the young leave their warm abode, dispersing among the surrounding trees and shrubs. As warm summer nights slip away to be replaced by cooler fall temperatures, Northern Parulas migrate to the warmer climes of Central America or the Florida Keys. • Nesting Northern Parulas are typically found in older forests where *Usnea* lichens (Old Man's Beard), or Spanish moss (south of the Fall Line), occur. The lichens or moss are an essential component of their nests. When the young are hatched, Northern Parulas expand their foraging areas to include deciduous trees, or from only deciduous trees to include understory shrubs, to obtain the extra food needed for the new family. Males spend most of their time singing and foraging among the tops of taller trees. • Parula means "little titmouse," an odd, yet distinctive name for one of the smallest American warblers.

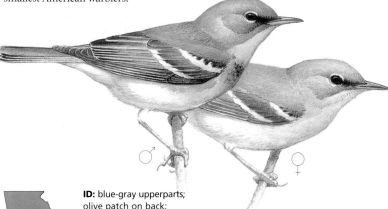

ID: blue-gray upperparts; olive patch on back; 2 bold white wing bars; bold white eye ring is broken by black eye line; yellow "chin," throat and breast; white belly and flanks. *Male:* 1 black and 1 orange breast band.

Size: *L* 4½ in; *W* 7 in.

Status: uncommon breeder north of the Fall Line to 3400 ft, to common breeder south of the Fall Line and barrier islands from March to October; rare in winter near the Coast.

Habitat: *Breeding:* humid riparian woodlands and swampy deciduous woodlands, especially where lichens hang from branches. *In migration:* woodlands or areas with tall shrubs.

Nesting: female weaves a small hanging nest into hanging strands of tree lichens; may add lichens to a dense cluster of conifer boughs; pair incubates 4–5 brown-marked, whitish eggs for 12–14 days.

Feeding: forages for insects and other invertebrates by hovering, gleaning or hawking; feeds from the tips of branches and occasionally on the ground.

Voice: *chip* and *tseep* calls; song is a rising, buzzy trill ending with an abrupt, lower-pitched *zip*.

Similar Species: *Cerulean Warbler* (p. 294): streaking on breast and sides; lacks white eye ring. *Blue-winged Warbler* (p. 274): yellow underparts. *Yellow-rumped Warbler* (p. 285): yellow rump and crown; lacks yellow throat. *Yellow-throated Warbler* (p. 288) and *Kirtland's Warbler* (p. 366): heavy black streaking along sides.

Best Sites: Ocmulgee NM; Eufaula NWR; Beaverdam WMA; Savannah–Ogeechee Canal; Cumberland I. (HC-spring: 70), and all barrier islands.

YELLOW WARBLER

Dendroica petechia

Yellow Warblers usually arrive here in April, searching for caterpillars, aphids, beetles and other invertebrates. Flitting from branch to branch among open woodland edges and riparian shrubs, these inquisitive birds seem to be in perpetual motion. • Yellow Warblers are among the most frequent victims of nest parasitism by Brown-headed Cowbirds. Unlike many birds, they can recognize the foreign eggs, and these warblers sometimes build another nest overtop the old nest that contained the cowbird eggs! Some persistent Yellow Warblers build over and over, creating bizarre, multilayered, high-rise nests. • During fall migration, silent, plain-looking Yellow Warblers and other similar-looking warblers can cause confusion for birders who have been lulled into a false sense of familiarity with these birds. Watch for the unique yellow flashes on the sides of the Yellow Warblers' tails. • Because of their bright yellow plumage, Yellow Warblers are often mistakenly called "Wild Canaries."

ID: bright yellow body; yellowish legs; black bill and eyes; bright yellow highlights on dark yellow olive tail and wings. *Male:* red breast streaks. *Female:* faint, red breast streaks.

Size: *L* 5 in; *W* 8 in.

Status: uncommon summer breeding resident north of the Fall Line, and local in the Piedmont; uncommon migrant statewide, except common on the Coast from March to November.

Habitat: moist, open woodlands with dense, low scrub; also shrubby meadows, willow tangles, shrubby fencerows and riparian woodlands; usually near water.

Nesting: in a fork in a deciduous tree or small shrub; female builds a compact cup nest of grass, weeds and shredded bark and lines it with plant down and fur; female incubates 4–5 speckled or spotted, greenish white eggs for 11–12 days.

Feeding: gleans foliage and vegetation for invertebrates, especially caterpillars, inchworms, beetles, aphids and cankerworms; occasionally hover-gleans.

Voice: *chip* call; song is a fast, frequently repeated *sweet-sweet-sweet summer sweet.*

Similar Species: *Orange-crowned Warbler* (p. 277): darker olive plumage overall; lacks reddish breast streaks. *American Goldfinch* (p. 356): black wings and tail; male often has black forehead. *Wilson's Warbler* (p. 308): shorter, darker tail; male has black "cap"; female has darker crown and upperparts. *Common Yellowthroat* (p. 306): darker face and upperparts; female lacks yellow highlights on wings.

Best Sites: *Summer:* Ivy Log Gap; Lake Winfield Scott; Rabun Bald. *Fall:* the Coast; Altamaha WMA (HC: 25).

CHESTNUT-SIDED WARBLER

Dendroica pensylvanica

When colorful waves of warbler migrants flood across the landscape each April, the Chestnut-sided Warbler is consistently ranked among the most anticipated arrivals. The boldly patterned males never fail to dazzle onlookers as they flit about at eye level. Chestnut-sided Warblers are common nesters in the mountains of Georgia, where they are also common in migration. • Chestnut-sided Warblers tend to favor early-succession forests, which have become abundant over the past century. Although clear-cut logging has had a negative impact on other warbler species, it has created suitable habitat for the Chestnut-sided Warbler in many parts of its range. • Other warblers lose some of their brighter colors in fall, yet still look familiar, but the Chestnut-sided Warbler undergoes a complete transformation, looking more like a flycatcher or kinglet in its green and gray coat.

breeding

ID: *Breeding male:* chestnut brown line along sides; white underparts; yellow "cap"; black "mask" and legs; yellowish wing bars. *Breeding female:* similar to male; washed-out colors; dark streaking on yellow "cap." *Nonbreeding:* yellow-green crown, nape and back; white eye ring; gray face and sides; white underparts; may retain chestnut line along sides. *Immature:* similar to nonbreeding adult but has brighter yellow wing bars.

Size: *L* 5 in; *W* 8 in.

Status: common summer breeding resident in the Mountains above 2800 ft from April to October; common migrant north of the Fall Line from March to May and from July to November; rare spring migrant and uncommon fall migrant south of the Fall Line.

Habitat: shrubby, deciduous second-growth woodlands, abandoned fields and orchards, especially in areas that are regenerating after logging or fire.

Nesting: low in a shrub or sapling; small cup nest is made of bark strips, grass, roots and weed fibers and lined with fine grasses, plant down and fur; female incubates 4 brown-marked, whitish eggs for 11–12 days.

Feeding: gleans trees and shrubs at midlevel for insects.

Voice: musical *chip* call; loud, clear song: *so pleased, pleased, pleased to MEET-CHA!*

Similar Species: *Bay-breasted Warbler* (p. 292): black face; dark chestnut hindcrown, upper breast and sides; buff belly and undertail coverts; white wing bars. *American Redstart* (p. 296): female has large, yellow patches on wings and tail; more grayish overall.

Best Sites: Lake Conasauga; Cooper's Creek WMA; Brasstown Bald; Rabun Bald; Atlanta (HC-fall: 100+).

MAGNOLIA WARBLER

Dendroica magnolia

The Magnolia Warbler is widely regarded as one of the most beautiful wood-warblers. It possesses bold "eyebrows," flashy wing bars and tail patches, an elegant "necklace," a bright yellow rump and breast and a dark "mask." As it migrates through Georgia in the spring and fall, it frequently forages along the lower branches of trees and among shrubs, allowing for reliable, close-up observations. • Male Magnolias flash their white wing and tail patches, snap bills, chase and use *chip* notes to discourage intruders, but competitive singing is used to settle the most intense disputes. • This species was given its current name in 1810, when Alexander Wilson collected the first specimen from a magnolia tree.

breeding

Habitat: woodlands or areas with tall shrubs.

Nesting: does not nest in Georgia.

Feeding: gleans vegetation and buds; occasionally flycatches for beetles, flies, wasps, caterpillars and other insects; sometimes eats berries.

ID: *Breeding male:* yellow underparts with bold black streaks; black "mask"; white "eyebrow"; blue-gray crown; dark upperparts; white wing bars often blend into larger patch. *Female and nonbreeding male:* duller overall; pale "mask"; 2 distinct white wing bars; streaked, olive back. *In flight:* yellow rump; white tail patches; unlike other warblers, white patches in tail are near base, not tip.

Size: *L* 4½–5 in; *W* 7½ in.

Status: uncommon migrant from April to May and common migrant from August to October north of the Fall Line; rare spring migrant and uncommon fall migrant south of the Fall Line; accidental in winter.

Voice: call is a *clank;* song is a quick, rising *pretty pretty lady* or *wheata wheata wheet-zu.*

Similar Species: *Yellow-rumped Warbler* (p. 285): white throat and belly; yellow hindcrown patch. *Cape May Warbler* (p. 283): chestnut "cheek" patch on yellow face; lacks white tail patches. *Prairie Warbler* (p. 290): dusky jaw stripe; faint, yellowish wing bars; immature lacks white tail patches. *American Redstart* (p. 296): tail pattern looks similar from underneath but light patches are colored yellow or orange, not white.

Best Sites: Chattahoochee River NRA; Kennesaw Mt.; Columbus (HC-fall: 82); Atlanta (HC-fall: 50).

CAPE MAY WARBLER

Dendroica tigrina

You may find yourself with "a pain in the neck" when you strain your head back for a glimpse of these warblers as they forage and sing at the very tops of tall trees. Cape May Warblers require mature forests that are at least 50 years old for secure nesting habitat and an abundance of canopy-dwelling insects. • In spring, the Cape May Warbler frequents hickory, tulip tree and oak stands when the trees shed pollen, and it also feeds on the swarms of insects attracted to blooming ornamentals. The Cape May's semitubular tongue is unique among wood-warblers and allows it to feed on nectar and fruit juices, both during migration and on its tropical wintering grounds. • Over much of their breeding range in Canada, these small birds are spruce budworm specialists. In years of budworm outbreaks, Cape Mays successfully fledge more young. • Named after Cape May, New Jersey, where the first scientific specimen was collected in 1811, this bird was not recorded there again for more than 100 years!

breeding

ID: dark streaking on yellow underparts; yellow side "collar"; dark olive green upperparts; yellow rump; clean white undertail coverts. *Breeding male:* chestnut "cheek" on yellow face; dark crown; large, white wing patch. *Female:* paler overall; 2 faint, thin, white wing bars; grayish "cheek" and crown.
Size: *L* 5–5½ in; *W* 7½ in.
Status: uncommon migrant from March to May and rare migrant from August to November statewide, except fairly common on the Coast in fall.
Habitat: high in the canopy; found in oak, hickory and other flowering ornamental trees; mature, coniferous and mixed forests.
Nesting: does not nest in Georgia.
Feeding: gleans treetop branches and foliage for spruce budworms, flies, beetles, moths, wasps and other insects; occasionally hover-gleans.
Voice: call is a very high-pitched *tsee;* song is a very high-pitched, weak *see see see see.*

Similar Species: *Bay-breasted Warbler* (p. 292): male has black face and chestnut throat, upper breast and sides; 2 white wing bars; buff underparts lack black streaking. *Black-throated Green Warbler* (p. 286): black throat or upper breast or both; white lower breast and belly; lacks chestnut "cheek" patch; 2 white wing bars. *Magnolia Warbler* (p. 282): white tail patches; less streaking on underparts; lacks chestnut "cheek" patch and yellow side "collar." *Pine Warbler* (p. 289): dull females are similar to dull Cape Mays but have larger bills and are larger overall.
Best Sites: *Spring:* Atlanta (HC-spring: 50). *Fall:* Along the Coast and barrier islands (HC-Jekyll: 53).

BLACK-THROATED BLUE WARBLER

Dendroica caerulescens

Dark and handsome, the male Black-throated Blue Warbler is a treasured sight to the eyes of any bird enthusiast or casual admirer. • When foraging, this warbler prefers to work methodically over a small area, snatching up insects from branches and foliage and gleaning insects from the undersides of leaves. It is generally shy and inconspicuous, foraging secretly within the dense confines of low shrubs and saplings. • Typical of warblers, the Black-throated Blue female can construct a highly sophisticated nest within three to five days using cobwebs and saliva to glue strips of bark together. The inside of the nest is usually padded with shredded bark, moss, pine needles and any available mammal hair, such as skunk and human hair. • In Georgia, Black-throated Blues are easily seen at higher elevations in the Mountains.

ID: *Male:* black face, throat, upper breast and sides; dark blue upperparts; clean white underparts and wing patch. *Female:* olive brown upperparts; unmarked buff underparts; faint white "eyebrow"; small, buff to whitish wing patch (may not be visible).
Size: *L* 5–5½ in; *W* 7½ in.
Status: common summer breeding resident in the Mountains above about 2600 ft from April to October; uncommon migrant in the Coastal Plain but common migrant in the Piedmont and the Coast; accidental in winter.
Habitat: *Breeding:* upland deciduous and mixed forests with a dense understory of deciduous saplings and shrubs; second-growth woodlands and brushy clearings. *In migration:* shrubby woodlands or areas with tall shrubs.

Nesting: in the fork of a dense shrub or sapling, usually within 3 ft of the ground; female builds an open cup nest of weeds, bark strips and spiderwebs and lines it with moss, hair and pine needles; female incubates 4 creamy white eggs, blotched with reddish brown and gray toward the larger end, for 12–13 days.
Feeding: thoroughly gleans the understory for caterpillars, moths, spiders and other insects; occasionally eats berries and seeds; feeds less energetically than other wood-warblers.
Voice: call is a short *tip;* song is a slow, wheezy *zee-zee-zee-zreeee* (*I am soo lay-zeee*), rising slowly throughout.
Similar Species: male is distinctive. *Tennessee Warbler* (p. 276): lighter "cheek"; greener back; lacks white wing patch. *Philadelphia Vireo* (p. 234): stouter bill; lighter "cheek"; more yellowish white below; lacks white wing patch. *Cerulean Warbler* (p. 294): female has 2 white wing bars; broader, yellowish "eyebrow."
Best Sites: Lake Conasauga; Brasstown Bald; Rabun Bald; Swallow Creek WMA (HC-breeding: 29).

YELLOW-RUMPED WARBLER

Dendroica coronata

The Yellow-rumped Warbler is the most abundant and widespread wood-warbler in North America. Your greatest chance of meeting this bird in Georgia is from late September to May, during the first few hours after dawn, when most Yellow-rumps forage among streamside and lakeshore trees or in wax myrtles near the Coast. • Two races of the Yellow-rumped Warbler occur and were once considered separate species: the white-throated race, formerly called "Myrtle Warbler," and the very rarely seen yellow-throated western race, formerly called "Audubon's Warbler." • The Yellow-rump is unique among warblers for its ability to digest the waxes in bayberry and wax myrtle fruits. • A long-standing name for Yellow-rumps among birders is "Butter-butts."

"Myrtle Warbler"

ID: yellow foreshoulder patches and rump; white underparts; dark "cheek"; faint white wing bars; thin "eyebrow." *Male:* yellow crown; blue-gray upperparts with black streaking; black "cheek," breast band and streaking along sides and flanks. *Female:* gray-brown upperparts with dark streaking; dark streaking on breast, sides and flanks.
Size: *L* 5–6 in; *W* 9 in.
Status: common migrant and winter resident statewide from September to May; abundant in the lower Coastal Plain in spring and winter.
Habitat: woodlands or shrubby areas.
Nesting: does not nest in Georgia.
Feeding: hawks and hovers for beetles, flies, wasps, caterpillars, moths and other insects; also gleans vegetation; sometimes

eats berries, especially wax myrtle and poison ivy in winter.
Voice: call is a sharp *chip* or *check;* song is a tinkling trill, often given in 2-note phrases that rise or fall at the end (there can be much variation among individuals).
Similar Species: *Magnolia Warbler* (p. 282): yellow underparts and throat; bold, white "eyebrow"; lacks yellow crown; white patches on tail. *Chestnut-sided Warbler* (p. 281): chestnut sides on otherwise clean white underparts; lacks yellow rump. *Cape May Warbler* (p. 283): heavily streaked yellow throat, breast and sides; lacks yellow crown. *Yellow-throated Warbler* (p. 288): yellow throat; bold, white "eyebrow," ear patch and wing bars; lacks yellow crown and rump.
Best Sites: ubiquitous south of the Mountains in winter.

BLACK-THROATED GREEN WARBLER

Dendroica virens

Before the first warm rays of dawn brighten the spires of our mountain forests and Piedmont uplands, male Black-throated Green Warblers offer up their distinctive *see-see-see SUZY!* tunes. On their breeding grounds, not only do males use song to defend their turf, but they also seem to thrive on chasing each other, and even other songbirds, from their territories. • When foraging among the forest canopy, males are highly conspicuous as they dart from branch to branch, chipping noisily as they go. Females often prefer to feed at lower levels among the foliage of tall shrubs and sapling trees. • Black-throated Green females will lay one egg every day for four or five days, and they will not begin to brood the eggs until the last egg is laid.

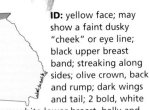

ID: yellow face; may show a faint dusky "cheek" or eye line; black upper breast band; streaking along sides; olive crown, back and rump; dark wings and tail; 2 bold, white wing bars; white lower breast, belly and undertail coverts. *Male:* black throat. *Female:* white throat with varying amounts of black, from large black spots on either side to almost none; thinner wing bars.
Size: L 4½–5 in; W 7½ in.
Status: uncommon to common summer breeding resident in the northeastern Mountains above 1800 ft, uncommon in the far northwest and rare in remainder of the northwestern Mountains from March to October; also nests rarely in the Piedmont uplands; rare to uncommon migrant statewide from March to May and from July to November.
Habitat: *Breeding:* coniferous and mixed forests; also in some deciduous woodlands

composed of beech, maple or birch; may inhabit cedar swamps, hemlock ravines and conifer plantations. *In migration:* woodlands or areas with tall shrubs.
Nesting: usually in a conifer; compact cup nest of grass, weeds, twigs, bark, lichens and spider silk is lined with moss, fur, feathers and plant fibers; female incubates 4–5 creamy white to gray eggs, scrawled or spotted with reddish brown, for 12 days.
Feeding: gleans vegetation and buds for beetles, flies, wasps, caterpillars and other insects; sometimes takes berries; frequently hover-gleans.
Voice: call is a fairly soft *tick;* fast *see-see-see SUZY!* or *zoo zee zoo zoo zee.*
Similar Species: *Blackburnian Warbler* (p. 287): female has yellowish underparts and angular, dusky facial patch. *Cape May Warbler* (p. 283): heavily streaked yellow throat, breast and sides. *Pine Warbler* (p. 289): yellowish breast and upper belly; lacks black upper breast band.
Best Sites: Brasstown Bald; Rabun Bald; Sosebee Cove; Pine Log WMA; Cloudland Canyon SP; Kennesaw Mt. (HC-fall: 41).

BLACKBURNIAN WARBLER

Dendroica fusca

High among towering coniferous spires of the Appalachian Mountains lives the colorful Blackburnian Warbler, its fiery orange throat ablaze in spring. • Different species of wood-warblers are able to coexist by feeding in separate areas of a tree and by using unique feeding strategies. This intricate partitioning reduces competition for food sources and allows each resource to last longer. Some warblers inhabit high treetops, a few feed and nest along outer tree branches—some at higher levels and some at lower levels—and others restrict themselves to inner branches and tree trunks. Blackburnians have found their niche predominantly in the outermost branches of the crowns of mature trees. • This bird's name is thought to honor the Blackburne family of England, whose members collected the type specimen and managed the museum in which it was housed.

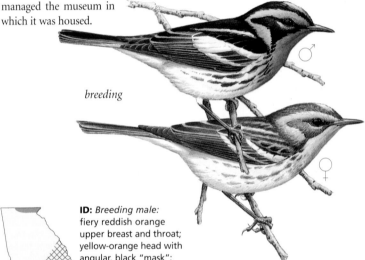

breeding

ID: *Breeding male:* fiery reddish orange upper breast and throat; yellow-orange head with angular, black "mask"; 2 broad, black crown stripes; blackish upperparts; large, white wing patch; yellowish to whitish underparts; dark streaking on sides and flanks. *Female:* brown version of male; yellower upper breast and throat than male.
Size: *L* 4½–5½ in; *W* 8½ in.
Status: uncommon summer breeding resident in the northeastern Mountains above 2600 ft from April to October; uncommon migrant statewide, except rare south of the Fall Line, from March to May and from July to October.
Habitat: *Breeding:* mature coniferous and mixed forests. *In migration:* woodlands or areas with tall shrubs.
Nesting: high in a mature conifer, often near a branch tip; female builds a cup nest of bark, twigs and plant fibers; female incubates 3–5 white to greenish white

eggs, blotched with reddish brown, for about 13 days.
Feeding: forages on uppermost branches, gleaning budworms, flies, beetles and other invertebrates; occasionally hover-gleans.
Voice: call is a short *tick;* song is a soft, faint, high-pitched *ptoo-too-too-too tititi zeee* or *see-me see-me see-me see-me.*
Similar Species: *Cerulean Warbler* (p. 294): drab immature fall female almost impossible to distinguish; unstreaked back and pale colors of head do not fully wrap around dark ear patch. *Yellow-throated Warbler* (p. 288): blue-gray upperparts; white "eyebrow," ear patch and eye crescent; lacks orange throat. *Prairie Warbler* (p. 290): faint, yellowish wing bars; black facial stripes do not form a solid angular patch.
Best Sites: Lake Conasauga; Ivy Log Gap; Neel's Gap; Burnt Mt.; Kennesaw Mt. (HC-spring: 24); Columbus (HC-fall: 60).

YELLOW-THROATED WARBLER

Dendroica dominica

The loud song of the Yellow-throated Warbler is one of the first signs of spring in the southeastern U.S. This warbler divides its time between two distinct habitats: wet, wooded lowlands or cypress swamps and drier pine or mixedwood forests. Most foraging and nesting occurs in the upper canopy of the latter. The Yellow-throat forages more like a Brown Creeper than a warbler, inserting its unusually long bill into cracks and crevices in bark. It often forages on the undersides of horizontal branches and sometimes on the trunk, techniques also used by the Black-and-white Warbler. • Two subspecies occur in Georgia: *D. d. dominica* breeds in all areas except the far northwest Mountain region, where *D. d. albilora* likely breeds. The latter subspecies, with its white lores, is often called the "Sycamore Warbler" because of its preference for nesting in sycamore trees.

yellow-lored morph

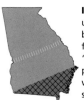

ID: yellow throat and upper breast; triangular, black face "mask"; black forehead; bold white "eyebrow" and ear patch; white underparts with black streaking on sides; 2 white wing bars; bluish gray upperparts.

Size: *L* 5–5½ in; *W* 8 in.

Status: uncommon summer breeding resident in the Piedmont and the Mountains to 2300 ft but common in the Coastal Plain and the Coast from March to November; in winter, rare in the Coastal Plain and uncommon on the Coast.

Habitat: primarily riparian woodlands; hardwood, pine and cypress forests.

Nesting: high in a sycamore, oak, cypress or pine tree, often near a branch tip; female builds a cup nest in Spanish moss and lines it with plant down and feathers; female incubates 4 greenish white or gray-white eggs, blotched and speckled with lavender, gray and wine red, for 12–13 days.

Feeding: primarily insectivorous; gleans insects from tree trunks and foliage by creeping along tree surfaces; often fly-catches insects in midair; wintering birds may eat suet from backyard feeders.

Voice: call is a loud *churp;* boisterous song is a series of down-slurred whistles with a final rising note: *tee-ew tee-ew tee-ew tew-wee.*

Similar Species: *Magnolia Warbler* (p. 282): black "necklace"; yellow breast, belly and rump; lacks white ear patch. *Blackburnian Warbler* (p. 287): yellow-orange to orange-red throat, "eyebrow," ear patch and crown stripe; dark brown to blackish upperparts; often shows yellowish underparts. *Yellow-throated Vireo* (p. 231): lacks black and white on face and dark streaking on sides. *Kentucky Warbler* (p. 303): unmarked, all-yellow underparts; yellow "eyebrow"; lacks white ear patch and wing bars.

Best Sites: Beaverdam WMA; Savannah–Ogeechee Canal; barrier islands and the Coast; McIntosh Co. (HC-breeding: 90); Glynn Co. (HC-winter: 23).

PINE WARBLER

Dendroica pinus

This well-named warbler is often difficult to find because it typically forages near the tops of very tall, mature pine trees. Its modest appearance, which is very similar to that of a number of immature and fall-plumaged vireos and warblers, forces birders to obtain a good, long look before making a positive identification. The Pine Warbler is most often confused with the Bay-breasted Warbler or Blackpoll Warbler in drab fall plumage. • The Pine Warbler is peculiar among the wood-warblers in that both its breeding and wintering ranges are located almost entirely within Canada and the United States. • The Pine Warbler is one of our earliest warblers to arrive and set up territories, and males can often be heard singing their persistent trilling song as early as late December. Occasionally, foraging Pine Warblers can be seen smeared with patches of sticky pine resin.

ID: *Male:* olive green head and back; dark grayish wings and tail; whitish to dusky wing bars; yellow throat and breast; faded, dark streaking or dusky wash on sides of breast; white undertail coverts and belly; faint dark line through eye; faint yellow, broken eye ring. *Female:* similar to male but duller, especially in fall. *Immature:* duller; brownish olive head and back; pale yellow (male) to creamy white (female) throat and breast; brown wash on flanks.
Size: *L* 5–5½ in; *W* 8½ in.
Status: common permanent breeding resident statewide, except rare and local in the Mountains below 2300 ft.
Habitat: open, mature pine woodlands and mature pine plantations.
Nesting: toward the end of a pine limb; female builds a deep, open cup nest of twigs, bark, weeds, grasses, pine needles and spiderwebs and lines it with feathers; pair incubates 3–5 whitish eggs, with brown specks toward the larger end, for about 10 days.
Feeding: gleans from the ground or foliage by climbing around trees and shrubs; may hang upside down on branch tips like a chickadee or titmouse; eats mostly insects, berries and seeds.
Voice: call note is a sweet *chip;* song is a short, musical trill.
Similar Species: *Prairie Warbler* (p. 290): distinctive, dark facial stripes; darker streaking on sides; yellowish wing bars; smaller bill. *Kirtland's Warbler* (p. 366): darker streaking on sides; broken, white eye ring; bluish gray upperparts. *Bay-breasted Warbler* (p. 292) and *Blackpoll Warbler* (p. 293): nonbreeding and immatures have dark streaking on head or back or both; long, thin, yellow "eyebrow." *Yellow-throated Vireo* (p. 231): bright yellow "spectacles"; gray rump; lacks streaking on sides.
Best Sites: almost any rural or urban, open, mature pine woodlands statewide.

PRAIRIE WARBLER

Dendroica discolor

The Prairie Warbler is not a bird of the prairies—it occupies early successional areas with such poor soil conditions that the vegetation remains short and scattered. • The Prairie Warbler was probably rare over much of its current breeding range in the early 1800s, before North America was widely colonized. As settlers cleared land, Prairie Warbler populations increased in the eastern states. Because this bird uses early successional habitats, which change over time, its breeding locations change as well. A male Prairie Warbler may return each year to a favored nest site until the vegetation in that area grows too tall and dense, at which point he moves to a new area. • On their nesting territories, song wars occasionally result in physical fights between competing males. When the dust and feathers clear, the victor resumes his slow, graceful, butterfly-like courtship flight.

ID: *Male:* bright yellow face and underparts, except for white under-tail coverts; dark "cheek" stripe and eye line; black streaking on sides; olive gray upperparts; inconspicuous chestnut streaks on back; 2 faint, yellowish wing bars. *Female* and *immature:* similar to male but duller in color.
Size: *L* 4½–5 in; *W* 7 in.
Status: common summer breeding resident statewide, except rare in the far southeast from April to October; in winter, rare in the Coastal Plain and the Coast; accidental in winter north of the Fall Line.
Habitat: dry, open scrubby sand dunes; young jack pine plains; shrubby, small tree, burned-over sites; young pine plantations with deciduous scrub.

Nesting: small, loose nesting colonies may form; low in a shrub or small tree; female builds an open cup nest of soft vegetation and lines it with animal hair; female incubates 4 whitish eggs, with brown spots toward the larger end, for 11–14 days; pair raises the young together.
Feeding: gleans, hover-gleans and occasionally hawks for prey; mainly insectivorous; will also eat berries and tree sap exposed by sapsuckers; caterpillars are a favored item for nestlings.
Voice: call is sweet *chip;* buzzy song is an ascending series of *zee* notes.
Similar Species: *Pine Warbler* (p. 289): lighter streaking on sides; whitish wing bars; lacks distinctive dark streaking on face; larger bill. *Yellow-throated Warbler* (p. 288): white belly; bold white wing bars, "eyebrow" and ear patch. *Bay-breasted Warbler* (p. 292) and *Blackpoll Warbler* (p. 293): nonbreeding and immature birds have white bellies and wing bars, and lighter upperparts with dark streaking.
Best Sites: Pine Log WMA; Piedmont NWR; Bartow Co. (HC-breeding: 100+); Okefenokee NWR (HC-winter: 5).

PALM WARBLER

Dendroica palmarum

The Palm Warbler doesn't actually forage in palm trees, but considering this bird's subtropical wintering range, the name may make sense. Despite its tropical name, the Palm Warbler nests farther north than all other wood-warblers except the Blackpoll Warbler. • Palm Warblers forage on the ground or in low shrubs and vegetation, which is an unusual strategy for warblers. • Whether hopping on the ground or perched momentarily on an elevated limb, the Palm Warbler's tail is always bobbing. For birders, this prominent trait is particularly useful for identification in fall, when the Palm Warbler's distinctive chestnut crown fades to a dull olive brown. • Two subspecies are present in Georgia: *D. p. palmarum,* the "western" race, has yellow restricted to the throat and undertail coverts, whereas the "eastern" race, *D. p. hypochrysea,* is more yellow overall. The "western" race is a common migrant and winter resident statewide, whereas the "eastern" race is a rare to uncommon migrant and winter resident, found mostly inland.

breeding
"eastern" race

ID: *Breeding:* chestnut brown "cap" (may be inconspicuous in fall); yellow "eyebrow," throat and undertail coverts; yellow or white breast and belly; dark streaking on breast and sides; olive brown upperparts; may show dull, yellowish rump; frequently bobs its tail. *Nonbreeding:* duller plumage.
Size: *L* 4–5½ in; *W* 8 in.
Status: common spring and uncommon fall migrant from August to May; uncommon (north of the Fall Line) to abundant (on the Coast) in winter.
Habitat: woodlands or areas with tall shrubs; also coastal areas, agricultural fields, parks and ditches.
Nesting: does not nest in Georgia.
Feeding: gleans the ground and vegetation for a wide variety of insects and berries while perched or hovering; occasionally hawks for insects; may take some seeds.
Voice: call is a sharp *sup* or *check;* song is a weak, buzzy trill with a quick finish.
Similar Species: *Yellow-rumped Warbler* (p. 285): white wing bars, throat and undertail coverts; female has bright yellow rump, crown patch and foreshoulder patch. *Prairie Warbler* (p. 290): dark jaw stripe; darker eye line; lacks chestnut crown and dark streaking on breast. *Chipping Sparrow* (p. 315) and *American Tree Sparrow:* stouter bodies; unstreaked, grayish underparts; lack yellow plumage. *Pine Warbler* (p. 289): faint, whitish wing bars; white undertail coverts; lacks chestnut "cap" and bold yellow "eyebrow."
Best Sites: Kennesaw Mt. in spring (HC: 76); Laurens Co.; Onslow I. and along the Coast; Jekyll I. (HC-"western": 500+); Lake Seminole WMA (HC-"eastern": 24).

BAY-BREASTED WARBLER

Dendroica castanea

Deep within stands of old-growth spruce and fir is where you will have to search to find the handsome Bay-breasted Warbler. It typically forages midway up a tree, often on the inner branches, so it's difficult to spot. The largest numbers of these multicolored birds typically pass through Georgia in fall migration. • Most Bay-breasted Warblers spend the winter close to the equator, where seasons and day length are similar year-round. At these tropical latitudes, birds rely heavily on their internal clocks, rather than external clues, to spark the spring migration northward. • Bay-breasted Warblers are spruce budworm specialists, and their populations fluctuate from year to year along with the cyclical rise and fall of budworm populations on their nesting grounds in Canada and the northeastern U.S. In outbreak years, one Bay-breasted Warbler can likely eat over 5000 budworms per acre through the breeding season! • Although Bay-breasts are insectivorous on their breeding grounds, they switch to an almost all-fruit diet while they winter in Panama and Colombia.

breeding

Habitat: woodlands or areas with tall shrubs; coastal areas.

Nesting: does not nest in Georgia.

Feeding: usually forages at the midlevel of trees; gleans vegetation and branches for caterpillars and adult invertebrates; eats berries and seeds in fall.

ID: dark legs and feet. *Breeding male:* black face and "chin"; chestnut crown, throat, sides and flanks; creamy yellow belly, undertail coverts and patch on side of neck; 2 white wing bars. *Breeding female:* paler colors overall; dusky face; whitish to creamy underparts and neck patch; faint chestnut "cap"; rusty wash on sides and flanks. *Nonbreeding:* yellow olive head and back; dark streaking on crown and back; buff-tinged underparts.

Size: *L* 5–6 in; *W* 9 in.

Status: rare to uncommon migrant from April to May and uncommon to common migrant from August to November, north of the Fall Line; rare spring and rare to uncommon fall migrant elsewhere.

Voice: call is a high *see;* song is an extremely high-pitched *seee-seese-seese-seee.*

Similar Species: *Cape May Warbler* (p. 283): chestnut "cheek" on yellow face; dark streaking on mostly yellow underparts; lacks reddish flanks and crown. *Chestnut-sided Warbler* (p. 281): yellow crown; white "cheek" and underparts; fall birds have a white eye ring, unmarked whitish face and underparts and lack bold streaking on lime green upperparts. *Blackpoll Warbler* (p. 293): white undertail coverts; nonbreeding and immature birds have dark streaking on breast and sides and lack chestnut on sides and flanks; often have yellowish legs and feet.

Best Sites: Kennesaw Mt. (HC-fall: 39); Chattahoochee River NRA.

BLACKPOLL WARBLER

Dendroica striata

The Blackpoll Warbler is the greatest warbler migrant: weighing less than a wet teabag, this bird is known to fly south over the Atlantic during its fall migration, leaving land at Cape Cod and flying for 88 nonstop hours (more than 3 days!) until it reaches the northern coast of Venezuela. In such a trip, a Blackpoll Warbler will cover 2500 miles, and in a single year, it may fly up to 15,000 miles! In migration, the Blackpoll Warbler adjusts its flying altitude—sometimes flying at heights of 20,000 feet—to best use shifting prevailing winds to reach its destination. In spring, Blackpolls take a more direct northerly route across the Gulf of Mexico. Some fly to Florida, and then to Georgia, as they head for their Canadian breeding grounds. They are most commonly seen migrating through Georgia in spring, from April to mid-May. This bird is truly an international resident, so conservation of its habitat requires the efforts of several nations. • Blackpoll Warblers in fall plumage are easily confused with very similar-looking Bay-breasted Warblers. Most Blackpolls, however, migrate later in fall than their Bay-breasted counterparts and most are offshore or along the coast, whereas almost all Bay-breasts are inland.

breeding

ID: 2 white wing bars; black streaking on underparts; white under-tail coverts. *Breeding male:* black "cap" and "mustache" stripe; white "cheek"; black-streaked, olive gray upperparts; white underparts; orange legs. *Breeding female:* streaked, yellow olive head and back; white underparts; small, dark eye line; pale "eyebrow." *Nonbreeding:* olive yellow head, back, rump, breast and sides; yellow "eyebrow"; dark legs and yellow feet or at least soles.
Size: *L* 5–5½ in; *W* 9 in.
Status: common migrant statewide from March to June; rare migrant inland and casual migrant on the Coast from August to November.
Habitat: mixed woodlands.
Nesting: does not nest in Georgia.

Feeding: gleans buds, leaves and branches for aphids, mosquitoes, beetles, wasps, caterpillars and many other insects; often flycatches for insects.
Voice: call is a loud *chip;* song is an extremely high-pitched, uniform trill: *tsit tsit tsit.*
Similar Species: *Black-and-white Warbler* (p. 295): dark legs; black-and-white-striped crown; male has black "chin," throat and "cheek" patch. *Bay-breasted Warbler* (p. 292): chestnut sides and flanks; buff undertail coverts; nonbreeding and immatures lack dark streaking on underparts.
Best Sites: Kennesaw Mt. (HC-spring: 60); any mixed woodlands, including urban shade trees in spring.

293

CERULEAN WARBLER

Dendroica cerulea

The handsome blue-and-white male is particularly difficult to observe as he blends into the sunny sky while foraging among treetop foliage. Often the only evidence of it is the precious sound of his buzzy, trilling voice. • Only in the last few decades have ornithologists been able to document this bird's breeding behavior. Courtship, mating, nesting and the rearing of young all tend to take place high in the canopy, well out of sight of most casual observers. Cerulean Warblers also attack each other high in the canopy; flying aggressively toward one another, they collide with an audible thud, then spiral together toward the ground. Females also fight, and an aggressive female may even knock her own mate off his perch in a similar manner. • The Cerulean has recently been found breeding in fair numbers at Ivy Log Gap near Young Harris. • *Cerulea* is Latin for "sky blue", an exceptionally appropriate name for this azure warbler.

ID: white undertail coverts and wing bars; short tail. *Male:* blue upperparts; white throat and underparts; blue "necklace" and streaking on sides. *Female:* blue-green crown, nape and back; dark eye line; yellow "eyebrow," throat and breast; pale streaking on sides.

Size: L 4½–5 in; W 7 in.

Status: uncommon migrant from March to May and from June to October north of the Fall Line; rare migrant south of the Fall Line, mostly in fall; rare breeder in the Mountains.

Habitat: mature deciduous hardwood forests and extensive woodlands with a clear understory; particularly drawn to riparian stands.

Nesting: high on the end of a deciduous branch; open cup nest is built with bark strips, weeds, grass, lichen and spider silk and is lined with fur and moss; female incubates 3–5 brown-spotted, gray to creamy whitish eggs for about 12–13 days.

Feeding: insects are gleaned from upper canopy foliage and branches; often hawks for insects.

Voice: call is a sharp *chip;* song is a rapid, accelerating sequence of buzzy notes leading into a higher-trilled note.

Similar Species: *Black-throated Blue Warbler* (p. 284): male has black face, "chin" and throat; female has small, white wing patch; lacks wing bars. *Blackburnian Warbler* (p. 287): drab immature fall female almost impossible to distinguish; streaked back and pale colors of head wrap around dark ear patch. *Blackpoll Warbler* (p. 293) and *Bay-breasted Warbler* (p. 292): similar to female but have more yellow than green on mantle.

Best Sites: *Breeding:* Ivy Log Gap (HC: 10); Gumlog Gap. *In migration:* Kennesaw Mt. is the best site in the eastern U.S. (HC-fall: 32).

BLACK-AND-WHITE WARBLER

Mniotilta varia

The foraging behavior of the Black-and-white Warbler stands in sharp contrast to that of most of its kin. Rather than dancing or flitting quickly between twig perches, Black-and-white Warblers behave like creepers and nuthatches—distantly related families of birds. Birders with frayed nerves and tired eyes from watching flitty warblers will be refreshed by the sight of this bird as it methodically creeps up and down tree trunks, probing bark crevices. • Novice birders can easily identify this unique, two-toned warbler, which is a breeder in northern Georgia and a statewide migrant. A keen ear also helps to identify this forest-dweller: its gentle oscillating song—like a wheel in need of greasing—is easily recognized and remembered.

ID: black-and-white-striped crown; dark upperparts with white streaking; 2 white wing bars; white underparts with black streaking on sides, flanks and under-tail coverts; black legs. *Male:* black "cheek" and throat. *Female:* gray "cheek"; white throat.
Size: *L* 4½–5½ in; *W* 8 in.
Status: common summer breeding resident in the Mountains; uncommon in the Piedmont and localized in the upper Coastal Plain; common migrant statewide from February to May and from July to November; uncommon winter resident in the Coastal Plain and the Coast; accidental in the Piedmont.
Habitat: deciduous or mixed forests, often near water.

Nesting: usually on the ground next to a tree, log or large rock; in a shallow scrape, often among a pile of dead leaves; female builds a cup nest with grass, leaves, bark strips, rootlets and pine needles and lines it with fur and fine grass; female incubates 5 creamy white eggs, with brown flecks toward the larger end, for 10–12 days.
Feeding: gleans insect eggs, larval insects, beetles, spiders and other invertebrates while creeping along tree trunks and branches.
Voice: call is a sharp *pit* and a soft, high *seet;* song is a series of high, thin, 2-syllable notes: *weetsee weetsee weetsee weetsee weetsee weetsee.*
Similar Species: *Blackpoll Warbler* (p. 293): breeding male has solid black "cap" and clean white undertail coverts.
Best Sites: Brasstown Bald; Rabun Bald; Kennesaw Mt. (HC-spring: 23); Harris Neck NWR (HC-winter: 15).

295

AMERICAN REDSTART

Setophaga ruticilla

American Redstarts are a consistent favorite among birders. These supercharged birds flit from branch to branch in dizzying pursuit of prey. Even when perched, their tails sway rhythmically back and forth. Few birds can rival a mature male redstart for his contrasting black-and-orange plumage and amusing behavior. • A common foraging technique used by the American Redstart is to flash its wings and tail patches to flush prey. If a concealed insect tries to flee, the redstart will give chase. The American Redstart behaves much the same way on its Central American wintering grounds, where it is known locally as "candelita," meaning "little candle." • Although Lake Winfield Scott is a fairly reliable location for finding breeding American Redstarts, the beautiful, trilly songs of these birds are so variable that identification is a challenge to birders of all levels.

ID: *Male:* black overall; red-orange foreshoulder, wing and tail patches; white belly and undertail coverts. *Female:* olive brown upperparts; gray-green head; yellow foreshoulder, wing and tail patches; clean white underparts.

Size: *L* 5 in; *W* 8 in.

Status: uncommon to common summer local breeding resident in the Mountains, Piedmont and upper Coastal Plain; common migrant statewide from April to May and from July to November.

Habitat: shrubby woodland edges, open and semi-open deciduous and mixed forests with a regenerating deciduous understory of shrubs and saplings; often near water; breeding populations away from the Mountains are almost exclusively along forested riparian corridors.

Nesting: in the fork of a shrub or sapling, usually 3–23 ft above the ground; female builds an open cup nest of plant down, bark shreds, grass and rootlets and lines it with feathers; female incubates 4 whitish eggs, marked with brown or gray, for 11–12 days.

Feeding: actively gleans foliage and hawks for insects and spiders on leaves, buds and branches; often hover-gleans.

Voice: call is a sharp, sweet *chip;* song is a highly variable series of *tseet* or *zee* notes, often given at different pitches.

Similar Species: *Magnolia Warbler* (p. 282): similar tail pattern, but tail bands are white. *Orioles* (pp. 350–51): larger; less black on plumage.

Best Sites: Lake Winfield Scott; Ivy Log Gap; Byron Herbert Reese Memorial Park; Columbus and Augusta (HC-fall: 100+).

PROTHONOTARY WARBLER

Protonotaria citrea

The Prothonotary Warbler is the only eastern wood-warbler to nest in cavities. Standing dead trees and stumps riddled with cavities provide perfect nesting habitat for this bird, especially if the site is near stagnant, swampy water. Much of the Prothonotary's swampy habitat is inaccessible to most birders, but if you are lucky, you may come across this bird as it forages for insects along tree trunks and decaying logs, in low, tangled thickets and on debris floating on the water's surface. • The male can be very aggressive when defending his territory, and he often resorts to combative aerial chases when songs and warning displays fail to intimidate an intruder. Unfortunately for neighboring birds, this scorn is unprejudiced—other cavity-nesting birds such as woodpeckers, wrens and bluebirds are often victims of this fury. • This bird acquired its unusual name because its plumage was thought to resemble the yellow hoods worn by prothonotaries, high-ranking clerics in the Catholic Church. It is also commonly called the "Swamp Canary" in rural areas.

Size: *L* 5½ in; *W* 8½ in.

Status: common summer breeding resident near water south of the Fall Line, and local in the Piedmont and northwestern Georgia from April to September; absent from the Mountains.

Habitat: wooded deciduous swamps and riparian woodlands.

Nesting: cavities in standing dead trees, rotten stumps, birdhouses or abandoned woodpecker nests, from water level to 10 ft above the ground; often returns to the same nest site; mostly the male builds a cup nest of twigs, leaves, moss and plant down and lines it with soft plant material; female

ID: large, dark eyes; long bill; unmarked, yellow head; yellow undersides except for gleaming white undertail coverts; olive green back; unmarked, bluish gray wings and tail.

incubates 4–6 brown-spotted, creamy to pinkish eggs for 12–14 days.

Feeding: forages for a variety of insects and small mollusks; gleans from vegetation; may hop on floating debris or creep along tree trunks.

Voice: call is a brisk *tink;* flight song is *chewee chewee chee chee;* song is a loud, ringing series of *sweet* or *zweet* notes issued on a single pitch.

Similar Species: *Blue-winged Warbler* (p. 274): white wing bars; black eye line; yellowish white undertail coverts. *Yellow Warbler* (p. 280): dark wings and tail with yellow highlights; yellow undertail coverts; male has reddish streaking on breast. *Hooded Warbler* (p. 307): female has yellow undertail coverts and yellow olive upperparts.

Best Sites: Ocmulgee NM; Phinizy Swamp Nature Park; Beaverdam WMA; Altamaha WMA; Savannah-Ogeechee Canal; Okefenokee NWR (HC: 100+).

297

WORM-EATING WARBLER

Helmitheros vermivora

People wishing to see this bird have a challenge ahead of them because the Worm-eating Warbler's subdued colors allow it to blend in with the decomposing twigs, roots and leaves that litter the forest floor. Most of this bird's time is spent foraging for caterpillars, small terrestrial insects and spiders among dense undergrowth and dead leaves in deciduous forests. This species is truly a "dead-leaf" specialist, and it can often be found by scanning clusters of dead leaves. • During the breeding season, this warbler may be found in the mountainous regions of Georgia. The Worm-eating Warbler is part of a small group of eastern warblers that nest on the ground. Nests are typically built on slopes and near water. The female becomes completely still if she is approached while on the nest, relying on her striped crown for concealment. • The Worm-eating Warbler is yet another trilling singer. Its trill is faster and more insectlike than the Chipping Sparrow's, and it seems louder in the middle of the trill and weaker at the beginning and end.

ID: black and buff orange head stripes; brownish olive upperparts; rich buff orange breast; whitish undertail coverts.
Size: *L* 5 in; *W* 8½ in.
Status: common summer breeding resident in most of the Mountains and uncommon in the northwestern Mountains, upper Piedmont and Coastal Plain; uncommon migrant elsewhere from March to October.
Habitat: steep, deciduous woodland slopes, ravines and swampy woodlands with shrubby understory cover.
Nesting: usually on a hillside or ravine bank, often near water; on the ground hidden under leaf litter; female builds a cup nest of decaying leaves and lines it with fine grass, moss stems and hair; female incubates 3–5 white eggs, speckled with reddish brown, for about 13 days.
Feeding: forages on the ground and in trees and shrubs; eats mostly small insects.
Voice: call is a buzzy *zeep-zeep;* song is a faster, thinner version of the Chipping Sparrow's chipping trill.
Similar Species: *Swainson's Warbler* (p. 299): very similar overall but has solid brown "cap" instead of head stripes. *Red-eyed Vireo* (p. 235): gray crown; white "eyebrow"; red eyes; yellow undertail coverts. *Louisiana Waterthrush* (p. 302) and *Northern Waterthrush* (p. 301): darker upperparts; bold white or yellowish "eyebrow"; dark streaking on white breast; lacks striped head.
Best Sites: Cloudland Canyon SP; Cohutta WMA; Ivy Log Gap; Harris Co. (HC-spring: 15).

SWAINSON'S WARBLER

Limnothlypis swainsonii

Plain looks and a large bill distinguish the Swainson's Warbler from other members of the colorful wood-warbler clan. With inconspicuous attire, the Swainson's Warbler blends into the shady undergrowth of rhododendron thickets and riparian woodlands to escape detection and identification by predators and birders alike. However, few can miss its loud, musical song echoing through the lush, dense vegetation of May and June. • Although the Swainson's Warbler forages alone in winter, pairs forage together in summer. Mates reinforce bonds by searching together for juicy insects hidden along the forest floor or among low understory vegetation. • The Swainson's Warbler and the likely extinct Bachman's Warbler are the only members of the wood-warbler family to lay white, unmarked eggs—most warblers lay eggs with dark blotches, spots or a wreath of markings. • This warbler, the Swainson's Thrush and the Swainson's Hawk are all named after William Swainson, a well-known and accomplished naturalist of the early 1800s.

ID: reddish brown crown; pale "eyebrow"; thin, black eye line; olive brown above; buffy gray underparts; long, sharp bill.
Size: *L* 5½ in; *W* 9 in.
Status: common summer breeding resident in the Coastal Plain and local in the Piedmont and northeastern Mountains from March to October; difficult to find in migration.
Habitat: two very different habitats: dense swamps, bottomlands and riparian floodplains south of the Fall Line; rhododendron thickets and oak, maple and poplar stands with dense understory growth in the Appalachians.
Nesting: female builds a large, inconspicuous open cup nest of various vegetative materials placed near or over water in dense understory plants (often vines, cane or rhododendron); female incubates 3–5 white to pale buff eggs for 13–15 days; pair raise the young together.

Feeding: probes leaf litter and foliage while walking rapidly along the ground; flips over leaves of infrequently flooded areas along rivers with its large bill; occasionally forages among tree trunks or hawks for flying insects; insects and other invertebrates (both adults and larvae) form bulk of diet.
Voice: call is a loud *chip;* slurred, whistling song ends with a rising *tea-o.*
Similar Species: *Worm-eating Warbler* (p. 298): stripes on head instead of solid "cap." *Louisiana Waterthrush* (p. 302): dark streaking on sides and breast; lacks reddish brown crown. *Warbling Vireo* (p. 233): stubby, thicker bill; whiter breast; lacks reddish brown crown. *Red-eyed Vireo* (p. 235): red eyes; thicker bill; black line separates gray crown from white "eyebrow."
Best Sites: Burrell's Ford; Beaverdam WMA; Big Hammock WMA; Bond Swamp in Bibb Co. (HC: 26).

OVENBIRD

Seiurus aurocapilla

The common name refers to this bird's unusual, dome-shaped ground nest. An incubating female nestled within her woven dome usually feels so secure that she will choose to sit tight rather than flee when approached. The nest is so well camouflaged that few people ever find one, even though nests are often located near hiking trails and bike paths. The Ovenbird itself is equally elusive: it will rarely expose itself, and even when it does, active searching and patience is necessary to get a good look at it. • In spring, the Ovenbird's loud and joyous "ode to teachers" is a common sound that echoes through the hardwood forests in our mountainous and upper Piedmont regions. • For night migrants, including warblers, collisions with human-made structures such as buildings and towers cause about a million fatalities each year. Unfortunately, the high count for migrating Ovenbirds in Georgia is 236 Ovenbirds collected at the base of a tower over two nights at Warner Robbins.

ID: olive brown upperparts; white eye ring; heavy, dark streaking on white breast, sides and flanks; rufous crown has black border; pink legs; white undertail coverts; no wing bars.

Size: *L* 6 in; *W* 9½ in.

Status: common summer breeding resident in the Mountains and the upper Piedmont, south to Macon; common migrant north of the Fall Line from March to June and from July to November; rare spring and uncommon fall migrant south of the Fall Line; accidental in winter.

Habitat: *Breeding:* undisturbed, mature, deciduous, mixed and coniferous forests with a closed canopy and very little understory; often in ravines and riparian areas. *In migration:* dense riparian shrubbery and thickets and a variety of woodlands; often

walks along the ground; requires leaf litter for foraging.

Nesting: on the ground; female builds an oven-shaped, domed nest of grass, weeds, bark, twigs and dead leaves and lines it with animal hair; female incubates 4–5 white eggs, spotted with gray and brown, for 11–13 days.

Feeding: gleans the ground for worms, snails, insects and occasionally seeds.

Voice: call is a brisk *chip, cheep* or *chock;* loud, distinctive *tea-cher tea-cher Tea-CHER Tea-CHER,* increasing in speed and volume; night song is an elaborate series of bubbly, warbled notes, often ending in *teacher-teacher.*

Similar Species: *Northern Waterthrush* (p. 301) and *Louisiana Waterthrush* (p. 302): bold, yellowish or white "eyebrow"; darker upperparts; lack rufous crown. *Thrushes* (pp. 262–67): all are larger and lack rufous crown outlined in black.

Best Sites: Brasstown Bald; Rabun Bald; Pine Log WMA; Dawson Forest WMA; Ocmulgee NM.

NORTHERN WATERTHRUSH

Seiurus noveboracensis

Although this bird's long body looks "thrushlike," the Northern Waterthrush is actually a large wood-warbler. This bird skulks along the shores of deciduous swamps or coniferous bogs, often wagging or bobbing its tail. During spring and fall, migrating Northern Waterthrushes also appear among drier, upland forests or along lofty park trails and boardwalks. Backyards featuring a small garden pond may also attract migrating waterthrushes. Typically, Northern Waterthrushes migrate later than the similar-looking Louisiana Waterthrushes. • The voice of the Northern Waterthrush is loud and raucous for such a small bird, so it seems fitting that this bird was once known as the New York Warbler, in reference to the city so well known for its decibels. The scientific name *noveboracensis* means "of New York."

ID: pale yellowish to buff "eyebrow"; pale yellowish to buff underparts with dark streaking; finely spotted throat; olive brown upperparts; pinkish legs; frequently bobs its tail.

Size: *L* 5–6 in; *W* 9½ in.

Status: uncommon migrant statewide from March to June; common migrant statewide from July to November; accidental in winter.

Habitat: wooded edges of swamps, lakes, beaver ponds, bogs and rivers; also in moist, wooded ravines and riparian thickets.

Nesting: does not nest in Georgia.

Feeding: gleans foliage and the ground for invertebrates, frequently tossing aside ground litter with its bill; may also take aquatic invertebrates and small fish from shallow water.

Voice: call is a brisk *chip* or *chuck;* song is a loud, 3-part *sweet sweet sweet, swee wee wee, chew chew chew chew.*

Similar Species: *Louisiana Waterthrush* (p. 302): broader, white "eyebrow"; larger bill; fewer but wider stripes; unspotted, white throat; buff orange wash on flanks. *Ovenbird* (p. 300): rufous crown bordered by black stripes; white eye ring; unspotted throat; lacks pale "eyebrow."

Best Sites: Chattahoochee River NRA; Newman Wetlands Center; Dawson Forest WMA; Altamaha WMA; Jekyll I. (HC: 15).

301

LOUISIANA WATERTHRUSH

Seiurus motacilla

The Louisiana Waterthrush is often seen sallying along the shorelines of babbling streams and gently swirling pools in search of its next meal. This bird inhabits swamps and sluggish streams throughout much of its North American range, but where its range overlaps with the Northern Waterthrush it inhabits shorelines near fast-flowing water. • The Louisiana Waterthrush has a larger bill, pinker legs, whiter eye stripes and less streaking on its throat than the Northern Waterthrush. Both waterthrushes are easily identified by their habit of bobbing their heads and moving their tails up and down as they walk, but the Louisiana Waterthrush bobs its tail more slowly, and also tends to sway from side to side. • It is one of the earliest departing warblers from Georgia, with many leaving as early as July, and few being seen after the end of August. • This bird's scientific name *motacilla* is Latin for "wagtail."

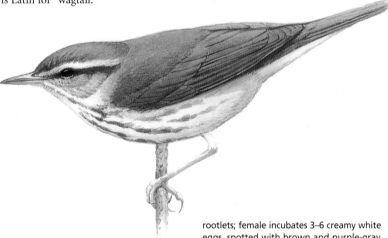

ID: brownish upperparts; long bill; pink legs; white underparts with buff orange wash on flanks; long, dark streaks on breast and sides; bicolored, buff-and-white "eyebrow"; clean white throat.

Size: *L* 6 in; *W* 10 in.

Status: uncommon to common migrant and summer breeding resident statewide, except in the southeast, from March to October.

Habitat: moist, forested ravines, alongside fast-flowing streams; rarely along wooded swamps.

Nesting: concealed within a rocky hollow or within a tangle of tree roots; pair builds a cup nest of leaves, bark strips, twigs and moss and lines it with animal hair, ferns and rootlets; female incubates 3–6 creamy white eggs, spotted with brown and purple-gray, for about 14 days.

Feeding: terrestrial and aquatic insects and crustaceans are gleaned from rocks and debris in or near shallow water; dead leaves and other debris may be flipped and probed for food; occasionally catches flying insects over water.

Voice: call is a brisk *chick* or *chink;* song begins with 3–4 distinctive, shrill, slurred notes followed by a warbling twitter.

Similar Species: *Northern Waterthrush* (p. 301): yellowish to buff "eyebrow" narrows behind eye; underparts are usually all yellowish or buff (occasionally all white); streaks are more numerous and thinner; finely spotted throat; lacks buff orange flanks. *Ovenbird* (p. 300) and *thrushes* (pp. 262–67): lack broad, white "eyebrow."

Best Sites: Cloudland Canyon SP; Pine Log WMA; Newman Wetlands Center; Beaverdam WMA; Flint R. (HC: 15).

KENTUCKY WARBLER

Oporornis formosus

Kentucky Warblers spend much of their time on the ground, turning over leaves and scurrying through dense thickets in search of insects. These birds are shy and elusive as they sing their loud springtime song from secluded perches. As a general rule, male warblers sing most actively in the morning, feeding only intermittently, but in the afternoon they quiet down and feed more actively. Once the young hatch, singing becomes rare as both the male and female spend much of their time feeding the young. Unmated males, however, may continue to sing throughout summer. • The Kentucky Warbler's song may be confused with that of the Carolina Wren, but the Kentucky Warbler will sing the same song pattern repeatedly, whereas the Carolina Wren varies its song constantly. • Like waterthrushes and Ovenbirds, Kentucky Warblers bob their tails up and down as they walk. • The Kentucky Warbler breeds over most of Georgia, south to Effingham, Bulloch, Appling and Thomas counties.

ID: bright yellow "spectacles" and underparts; black crown, "sideburns" and half "mask"; olive green upperparts.
Size: *L* 5–5½ in; *W* 8½ in.
Status: uncommon local summer breeding resident, except in the southeast, from April to October; secretive in migration.
Habitat: moist, deciduous and mixed woodlands with dense, shrubby cover and herbaceous plant growth, including wooded ravines, swamp edges and creek bottomlands.
Nesting: placed on or close to the ground; pair builds a cup nest of plant material and hair and lines it with rootlets and hair;

female incubates 4–5 cream-colored eggs, spotted or blotched with reddish brown, for 12–13 days.
Feeding: gleans insects while walking along the ground, flipping over leaf litter, or by snatching prey from the undersides of low foliage.
Voice: call is a sharp *chick, chuck* or *chip*; musical song is a series of 2-syllable notes: *chur-ree chur-ree* (less varied than the song of the Carolina Wren).
Similar Species: *Canada Warbler* (p. 309): dark, streaky "necklace"; bluish gray upperparts.
Best Sites: Pine Log WMA; Piedmont NWR (HC: 9); Ocmulgee NM; Beaverdam WMA; Big Hammock WMA.

CONNECTICUT WARBLER

Oporornis agilis

Soggy, impenetrable bogs, pine forests and mixed woodlands are all favored habitats for the mysterious and secretive Connecticut Warbler. This bird does a good job of avoiding detection as it migrates through Georgia. In fact, the Connecticut Warbler's elusive nature has made it one of the most sought-after birds around. In spring, this bird may show up just about anywhere in Georgia, but pinpointing its location takes patience and good fortune. • Though this bird was first described in 1813, a nest was not discovered for almost 70 more years. Because of the difficulty in finding active Connecticut Warbler nests, much of this bird's breeding biology remains unknown even today. • Like many other North American birds, the Connecticut Warbler was named for the place where it was first collected, even though it only visits Connecticut during fall migration. • These elusive birds use alternate migration routes each season, migrating up the Mississippi Valley in spring and down the Atlantic coastline in fall. They tend to be late migrants in Georgia, in both spring and fall.

1st winter

ID: bold, white eye ring; yellow underparts; olive green upperparts; long undertail coverts make tail look short; pink legs; longish bill. *Male:* blue-gray "hood." *Female* and *immature:* gray-brown "hood"; light gray throat.
Size: *L* 5–6 in; *W* 9 in.
Status: rare spring migrant statewide from early to late May; very rare migrant statewide from August to October (mostly from mid-September to mid-October); in fall, occurs primarily along the Coast.
Habitat: *Breeding:* open pine forests and fairly open spruce bogs and tamarack fens with well-developed understory growth. *In migration:* dense, shrubby thickets.
Nesting: does not nest in Georgia.

Feeding: gleans caterpillars, beetles, spiders and other invertebrates from ground leaf litter; occasionally forages among low branches.
Voice: call is a brisk, metallic *cheep* or *peak;* song is a loud, clear and explosive *chipity-chipity-chipity chuck* or *per-chipity-chipity-chipity choo.*
Similar Species: *Mourning Warbler* (p. 305): no eye ring or thin, incomplete eye ring; shorter undertail coverts; male has blackish breast patch; immature has pale gray to yellow "chin" and throat. *Nashville Warbler* (p. 278): bright yellow throat; shorter, dark legs and bill. *Common Yellowthroat* (p. 306): nonbreeding adult has yellow throat; olive breast band.
Best Sites: Kennesaw Mt. (9 spring records); Chattahoochee River NRA; Jekyll Island Banding Station (in fall).

MOURNING WARBLER

Oporornis philadelphia

Mourning Warblers are challenging to find in Georgia. These rare migrants seldom leave the protection of their dense, shrubby, often impenetrable habitat, and they tend to sing only on their breeding grounds in Canada and the northeastern United States. Mourning Warblers are best seen during migration, when backyard shrubs and raspberry thickets may attract small, silent flocks. • This bird's dark "hood" and black breast patch reminded pioneering ornithologist Alexander Wilson of someone dressed in mourning. The genus name is derived from the Greek word *opora*, which means "end of summer," when these birds are most abundant. Other birds in the same genus include the Kentucky, Connecticut and MacGillivray's (*O. tolmiei*) warblers. • The Mourning Warbler will make you wish that it wasn't the least common warbler on the list of birds regularly seen in Georgia.

breeding

ID: yellow underparts; olive green upperparts; short tail; pinkish legs. *Breeding male:* usually no eye ring but may have broken eye ring; blue-gray "hood"; black upper breast patch. *Female:* gray "hood"; whitish "chin" and throat; may show thin eye ring. *Immature:* gray-brown "hood"; pale gray to yellow "chin" and throat; thin, incomplete eye ring.
Size: *L* 5–5½ in; *W* 7½ in.
Status: rare migrant statewide from May to early June (mostly in the northeast) and from September to November.
Habitat: dense and shrubby thickets, tangles and brambles, often in moist areas of forest

clearings and along the edges of ponds, lakes and streams.
Nesting: does not nest in Georgia.
Feeding: forages in dense, low shrubs for caterpillars, beetles, spiders and other invertebrates.
Voice: call is a loud, low *check;* husky, 2-part song is variable and lower pitched at the end: *churry, churry, churry, churry, chorry, chorry.*
Similar Species: *Connecticut Warbler* (p. 304): bold, complete eye ring; lacks black breast patch; long undertail coverts make tail look very short; immature has light gray throat. *Nashville Warbler* (p. 278): bright yellow throat; dark legs.
Best Sites: Kennesaw Mt. (9 records); Jekyll Island Banding Station.

COMMON YELLOWTHROAT

Geothlypis trichas

This energetic songster of our wetlands is a favorite among birders—its small size, bright plumage and spunky disposition quickly endear it to all observers. • The Common Yellowthroat favors shrubby marshes and wet, overgrown meadows, shunning the forest habitat preferred by most of its wood-warbler relatives. In April and May, the male yellowthroat issues his distinctive *witchity-witchity-witchity* songs while perched atop tall cattails or shrubs. Observing a male in action will reveal the location of his favorite singing perches, which he visits in rotation. These strategic outposts mark the boundary of his territory, which is fiercely guarded from intrusion by other males. • The Common Yellowthroat is certainly one of our most common warblers and, unfortunately, its nests are commonly parasitized by Brown-headed Cowbirds.

ID: yellow throat, breast and undertail coverts; dingy white belly; olive green to olive brown upperparts; orangy legs. *Breeding male:* broad, black "mask" with white upper border. *Female:* no "mask"; may show faint, white eye ring. *Immature:* duller overall.

Size: *L* 5 in; *W* 6½ in.

Status: common permanent breeding resident statewide, though rare to uncommon north of the Fall Line in winter.

Habitat: cattail marshes, riparian willow and alder clumps, sedge wetlands, beaver ponds and wet overgrown meadows; sometimes dry, abandoned fields.

Nesting: on or near the ground in a small shrub or among emergent aquatic vegetation; female builds a bulky, open cup nest of weeds, grass, sedges and other materials and lines it with hair and soft plant fibers; female incubates 3–5 creamy white eggs, spotted with brown and black, for 12 days.

Feeding: gleans vegetation and hovers for adult and larval insects, including dragonflies, spiders and beetles; occasionally eats seeds.

Voice: call is a sharp *tcheck* or *tchet;* song is a clear, oscillating *witchety witchety witchety-witch.*

Similar Species: male's black "mask" is distinctive. *Kentucky Warbler* (p. 303): yellow "spectacles"; all-yellow underparts; half "mask." *Yellow Warbler* (p. 280): brighter yellow overall; yellow highlights on wings; all-yellow underparts. *Wilson's Warbler* (p. 308): forehead, "eyebrow" and "cheek" are as bright as all-yellow underparts; may show dark "cap." *Orange-crowned Warbler* (p. 277): dull yellow olive overall; faint breast streaks. *Nashville Warbler* (p. 278): bold, complete eye ring; blue-gray crown.

Best Sites: found in appropriate habitat statewide, except absent from upper mountain elevations.

HOODED WARBLER

Wilsonia citrina

Despite nesting low to the ground, Hooded Warblers require extensive mature forests, where fallen trees have opened gaps in the canopy, encouraging understory growth. • Different species of wood-warblers can coexist in a small area because they partition their food supplies, with each species foraging exclusively in certain microhabitats. Hooded Warblers also partition between the sexes: males tend to forage in treetops, whereas females forage near the ground. When Hooded Warblers arrive on their wintering grounds in Mexico and South America, the males and females again segregate—a practice unknown in any other warbler species—with males using mature forests, and females using shrubby and disturbed areas. • Unlike their female counterparts, male Hooded Warblers may return to the same nesting territory year after year. Once the young have left the nest, each parent takes on guardianship of half of the fledged young.

ID: fans tail, showing partially white outer tail feathers, bright yellow underparts; olive green upperparts; pinkish legs. *Male:* black "hood"; bright yellow face. *Female:* yellow face and olive crown; may show faint traces of black "hood."
Size: *L* 5½ in; *W* 7 in.
Status: common summer breeding resident statewide from April to October; uncommon summer breeding resident in the southern Coastal Plain and near the Coast.
Habitat: openings with dense, low shrubs in mature upland deciduous and mixed forests; occasionally in moist ravines or mature white pine plantations with a dense understory of deciduous shrubs.
Nesting: low in a deciduous shrub; mostly the female builds an open cup nest of fine grass, bark strips, dead leaves, animal hair,

spiderwebs and plant down; female incubates 4 creamy white eggs, spotted with brown toward the larger end, for about 12 days.
Feeding: gleans insects and other forest invertebrates from the ground or shrub branches; may scramble up tree trunks or flycatch.
Voice: call note is a metallic *tink*, given frequently; clear, whistling song is some variation of *whitta-witta-wit-tee-yo*.
Similar Species: *Wilson's Warbler* (p. 308), *Yellow Warbler* (p. 280) and *Common Yellowthroat* (p. 306): females lack white undertail feathers. *Kentucky Warbler* (p. 303): yellow "spectacles"; dark, triangular half "mask."
Best Sites: Brasstown Bald; Rabun Bald; Pine Log WMA; Ocmulgee NM; Big Hammock WMA; Kennesaw Mt. (HC: 66).

307

WILSON'S WARBLER

Wilsonia pusilla

Catching sight of the energetic Wilson's Warbler is a rare treat in Georgia, though this wood-warbler is occasionally reported at migration hotspots above the Fall Line, including Kennesaw Mountain or along the Chattahoochee River. This lively bird flickers quickly through tangles of leaves and trees, darting frequently into the air to catch flying insects. Birders often become exhausted while pursuing a Wilson's Warbler, but the bird itself never seems to tire during its lightning-fast performances. • Because these birds migrate at night, they run a greater risk of colliding with structures such as buildings or towers. • The Wilson's Warbler is richly deserving of its name. Named after Alexander Wilson, this species epitomizes the energetic devotion that the pioneering ornithologist exhibited in the study of North American birds.

Nesting: does not nest in Georgia.

Feeding: hovers, flycatches and gleans vegetation for insects.

Voice: call is a flat, low *chet* or *chuck;* song is a rapid chatter that drops in pitch at the end: *chi chi chi chi chet chet.*

Similar Species: male's black "cap" is distinctive. *Hooded Warbler* (p. 307): larger; larger bill; dark spot between bill and eye; white flashes in tail. *Yellow Warbler* (p. 280): brighter yellow upperparts; male has red breast streaks. *Orange-crowned Warbler* (p. 277): dull yellow olive overall; faint breast streaks. *Kentucky Warbler* (p. 303): yellow "spectacles"; dark, angular half "mask."

Best Sites: Kennesaw Mt. (20+ records); Chattahoochee River NRA; Harris Co. (HC-winter: 4).

ID: yellow underparts; yellow-green upperparts; beady, black eyes; thin, pointed, black bill; orange legs. *Male:* black "cap." *Female:* "cap" is very faint or absent.

Size: *L* 4½–5 in; *W* 7 in.

Status: rare to uncommon migrant, mostly north of the Fall Line, from March to May; uncommon migrant, mostly north of the Fall Line, from August to October; rare in winter mostly in the Coastal Plain (30+ records).

Habitat: riparian woodlands or areas with tall shrubs; occasionally in agricultural fields or suburbs.

CANADA WARBLER

Wilsonia canadensis

Male Canada Warblers, with their bold yellow eye rings, have a wide-eyed, alert appearance. Both sexes are fairly inquisitive, and these wood-warblers occasionally pop up from dense shrubs in response to passing hikers. Canada Warblers can be found in a wide variety of habitats, but you will almost always come across this "necklaced" warbler where there are dense understories. • Canadas nest only above 3800 ft on Brasstown Bald, Rabun Bald, Grassy Ridge and on Blood, Tray and Cowpen mountains in Georgia. • Canada Warblers live in open defiance of winter: they never stay in one place long enough to experience it! They are often the last of the warblers to arrive on their breeding grounds and the first to leave. As the summer nesting season in the Appalachian Mountains ends, these warblers migrate to South America. • Canada Warblers sing later in the breeding season than most warblers and can even be heard singing while on migration.

ID: white "spectacles"; yellow underparts (except white undertail coverts); blue-gray upperparts; pale legs. *Male:* streaky black "necklace"; dark, angular half "mask."
Female: blue-green back; faint gray "necklace."
Size: *L* 5–6 in; *W* 8 in.
Status: uncommon summer breeding resident in the northeastern Mountains above 3800 ft; uncommon migrant in the Mountains and Piedmont and rare migrant on the Coastal Plain and the Coast from late April to May and from August to September.
Habitat: *Breeding:* wet, low-lying areas of mixed forests with a dense understory, especially riparian willow-alder thickets; also cedar woodlands and swamps. *In migration:* woodlands or areas with tall shrubs.

Nesting: on a mossy hummock or upturned root or stump; female builds a loose, bulky cup nest made of leaves, grass, ferns and bark and lines it with animal hair and soft plant fibers; 4 brown-spotted, creamy white eggs are incubated for 10–14 days.
Feeding: gleans the ground and vegetation for beetles, flies, hairless caterpillars, mosquitoes and other insects; occasionally hovers.
Voice: call is a loud, quick *chip*; song begins with 1 sharp *chip* note and continues with a rich, variable warble.
Similar Species: *Kentucky Warbler* (p. 303): yellow undertail coverts; greenish upperparts; half eye ring; lacks black "necklace." *Northern Parula* (p. 279): white wing bars; broken, white eye ring; white belly. *Kirtland's Warbler* (p. 366): black streaking on sides and flanks; broken, white eye ring; dark streaking on back.
Best Sites: *Breeding:* Brasstown Bald; Rabun Bald. *In migration:* Kennesaw Mt. (HC-fall: 12); Ocmulgee NM; Chattahoochee River NRA.

YELLOW-BREASTED CHAT

Icteria virens

The unique Yellow-breasted Chat, measuring over 7 inches in length, is almost a warbler-and-a-half. Despite DNA evidence connecting the Chat with the wood-warbler family, its odd vocalizations and noisy thrashing behavior suggest a closer relationship to mimic thrushes such as the Gray Catbird or Northern Mockingbird. Chats typically thrash about in dense undergrowth, and they rarely hold back their strange vocalizations, often drawing attention to themselves. • During courtship, the male advertises for a mate by launching off his perch to hover in the air with head held high and legs dangling, chirping incessantly until he drops back down.

♂

ID: white "spectacles"; white jaw line; heavy, black bill; yellow breast; white undertail coverts; olive green upperparts; long tail; gray-black legs; large size. *Male:* black lores. *Female:* gray lores.

Size: *L* 7½ in; *W* 9½ in.

Status: common summer breeding resident statewide from May to October, except rare in the southeast and absent in the Mountains above 2300 ft; very difficult to find in migration; accidental to rare in winter south of the Mountains.

Habitat: riparian thickets, brambles and shrubby tangles.

Nesting: low in a shrub or deciduous sapling; well-concealed, bulky base of leaves and weeds holds an inner woven cup nest of vine bark, which is lined with fine grass and plant fibers; female incubates 3–4 creamy white eggs, spotted with brown toward the larger end, for about 11 days.

Feeding: gleans insects from low vegetation; eats berries in fall.

Voice: calls include a *whoit, chack* and *kook;* song is an assorted series of whistles, "laughs," squeaks, grunts, rattles and mews.

Similar Species: none.

Best Sites: Pine Log WMA, Dawson Forest WMA; Piedmont NWR; Beaverdam WMA; Bartow Co. (HC: 100+).

SUMMER TANAGER

Piranga rubra

Most of North America only gets a glimpse of these beauties if a rare individual flies off track, but these striking birds breed throughout Georgia's forested areas, edge habitats, pine-oak forests and riparian areas. • Summer Tanagers thrive on a wide variety of insects, but they are best known for their courageous attacks on wasps. These birds snatch flying bees and wasps from menacing swarms. They may even harass the occupants of a wasp nest until the nest is abandoned and the larvae inside are left free for the picking. • A courting male tanager will try to win a mate by offering her food and fanning his handsome crest and tail feathers. To ensure she notices him, the male hops persistently in front of the female and sometimes jumps right over her. • Most Georgian birders can experience the delightful "Summer Redbird," as it is sometimes called, because it is present statewide, except in the high Mountains. • *Rubra* refers to the brilliant red color of the male.

ID: *Male:* rose red overall; pale bill. *Female:* grayish yellow to greenish yellow upperparts; dusky yellow underparts; may have orange or reddish wash overall. *Immature male:* patchy, red and greenish plumage.

Size: *L* 7–8 in; *W* 12 in.

Status: common summer breeding resident statewide, except in the Mountains above 2500 ft, from April to October.

Habitat: mixed coniferous and deciduous woodlands, especially those with oak or hickory, or riparian woodlands with cottonwoods; occasionally in wooded backyards.

Nesting: constructed on a high, horizontal tree limb; female builds a flimsy, shallow cup nest of grass, Spanish moss and twigs and lines it with fine grass; female incubates 3–4 pale blue-green eggs, spotted with reddish brown, for 11–12 days.

Feeding: gleans insects from the tree canopy; may hover-glean or hawk insects in midair; also eats berries and small fruits; known to raid wasp nests.

Voice: call is *pit* or *pit-a-tuck;* song is a series of 2–3 sweet, clear, whistled phrases.

Similar Species: *Scarlet Tanager* (p. 312): smaller bill; male has black tail and wings; female has smaller bill, darker wings, brighter underparts and uniformly olive upperparts. *Northern Cardinal* (p. 334): red bill; prominent head crest; male has black "mask" and "bib." *Orchard Oriole* (p. 350) and *Baltimore Oriole* (p. 351): females have wing bars and sharper bills.

Best Sites: Pine Log WMA; Kennesaw Mt. (HC-migration: 20); Dawson Forest WMA; Harris Neck NWR; Glynn Co. (HC: 50+).

SCARLET TANAGER

Piranga olivacea

The Scarlet Tanager migrates farther than any other tanager. The return of the black-winged, brilliant red male to wooded ravines and traditional migrant stopover sites in spring is always a much-anticipated event. Birders eagerly await the lovely Scarlet Tanager's sweet, rough-edged song, which is often the only thing that gives away the presence of this unobtrusive bird. • When cold and rainy weather dampens spring birding, you may find a Scarlet Tanager at eye level, foraging in the forest understory. At other times, however, this bird can be surprisingly difficult to spot as it darts through the forest canopy in pursuit of insect prey. • *Piranga* is a South American name for the tanager. In Central and South America there are over 200 tanager species representing every color of the rainbow. • Pine Log Wildlife Management Area is home to both Scarlet Tanagers and Summer Tanagers—if you are lucky, you can check off both species on your birdlist in the same day. • *Olivacea* refers to the olive green color of the adult female, and the verdant color of both the immature and adult males in fall.

breeding

ID: *Breeding male:* bright red overall with pure black wings and tail; pale bill. *Fall male:* patchy, red and greenish yellow plumage; black wings and tail. *Nonbreeding male:* bright yellow underparts; olive upperparts; black wings and tail. *Female:* uniformly olive upperparts; yellow underparts; grayish brown wings.

Size: *L* 7 in; *W* 11½ in.

Status: common summer breeding resident in the Mountains and upper Piedmont up to 4400 ft from April to November; uncommon migrant south of the Fall Line from April to May and from July to November.

Habitat: fairly mature, upland deciduous and mixed forests and large woodlands.

Nesting: on a high branch, usually in a deciduous tree, well away from the trunk; female builds a flimsy, shallow cup of grass, weeds and twigs and lines it with rootlets

and fine grass; female incubates 2–5 pale blue-green eggs, spotted with reddish brown, for 12–14 days.

Feeding: gleans insects from the tree canopy; may hover-glean or hawk insects in midair; may forage at lower levels during cold weather; also takes some seasonally available berries.

Voice: call is a *chip-burrr* or *chip-churrr*; song is a series of 4–5 sweet, whistled phrases; more burry and shorter than Summer Tanager's song.

Similar Species: *Summer Tanager* (p. 311): larger bill; male has red tail and wings; female has paler wings and is duskier overall, often with orange or reddish tinge. *Northern Cardinal* (p. 334): red bill, wings and tail; prominent head crest; male has black "mask" and "bib." *Orchard Oriole* (p. 350) and *Baltimore Oriole* (p. 351): females have wing bars and sharper bills.

Best Sites: Brasstown Bald and Rabun Bald (mid-elevations); Crockford-Pigeon Mountain WMA; Pine Log WMA; Kennesaw Mt. (HC-migration: 50).

EASTERN TOWHEE

Pipilo erythrophthalmus

Eastern Towhees are often heard before they are seen. These noisy foragers rustle about in dense undergrowth, craftily scraping back layers of dry leaves to expose the seeds, berries or insects hidden beneath, though they also take insects and fruit from vegetation above ground. They employ an unusual two-footed technique to uncover food items—a strategy that is especially important in winter when virtually all of their food is taken from the ground. • Although you wouldn't guess it, this colorful bird is a member of the American Sparrow family—a group that is usually drab in color. • The Eastern Towhee and its similar western relative, the Spotted Towhee, were once grouped together as a single species called the "Rufous-sided Towhee." • The scientific name *Pipilo* is derived from the Latin *pipo*, meaning "to chirp or peep." *Erythrophthalmus* is derived from Greek words that mean "red eye." • A "white-eyed" subspecies of the Eastern Towhee, *P. e. rileyi*, is resident in the extreme southeast, and on the coast of Georgia.

ID: rufous sides and flanks; white outer tail corners, lower breast and belly; buff under-tail coverts; red eyes; dark bill. *Male:* black "hood" and upperparts. *Female:* brown "hood" and upperparts.

Size: *L* 7–8½ in; *W* 10½ in.

Status: common permanent breeding resident statewide.

Habitat: along woodland edges and in shrubby, abandoned fields.

Nesting: on the ground or low in a dense shrub; female builds a camouflaged cup nest of twigs, bark strips, grass, weeds, rootlets and animal hair; mostly the female

incubates 3–4 creamy white to pale gray eggs, spotted with brown toward the larger end, for 12–13 days.

Feeding: scratches at leaf litter for insects, seeds and berries; sometimes forages in low shrubs and saplings.

Voice: call is a scratchy, slurred *cheweee (towheee)!* or *chewink!;* song is 2 high, whistled notes followed by a trill: *drink your teeeee.*

Similar Species: *Dark-eyed Junco* (p. 333): much smaller; pale bill; black eyes; white outer tail feathers.

Best Sites: statewide at woodland edges, thick shrubby areas and backyards.

BACHMAN'S SPARROW

Aimophila aestivalis

Hiding in the grass of mature pine forests and open fields is the reclusive Bachman's Sparrow, a shy little bird that will drop out of sight at the first sound of a birder's pishing. For those with enough patience, this bird will quietly perch on a small branch on early April evenings and grace the listeners with a varied and clear song. • The Bachman's Sparrow depends on grass for nest material, cover and winter forage. Before heavy logging, mature southern pine forests provided an ideal meadowlike understory, but today the Bachman's Sparrow is often found in cleared fields or utility rights-of-way. The population and range of the Bachman's Sparrow expands as fire or humans open grassy pastures but often crashes as the understory regrows. • In 1837, William Swainson named this sparrow after John Bachman, an ornithologist and good friend of John James Audubon.

ID: long, dark tail; white belly; buffy breast and sides; heavy gray and rust streaking above. *In flight:* buffy "wing pits."
Size: *L* 5–6 in; *W* 7¼ in.
Status: permanent breeding resident south of the Fall Line; locally common permanent breeding resident in the Coastal Plain; rare permanent breeding resident in the Piedmont, the northwest and along the Coast; uncommonly overwinters in the Coastal Plain, but status is poorly known in winter.
Habitat: grassy understory of mature pine forests; open fields.

Nesting: on the ground, at base of a grass clump or shrub; domed nest is made of grass, small roots and animal hair; female incubates 2–5 white eggs for 12–14 days.
Feeding: forages on the ground; sometimes jumps for seeds and insects.
Voice: varied; long, clear note followed by a trill in a different pitch; will also mimic other birds.
Similar Species: *Chipping Sparrow* (p. 315): red "paint chip" on crown; gray nape and "cheek"; solid gray chest.
Best Sites: Piedmont NWR; Okefenokee NWR (HC-winter: 9); Lake Seminole WMA.

CHIPPING SPARROW

Spizella passerina

The Chipping Sparrow and Dark-eyed Junco do not share the same tailor, but they must have attended the same voice lessons, because their songs are very similar. Though the rapid trill of the Chipping Sparrow is slightly faster, drier and less musical than the junco's, even experienced birders can have difficulty identifying this bird by song alone. • Chipping Sparrows commonly nest at eye level, so you can easily watch their breeding and nest-building rituals. They are well known for their preference for conifers as a nest site and for hair as a lining material for the nest. By planting conifers in your backyard and offering samples of your pet's hair—or even your own—in backyard baskets in spring, you could attract nesting Chipping Sparrows to your area and contribute to their nesting success. • The Chipping Sparrow is the smallest and tamest of sparrows. "Chipping" refers to this bird's call and *passerina* is Latin for "little sparrow." The word "sparrow" comes from Old English meaning "a flutterer."

breeding

ID: *Breeding:* prominent rufous "cap"; white "eyebrow"; black eye line; light gray, unstreaked underparts; mottled brown upperparts; all-dark bill; 2 faint wing bars; pale legs. *Nonbreeding:* paler crown with dark streaks; brown "eyebrow" and "cheek"; pale lower mandible. *Immature:* brown gray overall with dark brown streaking; pale lower mandible.
Size: *L* 5–6 in; *W* 8½ in.
Status: common permanent breeding resident north of the Fall Line; uncommon permanent breeding resident in the Coastal Plain, except rare in the southern portion; common statewide in winter, except in the Mountains.

Habitat: open conifers or mixed woodland edges; often in yards and gardens with tree and shrub borders.
Nesting: usually at midlevel in a coniferous tree; female builds a compact cup nest of woven grass and rootlets, often lined with hair; female incubates 4 pale blue eggs for 11–12 days.
Feeding: gleans seeds from the ground and from the outer branches of trees or shrubs; prefers seeds from grasses, dandelions and clovers; also eats adult and larval invertebrates; occasionally visits feeders.
Voice: call is a high-pitched *chip;* song is a rapid, dry trill of *chip* notes.
Similar Species: *Swamp Sparrow* (p. 330): lacks white "eyebrow," white wing bars and dark line behind eye. *Field Sparrow* (p. 317): rufous stripe extends behind eye; white eye ring; gray throat; orange-pink bill; lacks bold white "eyebrow."
Best Sites: Cloudland Canyon SP; Pine Log WMA; Beaverdam WMA. *Winter:* old fields and backyards; Peachtree City (HC: 1400+).

315

CLAY-COLORED SPARROW

Spizella pallida

immature

For the most part, Clay-colored Sparrows go completely unnoticed because their plumage, habits and voice all contribute to a cryptic lifestyle. Even when males are singing at the top of their vocal cords they are usually mistaken for buzzing insects. • Although subtle in plumage, the Clay-colored Sparrow still possesses an unassuming beauty. Birders looking closely at this sparrow to confirm its identity can easily appreciate its delicate shading, texture and form—features so often overlooked in birds with more colorful plumage. • Small flocks of Clay-colored Sparrows migrate along the Atlantic Coast in late fall and occasionally overwinter in Georgia, but these obscure birds are a challenge to locate. Watch roadsides and fields, where foraging individuals may join a group of Chipping Sparrows.

ID: unstreaked, white underparts; buff breast wash; gray nape; light brown "cheek" edged with darker brown; brown crown with dark streak and pale, central stripe; white "eyebrow" and throat; white jaw stripe is bordered with brown; mostly pale bill. *Immature:* dark streaks on buff breast, sides and flanks.
Size: *L* 5–6 in; *W* 7½ in.
Status: rare to uncommon fall migrant south of the Mountains; rare winter resident in the Coastal Plain from September to February; accidental in spring south of the Mountains.
Habitat: brushy open areas along forest and woodland edges; roadsides; in forest openings, regenerating burn sites, abandoned fields and riparian thickets.
Nesting: does not nest in Georgia.
Feeding: forages for seeds and insects on the ground and in low vegetation; also eats berries.
Voice: generally silent in Georgia; call is a soft *chip;* song is a series of 2–5 slow, low-pitched, insectlike buzzes.
Similar Species: *Chipping Sparrow* (p. 315): breeding adult has prominent rufous "cap," gray "cheek" and underparts; 2 faint white wing bars; all-dark bill; juvenile lacks gray nape and buff sides and flanks.
Best Sites: along the Coast and barrier islands in fall; Altamaha WMA; Gould's Inlet (HC: 3).

FIELD SPARROW

Spizella pusilla

The pink-billed Field Sparrow frequents overgrown fields, pastures and forest clearings. Deserted farmland may seem unproductive to some people, but the Field Sparrow considers it heaven. For nesting purposes, the usual pastures that these birds inhabit must be scattered with shrubs, herbaceous plants and plenty of tall grass. • Unlike most songbirds, a nestling Field Sparrow will leave its nest prematurely if disturbed. Also, over time the Field Sparrow has learned to recognize when the Brown-headed Cowbird has parasitized its nest. The unwelcome eggs are usually too large for this small sparrow to eject, so the nest is simply abandoned. Affected pairs of Field Sparrows may make numerous nesting attempts in a single season to avoid raising cowbird young.

ID: orange-pink bill; gray face and throat; rusty crown with gray central stripe; rusty streak behind eye; white eye ring; 2 white wing bars; gray, unstreaked under-parts with buffy red wash on breast, sides and flanks; pinkish legs. *Immature:* duller version of adult with streaked breast and faint, buff white wing bars.

Size: *L* 5–6 in; *W* 8 in.

Status: common permanent breeding resident, more abundant north of the Fall Line than south of it; common in winter, except uncommon on the Coast.

Habitat: abandoned or weedy and over-grown fields and pastures, woodland edges and clearings, extensive shrubby riparian areas and young conifer plantations.

Nesting: on or near the ground, often sheltered by a grass clump, shrub or sapling; female weaves an open cup nest of grass and lines it with animal hair and soft plant material; female incubates 3–5 brown-spotted, whitish to pale bluish white eggs for 10–12 days.

Feeding: forages on the ground; takes mostly insects in summer and seeds in spring and fall.

Voice: call is a *chip* or *tsee;* song is a series of woeful, musical, down-slurred whistles accelerating into a trill.

Similar Species: most other sparrows lack pinkish bill. *Swamp Sparrow* (p. 330): white throat; dark upper mandible; lacks 2 white wing bars and white eye ring. *Chipping Sparrow* (p. 315): all-dark bill; white "eyebrow"; black eye line; lacks buffy red wash on underparts.

Best Sites: Cloudland Canyon SP; Pine Log WMA; Dawson Forest WMA; Piedmont NWR; Bulloch Co. sod farms in winter; Atlanta (HC: 1100+).

VESPER SPARROW

Pooecetes gramineus

For birders who live near grassy fields and agricultural lands with multitudes of confusing little brown sparrows, the Vesper Sparrow offers welcome relief—white outer tail feathers and a chestnut shoulder patch announce its identity whether the bird is perched or in flight. The Vesper Sparrow is also known for its bold and easily distinguished song, which begins with two sets of unforgettable, double notes: *here-here! there-there!* • These ground-dwelling birds expanded their range into the eastern U.S. when European settlers began clearing forests for farmland. Today, Vesper Sparrows are declining in the southeastern United States as agricultural land reverts back to forests. • "Vesper" is Latin for "evening," a time when this bird often sings. *Pooecetes* is Greek for "grass dweller."

ID: chestnut shoulder patch; white outer tail feathers; pale yellow lores; weak flank streaking; white eye ring; dark upper mandible; lighter lower mandible; pale legs.

Size: *L* 6 in; *W* 10 in.

Status: uncommon winter resident statewide, except rare in the Mountains, from September to May.

Habitat: open fields bordered or interspersed with shrubs, semi-open shrublands and grasslands; also in agricultural areas, open, dry conifer plantations and scrubby gravel pits.

Nesting: does not nest in Georgia.

Feeding: walks and runs along the ground, picking up grasshoppers, beetles, cutworms, other invertebrates and seeds.

Voice: *chip* call; song is 4 characteristic, preliminary notes, with the second higher in pitch, followed by a bubbly trill: *here-here there-there, everybody-down-the-hill.*

Similar Species: *Song Sparrow* (p. 328) and *Savannah Sparrow* (p. 320): smaller; lack eye ring. *Other sparrows* (pp. 313–333): lack white outer tail feathers and chestnut shoulder patch. *American Pipit* (p. 272): thinner bill; grayer upperparts lack brown streaking; lacks chestnut shoulder patch. *Lapland Longspur* (p. 367): blackish or buff wash on upper breast; nonbreeding has broad, pale "eyebrow" and reddish edgings to wing feathers.

Best Sites: Lake Seminole WMA; Beaverdam WMA; Harris Neck NWR; Bulloch Co. agricultural and sod fields; Pine Mt. (HC: 178).

LARK SPARROW

Chondestes grammacus

Prime Lark Sparrow habitat is easy to spot: grasses and low shrubs dominate the arid, sun-baked landscape, and the full-crowned forms of scattered oaks stand widely separated against the sky. In such rural haunts, male Lark Sparrows sing atop small bushes or low rock outcrops, proclaiming themselves to the world. • Male Lark Sparrows fluff their chestnut feathers, spread their tails, droop their wings and bubble with song in the presence of potential mates. Their beautiful arias reminded early naturalists of the famed Sky Lark of Europe. • Although these birds are typically seen in open shrubby areas and "edge" habitat, they occasionally venture into meadows, grassy forest openings and densely wooded areas. In winter, Lark Sparrows may be sighted foraging alongside juncos, other sparrows and towhees in suburban parks and gardens. Lark Sparrows are very rare along the Atlantic Coast but individuals are seen each year.

1st winter

Status: rare and irregular late summer and winter visitor to Georgia, including barrier islands; rare in spring.

Habitat: arid grasslands, borders of pastures and agricultural fields, brushy fields, lawns, parks and gardens, weedy roadsides.

Nesting: does not nest in Georgia.

Feeding: walks or hops on the ground, gleaning for seeds; also eats grasshoppers and other invertebrates.

Voice: generally silent in Georgia; melodious and variable song consists of short trills, buzzes, pauses and clear notes; song may incorporate notes of other species common in the area.

Similar Species: no other sparrow has the distinctive head and tail pattern.

Best Sites: barrier islands; Altamaha WMA.

ID: distinctive "helmet" created by white throat, "eyebrow" and crown stripe, and black lines on chestnut red head; unstreaked, pale breast with central spot; rounded black tail with flashy white corners; soft brown, mottled back and wings; pale legs. *1st winter:* more brownish facial markings; some brown streaks on nape.

Size: *L* 6 in; *W* 11 in.

SAVANNAH SPARROW

Passerculus sandwichensis

The Savannah Sparrow is one of our more common open-country birds in winter. At one time or another, most people have probably seen or heard one, although they may not have been aware of it—this bird's streaky, dull brown, buff and white plumage resembles so many of the other grassland sparrows that it is easily overlooked. • Peak numbers of Savannah Sparrows occur during fall migration, from mid-October to mid-November. You may see them darting across roads, foraging in open fields, marshes and sand dunes or perched on a fence. But like most sparrows, Savannahs generally stay out of sight. When danger appears, they take flight only as a last resort, preferring to run swiftly and inconspicuously through the grass, almost like feathered voles. • The common and scientific names of this bird reflect its broad North American distribution: "Savannah" refers to the city in Georgia, and *sandwichensis* is derived from Sandwich Bay in the Aleutian Islands off Alaska. • The pale, sandy-colored, "Ipswich Sparrow" (*P. s. princeps*) subspecies that breeds in Nova Scotia, Canada, is a rare winter visitor on Georgia's barrier islands from October to April.

ID: finely streaked breast, sides and flanks; pale, streaked underparts; mottled brown upperparts; yellow lores; light jaw line; pale legs and bill; may show dark breast spot.

Size: *L* 5–6 in; *W* 6½ in.

Status: common winter resident statewide from August to June; accidental in summer.

Habitat: agricultural fields, moist sedge and grass meadows, pastures, beaches, bogs and fens.

Nesting: does not nest in Georgia.

Feeding: gleans insects and seeds while walking or running along the ground; occasionally scratches.

Voice: generally silent in Georgia; call is a high, thin *tsit; song* is a high-pitched, clear, buzzy *tea tea teeeeea today.*

Similar Species: *Vesper Sparrow* (p. 318): white outer tail feathers; chestnut shoulder patch. *Lincoln's Sparrow* (p. 329): buff jaw line; buff wash across breast; broad, gray "eyebrow." *Grasshopper Sparrow* (p. 321): unstreaked breast. *Song Sparrow* (p. 328): triangular "mustache" stripes; pale central crown stripe; rounded tail; lacks yellow lores.

Best Sites: agricultural fields, meadows and beaches statewide.

GRASSHOPPER SPARROW
Ammodramus savannarum

The Grasshopper Sparrow is named not for its diet, but rather for its buzzy, insect-like song. During courtship flights, males chase females through the air, buzzing at a frequency that is usually inaudible to human ears. The males sing two completely different courtship songs: one ends in a short trill and the other is a prolonged series of high trills that vary in pitch and speed. • The Grasshopper Sparrow is an open-country bird that prefers grassy expanses free of trees and shrubs. Wide, well-drained, grassy ditches occasionally attract nesting Grasshopper Sparrows, so mowing or harvesting these grassy margins early in the nesting season may be detrimental to their nesting success. Convincing local landowners and state governments to delay cutting until mid-August or September would benefit the Grasshopper Sparrow. • The scientific name *Ammodramus* is Greek for "sand runner," and *savannarum* is Latin for "of the savanna," after this bird's grassy, open habitat.

ID: unstreaked, white underparts with buff wash on breast, sides and flanks; flattened head profile; dark crown with pale central stripe; buff "cheek"; mottled brown upperparts; beady, black eyes; sharp tail; pale legs; may show small yellow patch on edge of forewing. *Immature:* less buff on underparts; faint streaking across breast.

Size: *L* 5–5½ in; *W* 7½ in.

Status: uncommon to common summer breeding resident north of the Fall Line, but absent from the northeastern Mountains; rare breeder south of the Fall Line; probable winter resident in parts of the Piedmont; uncommon winter resident on the Coastal Plain and Coast from September to April.

Habitat: grasslands and grassy fields with little or no shrub or tree cover.

Nesting: in a shallow depression on the ground, usually concealed by grass; female builds a small cup nest of grass and lines it with rootlets, fine grass and hair; female incubates 4–5 creamy white eggs, spotted with gray and reddish brown, for 11–13 days.

Feeding: gleans insects and seeds from the ground and grass; eats a variety of insects, including grasshoppers.

Voice: song is a high, faint, buzzy trill preceded by 1–3 high, thin whistled notes: *tea-tea-tea zeeeeeeeeee.*

Similar Species: *Le Conte's Sparrow* (p. 323): buff-and-black-striped head with white central crown stripe; gray "cheek"; dark streaking on sides and flanks. *Nelson's Sharp-tailed Sparrow* (p. 324): buff orange face and breast; gray, central crown stripe; gray "cheek" and shoulders.

Best Sites: Sod Atlanta Inc.; Oconee River RA; Laurens Co.; Stephens Co./Franklin Co. (HC-summer: 40).

HENSLOW'S SPARROW

Ammodramus henslowii

It's difficult to predict when you'll see the next Henslow's Sparrow in Georgia—this bird makes regular winter visits here and is probably more common than reported, but it is very secretive. The Henslow's furtive nature has made it a difficult species to study, so we have much more to learn about the reasons for its recent, widespread decline. • Henslow's Sparrows breed in the northeastern U.S., where they are known for their unusual habit of singing at night. On wintering grounds, without the male's lyrical advertisements, the inconspicuous Henslow's Sparrow is almost impossible to observe as it forages alone along the ground. • This bird is best found when a large group of birders forms a long search-line and walks through likely winter habitat, while carefully observing any sparrow that flushes. When done in the proper habitat, this trick nearly always scares up a Henslow's, much to everyone's delight, even though most get only a quick glimpse before it drops back into cover. Try this technique along power line rights-of-way on public lands. • John J. Audubon named this sparrow after his friend John Stevens Henslow, a naturalist and one-time teacher of Charles Darwin.

Habitat: large, fallow or wild, grassy fields and meadows with a matted ground layer of dead vegetation and scattered shrub or herb perches (e.g., under power lines); often in moist, grassy areas.

Nesting: does not nest in Georgia.

Feeding: gleans insects and seeds from the ground.

ID: flattened head profile; olive green face, central crown stripe and nape; dark crown and "whisker" stripes; rusty tinge on back, wings and tail; white underparts with dark streaking on buff breast, sides and flanks; thick bill; deeply notched, sharp-edged tail. *Immature:* buff wash on most of underparts; faint streaking on sides only.

Size: *L* 5–5½ in; *W* 6½ in.

Status: uncommon winter resident in the Coastal Plain, Coast and barrier islands from October to April; rare migrant and winter resident north of the Fall Line.

Voice: generally silent in Georgia; sharp *tsip* alarm call; weak, liquidy, cricketlike *tse-lick* song is distinctive, given during periods of rain or at night.

Similar Species: *Other sparrows* (pp. 313–33): lack greenish face, central crown stripe and nape. *Grasshopper Sparrow* (p. 321): lacks dark "whisker" stripe and prominent streaking on breast and sides. *Savannah Sparrow* (p. 320): lacks buff breast. *Le Conte's Sparrow* (p. 323): buff-and-black-striped head with white central crown stripe; gray "cheek."

Best Sites: grassy pinelands; Paulks Pasture WMA; Harris Neck NWR; under power lines; Glynn Co. (HC: 17).

LE CONTE'S SPARROW

Ammodramus leconteii

These sparrows are difficult to find because of their remote breeding habitat, scattered distribution and secretive behavior. They prefer to scurry along the ground in thick cover and will only resort to flight for short distances before dropping out of sight again. • Except for a high-pitched alarm call, the Le Conte's Sparrow is generally silent in winter. Skilled birders may follow the buzzy call to its source to catch a fleeting glimpse of the bird before it dives into tall vegetation and disappears from view. • This species was first discovered in Georgia, and described by John Latham, in 1790. Its namesake, John Le Conte, is best remembered as one of the preeminent American entomologists of the 19th century, though he was interested in all areas of natural history.

ID: buff orange face; gray "cheek"; black line behind eye; pale central crown stripe bordered by black stripes; buff orange upper breast, sides and flanks; dark streaking on sides and flanks; white throat, lower breast and belly; mottled, brown-black upperparts; buff streaks on back; pale legs. *Immature:* duller overall; more streaking on breast.
Size: L 4½–5 in; W 6½ in.
Status: rare migrant and winter resident south of the Mountains, but uncommon on the western Coastal Plain, from October to April.
Habitat: grassy meadows with dense vegetation, drier edges of wet sedge and grass meadows, willow and alder flats and forest openings.
Nesting: does not nest in Georgia.
Feeding: gleans the ground and low vegetation for insects, spiders and seeds.
Voice: alarm call is a high-pitched whistle.
Similar Species: *Nelson's Sharp-tailed Sparrow* (p. 324): gray central crown stripe and nape; white streaks on dark back. *Grasshopper Sparrow* (p. 321): lacks buff orange face and streaking on underparts.
Best Sites: Bradley Unit of Eufaula NWR (HC: 51); Paulks Pasture WMA; under power lines.

323

NELSON'S SHARP-TAILED SPARROW
Ammodramus nelsoni

It's hard to find a Nelson's Sharp-tailed Sparrow without getting your feet wet. This relatively colorful sparrow conceals itself in low, coastal marsh grass then unexpectedly pops out of a soggy hiding place to perch completely exposed at a close distance. A few even venture into inland freshwater marshes and riparian margins. Like most other sparrows, the Nelson's Sharp-tail is best identified by sound. It produces a single sharp note followed by a buzzy trill—a unique combination among our birds. • Edward William Nelson was the chief of the U.S. Biological Survey and former president of the American Ornithologists' Union. His greatest contribution was the creation of the Migratory Bird Treaty, which is still in effect today. • This species was formerly grouped together with the Saltmarsh Sharp-tailed Sparrow as a single species, known as the Sharp-tailed Sparrow.

ID: orangish face; gray "cheek" and nape; breast streaked with buffy gray; white stripes on back; bluish bill. **Size:** *L* 5 in; *W* 7 in. **Status:** uncommon to common winter resident in salt marshes and brackish or freshwater impoundments of the Coast from September to May; rare migrant inland. **Habitat:** marshlands with tall emergent vegetation and shoreline vegetation; coastal salt marshes and dunes.

Nesting: does not nest in Georgia.
Feeding: runs or walks along the ground, gleaning ants, beetles, grasshoppers and often invertebrates; also eats seeds.
Voice: raspy *ts tse-sheeeeeush* at beginning and end.
Similar Species: *Le Conte's Sparrow* (p. 323): lacks gray nape and white stripes on back. *Grasshopper Sparrow* (p. 321): lacks streaking on breast. *Savannah Sparrow* (p. 320): yellow color on head is restricted to lores. *Saltmarsh Sharp-tailed Sparrow* (p. 325): pinkish bill and dark streaks on breast.
Best Sites: Ft. Pulaski; Sapelo, Andrews, Jekyll and Cumberland islands; Harris Neck NWR (HC: 53).

SALTMARSH SHARP-TAILED SPARROW

Ammodramus caudacutus

Confirming the specific identity of those little brown birds known as sparrows may seem to be a nightmarish challenge...don't they all look the same? Fortunately, all you have to do is look this sparrow in the eye to see the unique orange facial triangle that encompasses its gray ear patch and adjacent eye. Its streaky, buff-colored breast and sides also separate it from many of the sparrows that sport a clear, unstreaked breast. Another clue to its identity is its choice of habitat: the tidal salt marshes of the Atlantic Coast. • When flushed, sharp-tailed sparrows fly off using a low, erratic flight pattern then touch down and run along the ground before disappearing into the reeds. • Until recently, this bird was lumped together with the interior Nelson's Sharp-tailed Sparrow as a single species called the Sharp-tailed Sparrow.

ID: small sparrow; breast and flanks streaked with dark brown; gray ear patch surrounded by orange triangle on face; gray central crown stripe and nape; long, pinkish bill.

Size: *L* 5¼ in; *W* 7 in.

Status: uncommon to common winter resident in salt marshes and brackish impoundments on the Coast from September to May.

Habitat: confined to freshwater and saltwater marshes along or adjacent to the coast.

Nesting: does not nest in Georgia.

Feeding: insects, other invertebrates and seeds are obtained by gleaning them from the ground and marsh vegetation; occasionally probes for food in mud.

Voice: variety of soft trills, buzzes and other notes.

Similar Species: *Nelson's Sharp-tailed Sparrow* (p. 324): bluish bill and buffy streaking on breast. *Le Conte's Sparrow* (p. 323): pale crown stripe; gray nape is streaked. *Henslow's Sparrow* (p. 322): lacks gray nape and ear patch. *Field Sparrow* (p. 317), *Seaside Sparrow* (p. 326) and nonbreeding *Swamp Sparrow* (p. 330): all lack the orange facial triangle.

Best Sites: along the coast and barrier islands; Ft Pulaski; Harris Neck NWR (HC: 60+); St. Catherines I. (HC: 89)

SEASIDE SPARROW

Ammodramus maritimus

Fortunate birdwatchers may delight in an encounter with a courting male Seaside Sparrow as he projects his cheery buzzing song from atop a nearby shrub or during a courtship flight. But for most observers, meeting this bird may be brief and seemingly unrewarding as most flushed birds flutter only a short distance before disappearing into the thick vegetation of their marshy home. Your best chance of meeting this secretive bird is to visit the tidal salt marshes of the Atlantic Coast where tall stands of marsh grasses, rushes and shrubs create a habitat that provides the Seaside Sparrow with everything it needs to survive. • Foraging primarily on the ground, this stocky bird enjoys a diverse diet of insects, spiders, small aquatic invertebrates and seeds. • Small, widely separated populations of Seaside Sparrows living in slightly different salt marshes along the species' coastal range have produced a number of distinctive races or "subspecies" that, given time, may develop into fully separate and unique species.

grayish white eggs for 12 days; pair feeds young.

ID: midsized sparrow; long bill; yellow lores; white "chin"; gray "whisker" stripes; olive gray upperparts; streaked pale gray underparts.

Size: *L* 6 in; *W* 7½ in.

Status: uncommon permanent breeding resident of the Coast and barrier islands.

Habitat: restricted to tidal salt marshes along the Coast.

Nesting: in low marsh vegetation just above the high tide mark; female builds a cup-shaped nest with a sheltering canopy; female incubates 2–5 brown-blotched,

Feeding: insects, invertebrates and seeds are obtained by foraging on the ground among marsh vegetation or at the water's edge; occasionally probes in mud.

Voice: varied calls; a series of soft notes followed by buzzes; sounds akin to the song of the Red-winged Blackbird: *tup-tup zee-reeee.*

Similar Species: *Savannah Sparrow* (p. 320): lighter undersides; streaked head and back. *Song Sparrow* (p. 328): darker streaking; spot on breast; lacks yellow lores. *Saltmarsh Sharp-tailed Sparrow* (p. 325): orange facial triangle.

Best Sites: along the Coast and barrier islands; Harris Neck NWR; St. Catherines I. (HC: 600+); Glynn Co. (HC: 800+).

FOX SPARROW

Passerella iliaca

Like the Eastern Towhee, the Fox Sparrow eagerly scratches out a living, using both feet to stir up leaves and scrape the organic matter littered on the forest floor. This large sparrow's preference for impenetrable, brushy habitat makes it a difficult species to observe, even though its noisy foraging habits often reveal its whereabouts in winter here. • The Fox Sparrow's range covers most of North America, and this species exhibits considerable variation in characteristics such as plumage, song or bill shape and size throughout North America—in fact, Fox Sparrows have been divided into 18 subspecies. • The overall reddish brown appearance of the common eastern subspecies of this bird inspired taxonomists to name it after the red fox.

ID: whitish underparts; heavy, reddish brown spotting and streaking often converges into central breast spot; reddish brown wings, rump and tail; brown-streaked back; gray crown, "eyebrow" and nape; stubby, conical bill; pale legs.

Size: *L* 6½–7 in; *W* 10½ in.

Status: uncommon winter resident statewide; rare to uncommon in the southern Coastal Plain and the Coast from October to April.

Habitat: riparian thickets and brushy woodland clearings, edges and parklands.

Nesting: does not nest in Georgia.

Feeding: scratches the ground to uncover seeds, berries and invertebrates; visits backyard feeders in migration and winter.

Voice: does not sing in migration; calls include an explosive *smack*.

Similar Species: *Song Sparrow* (p. 328): pale central crown stripe; dark "mustache"; dark brownish rather than reddish streaking on upperparts. *Hermit Thrush* (p. 265): longer, thinner bill; pale eye ring; dark breast spots; unstreaked, olive brown and reddish brown upperparts; lacks heavy streaking on underparts.

Best Sites: Chattahoochee River NRA; Beaverdam WMA; Savannah NWR; Atlanta (HC: 43).

SONG SPARROW

Melospiza melodia

The Song Sparrow's heavily streaked, low-key plumage doesn't prepare you for its symphonic song. This well-named sparrow is known for the complexity, rhythm and emotion of its springtime rhapsodies, although some people will insist that the Fox Sparrow and the Lincoln's Sparrow carry the best tunes. • Young Song Sparrows and many other songbirds learn to sing by eavesdropping on their fathers or on rival males. By the time a young male is a few months old, he will have formed the basis for his own courtship tune. • Most songbirds are lucky if they are able to produce one brood per year. In some years, Song Sparrows in our region will successfully raise three broods. There are about 31 different subspecies of the Song Sparrow, from the pale desert birds to the larger and darker Alaskan forms.

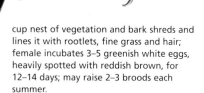

ID: whitish underparts with heavy brown streaking that converges into central breast spot; grayish face; dark line behind eye; white jaw line is bordered by dark "whisker" and "mustache" stripes; dark crown with pale central stripe; mottled brown upperparts; rounded tail tip.

Size: *L* 5½–7 in; *W* 8½ in.

Status: common permanent breeding resident in the Mountains and upper Piedmont south to Milledgeville and Macon; common winter resident statewide from October to May outside its breeding range.

Habitat: shrubby areas, often near water, including willow shrublands, riparian thickets, forest openings and pastures.

Nesting: usually on the ground or low in a shrub or small tree; female builds an open cup nest of vegetation and bark shreds and lines it with rootlets, fine grass and hair; female incubates 3–5 greenish white eggs, heavily spotted with reddish brown, for 12–14 days; may raise 2–3 broods each summer.

Feeding: gleans the ground, shrubs and trees for cutworms, beetles, grasshoppers, ants, other invertebrates and seeds; also eats wild fruit and visits feeders.

Voice: calls include a short *tsip* and a nasal *tchep;* song is 1–4 bright, distinctive introductory notes, such as *sweet, sweet, sweet,* followed by a buzzy *towee,* then a short, descending trill.

Similar Species: *Fox Sparrow* (p. 327): heavier breast spotting and streaking; lacks pale, central crown stripe and dark "mustache"; reddish rather than dark brownish streaking on upperparts. *Lincoln's Sparrow* (p. 329): lightly streaked breast with buff wash; buff jaw line. *Savannah Sparrow* (p. 320): lightly streaked breast; yellow lores; notched tail; lacks grayish face and dark, triangular "mustache."

Best Sites: rural and urban sites north of the Fall Line in summer; Atlanta (HC: 600+).

LINCOLN'S SPARROW

Melospiza lincolnii

There is a certain beauty in the plumage of a Lincoln's Sparrow that is greater than the sum of its feathers. Sightings of Lincoln's Sparrows in Georgia are rare because their migration route falls to the west of our state, and most birds continue farther south to wintering grounds in Mexico or Central America. Nonetheless, observations of this bird, linked with the sounds and smells of its natural habitat, can bring joy to the hearts of perceptive birders. • Lincoln's Sparrows seem to be more timid than other sparrows. During winter and migration, they remain well hidden in tall grass and dense, bushy growth. Their remote breeding grounds and secretive behavior conspire to keep this species one of the least-known sparrows. • This sparrow bears the name of Thomas Lincoln, a young companion of John James Audubon on his voyage to Labrador, Canada.

ID: buff breast band, sides and flanks with fine, dark streaking; buff jaw stripe; gray "eyebrow," face and "collar"; dark line behind eye; dark, reddish "cap" with gray central stripe; white throat and belly; mottled, gray-brown to reddish brown upperparts; very faint white eye ring.
Size: *L* 5½ in; *W* 7½ in.
Status: rare to uncommon migrant and winter resident statewide, except the higher Mountains, from September to May.
Habitat: brushy woodlands and shrubby fencerows.
Nesting: does not nest in Georgia.

Feeding: scratches at the ground to expose invertebrates and seeds; occasionally visits feeders.
Voice: generally silent in Georgia; calls include a buzzy *zeee* and *tsup*; song is a wrenlike musical mixture of buzzes, trills and warbled notes.
Similar Species: *Song Sparrow* (p. 328): heavier breast streaking; dark triangular "mustache"; lacks buff wash on breast, sides and flanks. *Savannah Sparrow* (p. 320): yellow lores; white "eyebrow" and jaw line. *Swamp Sparrow* (p. 330): generally lacks breast streaking; more contrast between red and gray crown stripes.
Best Sites: Altamaha WMA; Chattahoochee River NRA; Pendergrass (HC: 5).

329

SWAMP SPARROW

Melospiza georgiana

Swamp Sparrows are well adapted to life near water. These wetland inhabitants skulk among the emergent vegetation of cattail marshes, foraging for a variety of invertebrates, including beetles, caterpillars, spiders, leafhoppers and flies. Like other sparrows, they are unable to swim, but that is no deterrent—many of their meals are snatched directly from the water's surface as they wade through the shallows. • The Swamp Sparrow must keep a lookout for daytime predators such as Northern Harriers, Great Blue Herons and large snakes. At night, the key to survival is finding a secluded, concealing perch that will keep it safe from raccoons, skunks and weasels. • The males' metallic trills are occasionally heard in spring, just before Swamp Sparrows depart for their northern breeding grounds, but their *chink* calls are heard throughout winter. • Birders can "squeak" to draw the curious Swamp Sparrow in for closer observation.

nonbreeding

ID: gray face; reddish brown wings; brownish upperparts; dark streaking on back; dull gray breast; black stripes outline white throat and jaw; dark line behind eye. *Breeding:* rusty "cap"; streaked, buff sides and flanks. *Nonbreeding:* streaked, brown "cap" with gray central stripe; more brownish sides. *Immature:* buffy "eyebrow" and nape; faint streaking on breast.
Size: *L* 5–6 in; *W* 7½ in.
Status: common winter resident statewide, but uncommon in the higher Mountains, from September to May.

Habitat: cattail marshes, open wetlands, wet meadows and open deciduous riparian thickets.
Nesting: does not nest in Georgia.
Feeding: gleans insects from the ground, vegetation and the water's surface; takes seeds in late summer and fall.
Voice: call is a harsh *chink;* song, occasionally heard in spring, is a slow, sharp, metallic trill: *weet-weet-weet-weet.*
Similar Species: *Chipping Sparrow* (p. 315): clean white "eyebrow"; full, black eye line; uniformly gray underparts; white wing bars. *American Tree Sparrow:* dark central breast spot; white wing bars; 2-tone bill. *Song Sparrow* (p. 328): heavily streaked underparts; lacks gray "collar." *Lincoln's Sparrow* (p. 329): fine breast streaking; less contrast between brown and gray crown stripes.
Best Sites: Chattahoochee River NRA; Newman Wetlands Center; Sapelo I. (HC: 292).

WHITE-THROATED SPARROW

Zonotrichia albicollis

The handsome White-throated Sparrow is easily identified by its bold, white throat and striped crown. Two color morphs are common: one has black and white stripes on its head; the other has brown and tan stripes. White-striped males are more aggressive than tan-striped males, and tan-striped females are more nurturing than white-striped females. These two color morphs are perpetuated because each morph almost always breeds with the opposite color morph. • In winter, White-throated Sparrows may appear anywhere in Georgia. Urban backyards dressed with brushy fenceline tangles and a bird feeder brimming with seeds can attract good numbers of these delightful sparrows. • *Zonotrichia* means "hairlike," a reference to the striped heads of birds in this genus; *albicollis* is Latin for "white neck"—not quite accurate, as it is the bird's throat and not its neck that is white.

tan-striped morph

white-striped morph

ID: black-and-white-striped or brown-and-tan-striped head; white throat; gray "cheek"; yellow lores; black eye line; unstreaked, gray underparts; mottled brown upperparts; grayish bill.

Size: *L* 6½–7½ in; *W* 9 in.

Status: abundant winter resident statewide from October to May; accidental in summer.

Habitat: backyards, woodlots and wooded parks with thick understory; riparian brush.

Nesting: does not nest in Georgia.

Feeding: scratches the ground to expose invertebrates, seeds and berries; also gleans insects from vegetation and while in flight; eats seeds from bird feeders in winter.

Voice: call is a sharp *chink;* variable song, whistled: *Old Sam Peabody, Peabody, Peabody.*

Similar Species: *White-crowned Sparrow* (p. 332): pinkish bill; gray "collar"; lacks bold white throat and yellow lores. *Swamp Sparrow* (p. 330): smaller; gray and chestnut on crown; streaked underparts; lacks head pattern.

Best Sites: ubiquitous statewide in backyards, parks and woodlots.

WHITE-CROWNED SPARROW
Zonotrichia leucophrys

Mixed sparingly among the legions of White-throated Sparrows found in low-lying areas from October to May are scattered White-crowned Sparrows. They typically appear singly, or in twos or threes, flitting through brushy fencerows and overgrown fields. White-crowns are more likely to venture out into open lawns and crop fields than are White-throats. As well, White-crowned Sparrows may be distinguished by their larger size and more erect stance. • The White-crowned Sparrow is one of North America's most studied sparrows. Research on this bird has given science tremendous insight into bird physiology, homing behavior and the geographic variability of song dialects. • White-crowns breed in the Far North, in alpine environments or along the California coast. This bird has a widespread distribution in North America, and populations in different parts of its range vary significantly in behavior, and in migratory and nesting habits. • The western subspecies, *Z. l. gambelli*, which has white rather than black lores and a smaller, orange-yellow bill, is an accidental winter resident and may be more common than reported.

ID: black-and-white-striped head; black eye line; pinkish or orange bill; gray face; unstreaked, gray underparts; pale gray throat; mottled, gray-brown upperparts; 2 faint white wing bars. *Immature:* broad, gray "eyebrow" bordered by brown eye line and crown.
Size: *L* 5½–7 in; *W* 9½ in.
Status: uncommon migrant and local winter resident statewide from October to May; uncommon migrant and local winter resident near the Coast, but more common in western Coastal Plain.

Habitat: woodlots, brushy tangles and riparian thickets.
Nesting: does not nest in Georgia.
Feeding: scratches the ground to expose insects and seeds; also eats berries, buds and moss caps; may take seeds from bird feeders.
Voice: call is a high, thin *seet* or sharp *pink*; song is a frequently repeated variation of *I gotta go wee-wee now.*
Similar Species: *White-throated Sparrow* (p. 331): bold white throat; grayish bill; yellow lores; browner overall. *Swamp Sparrow* (p. 330): smaller, reddish tinge to wings.
Best Sites: barrier islands; Altamaha WMA; Albany (HC: 44); Pendergrass (HC: 35+); Elmodel WMA (HC: 25); Bulloch Co. (HC: 20).

DARK-EYED JUNCO

Junco hyemalis

Wintering juncos usually congregate in backyards with bird feeders and sheltering conifers—with such amenities at their disposal, more and more juncos are appearing in urban areas. Georgians get to enjoy more of the brownish female juncos in winter, because they migrate farther south than the males. • Juncos rarely perch at feeders, preferring to snatch up seeds that are knocked to the ground by other visitors such as chickadees, sparrows, nuthatches and jays. They are readily flushed from wooded trails and backyard feeders, flashing their distinctive, white outertail feathers in alarm as they seek cover in a nearby tree or shrub. • In 1973, the American Ornithologists' Union grouped five junco species into a single species called the Dark-eyed Junco. The five subspecies are closely related and have similar habits, but differ in coloration and range, though they interbreed where their ranges meet. • In the Mountains, above 3200 ft, is the only place in Georgia where you can observe breeding juncos in summer. • The Dark-eyed Junco is often called the "Snow Bird"; the species name, *hyemalis*, is equally suiting—it means "winter" in Greek.

"Slate-colored Junco"

ID: white outer tail feathers; pale bill. *Male:* dark slate gray overall, except for white lower breast, belly and under-tail coverts. *Female:* brown rather than gray. *Immature:* brown like female, but streaked with darker brown.
Size: *L* 5½–7 in; *W* 9½ in.
Status: common summer breeding resident in the Mountains above 3200 ft; common to abundant winter resident in most of the state but erratic in the southern half.
Habitat: *Breeding:* coniferous and mixed forests; young jack pine stands, burned areas and shrubby regenerating clearings. *In migration* and *winter:* shrubby woodland borders; also backyard feeders.

Nesting: on the ground, usually concealed by a shrub, tree, root, log or rock; female builds a cup nest of twigs, bark shreds, grass and moss and lines it with fine grass and hair; female incubates 3–5 whitish to bluish white eggs, marked with gray and brown, for 12–13 days.
Feeding: scratches the ground for invertebrates; also eats berries and seeds.
Voice: call is a smacking *chip* note, often given in series; song is a long, dry trill.
Similar Species: *Eastern Towhee* (p. 313): larger; female has rufous sides, red eyes and grayish bill.
Best Sites: Lake Conasauga; Brasstown Bald; Rabun Bald; at feeders and ecotones in winter; Atlanta and Columbus (HC-winter: 1000+).

NORTHERN CARDINAL

Cardinalis cardinalis

A bird as beautiful as the Northern Cardinal rarely fails to capture our attention and admiration: it is often the first choice for calendars and Christmas cards. Most people can easily recognize this delightful year-round neighbor even without the help of a bird field guide. • Cardinals prefer the tangled shrubby edges of woodlands and are easily attracted to backyards with feeders and sheltering trees and shrubs. • Northern Cardinals form one of the bird world's most faithful pair bonds. The male and female remain in close contact year-round, singing to one another through the seasons with soft, bubbly whistles. The female is known to sing while on the nest, and it is believed that she is informing her partner whether or not she and the young need food. The male is highly territorial and will even challenge his own reflection in a window or shiny hubcap! • The Northern Cardinal owes its name to the vivid red plumage of the male, which resembles the red robes of Roman Catholic cardinals.

ID: *Male:* red overall; pointed crest; black "mask" and throat; red, conical bill. *Female:* brown buff to buff olive overall; red bill, crest, wings and tail. *Immature male:* similar to female but has dark bill and crest.
Size: *L* 7½–9 in; *W* 12 in.
Status: common to abundant permanent breeding resident statewide.
Habitat: brushy thickets and shrubby tangles along forest and woodland edges; also in backyards and suburban and urban parks.
Nesting: in a dense shrub, thicket, vine tangle or low in a coniferous tree; female builds an open cup nest of twigs, bark shreds, weeds, grass, leaves and rootlets and lines it with hair and fine grass; female incubates 3–4 whitish to bluish or greenish white eggs, marked with gray, brown and purple, for 12–13 days.
Feeding: gleans seeds, insects and berries from low shrubs or while hopping along the ground; visits feeders.
Voice: call is a metallic *chip;* song is a variable series of clear, bubbly whistled notes: *what cheer! what cheer! birdie-birdie-birdie what cheer!*
Similar Species: *Summer Tanager* (p. 311) and *Scarlet Tanager* (p. 312): lack head crest, black "mask" and throat and red, conical bill; Scarlet Tanager has black wings and tail.
Best Sites: backyard feeders statewide.

ROSE-BREASTED GROSBEAK

Pheucticus ludovicianus

The boisterous, whistled tune of the Rose-breasted Grosbeak echoing through northern Georgia's deciduous forests is difficult to miss in spring and summer. The bird's hurried song sounds like a robin that has taken singing lessons. Although the female lacks the magnificent colors of the male, she shares his talent for beautiful song. Mating grosbeaks appear pleasantly affectionate toward each other, often touching bills during courtship and after absences. • Rose-breasted Grosbeaks usually build their nests low in a tree or tall shrub but typically forage high in the canopy where they can be difficult to spot. Luckily for birders, the abundance of berries in fall often draws these birds to ground level. • The species name *ludovicianus*, Latin for "from Louisiana," is misleading because this bird is only a migrant through Louisiana and other southern states.

♀

breeding

♂

ID: pale, conical bill; dark wings with small white patches; dark tail. *Male:* black "hood" and back; red breast and inner underwings; white underparts and rump. *Female:* bold, whitish "eyebrow"; thin crown stripe; brown upperparts; buff underparts with dark brown streaking.

Size: *L* 7–8½ in; *W* 12½ in.

Status: uncommon summer breeding resident in the northeastern Mountains above 2800 ft (some lower) from April to October; uncommon to common migrant from April to May and from September to November elsewhere; accidental in summer in the upper Piedmont; accidental in winter.

Habitat: deciduous and mixed forests.

Nesting: fairly low in a tree or tall shrub, often near water; mostly the female builds a flimsy cup nest of twigs, bark strips, weeds, grass and leaves and lines it with rootlets and hair; pair incubates 3–5 pale, greenish blue eggs, spotted with reddish brown, for 13–14 days.

Feeding: gleans vegetation for insects, seeds, buds, berries and some fruit; occasionally hover-gleans or catches flying insects on the wing; may also visit feeders.

Voice: song is a long, melodious series of whistled notes, much like a fast version of a robin's song; call is a distinctive *squeak*.

Similar Species: male is distinctive. *Purple Finch* (p. 352) or *House Finch* (p. 353): females are much smaller and have heavier streaking on underparts. *Sparrows* (pp. 313–33): smaller; all lack large, conical bill.

Best Sites: Brasstown Bald; Rabun Bald; Kennesaw Mt. (HC-migration: 40); Chattahoochee River NRA.

BLUE GROSBEAK

Passerina caerulea

Male Blue Grosbeaks owe their spectacular spring plumage not to a fresh molt but, oddly enough, to feather wear. While Blue Grosbeaks are wintering in Mexico and Central America, their brown feather tips slowly wear away, leaving the crystal blue plumage that is seen as they arrive on their breeding grounds. Surprisingly, the blue color of the plumage of this and all blue-colored birds (buntings, jays, bluebirds, etc.) is not produced by a blue feather pigment, but instead by tiny melanin particles in the feathers that reflect only the short blue wavelengths in the visible light spectrum. • Blue Grosbeaks are very expressive during courtship. If you are lucky enough to spot one of these birds in spring, watch for the tail-spreading, tail-flicking and crown-raising behaviors that suggest the bird might be breeding. • Birders are advised to look carefully for the rusty wing bars that will distinguish this bird from the similar-looking and much more common Indigo Bunting. • *Caerulea* is Latin for "blue," a description that doesn't quite grasp this bird's true beauty.

ID: large, pale grayish conical bill. *Male:* blue overall; 2 rusty wing bars; black around base of bill. *Female:* soft brown plumage overall; whitish throat; rusty wing bars; rump and shoulders are faintly washed with blue. *1st-spring male:* like female but has blue head.
Size: *L* 6–7½ in; *W* 11 in.
Status: common summer breeding resident from April to November statewide, except rare in the southeast, adjacent to the Coast, and in the Mountains above 2500 ft.
Habitat: thick brush, riparian thickets, shrubby areas and dense weedy fields near water.

Nesting: in a shrub or low tree; cup nest is woven with twigs, roots and grass and lined with finer materials, including paper and occasionally shed reptile skins; female incubates 2–5 pale blue eggs for 11–12 days.
Feeding: gleans insects from the ground while hopping; occasionally takes seeds; may visit feeding stations.
Voice: call is a loud *chink;* sweet, melodious, warbling song with phrases that rise and fall.
Similar Species: *Indigo Bunting* (p. 337): smaller body and bill; male lacks rusty wing bars; female has dark brown streaking on breast.
Best Sites: Beaverdam WMA; Piedmont NWR; Rum Creek WMA; River Bend WMA; Eufaula NWR; Bartow Co. (HC: 42).

INDIGO BUNTING

Passerina cyanea

In the shadow of a towering tree, a male Indigo Bunting can look almost black. In such a case, reposition yourself quickly so that you can see the sun strike and enliven this bunting's incomparable indigo plumage—the rich shade of blue is rivaled only by the sky. • Thickets are a favored nesting location for many of our Indigo Buntings. The dense, thorny stems provide the nestlings with protection from many predators, and the berries are a convenient source of food. • The Indigo Bunting employs a clever and comical foraging strategy to reach the grass and weed seeds upon which it feeds. The bird lands midway on a stem and then shuffles slowly toward the seed head, which eventually bends under the bird's weight, giving the bunting easier access to the seeds. • Only male Indigo Buntings sing, and they do not learn their musical warble from their fathers but rather from neighboring males during their first spring.

breeding

ID: stout, gray, conical bill; black legs; no wing bars. *Breeding Male:* blue overall; black lores; wings and tail may show some black. *Female:* brown streaks on breast; whitish throat. *Nonbreeding male:* similar to female, but usually with some blue in wings and tail.
Size: *L* 5½ in; *W* 8 in.
Status: common summer breeding resident from March to November, except rare in the southeast adjacent to the Coast; accidental in winter.
Habitat: deciduous forest and woodland edges, regenerating forest clearings, shrubby fields, orchards, abandoned pastures and hedgerows; occasionally along mixed woodland edges.

Nesting: usually in an upright fork of a small tree or shrub or within a vine tangle; female builds a cup nest of grass, leaves and bark strips and lines it with rootlets, hair and feathers; female incubates 3–4 white to bluish white eggs, rarely spotted with brown or purple, for 12–13 days.
Feeding: gleans low vegetation and the ground for insects, especially grasshoppers, beetles, weevils, flies and larvae; also eats the seeds of thistles, dandelions, goldenrods and other native plants.
Voice: call is a quick *spit;* song consists of paired warbled whistles: *fire-fire, where-where, here-here, see-it see-it.*
Similar Species: *Blue Grosbeak* (p. 336): larger overall; larger, more robust bill; 2 rusty wing bars; male has black around base of bill; female lacks streaking on breast. *Eastern Bluebird* (p. 261): larger; slimmer bill; orange or rufous below; male has pure blue wings and tail.
Best Sites: open areas of wildlife management areas, national wildlife refuges and rural woodlands; Greene Co. (HC-fall: 168); McIntosh Co. (HC-fall: 80).

PAINTED BUNTING

Passerina ciris

Brilliantly colored male Painted Buntings look like living fragments of precious rainbows, a characteristic more typical of birds found in the warm tropical forests of Central and South America. Though a few Painted Buntings spend their winters on the coast of Georgia, most of these nonpareil buntings spend their winters in more tropical homes. • Each spring, these birds traverse the Gulf of Mexico to grace southern thickets and tangles with their colors and sweet songs. Along with the more subdued greenish females, bright males may be seen migrating alongside pure blue Indigo Buntings, providing observers with a truly overwhelming feast of colors. • Once breeding begins, Painted Buntings tend to be rather secretive, hiding among dense foliage. During the short breeding season, singing males often find themselves caught in violent physical challenges over territory and breeding privileges.

• Unfortunately, overall numbers of Painted Buntings are declining along the Atlantic Coast, where their swampy breeding habitat is rapidly being lost to development. Though trapping of these birds is illegal in the U.S., regrettably, large numbers are still caged in Cuba, Mexico and Central America, then sold to the pet trade.

ID: *Male:* blue head; red eye ring, underparts and rump; green back; dark wings and tail with reddish highlights. *Female:* green upperparts and yellow-green underparts. *Immature:* overall drab plumage with green highlights on upperparts and yellow highlights on underparts.

Size: *L* 5½ in; *W* 8½ in.

Status: common summer breeding resident on and near the Coast and barrier islands from mid-March to mid-October; less common, but increasing summer breeding resident in the eastern Coastal Plain to Macon and Augusta; accidental outside breeding areas in spring and summer; accidental in winter on the Coast.

Habitat: semi-open areas, including roadside thickets, hedgerows, woodland edges, clearings and undergrowth, townsite parks, gardens and brushlands.

Nesting: in low trees, dense shrubbery or vines; female weaves an open cup nest from a variety of vegetative materials, lined with fine plant material and animal hair; female incubates 3–5 white eggs finely speckled with purple and red; female feeds nestlings; male may have more than one mate.

Feeding: seeds and insects are found while foraging on the ground or in low vegetation; may also eat fruits and berries.

Voice: call is a sharp *chip;* song is a sweet, clear series of warbling notes.

Similar Species: male is distinctive. *Other female and immature buntings* (pp. 337–38): brown overall.

Best Sites: Augusta Levee; Altamaha WMA; all barrier islands; McIntosh Co. (HC: 167).

DICKCISSEL

Spiza americana

Dickcissels are an irruptive species and may be here one year and absent the next. Arriving in suitable nesting habitat before the smaller females, breeding males bravely announce their presence with stuttering, trilled renditions of their own name. The territorial males perch atop tall blades of grass, fence posts or rocks to scour their turf for signs of potential mates or unwelcome males. Dickcissels are polygynous, and males may mate with up to eight females in a single breeding season. They provide no assistance to the females in nesting or brooding.

• This "miniature meadowlark" has a special fondness for fields of alfalfa. Though Dickcissels eat mostly insects on their breeding grounds, seeds and grain form the main part of their diet on their South American wintering grounds, making them unpopular with local farmers. Drought cycles, and consequent food shortages, in their normal breeding areas in the Great Plains likely explain the Dickcissel's pattern of absence and abundance in Georgia.

breeding

ID: yellow "eyebrow"; thin, dark malar stripe; gray head, nape and sides of yellow breast; brown upperparts; pale, grayish underparts; rufous shoulder patch; dark, conical bill. *Breeding Male:* white "chin" and black "bib"; duller colors in nonbreeding plumage. *Female:* duller version of male; white throat. *Nonbreeding Male:* less distinct black "bib."
Size: *L* 6–7 in; *W* 9½ in.
Status: rare, irruptive summer breeding resident in the northwest Ridge and Valley, Piedmont and upper Coastal Plain from March to November; rare migrant statewide, mostly in fall; accidental in winter.
Habitat: abandoned fields dominated by forbs, weedy meadows, croplands, grasslands and grassy roadsides.
Nesting: on or near the ground; well concealed among tall, dense vegetation;

female builds a bulky, open cup nest of grass, weed stems and leaves and lines it with rootlets, fine grass or hair; female incubates 4 pale blue eggs for 11–13 days.
Feeding: gleans insects and seeds from the ground and low vegetation.
Voice: flight call is a buzzerlike *bzrrrrt;* song consists of 2–3 single notes followed by a trill, often paraphrased as *dick dick dick-cissel.*
Similar Species: *House Sparrow* (p. 358): black bill, "bib" and lores; gray throat; lacks yellow "eyebrow," dark malar stripe and yellow breast. *Eastern Meadowlark* (p. 342): much larger; long, pointed bill; yellow "chin" and throat with black "necklace." *American Goldfinch* (p. 356): lacks black "bib"; white or buff yellow bars on dark wings; may show black forecrown.
Best Sites: very irruptive; Athens (HC-breeding: 50); Laurens Co. (HC-breeding: 6); Resaca (HC-breeding: 16).

BOBOLINK

Dolichonyx oryzivorus

At first glance, the female Bobolink resembles a sparrow, but the male, with his dark belly and his buff-and-black upperparts, is colored like no other bird in Georgia. Roger Tory Peterson likened the male Bobolink's plumage to a backward tuxedo. • Traveling an incredible 12,400 miles annually from its breeding grounds in the northern U.S. to winter in southern South America, the Bobolink migrates farther than any other passerine in the Western Hemisphere. One banded female made the round-trip nine times throughout her lifetime, the equivalent of circling the Earth at the equator 4½ times! To guide them during their night migration, Bobolinks use the Earth's magnetic field (they possess magnetite in their heads), as well as the rotation axis of the stars. • Most people believe that the name of this bird is a reference to the bird's *bob-o-link* song.

breeding

ID: *Breeding male:* black bill, head, wings, tail and underparts; buff nape; white rump and wing patch. *Breeding female:* yellowish bill; buff brown overall; streaked back, sides, flank and rump; pale "eyebrow"; dark eye line; pale central crown stripe bordered by dark stripes; whitish throat. *Nonbreeding male:* similar to breeding female but darker above and rich golden buff below.
Size: *L* 6–8 in; *W* 11½ in.
Status: common migrant statewide to abundant migrant on the Coast from March to June and from July to October; rare or absent in the Mountains.
Habitat: tall, grassy meadows and ditches, rice fields and some croplands.
Nesting: does not nest in Georgia.
Feeding: gleans the ground and low vegetation for adult and larval invertebrates; also eats many seeds.

Voice: issues a *pink* call in flight; song is a series of banjolike twangs: *bobolink bobolink spink spank spink*, often given in flight.
Similar Species: breeding male is distinctive. *Savannah Sparrow* (p. 320): dark breast streaking; yellow lores. *Vesper Sparrow* (p. 318): breast streaking; white outer tail feathers. *Grasshopper Sparrow* (p. 321): white belly; unstreaked sides and flanks.
Best Sites: Ocmulgee NM; Savannah NWR; Harris Neck NWR; Altamaha WMA; Jekyll I. (HC-fall: 1000s); Greene Co. (HC-spring: 1600).

RED-WINGED BLACKBIRD

Agelaius phoeniceus

Nearly every cattail marsh worthy of description in Georgia plays host to Red-winged Blackbirds during at least some part of the year. Red-wings are year-round residents of Georgia, and few people have been denied a meeting with these abundant and widespread birds. • The male's bright red shoulders and short, raspy song are his most important tools in the strategy he employs to defend his territory from rivals. A flashy and richly voiced male who has managed to establish a large and productive territory can attract several mates to his cattail kingdom. In field experiments, males whose red shoulders were painted black soon lost their territories to rivals they had previously defeated. • After a female has been wooed by the polygynous male, she starts the busy work of weaving a nest amid the cattails. Cryptic coloration allows her to sit inconspicuously upon her nest, blending in perfectly with the surroundings. • *Agelaius* is a Greek word meaning "flocking," which is an accurate description of this bird's winter behavior, when impressive flocks can sometimes be seen.

ID: *Male:* all black, except for large, red shoulder patch edged in yellow (occasionally concealed). *Female:* heavily streaked underparts; mottled brown upperparts; faint, red shoulder patch; light "eyebrow."
Size: *L* 7–9½ in; *W* 13 in.
Status: common year-round resident statewide; abundant in winter, except rare or uncommon in the Mountains.
Habitat: cattail marshes, wet meadows and ditches, croplands and shoreline shrubs.
Nesting: colonial; in cattails or shoreline bushes; female weaves an open cup nest of dried cattail leaves and grass and lines it with fine grass; female incubates 3–4 darkly marked, pale blue-green eggs for 10–12 days.

Feeding: gleans the ground for seeds, waste grain and invertebrates; also gleans vegetation for seeds, insects and berries; occasionally catches insects in flight; may visit feeders.
Voice: calls include a harsh *check* and a high *tseert;* song is a loud, raspy *konk-a-ree* or *ogle-reeee. Female:* may give a loud *che-che-che chee chee chee.*
Similar Species: male is distinctive when shoulder patch shows. *Brewer's Blackbird* (p. 345) and *Rusty Blackbird* (p. 344): females lack streaked underparts. *Brown-headed Cowbird* (p. 349): juvenile is smaller, has stubbier, conical bill and is unstreaked.
Best Sites: near marshes and rural and urban areas in winter; Milledgeville (HC-winter: 4,000,000).

341

EASTERN MEADOWLARK

Sturnella magna

The male Eastern Meadowlark's bright yellow underparts, black V-shaped "necklace" and white outer tail feathers help attract mates. Females share these colorful attributes for a slightly different purpose: when a predator approaches too close to a nest, the incubating female explodes from the grass in a burst of flashing color. Most predators cannot resist chasing the moving target, and once the female has led the predator away from the nest, she simply folds away her white tail flags, exposes her camouflaged back and disappears into the grass without a trace. • Because of their bright plumage, Eastern Meadowlarks don't seem to fit in with the blackbird family. When they're seen in silhouette, however, the similarities become very apparent. • Eastern Meadowlarks are relatively common throughout Georgia, especially in winter when migrants join resident birds. Wintering birds join up with flocks of European Starlings, providing safety in numbers and a chance to feast on tasty morsels stirred up by so many feet.

breeding

ID: *Breeding:* yellow underparts; broad, black breast band; mottled, brown upperparts; short, wide tail with white outer tail feathers; long, pinkish legs; yellow lores; long, sharp bill; blackish crown stripes and eye line border; pale "eyebrow" and median crown stripe; dark streaking on white sides and flanks. *Nonbreeding:* duller plumage.
Size: *L* 9–11 in; *W* 13½–17 in.
Status: uncommon on the Coast to common statewide as a breeding resident; in winter, more common in the south and the Coast.
Habitat: *Breeding:* grassy meadows and pastures; also in some croplands, weedy fields, grassy roadsides and old orchards. *In migration* and *winter:* coastal barrens and fields, croplands and wasteland.

Nesting: in a depression or scrape on the ground, concealed by dense grass; domed grass nest, with a side entrance, is woven into the surrounding vegetation; female incubates 3–7 white eggs, heavily spotted with brown and purple, for about 13–15 days.
Feeding: gleans grasshoppers, crickets, beetles and spiders from the ground and vegetation; extracts grubs and worms by probing its bill into the soil; also eats seeds.
Voice: song is a rich series of 2–8 melodic, distinct, slurred whistles: *see-you at school-today* or *this is the year;* gives a rattling flight call and a high, buzzy *dzeart.*
Similar Species: *Dickcissel* (p. 339): much smaller; solid dark crown; white throat; lacks brown streaking on sides and flanks. *Bobolink* (p. 340): smaller; more conical bill; less yellow on underparts; lacks black breast band.
Best Sites: grassy and agricultural fields statewide, declining as these habitat types are lost to development.

YELLOW-HEADED BLACKBIRD

Xanthocephalus xanthocephalus

Handsome Yellow-headed Blackbirds stand out like beacons as they forage among mixed flocks of duller blackbirds. In winter, these highly social birds stray into Georgia from their western prairie strongholds to fatten up on waste grain and seeds. Though Yellow-headed Blackbirds occasionally visit backyard bird feeders, they are most often seen foraging together with Common Grackles, or other blackbirds, in agricultural fields, farmlands or sod farms. As dusk approaches, Yellow-headed Blackbirds return to roost at nearby wetlands. • Surprisingly, flocks are often sex specific. The majority of males overwinter in the southern United States and northern Mexico, whereas most females overwinter farther south. • You may expect Yellow-headed Blackbirds to have voices as splendid as their gold and black plumage. The shocking truth is revealed when noisy flocks call to each other with harsh, chain-saw-like wails and raspy croaks, sounding like a creaky door hinge.

Status: rare fall to spring visitor, and very rare in the Mountains, from September to June; accidental in summer.
Habitat: plowed agricultural fields, feedlots, pastures and residential areas; roosts near wetlands at night.
Nesting: does not nest in Georgia.
Feeding: gleans the ground for waste grain, seeds and insects; may visit bird feeders.
Voice: usually silent in Georgia; call is a deep *krrt* or *ktuk*; song is a strained, metallic grating note followed by a descending buzz.
Similar Species: male is distinctive. *Rusty Blackbird* (p. 344) and *Brewer's Blackbird* (p. 345): females lack yellow throat and face.
Best Sites: erratic statewide; most likely in blackbird flocks in the southwest in winter; Athens (HC: 14).

ID: *Male:* yellow head and breast; black body; white wing patches; black lores and bill; long tail. *Female:* dusky brown overall; yellow breast, throat and "eyebrow"; hints of yellow on face.
Size: *L* 8–11 in; *W* 15 in.

343

RUSTY BLACKBIRD

Euphagus carolinus

The Rusty Blackbird owes its name to the rusty color of its fall plumage, but the name could just as well reflect this bird's grating, squeaky song, which sounds very much like a rusty hinge. • Unlike many blackbirds, Rusty Blackbirds prefer flooded woodlands, swamps or wetlands. In winter these birds occasionally roost or forage with grackles and other blackbirds, though unmixed flocks are also common. • Rusty Blackbirds spend their days foraging along the wooded edges of fields and wetlands, and they occasionally pick through the manure-laden ground of cattle feedlots. At day's end, when feeding is curtailed, most birds seek the shelter of trees and shrubs as well as the stalks of emergent marshland vegetation. • Rusty Blackbirds are generally less abundant and less aggressive than their relatives, and they usually avoid human-altered environments.

nonbreeding

ID: yellow eyes; dark legs; long, sharp bill. *Breeding male:* dark plumage; subtle green gloss on body; subtle bluish or greenish gloss on head. *Breeding female:* paler than male; without gloss. *Nonbreeding male:* rusty wings, back and crown. *Nonbreeding female:* paler than male; buffy underparts; rusty "cheek."

Size: *L* 9 in; *W* 14 in.

Status: uncommon winter resident statewide, except rare near the Coast from September to May.

Habitat: marshes, open fields, feedlots and woodland edges near water.

Nesting: does not nest in Georgia.

Feeding: walks along shorelines gleaning waterbugs, beetles, dragonflies, snails,

grasshoppers and occasionally small fish; also eats waste grain and seeds.

Voice: call is a harsh *chack;* song is a squeaky, creaking *kushleeeh ksh-lay.*

Similar Species: *Brewer's Blackbird* (p. 345): male has glossier, iridescent plumage, greener body and shows more purple; female has dark eyes; nonbreeding birds lack conspicuous, rusty highlights. *Common Grackle* (p. 346): longer, keeled tail; larger body and bill; more iridescent. *European Starling* (p. 271): speckled appearance; dark eyes; yellow bill in summer.

Best Sites: E.L. Huie; Atlanta Motor Speedway; Phinizy Swamp Nature Park; Bibb Co. (HC: 2000+).

BREWER'S BLACKBIRD

Euphagus cyanocephalus

This bird of the western plains is a relatively new addition to our avifauna and is still not very common here. For the last century, the Brewer's Blackbird has been expanding its nesting range at an incredible rate of 11 miles per year by following roadways and taking advantage of cleared land. In Georgia, this blackbird occasionally shows up along roadsides where it searches for roadkilled insects, and squabbles with pigeons and starlings for scraps of food. • The feathers of this bird show an iridescent quality as rainbows of reflected sunlight move along the feather shafts. When it walks, the Brewer's Blackbird jerks its head back and forth like a chicken, enhancing the glossy effect and distinguishing it from other blackbirds. • John James Audubon named this bird after Thomas Mayo Brewer, a friend and prominent oologist (person who studies eggs).

ID: *Breeding male:* iridescent, blue-green body and purplish head often look black; yellow eyes; some nonbreeding males may show some faint, rusty feather edgings. *Female:* flat brown plumage; dark eyes. *Nonbreeding male:* black-brown plumage overall.
Size: *L* 8–10 in; *W* 15½ in.
Status: rare to uncommon migrant and winter resident, more abundant south of the Fall Line and rare near the Coast, from September to April.
Habitat: moist, grassy meadows and road-sides with nearby wetlands and patches of trees and shrubs.

Nesting: does not nest in Georgia.
Feeding: gleans invertebrates and seeds while walking along shorelines and open areas.
Voice: call is a metallic *chick* or *check*; song is a creaking, 2-noted *k-shee*.
Similar Species: *Rusty Blackbird* (p. 344): longer, more slender bill; iridescent plumage has subtler green gloss on body and subtle bluish or greenish gloss on head; female has yellow eyes. *Common Grackle* (p. 346): much longer, keeled tail; larger body and bill. *Brown-headed Cowbird* (p. 349): shorter tail; stubbier, thicker bill; male has dark eyes and brown head; female has paler, streaked underparts and very pale throat. *European Starling* (p. 271): speckled appearance; dark eyes; yellow bill in summer.
Best Sites: Laurens Co. pastures; Rome (HC: 2400).

COMMON GRACKLE

Quiscalus quiscula

The Common Grackle is a poor but spirited singer. Usually while perched in a shrub, a male grackle will slowly take a deep breath to inflate his breast, causing his feathers to spike outward, then close his eyes and give out a loud, strained *tssh-schleek*. Despite his lack of musical talent, the male remains smug and proud, posing with his bill held high. • Large flocks of Common Grackles are common year-round in rural areas where they forage on waste grain in open fields. Smaller bands occasionally venture into urban neighborhoods where they assert their dominance at backyard bird feeders. • Grackles are one of several species that squish ants into their feathers while preening. The formic acid contained in the ant's body acts as a disinfectant. Sometimes grackles will also clean their feathers with the oils found in a green lemon or walnut hull. • The Common Grackle is easily distinguished from the Rusty Blackbird and Brewer's Blackbird by its long, heavy bill and lengthy, wedge-shaped tail.

purple morph

ID: iridescent plumage (purple-blue head and breast, bronze back and sides and purple wings and tail) often looks blackish; long, keeled tail; yellow eyes; long, heavy bill; female is smaller, duller and browner than male.

Size: *L* 11–13½ in; *W* 17 in.

Status: common permanent breeding resident statewide; abundant in winter, except uncommon in the Mountains.

Habitat: wetlands, hedgerows, fields, wet meadows, riparian woodlands and along the edges of coniferous forests and woodlands; also shrubby urban and suburban parks and gardens.

Nesting: singly or in small colonies; in dense tree or shrub branches or emergent vegetation; often near water; female builds a bulky, open cup nest of twigs, grass, plant fibers and mud and lines it with fine grass or feathers; female incubates 4–5 brown-blotched, pale blue eggs for 12–14 days.

Feeding: slowly struts along the ground, gleaning, snatching and probing for insects, earthworms, seeds, waste grain and fruit; also catches insects in flight and eats small vertebrates; may take some bird eggs.

Voice: call is a quick, loud *swaaaack* or *chaack*; song is a series of harsh, strained notes ending with a metallic squeak: *tssh-schleek* or *gri-de-leeek*.

Similar Species: *Rusty Blackbird* (p. 344) and *Brewer's Blackbird* (p. 345): smaller overall; lack heavy bill and keeled tail. *European Starling* (p. 271): very short tail; long, thin bill (yellow in summer); speckled appearance; dark eyes.

Best Sites: widespread near farms and cities; Milledgeville (HC-winter: 1,000,000+).

BOAT-TAILED GRACKLE

Quiscalus major

Feathers fluffed, tail spread and wings fluttering above its back, the Boat-tailed Grackle issues harsh, grating calls across the marsh landscape. If an intruder dares to enter the aggressively guarded territory, the male grackle points his bill skyward in a threatening posture that warns of an impending attack. • Bold and seemingly carefree, the Boat-tailed Grackle may eat eggs from the unguarded nests of other birds, including much larger species such as herons and rails. It is closely associated with coastal waters, where it wades through the shallows or walks on top of floating vegetation while searching for snails and mussels. It also ranges inland to the Okefenokee National Wildlife Refuge and nearby counties. • The Boat-tailed Grackle and the southwestern Great-tailed Grackle were, until the 1970s, considered to be the same species. • The dark-eyed subspecies, *Q.m. westoni*, is present and breeds in southwestern Georgia in Thomas, Brooks, Lowndes, Colquitt and Cook counties.

ID: long, keel-shaped tail; long, dark bill; eye color variable, from yellow along the Coast to brown in the southwest. *Male:* iridescent, blue plumage usually looks black. *Female:* orangy brown undersides; brown face "mask" and crown; darker wings and tail; *Immature:* males are blackish; females have faint streaking or spotting on breast and pale "eyebrow."

Size: *Male: L* 16½ in; *W* 23 in. *Female: L* 14 in; *W* 17½ in.

Status: abundant permanent breeding resident on barrier islands and in coastal areas; dark-eyed subspecies is an uncommon permanent breeder in southwestern Georgia.

Habitat: usually near water; saltwater marshes, beaches, mudflats and other ocean-side habitats; inland near large lakes and rivers; urban environments.

Nesting: colonial nester; nests in vegetation at the edge of a marsh or other water body; males and females often have more than one mate; female builds bulky cup nest from marsh vegetation and mud; female incubates 2–3 often pale bluish eggs with bold, dark scrawl markings for 13 days and raises the young alone.

Feeding: walks on land or in shallow water, thrusting its bill forward to snatch up prey; omnivorous diet includes aquatic and terrestrial insects, crustaceans and other invertebrates; may also eat amphibians, fish, seeds, grain and the eggs and young of other birds.

Voice: a variety of calls, including rattles, chatters, squeaks and a soft *chuck;* song consists of harsh *jeeb* notes repeated in series.

Similar Species: *Common Grackle* (p. 346): smaller; yellow eyes; iridescent, purple head; darker throat and breast.

Best Sites: barrier islands; Savannah NWR; Harris Neck NWR; Andrews I. (HC-winter: 1200). *Dark-eyed subspecies:* Grand Bay WMA (HC-winter: 275).

SHINY COWBIRD
Molothrus bonariensis

The Shiny Cowbird, the South American counterpart to the Brown-headed Cowbird, hopped the Antilles Island chain to expand into Florida in 1985, and eventually into Georgia in 1999. • The female, who lays her eggs in other birds' nests and never raises her own brood, may puncture existing eggs in the nest, making hers the only offspring that the parasitized host bird will raise. Before arriving in the United States, the Shiny Cowbird parasitized Puerto Rico's Yellow-shouldered Blackbird so often that the bird is now endangered. American ornithologists are worried the same fate will befall many of Georgia's birds, but the Shiny Cowbird has yet to significantly affect our indigenous bird populations. • Cowbirds inherit their song, which ensures that they mate only with other cowbirds after they are fledged by their foster parents. • The scientific name *Molothrus* is a form of the Greek word "molobros," meaning greedy or parasitic, and is an accurate description of this bird's nesting habits.

ID: thin, pointed bill; rounded wings, long tail; dark eyes. *Male:* all black with purple iridescence. *Female:* brown overall; indistinct "eyebrow."
Size: *L* 7½–8 in; *W* 12 in.
Status: rare visitor (18 reports) to the Coast from April to August; accidental on the Coast in winter.
Habitat: agricultural areas, edge habitats, lightly treed areas, roadsides and bird feeders.
Nesting: only one known nesting record in Georgia so far; does not build a nest; females lay a variable number of eggs per year in the nests of other birds, usually laying 1 egg per nest; whitish eggs, marked with gray or red spots, brown blotches, or rarely all dark red, hatch after 10–13 days.
Feeding: eats mostly agricultural grains, seeds and insects.
Voice: silvery warble, broken with whistles and metallic trills; sings in flight.
Similar Species: *Brown-headed Cowbird* (p. 349): shorter tail and less pointy bill; pointed wings; male has brown head and green iridescence on black body; female has white throat, subtly streaked chest and gray-brown plumage.
Best Sites: barrier islands and the Coast.

BROWN-HEADED COWBIRD

Molothrus ater

The Brown-headed Cowbird's song, a bubbling, liquidy *glug-ahl-whee*, might be translated by other bird species as "here comes trouble!" Historically, Brown-headed Cowbirds followed bison herds across the Great Plains—they now follow cattle—and the birds' nomadic lifestyle made it impossible for them to construct and tend a nest. Instead, cowbirds engage in "brood parasitism," laying their eggs in the nests of other songbirds. Many of the parasitized songbirds do not recognize that the eggs are not theirs, so they incubate them and raise the cowbird young as their own. Cowbird chicks typically hatch first and develop much more quickly than their nestmates, which may be pushed out of the nest or simply outcompeted for food. • The expansion of livestock farming, the fragmentation of forests and the extensive network of transportation corridors in North America have increased the cowbird's range, and it now parasitizes more than 140 species of birds. Many eastern bird species have yet to evolve a defense against the cowbird's brood parasitism. • The endangered Kirtland's Warbler was saved from extinction only when an intensive cowbird control program was instituted on the warbler's breeding grounds in Michigan.

ID: thick, conical bill; short, squared tail; dark eyes. *Male:* iridescent, green-blue plumage usually looks glossy black; dark brown head. *Female:* brown plumage overall; faint streaking on light brown underparts; pale throat.

Size: *L* 6–8 in; *W* 12 in.

Status: uncommon permanent breeding resident statewide; common migrant and winter visitor; increasing.

Habitat: open agricultural and residential areas, including fields, woodland edges, utility cutlines, roadsides, landfills, campgrounds and areas near cattle.

Nesting: does not build a nest; each female may lay up to 40 eggs per year in the nests of other birds, usually laying 1 egg per nest (larger numbers, up to 8 eggs in a single nest, are probably from several different cowbirds); whitish eggs, marked with gray and brown, hatch after 10–13 days.

Feeding: gleans the ground for seeds, waste grain and invertebrates, especially grasshoppers, beetles and true bugs.

Voice: call is a squeaky, high-pitched *seep, psee* or *wee-tse-tse*, often given in flight; also a fast, chipping *ch-ch-ch-ch-ch-ch;* song is a high, liquidy gurgle: *glug-ahl-whee* or *bubbloozeee.*

Similar Species: *Rusty Blackbird* (p. 344) and *Brewer's Blackbird* (p. 345): slimmer, longer bills; longer tails; lack contrasting brown head and darker body; all have yellow eyes except for female Brewer's Blackbird. *Shiny Cowbird* (p. 348): thin, pointed bill; male lacks brown head; female is darker brown overall and lacks pale throat.

Best Sites: statewide in a variety of habitats.

ORCHARD ORIOLE

Icterus spurius

Orchards may have been favored haunts of this oriole at one time, but because orchards are now heavily sprayed and manicured, it is unlikely that you will ever see this bird in such a locale. Instead, the Orchard Oriole is most commonly found in large shade trees that line roads, paths and streams. Smaller than all other North American orioles, the Orchard Oriole is one of only two oriole species commonly found in the eastern United States. • These orioles are frequent victims of nest parasitism by Brown-headed Cowbirds. In some parts of their breeding range, over half of the Orchard Oriole nests are parasitized by cowbirds. • The Orchard Oriole is one of the first species to migrate following breeding and is usually absent by the end of August. • Orchard Orioles are best seen in spring when eager males hop from branch to branch, singing their quick and musical courtship songs.

ID: *Male:* black "hood" and tail; chestnut underparts, shoulder and rump; dark wings with white wing bar and feather edgings. *Female and immature:* olive upperparts; yellow to olive yellow underparts; faint, white wing bars on dusky gray wings.
Size: *L* 6–7 in; *W* 9½ in.
Status: common summer breeding resident statewide, except uncommon in the Mountains above 2000 ft, from March to October; very accidental in winter.
Habitat: open woodlands, suburban parklands, forest edges, hedgerows and groves of shade trees.
Nesting: in the fork of a deciduous tree or shrub; female builds a hanging pouch nest woven from grass and other fine plant fibers; female incubates 4–5 pale bluish white eggs, blotched with gray, brown and purple, for about 12–15 days.
Feeding: finds insects and berries while inspecting trees and shrubs; probes flowers for nectar; may visit hummingbird feeders and feeding stations that offer orange halves.
Voice: call is a quick *chuck;* song is a loud, rapid, varied series of whistled notes.
Similar Species: *Baltimore Oriole* (p. 351): male has brighter orange plumage with orange in tail; female has orange overtones. *Summer Tanager* (p. 311) and *Scarlet Tanager* (p. 312): females have thicker, pale bills and lack wing bars.
Best Sites: wildlife management areas, national wildlife refuges and rural and urban sites statewide; Eufaula NWR; Beaverdam WMA; Altamaha WMA; Columbus (HC: 50); Laurens Co. (HC: 30).

BALTIMORE ORIOLE

Icterus galbula

The male Baltimore Oriole has striking, black and orange plumage that flickers like smoldering embers among our neighborhood treetops. As if his brilliant plumage were not enough to secure our admiration, he also sings a rich, flute-like courtship song and will vocalize almost continuously until he finds a mate. • In Georgia, Baltimore Orioles currently nest only in Central City Park in Macon, where they are often difficult to find because they inhabit the forest heights along the Ocmulgee River. Developing an ear for their whistled *peter peter peter here peter* tune and frequently scanning the park's sycamore and elm trees may produce enchanting views of these beloved orioles. • Baltimore Orioles occasionally winter in the Coastal Plain, where they are most often seen in mature pecan orchards, especially where Yellow-bellied Sapsuckers have drilled fresh "sap-wells." • "Oriole" is derived from the Latin for "golden."

ID: *Male:* black "hood," back, wings and central tail feathers; bright orange underparts, shoulder, rump and outer tail feathers; white wing patch and feather edgings. *Female:* olive brown upperparts (darkest on head); dull yellow-orange underparts and rump; white wing bar.
Size: *L* 7–8 in; *W* 11½ in.
Status: rare breeding resident in Macon, and casual in the Mountains; uncommon migrant statewide from April to May and from August to December; rare north of the Fall Line and uncommon south of the Fall Line in winter; previously more common.
Habitat: deciduous and mixed forests, particularly riparian woodlands; natural openings, shorelines, roadsides, orchards, gardens and parks.

Nesting: high in a deciduous tree; female builds a hanging pouch nest made of grass, bark shreds, rootlets and plant stems and lines it with fine grass, rootlets and fur; female incubates 4–5 darkly marked, pale gray to bluish white eggs for 12–14 days.
Feeding: gleans canopy vegetation and shrubs for caterpillars, beetles, wasps and other invertebrates; also eats some fruit, nectar and sap; may visit sugarwater feeders and feeders that offer grape jelly or orange halves; eats cracked pecans in winter.
Voice: calls include a 2-note *tea-too* and a rapid chatter: *ch-ch-ch-ch-ch;* song consists of slow, loud, clear whistles: *peter peter peter here peter.*
Similar Species: *Orchard Oriole* (p. 350): male has darker chestnut plumage; female is olive yellow and lacks orange overtones. *Summer Tanager* (p. 311) and *Scarlet Tanager* (p. 312): females have thicker, pale bills and lack wing bars.
Best Sites: *Summer:* Macon Central City Park. *Winter:* Valdosta (HC: 12); Bulloch Co. (HC: 32 in a week).

351

PURPLE FINCH

Carpodacus purpureus

The Purple Finch's gentle nature and simple but stunning plumage endears it to many birders. In some winters this charming finch may delight feeder-watchers with regular visits, only to be completely absent the next year. The availability of natural food elsewhere is likely the reason for the irregularity of the Purple Finch's visits. • In winter, groups of Purple Finches forage alone or join mixed flocks of American Goldfinches and Pine Siskins. Your best chance of finding Purple Finches is at a backyard feeder, especially north of the Fall Line. Erecting a flat, table-style feeding station near tree cover may attract a small flock of Purple Finches to your backyard in winter. • "Purple" (*purpureus*) is simply a false description of this bird's reddish coloration. Roger Tory Peterson said it best when he described the Purple Finch as "a sparrow dipped in raspberry juice." Only the male is brightly colored, however, and the female is a rather drab, unassuming bird by comparison.

ID: *Male:* pale bill; raspberry red (occasionally yellow to salmon pink) head, throat, breast and nape; back and flanks are streaked with brown and red; reddish brown "cheek"; red rump; notched tail; pale, unstreaked belly and undertail coverts. *Female:* dark brown "cheek" and "jaw line"; white "eyebrow" and lower "cheek" stripe; heavily streaked underparts; unstreaked undertail coverts.
Size: *L* 5–6 in; *W* 10 in.
Status: uncommon and highly variable winter resident statewide from September to May; absent in many years; erratic south of the Fall Line.
Habitat: coniferous, mixed and deciduous forests, shrubby open areas and feeders with nearby tree cover.
Nesting: does not nest in Georgia.
Feeding: gleans the ground and vegetation for seeds, buds, berries and insects; readily visits table-style feeding stations.
Voice: call is a single metallic *cheep* or *weet;* song is a slightly raspy, continuous warble.
Similar Species: *House Finch* (p. 353): squared tail; male has brown flanks and lacks reddish "cap"; female lacks distinct "cheek" patch and has more heavily streaked underparts. *Red Crossbill* (p. 354): larger bill with crossed mandibles; male has more red overall and dark "V"s on whitish undertail coverts.
Best Sites: backyard feeders; Kennesaw Mt.; Black Rock Mountain SP; Columbus (HC: 400+).

HOUSE FINCH

Carpodacus mexicanus

A native to western North America, the House Finch was brought to eastern parts of the continent as an illegally captured cage bird known as the "Hollywood Finch." In the early 1940s, New York pet shop owners released their birds to avoid prosecution and fines, and it is the descendents of those birds that have colonized our area. In fact, the House Finch is now commonly found throughout the continental U.S. and southern Canada and has been introduced in Hawaii. • Only the resourceful House Finch has been aggressive and stubborn enough to successfully outcompete the House Sparrow. Like the House Sparrow, this finch has prospered in urban environments. Both birds often build their messy nests among eaves, rafters, chimneys and other human-fashioned habitats, and both birds thrive on seeds. In the west, this bird is often found in natural settings as well as urban centers; in the east, it is seldom found outside of urban and suburban settings. • The male House Finch's plumage varies in color from light yellow to bright red, but females will choose the reddest males with which to breed. The red color of the males is related to dietary carotenoid intake.

ID: streaked undertail coverts; brown-streaked back; square tail. *Male:* brown "cap"; bright red "eyebrow," forecrown, throat and breast; heavily streaked flanks. *Female:* indistinct facial patterning; heavily streaked underparts.
Size: *L* 5–6 in; *W* 9½ in.
Status: common permanent breeding resident statewide, except less abundant in the southeast Coast, and in the Mountains in winter.
Habitat: cities, towns and agricultural areas.
Nesting: in a cavity, building, dense foliage or an abandoned bird nest; especially in evergreens and ornamental shrubs or hanging plants near buildings; mostly the female builds an open cup nest of grass, twigs, leaves, hair and feathers, often adding string and other debris; female incubates 4–5 pale blue eggs, dotted with lavender and black, for 12–14 days.
Feeding: gleans vegetation and the ground for seeds; also takes berries, buds and some flower parts; often visits feeders.
Voice: flight call is a sweet *cheer*, given singly or in series; song is a bright, disjointed warble lasting about 3 seconds, often ending with a harsh *jeeer* or *wheer*.
Similar Species: *Purple Finch* (p. 352): notched tail; male has more burgundy red "cap," upper back and flanks; female has distinct "cheek" patch and less streaking below. *Red Crossbill* (p. 354): bill has crossed mandibles; male has more red overall and darker wings.
Best Sites: statewide at feeders.

RED CROSSBILL

Loxia curvirostra

Red Crossbills are the great gypsies of our bird community, wandering through forests in search of pine cones. They may breed at any time of year if they discover a bumper crop—it's not unusual to hear them singing and see them nest-building in midwinter. Their nomadic ways make them difficult birds to find, and even during years of plenty there is no guarantee that these birds will surface here. In Georgia, Red Crossbills are typically found only in the Mountains, though they have recently bred in the Pine Log Wildlife Management Area. • The crossbill's oddly shaped bill is an adaptation for prying open conifer cones. While holding the cone with one foot, the crossbill inserts its partially open bill between the cone and scales and pries them apart by using its powerful masseters (jaw muscles) when it closes its crossed bill. Once a cone is cracked, a crossbill uses its nimble tongue to extract the soft, energy-rich seeds hidden within. • The scientific name *Loxia* is Greek for "crooked," and *curvirostra* is Latin for "curve-billed."

twigs, grass, bark shreds and rootlets and lines it with moss, lichens, rootlets, feathers and hair; female incubates 3–4 pale bluish white to greenish white eggs, dotted with black and purple, for 12–18 days.

Feeding: eats primarily conifer seeds (especially pine); also eats buds, deciduous tree seeds and occasionally insects; often licks road salt or minerals in soil and along roadsides; rarely visits feeders.

Voice: distinctive *jip-jip* call note, often given in flight; song is a varied series of warbles, trills and chips (similar to other finches).

Similar Species: *Pine Siskin* (p. 355): similar to juvenile Red Crossbill but is smaller, lacks crossed bill and has yellow highlights on wings. *House Finch* (p. 353) and *Purple Finch* (p. 352): conical bills; less red overall; lighter brownish wings; lack red on lower belly.

Best Sites: Cohutta WMA; Pine Log WMA (HC-winter: 64); Burrell's Ford.

ID: bill has crossed tips. *Male:* dull orange red to brick red plumage; dark wings and tail; always has color on throat. *Female:* olive gray to dusky yellow plumage; plain, dark wings. *Immature:* streaky brown overall.

Size: *L* 5–6½ in; *W* 11 in.

Status: rare erratic summer and uncommon winter visitor in the Mountains and upper Piedmont; very erratic elsewhere.

Habitat: coniferous forests and plantations; favors red and white pines but is also found in other pine and spruce-fir forests.

Nesting: high on the outer branch of a conifer; female builds an open cup nest of

PINE SISKIN

Carduelis pinus

Occasionally, hundreds of Pine Siskins are reported at Georgia feeders in winter, only to be absent the next year. Perhaps the best way to meet these birds is to set up a finch feeder filled with black niger seeds in your backyard and wait for them to appear. • Tight flocks of these gregarious birds are frequently heard before they are seen. Once you recognize their characteristic rising *zzzreeeee* calls and boisterous chatter, you can confirm the presence of these finches simply by listening. • Aside from the Pine Siskin's occasional flashes of yellow, its wardrobe is drab and sparrowlike. But for those who get to know it, this bird's behavior reveals a gentle nature that radiates the playfulness and enthusiasm of a goldfinch.

ID: heavily streaked underparts; yellow highlights at base of tail feathers and on wings (easily seen in flight); dull wing bars; darker, heavily streaked upperparts; slightly forked tail; indistinct facial pattern. *Immature:* similar to adult, but overall yellow tint fades through summer.

Size: *L* 4½–5½ in; *W* 9 in.

Status: irruptive winter resident statewide, sometimes fairly common north of the Fall Line, from October to June; accidental in summer, with one record of possible nesting in Rabun Co.

Habitat: coniferous and mixed forests, forest edges, meadows, roadsides, agricultural fields and backyards with feeders.

Nesting: not known to nest in Georgia.

Feeding: gleans the ground and vegetation for seeds (especially thistle seeds), buds and some insects; attracted to road salts, mineral licks and ashes; regularly visits feeders.

Voice: call is a buzzy, rising *zzzreeeee*; song is a variable, bubbly mix of squeaky, raspy, metallic notes, sometimes resembling a jerky "laugh."

Similar Species: *American Goldfinch* (p. 356): nonbreeding male has yellow head and yellow "shoulder" patch; gray, unstreaked underparts; blacker tail. *Purple Finch* (p. 352) and *House Finch* (p. 353): females have thicker bills and no yellow on wings or tail. *Sparrows* (pp. 313–33): all lack yellow on wings and tail.

Best Sites: feeders near Black Rock Mountain SP; backyard feeders when present.

AMERICAN GOLDFINCH

Carduelis tristis

American Goldfinches are bright, cheery songbirds that are commonly seen in weedy fields, along roadsides and among backyard shrubs throughout the year. Goldfinches seem to delight in perching upon late-summer thistle heads as they search for seeds to feed their offspring. It's hard to miss the jubilant *po-ta-to-chip* they issue as they flutter over parks and gardens in a distinctive, undulating flight style. • It is a joy to observe a flock of goldfinches raining down to ground level to poke and prod the heads of dandelions. These birds can look quite comical as they attempt to step down on the flower stems to reach the crowning seeds. A dandelion-covered lawn always seems a lot less weedy with a flock of glowing goldfinches hopping through it. • The scientific name *tristis*, derived from Old English for "bold," likely refers to the goldfinch's bold colors.

breeding

ID: *Breeding male:* black "cap" (extends onto forehead), wings and tail; bright yellow body; white wing bars, undertail coverts and tail base; orange bill and legs. *Nonbreeding male:* olive brown back; yellow-tinged head; gray underparts. *Female:* yellow-green upperparts and belly; yellow throat and breast.
Size: *L* 4½–5½ in; *W* 9 in.
Status: common permanent breeding resident north of the Fall Line and in the southwestern and southeastern Coastal Plain; common in winter statewide.

Habitat: weedy fields, woodland edges, meadows, riparian areas, parks and gardens.
Nesting: in a fork in a deciduous shrub or tree, often in hawthorn, serviceberry or sapling maple; female builds a compact cup nest of plant fibers, grass and spider silk and lines it with plant down and hair; female incubates 4–6 pale bluish white eggs, occasionally spotted with light brown, for about 12–14 days.
Feeding: gleans vegetation for seeds, primarily thistle, birch and alder, as well as for insects and berries; commonly visits feeders.
Voice: calls include *po-ta-to-chip* or *per-chic-or-ee* (often delivered in flight) and a whistled *dear-me, see-me;* song is a long, varied series of trills, twitters, warbles and hissing notes.
Similar Species: *Evening Grosbeak* (p. 357): much larger; massive bill; lacks black forehead. *Wilson's Warbler* (p. 308): olive upperparts; olive wings without wing bars; thin, dark bill; black "cap" does not extend onto forehead.
Best Sites: backyard feeders, riparian areas or thistle and sunflower fields statewide.

EVENING GROSBEAK

Coccothraustes vespertinus

Stunning, gold and black Evening Grosbeaks were originally birds of western Canada and the Rocky Mountains. In the 1800s, flocks of these birds began periodic southeastward invasions, eventually reaching Georgia in 1955. Most Evening Grosbeaks breed in Canada then wander southward in search of wild berries and feeders that are well stocked with sunflower seeds. Today, Evening Grosbeaks are irruptive winter visitors to Georgia, mostly north of the Fall Line. • In 1969, one staggering irruption winter, numbers exceeded 3000 grosbeaks as far south as Thomas County, but in recent years there have been very few that have made it to our state. • The massive bill of this seedeater is difficult to ignore. In French, *gros bec* means "large beak," and any seasoned bird bander will tell you that the Evening Grosbeak's bill can exert an incredible force per unit area—it may be the most powerful bill of any North American bird. • It was once thought that the Evening Grosbeak sang only in the evening, a fact that is reflected in both its common and scientific names (*vespertinus* is Latin for "of the evening").

ID: massive, pale, conical bill; black wings and tail; broad, white wing patches. *Male:* black crown; bright yellow "eyebrow" and forehead band; dark brown head gradually fades into golden yellow belly and lower back. *Female:* gray head and upper back; yellow-tinged underparts; white undertail coverts.
Size: *L* 7–8¾ in; *W* 14 in.
Status: scarce and irruptive winter resident north of the Fall Line, and sometimes south of it, from September to May.

Habitat: coniferous, mixed and deciduous forests and woodlands; parks and gardens with feeders.
Nesting: does not nest in Georgia.
Feeding: gleans the ground and vegetation for seeds, buds and berries; also eats insects and licks mineral-rich soil; often visits feeders for sunflower seeds.
Voice: call is a loud, sharp *clee-ip* or a ringing *peeer;* song is a wandering, halting warble.
Similar Species: *American Goldfinch* (p. 356): much smaller; small bill; smaller wing bars; male has black "cap."
Best Sites: backyard feeders; Cohutta WMA, Lake Conasauga or Betty Gap; Acworth (HC: 75).

HOUSE SPARROW

Passer domesticus

House Sparrows were introduced to North America in the 1850s around Brooklyn, New York, as part of a plan to control the numbers of insects that were damaging grain and cereal crops. Contrary to popular opinion at the time, this sparrow's diet is largely vegetarian, so its effect on crop pests proved to be minimal. Since then, this Eurasian sparrow has managed to colonize most human-altered environments on the continent, and it has benefited greatly from a close association with humans. Unfortunately, its aggressive behavior has helped it to usurp territory from many native bird species, especially in rural habitats. • House Sparrows are not closely related to the other North American sparrows but belong to the family of Old World Sparrows or "Weaver Finches." • Surprisingly, the House Sparrow is relatively uncommon in southeastern Georgia, being found only near restaurant, grocery and mall parking lots. The reason for these paltry numbers is unknown but is probably related to the absence of native seeds, which are the usual staple of their diet. This hypothesis seems likely, considering their meager existence on "scraps" around parking lots and the few dead bugs they glean from car bumpers.

breeding

absent from undeveloped and heavily wooded areas.

ID: *Breeding male:* gray crown; black "bib" and bill; chestnut nape; light gray "cheek"; white wing bar; dark, mottled upperparts; gray under-parts. *Nonbreeding male:* smaller, black "bib"; pale bill. *Female:* plain gray brown overall; buffy "eyebrow"; streaked upper-parts; indistinct facial patterns; grayish, unstreaked underparts.

Size: *L* 5½–6½ in; *W* 9½ in.

Status: uncommon to common year-round resident.

Habitat: townsites, urban and suburban areas, farmyards and agricultural areas, railroad yards and other developed areas;

Nesting: often communal; in a human-made structure, ornamental shrub or natural cavity; pair builds a large, dome-shaped nest of grass, twigs, plant fibers and litter and often lines it with feathers; pair incubates 4–6 whitish to greenish white eggs, dotted with gray and brown, for 10–13 days.

Feeding: gleans the ground and vegetation for seeds, insects and fruit; frequently visits feeders for seeds.

Voice: call is a short *chill-up*; song is a plain, familiar *cheep-cheep-cheep-cheep*.

Similar Species: female is distinctively drab. *Brown-headed Cowbird* (p. 349): similar to female and immature House Sparrow; walks on ground instead of hops.

Best Sites: backyards; mall and food-related parking lots in the southeast.

OCCASIONAL BIRD SPECIES

FULVOUS WHISTLING-DUCK

Dendrocygna bicolor

This large, gooselike duck occurs very rarely in Georgia, with only about a dozen reports. It appears mostly along the coast and Coastal Plain as a rare fall transient and winter resident. Nonetheless, high counts of more than a hundred ducks have been reported in Thomas County and at Blackbeard Island. The Black-bellied Whistling-Duck (*D. autumnalis*), another member of this genus, has also been very rarely documented. In past years, the source of most sightings was from releases from breeders in south Georgia, but expansions from wild flocks in Florida have been the source of many records in the southeast in recent years.

BRANT

Branta bernicla

This cousin of the Canada Goose typically spends most of its time in saltwater environments, but it moves inland in migration, feeding on freshwater plants and waste grains. The Brant is accidental in Georgia in winter, when it is found primarily along the coast and near the barrier islands. The high count for the coast was 25 birds at Harris Neck National Wildlife Refuge. It has also been reported inland at Okefenokee National Wildlife Refuge.

TUNDRA SWAN

Cygnus columbianus

The Tundra Swan is a rare visitor to most of Georgia between November and April, but is quite rare in the mountains, with reports from Rome and Carters Lake (Murray County). This majestic bird has also been reported from the Savannah Wildlife Refuge, Little St. Simons Island, Darien and Griffin. • Lewis and Clark collected the first specimen on their trip westward near the Columbia River, hence the name *columbianus*.

CINNAMON TEAL

Anas cyanoptera

Adult male Cinnamon Teals are unmistakable in their beautiful cinnamon breeding plumage. The duller females, however, are readily confused with other teals.

• First reported in Georgia in 1977, this accidental winter visitor is generally seen in the Coastal Plain between October and March. It has also been an accidental visitor to the coast at Altamaha Wildlife Management Area.

COMMON MERGANSER

Mergus merganser

The Common Merganser is the most common North American merganser, but in Georgia it is only a rare migrant and winter resident, primarily in the interior, from September through April. It is only occasionally found in the mountains or along the coast. High winter counts for the state are 14 at Columbus, 10 at Lake Juliette (Monroe County) and 18 at Sapelo Island.

SOOTY SHEARWATER

Puffinus griseus

Sooty Shearwaters often travel in huge numbers from their breeding grounds in the Southern Hemisphere to their "wintering" grounds in the North Atlantic. These birds are accidental spring migrants to Georgia offshore of the continental shelf from May to June. Up to six Sooty Shearwaters at a time have been reported on several occasions, but regular pelagic trips would likely show this species to be more common than reported. Also, a number of specimens have been recovered from the shores of Cumberland Island in recent years.

MANX SHEARWATER

Puffinus puffinus

The Manx Shearwater is an accidental fall and winter visitor to offshore zones, primarily on the inner and middle shelf from August to February. Because this European sea-island nester has recently also begun to nest in the Northern Atlantic, it might become more readily seen on pelagic trips off the coast of Georgia.

BROWN BOOBY

Sula leucogaster

Brown Boobies nest and are permanent residents in the Dry Tortugas off the coast of the Florida Keys, and they rarely wander far from that area. As a result, the Brown Booby is only an accidental visitor on the outer shelf in Georgia during summer and early fall. • Although there are only two accepted records, this booby is probably more common than current reports indicate.

ROUGH-LEGGED HAWK

Buteo lagopus

This white-rumped hawk is often seen "hover-hunting" over harsh, wind-swept grasslands and open country. This hunting technique contrasts with the white-rumped, longer-tailed Northern Harrier's low-flying habits over similar habitats. The Rough-legged Hawk is a rare to uncommon winter visitor usually seen from November to May over most of Georgia, and light-morph birds predominate. The high count for the state is two immatures near Colbert (Madison County).

YELLOW RAIL

Coturnicops noveboracensis

The Yellow Rail is a very rare winter resident on the coast and lower Coastal Plain, where it is probably overlooked because of its incredibly secretive behavior. It is also a poorly known migrant statewide and an extremely rare fall migrant in the Piedmont and mountains. • Look for this reticent rail between September and April, especially in winter in dense grassy meadows or sedge marshes along the coast and adjacent Coastal Plain. In spring migration listen for the night call, a rhythmic mechanical *tic-tic tictictic*, which unfortunately, is quite similar to that of a cricket frog. But the rail's double *tic* followed by a rapid triple *tic* should be readily discernable, especially if recorded and played back for more careful listening.

LIMPKIN
Aramus guarauna

This rail is a large, nocturnal bird of fresh-water streams, swamps and lake edges in Florida, where it feeds primarily on snails, mussels and other aquatic animals. It was once thought to possibly breed in Georgia along the Altamaha River, and in the Okefenokee Swamp, but this has never been confirmed. There are a number of recent records for Georgia from counties mostly along the Ocmulgee River and Altamaha River. It has also been photographed recently on the coast at Harris Neck National Wildlife Refuge.

HUDSONIAN GODWIT
Limosa haemastica

This more westerly godwit is accidental in Georgia, with only four accepted winter records (from September to April), from mostly along the coast, including St. Simons, St. Catherines and Andrews islands. There also has been one inland sighting near Duluth (Gwinnett County). It is easily distinguished from the Marbled Godwit in flight by its white rump and black tail and its mostly black underwings. Its nonbreeding gray plumage contrasts with the cinnamon brownish plumage of the more common Marbled Godwit.

nonbreeding

ICELAND GULL
Larus glaucoides

The hardy arctic Iceland Gull is accidental on the coast, with eight documented records to date, primarily along the shores of the coast and barrier islands between December and March. It has recently been seen inland as well, at West Point Lake and the LaGrange land-fill. At landfills, which are in fact good places to look for this gull when it is inland, this "white-winged" gull is easily sep-arated from the other inland gulls, which typi-cally have black-tipped wings.

nonbreeding

ARCTIC TERN
Sterna paradisaea

Arctic Terns make annual round-trip migrations between their arctic breeding grounds and their wintering grounds in Antarctica that can cover nearly 20,000 miles! Most sightings of this tern in Georgia are far offshore during April and May, but there have been coastal sightings on Jekyll Island and St. Simons Island. Also, there has been one rare inland specimen taken on Suwannee Creek, as well as one fall record in the state.

nonbreeding

BURROWING OWL
Athene cunicularia

This small, long-legged owl is the only owl in North America to nest in underground burrows. It is only an accidental visitor to Georgia, mostly below the Fall Line, and many reports of of it in Georgia are from more than 50 years ago. Nevertheless, Burrowing Owls were seen in Georgia on Jekyll Island in 1980 and near Gainesville in 1988. More recently, in the mid-1990s, a pair of Burrowing Owls spent a year at an abandoned airfield near Bainbridge, but nesting was never confirmed.
• Many of these owls in the southeast probably appropriate unused or abandoned gopher tortoise burrows. Conversion of native grasslands and the loss of burrowing gopher tortoise habitats have likely greatly reduced nesting sites suitable for Burrowing Owls.

LONG-EARED OWL
Asio otus

Because the Long-eared Owl is a rather secretive bird, it is probably more common than is reflected in the nearly two dozen reports in Georgia. In fact, of the four most recent records of Long-eareds, all but one were birds found wounded or dead. This rare winter visitor should be looked for between October and May, near wooded edges and brushy meadows just about anywhere in the state.

NORTHERN SAW-WHET OWL
Aegolius acadicus

Of the owls that visit Georgia, the Saw-whet Owl is the smallest. It has been reported 13 times, generally north of the Fall Line from October to April, but it is likely more common than records would indicate. It is seldom heard in winter but can sometimes be found by looking for "white-wash" (excreta) buildup very low in small evergreens or vine tangles, where it usually roosts. Probably because of better owl surveys, this owl has recently been found in higher numbers, with more than 10 owls seen on Burrell's Ford Road in Rabun County over the past few years.

CALLIOPE HUMMINGBIRD
Stellula calliope

The Calliope Hummingbird is the smallest of the hummingbirds that breed in North America. It regularly winters along the Gulf Coast and is an accidental visitor to Georgia, mostly above the Fall Line from November to April. Our first record was in 1998, and this tiny hummer has since been recorded almost annually. All recorded individuals were banded, and surprisingly, two birds were recaptured at the same winter sites where they had been banded the year before.

ALLEN'S HUMMINGBIRD
Selasphorus sasin

Named for California bird collector Charles A. Allen, this West Coast bird commonly overwinters eastward to the Gulf Coast and is an accidental winter visitor from October to March, mostly above the Fall Line. Sightings of this hummingbird have increased in recent years, with reports almost every winter. Leaving freshly filled sugarwater feeders up in winter might attract one of these vagrants to your backyard.

ALDER FLYCATCHER
Empidonax alnorum

The Alder Flycatcher is often indistinguishable from other *Empidonax* flycatchers until it sings its *fee-be-o* or *free beer* song. It is often confused with the Willow Flycatcher, a look-alike that has a harsh, buzzy *fitz-bew* song. • The Alder Flycatcher is best seen in low brushy vegetation in wet areas, such as willow or alder thickets surrounding bogs or marshes. This flycatcher is a rare fall and spring migrant that is often easily overlooked in Georgia, but there a number of confirmed records for the state.

CAVE SWALLOW
Petrochelidon fulva

A "be-on-the-watch-for" accidental wanderer, this swallow has staged incursions into several southeastern states in the past few years, particularly in mid-December in Georgia. It has recently shown up near Macon, at the Altamaha Wildlife Management Area, on Wassaw Island and on Cumberland Island. • The Southwestern sub-species (*P.f. pelodoma*) has a pale throat and "cheeks," characteristics that were found on a specimen captured at Wassaw Island in 2002.

BICKNELL'S THRUSH
Catharus bicknelli

Long classified as a subspecies of the Gray-cheeked Thrush, this thrush, which breeds from eastern Canada south to New York state, was given full species status in 1995. The two species are very difficult to tell apart, and both thrushes may be seen in migration in Georgia. The best way to distin-guish the two species is by song. The Bicknell's Thrush has a higher-pitched, more nasal song, with the last note ris-ing. • Because of the recent species designation, little is known of this bird's status in Georgia. It is thought to be a rare but regular migrant along the coast, with only six confirmed records to date.

SPRAGUE'S PIPIT
Anthus spragueii

This streak-backed, pinkish-legged, American Pipit look-alike is an accidental winter visitor to Georgia. Look for the secretive and usually solitary Sprague's Pipit in grassy areas and prairies statewide from December to May. When flushed, the Sprague's Pipit flies steeply into the air before folding its wings and plummeting back to the ground. It has been found most recently on the barrier islands, at Eufaula National Wildlife Refuge and at Harris Neck National Wildlife Refuge.

KIRTLAND'S WARBLER

Dendroica kirtlandii

Only about 1300 singing male Kirtland's Warblers were tallied on their breeding grounds in northern Michigan in 2004, making this bird one of the rarest birds in North America. With such a restricted breeding range and such a small population, it isn't surprising that this rare bird is endangered nationwide. Although it breeds only in Michigan, it passes through Georgia twice a year, as it travels to and from its wintering grounds in the Bahamas. Most recent records have been in fall at Blairsville, Athens and Pendergrass as well as St. Simons, Jekyll and Cumberland islands. The population in Michigan seems to be increasing, which should result in additional records in Georgia.

WESTERN TANAGER

Piranga ludoviciana

The beautiful, red-headed male tanager is usually observed in Georgia in his nonbreeding plumage, with only a red-tinted face. Both the drab, olive female and the nonbreeding male are easily distinguished by their untanager-like pale but distinct wing bars. Western Tanagers are present in Georgia mostly from fall through spring, primarily on the

breeding

Coastal Plain. This tanager is accidental above and below the Coastal Plain, with one summer report in the Cohutta Mountains and one winter sighting on St. Catherines Island. Listen for this tanager's raspy *prididit* calls in woodlands, or look for the brilliant male in your backyard in early spring.

LARK BUNTING

Calamospiza melanocorys

This Great Plains breeder irregularly wanders eastward, often in late summer, with one confirmed winter record. Lark Buntings have been recorded only seven times in Georgia. Breeding males are easily recognizable, but females and nonbreeding males are much less conspicuous; most Georgia birds are seen in nonbreeding plumage. This bunting could appear almost anywhere in the state, in places such as grassy open country, agricultural fields or weedy vacant lots.

breeding

HARRIS'S SPARROW

Zonotrichia querula

The Harris's Sparrow breeds in north-central Canada and winters in the central Great Plains. It is an accidental winter and spring visitor to Georgia, with 10 state records. Most sightings are from above the Fall Line, but it has been recorded as far south as Okefenokee National Wildlife Refuge in winter. The Harris's Sparrow usually associates with other sparrows when it visits thickets, woodland edges, brushy fields and hedgerows in Georgia.

nonbreeding

LAPLAND LONGSPUR

Calcarius lapponicus

Lapland Longspurs are arctic breeders that are rare and irregular winter visitors to the Lookout Plateau, Ridge and Valley, Piedmont and Coast regions of Georgia from October to March. Longspurs spurn forested areas in all seasons and are denizens of open barren lands. The best place to look for them is at large, open farm fields, with sparse vegetation. Unfortunately for Georgia, they have been more infrequent in recent years. The highest count is 31 birds near Augusta.

nonbreeding

SNOW BUNTING

Plectrophenax nivalis

Snow Buntings are circumpolar arctic breeders, and one individual was even recorded near the north pole—the most northerly record for any songbird. Although they winter throughout the central United States, these buntings are rare and irregular winter visitors in the Piedmont and along the coast in Georgia, from November to February. Not surprisingly, because they often travel with Lapland Longspurs, they too have been more infrequent in recent years. The highest winter count is 16 Snow Buntings on Cumberland Island.

nonbreeding

BLACK-HEADED GROSBEAK

Pheucticus melanocephalus

The Black-headed Grosbeak is a western species that winters primarily in Mexico. Eastern stragglers are rare, so this grosbeak is only accidental in winter in Georgia. There have been a number of confirmed reports in the state, primarily from south of the Fall Line from December to March. Identification is complicated by many similarities between immature and female Rose-breasted Grosbeaks, but look for a distinctive bicolored bill (dark upper mandible) in both female and immature male Black-headed Grosbeaks.

GLOSSARY

accipiter: a forest hawk (genus *Accipiter*), characterized by a short, rounded wings and a long tail; feeds mostly on birds.

brood: *n.* a family of young from one hatching; *v.* to incubate the eggs.

brood parasite: a bird that lays its eggs in other birds' nests.

buteo: a high-soaring hawk (genus *Buteo*), characterized by broad wings and a short, wide tail; feeds mostly on small mammals and other land animals.

cere: on birds of prey, a fleshy area at the base of the bill that contains the nostrils.

clutch: the number of eggs laid by the female at one time.

corvid: a member of the crow family (Corvidae); includes crows, jays, magpies and ravens.

crop: an enlargement of the esophagus; serves as a storage structure and (in pigeons) has glands that produce secretions.

cryptic: a coloration pattern that helps to conceal the bird.

dabbling: a foraging technique used by ducks in which the head and neck are submerged but the body and tail remain on the water's surface; dabbling ducks can usually walk easily on land, can take off without running and have brightly colored speculums.

diurnal: most active during the day.

drake: a male duck.

"eclipse" plumage: a cryptic plumage, similar to that of females, worn by some male ducks in fall when they molt their flight feathers and consequently are unable to fly.

endangered: a species that is facing extirpation or extinction in all or part of its range.

extinct: a species that no longer exists.

extirpated: a species that no longer exists in the wild in a particular region but occurs elsewhere.

fledge: to grow the first full set of feathers.

flushing: when frightened, birds explode into flight in response to a disturbance.

flycatching: a feeding behavior in which a bird leaves a perch, snatches an insect in mid-air and then returns to the same perch; also known as "hawking" or "sallying."

hawking: attempting to capture insects through aerial pursuit.

irruption: a sporadic mass migration of birds into an unusual range.

lek: a place where males gather to display for females in the spring.

mantle: the area that includes the back and upersides of the wings.

molt: the periodic shedding and regrowth of worn feathers (often twice per year).

morph: one of several alternate color phases displayed by a species.

pelagic: open ocean habitat very far from land.

precocial: a bird that is relatively well developed at hatching; precocial birds usually have open eyes, extensive down and are fairly mobile.

primaries: the outermost flight feathers of a bird's wing.

raft: a gathering of birds.

raptor: a carnivorous (meat-eating) bird; includes eagles, hawks, falcons and owls.

riparian: habitat along rivers and streams.

sexual dimorphism: a difference in plumage, size or other characteristics between males and females of the same species.

speculum: a brightly colored patch on the wings of many dabbling ducks.

stage: to gather in one place during migration, usually when birds are flightless or partly flightless during molting.

stoop: a steep drive through the air, usually performed by birds of prey while foraging or during courtship displays.

threatened: a species likely to become endangered in the near future in all or part of its range.

vagrant: a transient bird found outside its normal range.

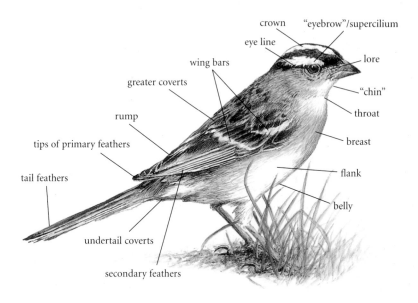

SELECT REFERENCES

American Ornithologists' Union. 1998. *Check-list of North American Birds.* 7th ed. (and its supplements). American Ornithologists' Union, Washington, D.C.

Beaton, G. 2000. *Birding Georgia.* Falcon Publishing, Helena, MT.

Beaton, G. 2004. *Birds of Kennesaw Mountain.* Occasional Publication No. 16, Georgia Ornithological Society.

Beaton, G., P.W. Sykes, Jr. and J.W. Parrish, Jr. 2003. *Annotated Checklist of Georgia Birds.* Occasional Publication No. 14, Georgia Ornithological Society.

Bell, M.K. 2004. *The Breeding Birds of Haralson County.* Occasional Publication No. 17, Georgia Ornithological Society.

Burleigh, T.D. 1958. *Georgia Birds.* The University of Oklahoma Press, Norman, OK.

Choate, E.A. 1985. *The Dictionary of American Bird Names.* Rev. ed. Harvard Common Press, Cambridge, MA.

Cox, R.T. 1996. *Birder's Dictionary.* Falcon Publishing, Helena, MT.

Ehrlich, P.R., D.S. Dobkin & D. Wheye. 1988. *The Birder's Handbook: A Field Guide to the Natural History of North American Birds.* Simon & Schuster, New York.

Jones, J.O. 1990. *Where The Birds Are: A Guide to All 50 States and Canada.* William Morrow and Company, New York.

Kaufman, K. 1996. *Lives of North American Birds.* Houghton Mifflin Co., Boston, MA.

Kaufman, K. 2000. *Birds of North America.* Houghton Mifflin Co., New York.

National Geographic Society. 2002. *Field Guide to the Birds of North America.* 4th ed. National Geographic Society, Washington, DC.

Patterson, T. K. *Birds of Laurens County.* Occasional Publication No. 15, Georgia Ornithological Society.

Peterson, R.T. 1996. *A Field Guide to the Birds: Including all species found in Eastern North America.* Houghton Mifflin Co., Boston, MA.

Sauer, J.R., J.E. Hines, I. Thomas and J. Fallon. 2004. *The North American Breeding Bird Survey, Results and Analysis 1966–2003, Version 2004.I.* USGS Patuxent Wildlife Research Center, Laurel, MD.

Sibley, D.A. 2000. *National Audubon Society: The Sibley Guide to Birds.* Alfred A. Knopf, New York.

Sibley, D.A. 2001. *National Audubon Society: The Sibley Guide to Bird Life and Behavior.* Alfred A. Knopf, New York.

Sibley, D.A. 2002. *Sibley's Birding Basics.* Alfred A. Knopf, New York.

Sandhill Crane

CHECKLIST

The following checklist contains 405 species of birds that have been officially recorded in Georgia, plus eight provisional species (species for which there has been no photographic verification and fewer than four accepted sight records) and four extirpated or extinct species. Species are grouped by family and listed in taxonomic order in accordance with the American Ornithologists' Union's *Check-list of North American Birds* and its supplements, through to *The Forty-fifth Supplement 2005*. Casual and accidental species (those that aren't seen on a yearly basis) are listed in italics. In addition, the following risk categories are noted: endangered (en) and threatened (th).

We would like to thank the Georgia Ornithological Society for their kind assistance in providing the information for this checklist.

Waterfowl (Anatidae)
- ❏ *Black-bellied Whistling-Duck*
- ❏ *Fulvous Whistling-Duck*
- ❏ Greater White-fronted Goose
- ❏ Snow Goose
- ❏ Ross's Goose
- ❏ *Brant*
- ❏ Canada Goose
- ❏ *Tundra Swan*
- ❏ Wood Duck
- ❏ Gadwall
- ❏ *Eurasian Wigeon*
- ❏ American Wigeon
- ❏ American Black Duck
- ❏ Mallard
- ❏ Mottled Duck
- ❏ Blue-winged Teal
- ❏ *Cinnamon Teal*
- ❏ Northern Shoveler
- ❏ Northern Pintail
- ❏ Green-winged Teal
- ❏ Canvasback
- ❏ Redhead
- ❏ Ring-necked Duck
- ❏ Greater Scaup
- ❏ Lesser Scaup
- ❏ King Eider
- ❏ Common Eider
- ❏ Harlequin Duck
- ❏ Surf Scoter
- ❏ White-winged Scoter
- ❏ Black Scoter
- ❏ Long-tailed Duck
- ❏ Bufflehead
- ❏ Common Goldeneye
- ❏ Hooded Merganser
- ❏ *Common Merganser*
- ❏ Red-breasted Merganser
- ❏ *Masked Duck*
- ❏ Ruddy Duck

Chachalacas (Cracidae)
- ❏ Plain Chachalaca

Grouse & Turkeys (Phasianidae)
- ❏ Ruffed Grouse
- ❏ Wild Turkey

New World Quail (Odontophoridae)
- ❏ Northern Bobwhite

Loons (Gaviidae)
- ❏ Red-throated Loon
- ❏ *Pacific Loon*
- ❏ Common Loon
- ❏ Yellow-billed Loon

Grebes (Podicipedidae)
- ❏ Pied-billed Grebe
- ❏ Horned Grebe
- ❏ Red-necked Grebe
- ❏ Eared Grebe
- ❏ *Western Grebe*

Petrels & Shearwaters (Procellariidae)
- ❏ *Black-capped Petrel*
- ❏ Cory's Shearwater
- ❏ Greater Shearwater
- ❏ *Sooty Shearwater*
- ❏ *Manx Shearwater*
- ❏ Audubon's Shearwater

Storm-Petrels (Hydrobatidae)
- ❏ Wilson's Storm-Petrel
- ❏ *Leach's Storm-Petrel*
- ❏ *Band-rumped Storm-Petrel*

Tropicbirds (Phaethontidae)
- ❏ *White-tailed Tropicbird*
- ❏ *Red-billed Tropicbird*

Boobies & Gannets (Sulidae)
- ❏ *Masked Booby*

❏ *Brown Booby*
❏ Northern Gannet

Pelicans (Pelecanidae)
❏ American White Pelican
❏ Brown Pelican (en)

Cormorants (Phalacrocoracidae)
❏ Double-crested Cormorant
❏ *Great Cormorant*

Anhingas (Anhingidae)
❏ Anhinga

Frigatebirds (Fregatidae)
❏ Magnificent Frigatebird

Bitterns, Herons & Egrets (Ardeidae)
❏ American Bittern
❏ Least Bittern
❏ Great Blue Heron
❏ Great Egret
❏ Snowy Egret
❏ Little Blue Heron
❏ Tricolored Heron
❏ Reddish Egret
❏ Cattle Egret
❏ Green Heron
❏ Black-crowned Night-Heron
❏ Yellow-crowned Night-Heron

Ibises & Spoonbills (Threskiornithidae)
❏ White Ibis
❏ Glossy Ibis
❏ *White-faced Ibis*
❏ Roseate Spoonbill

Storks (Ciconiidae)
❏ Wood Stork (en)

New World Vultures (Cathartidae)
❏ Black Vulture
❏ Turkey Vulture

Kites, Eagles & Hawks (Accipitridae)
❏ Osprey
❏ Swallow-tailed Kite
❏ Mississippi Kite
❏ Bald Eagle (th)
❏ Northern Harrier
❏ Sharp-shinned Hawk
❏ Cooper's Hawk
❏ *Northern Goshawk*
❏ Red-shouldered Hawk
❏ Broad-winged Hawk
❏ Red-tailed Hawk
❏ *Rough-legged Hawk*
❏ Golden Eagle

Falcons (Falconidae)
❏ American Kestrel
❏ Merlin
❏ Peregrine Falcon (en)

Rails (Rallidae)
❏ Yellow Rail
❏ Black Rail
❏ Clapper Rail
❏ King Rail
❏ Virginia Rail
❏ Sora
❏ Purple Gallinule
❏ Common Moorhen
❏ American Coot

Limpkins (Aramidae)
❏ *Limpkin* (en)

Cranes (Gruidae)
❏ Sandhill Crane
❏ Whooping Crane (en)

Plovers (Charadriidae)
❏ Black-bellied Plover
❏ American Golden-Plover
❏ *Snowy Plover*
❏ Wilson's Plover
❏ Semipalmated Plover
❏ Piping Plover (th)
❏ Killdeer

Oystercatchers (Haematopodidae)
❏ American Oystercatcher

Stilts & Avocets (Recurvirostridae)
❏ Black-necked Stilt
❏ American Avocet

Sandpipers & Phalaropes (Scolopacidae)
❏ Greater Yellowlegs
❏ Lesser Yellowlegs
❏ Solitary Sandpiper
❏ Willet
❏ Spotted Sandpiper
❏ Upland Sandpiper
❏ Whimbrel
❏ Long-billed Curlew
❏ Hudsonian Godwit
❏ Marbled Godwit
❏ Ruddy Turnstone
❏ Red Knot
❏ Sanderling
❏ Semipalmated Sandpiper
❏ Western Sandpiper
❏ Least Sandpiper
❏ White-rumped Sandpiper

❏ Baird's Sandpiper
❏ Pectoral Sandpiper
❏ Purple Sandpiper
❏ Dunlin
❏ *Curlew Sandpiper*
❏ Stilt Sandpiper
❏ Buff-breasted Sandpiper
❏ *Ruff*
❏ Short-billed Dowitcher
❏ Long-billed Dowitcher
❏ Wilson's Snipe
❏ American Woodcock
❏ Wilson's Phalarope
❏ Red-necked Phalarope
❏ Red Phalarope

Jaegers, Gulls & Terns (Laridae)
❏ South Polar Skua
❏ Pomarine Jaeger
❏ Parasitic Jaeger
❏ *Long-tailed Jaeger*
❏ Laughing Gull
❏ Franklin's Gull
❏ *Little Gull*
❏ *Black-headed Gull*
❏ Bonaparte's Gull
❏ Ring-billed Gull
❏ Herring Gull
❏ *Iceland Gull*
❏ Lesser Black-backed Gull
❏ Glaucous Gull
❏ Great Black-backed Gull
❏ *Sabine's Gull*
❏ Black-legged Kittiwake
❏ Gull-billed Tern (th)
❏ Caspian Tern
❏ Royal Tern
❏ Sandwich Tern
❏ Common Tern
❏ *Arctic Tern*
❏ Forster's Tern
❏ Least Tern
❏ Bridled Tern
❏ Sooty Tern

❏ Black Tern
❏ Brown Noddy
❏ Black Skimmer

Alcids (Alcidae)
❏ *Dovekie*
❏ *Razorbill*

Pigeons & Doves (Columbidae)
❏ Rock Pigeon
❏ Eurasian Collared-Dove
❏ White-winged Dove
❏ Mourning Dove
❏ Common Ground-Dove

Cuckoos & Anis (Cuculidae)
❏ Black-billed Cuckoo
❏ Yellow-billed Cuckoo
❏ *Smooth-billed Ani*

Barn Owls (Tytonidae)
❏ Barn Owl

Typical Owls (Strigidae)
❏ Eastern Screech-Owl
❏ Great Horned Owl
❏ *Snowy Owl*
❏ *Burrowing Owl*
❏ Barred Owl
❏ *Long-eared Owl*
❏ Short-eared Owl
❏ *Northern Saw-whet Owl*

Nightjars (Caprimulgidae)
❏ Common Nighthawk
❏ Chuck-will's-widow
❏ Whip-poor-will

Swifts (Apodidae)
❏ Chimney Swift

Hummingbirds (Trochilidae)
❏ Broad-billed Hummingbird
❏ *Magnificent Hummingbird*
❏ Ruby-throated Hummingbird
❏ Black-chinned Hummingbird
❏ *Anna's Hummingbird*
❏ *Calliope Hummingbird*
❏ *Broad-tailed Hummingbird*
❏ Rufous Hummingbird
❏ *Allen's Hummingbird*

Kingfishers (Alcedinidae)
❏ Belted Kingfisher

Woodpeckers (Picidae)
❏ Red-headed Woodpecker
❏ Red-bellied Woodpecker
❏ Yellow-bellied Sapsucker
❏ Downy Woodpecker
❏ Hairy Woodpecker
❏ Red-cockaded Woodpecker (en)
❏ Northern Flicker
❏ Pileated Woodpecker
❏ Ivory-billed Woodpecker

Flycatchers (Tyrannidae)
❏ Olive-sided Flycatcher
❏ Eastern Wood-Pewee
❏ Yellow-bellied Flycatcher
❏ Acadian Flycatcher
❏ *Alder Flycatcher*
❏ Willow Flycatcher
❏ Least Flycatcher

- ❏ Eastern Phoebe
- ❏ *Say's Phoebe*
- ❏ *Vermilion Flycatcher*
- ❏ *Ash-throated Flycatcher*
- ❏ Great Crested Flycatcher
- ❏ Western Kingbird
- ❏ Eastern Kingbird
- ❏ Gray Kingbird
- ❏ Scissor-tailed Flycatcher

Shrikes (Laniidae)
- ❏ Loggerhead Shrike

Vireos (Vireonidae)
- ❏ White-eyed Vireo
- ❏ *Bell's Vireo*
- ❏ Yellow-throated Vireo
- ❏ Blue-headed Vireo
- ❏ Warbling Vireo
- ❏ Philadelphia Vireo
- ❏ Red-eyed Vireo

Jays & Crows (Corvidae)
- ❏ Blue Jay
- ❏ *Florida Scrub-Jay*
- ❏ American Crow
- ❏ Fish Crow
- ❏ Common Raven

Larks (Alaudidae)
- ❏ Horned Lark

Swallows (Hirundinidae)
- ❏ Purple Martin
- ❏ Tree Swallow
- ❏ Northern Rough-winged Swallow
- ❏ Bank Swallow
- ❏ Cliff Swallow
- ❏ *Cave Swallow*
- ❏ Barn Swallow

Chickadees & Titmice (Paridae)
- ❏ Carolina Chickadee
- ❏ Tufted Titmouse

Nuthatches (Sittidae)
- ❏ Red-breasted Nuthatch
- ❏ White-breasted Nuthatch
- ❏ Brown-headed Nuthatch

Creepers (Certhiidae)
- ❏ Brown Creeper

Wrens (Troglodytidae)
- ❏ Carolina Wren
- ❏ *Bewick's Wren*
- ❏ House Wren
- ❏ Winter Wren
- ❏ Sedge Wren
- ❏ Marsh Wren

Kinglets (Regulidae)
- ❏ Golden-crowned Kinglet
- ❏ Ruby-crowned Kinglet

Gnatcatchers (Sylviidae)
- ❏ Blue-gray Gnatcatcher

Thrushes (Turdidae)
- ❏ *Northern Wheatear*
- ❏ Eastern Bluebird
- ❏ Veery
- ❏ Gray-cheeked Thrush
- ❏ *Bicknell's Thrush*
- ❏ Swainson's Thrush
- ❏ Hermit Thrush

- ❏ Wood Thrush
- ❏ American Robin
- ❏ *Varied Thrush*

Mockingbirds & Thrashers (Mimidae)
- ❏ Gray Catbird
- ❏ Northern Mockingbird
- ❏ *Sage Thrasher*
- ❏ Brown Thrasher

Starlings (Sturnidae)
- ❏ European Starling

Pipits (Motacillidae)
- ❏ American Pipit
- ❏ *Sprague's Pipit*

Waxwings (Bombycillidae)
- ❏ Cedar Waxwing

Wood-warblers (Parulidae)
- ❏ Blue-winged Warbler
- ❏ Golden-winged Warbler
- ❏ Tennessee Warbler
- ❏ Orange-crowned Warbler
- ❏ Nashville Warbler
- ❏ Northern Parula
- ❏ Yellow Warbler
- ❏ Chestnut-sided Warbler
- ❏ Magnolia Warbler
- ❏ Cape May Warbler
- ❏ Black-throated Blue Warbler
- ❏ Yellow-rumped Warbler
- ❏ *Black-throated Gray Warbler*

❏ Black-throated Green Warbler
❏ *Townsend's Warbler*
❏ Blackburnian Warbler
❏ Yellow-throated Warbler
❏ Pine Warbler
❏ *Kirtland's Warbler* (en)
❏ Prairie Warbler
❏ Palm Warbler
❏ Bay-breasted Warbler
❏ Blackpoll Warbler
❏ Cerulean Warbler
❏ Black-and-white Warbler
❏ American Redstart
❏ Prothonotary Warbler
❏ Worm-eating Warbler
❏ Swainson's Warbler
❏ Ovenbird
❏ Northern Waterthrush
❏ Louisiana Waterthrush
❏ Kentucky Warbler
❏ Connecticut Warbler
❏ Mourning Warbler
❏ *MacGillivray's Warbler*
❏ Common Yellowthroat
❏ Hooded Warbler
❏ Wilson's Warbler
❏ Canada Warbler
❏ Yellow-breasted Chat

Tanagers (Thraupidae)
❏ Summer Tanager
❏ Scarlet Tanager
❏ *Western Tanager*

Sparrows (Emberizidae)
❏ *Green-tailed Towhee*
❏ *Spotted Towhee*
❏ Eastern Towhee
❏ Bachman's Sparrow
❏ *American Tree Sparrow*

❏ Chipping Sparrow
❏ Clay-colored Sparrow
❏ Field Sparrow
❏ Vesper Sparrow
❏ Lark Sparrow
❏ *Lark Bunting*
❏ Savannah Sparrow
❏ Grasshopper Sparrow
❏ Henslow's Sparrow
❏ Le Conte's Sparrow
❏ Nelson's Sharp-tailed Sparrow
❏ Saltmarsh Sharp-tailed Sparrow
❏ Seaside Sparrow (en)
❏ Fox Sparrow
❏ Song Sparrow
❏ Lincoln's Sparrow
❏ Swamp Sparrow
❏ White-throated Sparrow
❏ *Harris's Sparrow*
❏ White-crowned Sparrow
❏ Dark-eyed Junco
❏ *Lapland Longspur*
❏ *Snow Bunting*

Cardinals & Grosbeaks (Cardinalidae)
❏ Northern Cardinal
❏ Rose-breasted Grosbeak
❏ *Black-headed Grosbeak*
❏ Blue Grosbeak
❏ Indigo Bunting
❏ Painted Bunting
❏ Dickcissel

Blackbirds & Orioles (Icteridae)
❏ Bobolink
❏ Red-winged Blackbird
❏ Eastern Meadowlark

❏ *Western Meadowlark*
❏ Yellow-headed Blackbird
❏ Rusty Blackbird
❏ Brewer's Blackbird
❏ Common Grackle
❏ Boat-tailed Grackle
❏ *Shiny Cowbird*
❏ Brown-headed Cowbird
❏ Orchard Oriole
❏ *Bullock's Oriole*
❏ Baltimore Oriole
❏ *Scott's Oriole*

Finches (Fringillidae)
❏ Purple Finch
❏ House Finch
❏ Red Crossbill
❏ *Common Redpoll*
❏ Pine Siskin
❏ American Goldfinch
❏ Evening Grosbeak

Old World Sparrows (Passeridae)
❏ House Sparrow

PROVISIONAL SPECIES
❏ *Northern Fulmar*
❏ *Swainson's Hawk*
❏ *Mountain Plover*
❏ *Roseate Tern* (en)
❏ *White-winged Tern*
❏ *Green Violet-Ear*
❏ *Virginia's Warbler*
❏ *Painted Redstart*

EXTINCT/EXTIRPATED SPECIES
❏ *Passenger Pigeon*
❏ *Carolina Parakeet*
❏ *Ivory-billed Woodpecker*
❏ *Bachman's Warbler*

INDEX OF SCIENTIFIC NAMES

This index references only the primary species accounts.

INDEX OF COMMON NAMES

Page numbers in **boldface** type refer to the primary, illustrated species accounts.

ABOUT THE AUTHORS

Dr. John Parrish became an avid birder in graduate school and has conducted most of his research on avian biology. He and his students have studied such diverse topics as near-UV vision in passerines, waterfowl and the kingfisher; avian hematology; bioenergetics in Scaled Quail and Greater Prairie-Chickens; population studies of introduced Psittacids in Florida; and for the past 11 years, demographics of the Southeastern American Kestrel in Georgia. He has taught animal physiology and ornithology in Kansas, at Emporia State University, and currently at Georgia Southern University. He was a member of the Editorial Board for *The Oriole*, the quarterly journal of the Georgia Ornithological Society, for eight years and has served as coeditor for the past six years. He is also a coauthor of the *Annotated Checklist of Georgia Birds*, has published numerous scientific articles and has presented his research at state, national and international scientific meetings. He is a life member of the American Ornithologists' Union, the Kansas Ornithological Society and the Georgia Ornithological Society. John has been active in the USGS Breeding Bird Survey program, assisted with the Georgia Breeding Bird Atlas project and is an active participant in the Audubon Christmas Bird Count program. He is an avid birder and photographer, and you won't see him in the field without both his binoculars and telephoto-equipped SLR camera (digital, in recent years).

Giff Beaton has been observing and photographing nature for almost 30 years, the last 15 in Georgia. He is the senior author of the *Annotated Checklist of Georgia Birds* and author of *Birding Georgia* and *Birds of Kennesaw Mountain*. He has also contributed to numerous other books and has written many magazine articles on both birds and insects, and is currently finishing his latest project, a photographic field guide to Georgia dragonflies to be published next year. He has been leading bird tours in Georgia and across North America for about 10 years, and he has been on the state Bird Record Committees for both Georgia and South Carolina. He and his wife Becky live in Marietta, Georgia, not far from the great migrant location Kennesaw Mountain.

Gregory Kennedy has been an active naturalist since he was very young. He is the author of many books on natural history and has produced television shows on environmental and indigenous concerns in Southeast Asia, New Guinea, South and Central America, the High Arctic and elsewhere. He has also been involved in countless research projects around the world, ranging from studies in the upper canopy of tropical and temperate rainforests to deepwater marine investigations.

ABOUT THE AUTHORS

Dr. John Parrish became an avid birder in graduate school and has conducted most of his research on avian biology. He and his students have studied such diverse topics as near-UV vision in passerines, waterfowl and the kingfisher; avian hematology; bioenergetics in Scaled Quail and Greater Prairie-Chickens; population studies of introduced Psittacids in Florida; and for the past 11 years, demographics of the Southeastern American Kestrel in Georgia. He has taught animal physiology and ornithology in Kansas, at Emporia State University, and currently at Georgia Southern University. He was a member of the Editorial Board for *The Oriole,* the quarterly journal of the Georgia Ornithological Society, for eight years and has served as coeditor for the past six years. He is also a coauthor of the *Annotated Checklist of Georgia Birds,* has published numerous scientific articles and has presented his research at state, national and international scientific meetings. He is a life member of the American Ornithologists' Union, the Kansas Ornithological Society and the Georgia Ornithological Society. John has been active in the USGS Breeding Bird Survey program, assisted with the Georgia Breeding Bird Atlas project and is an active participant in the Audubon Christmas Bird Count program. He is an avid birder and photographer, and you won't see him in the field without both his binoculars and telephoto-equipped SLR camera (digital, in recent years).

Giff Beaton has been observing and photographing nature for almost 30 years, the last 15 in Georgia. He is the senior author of the *Annotated Checklist of Georgia Birds* and author of *Birding Georgia* and *Birds of Kennesaw Mountain.* He has also contributed to numerous other books and has written many magazine articles on both birds and insects, and is currently finishing his latest project, a photographic field guide to Georgia dragonflies to be published next year. He has been leading bird tours in Georgia and across North America for about 10 years, and he has been on the state Bird Record Committees for both Georgia and South Carolina. He and his wife Becky live in Marietta, Georgia, not far from the great migrant location Kennesaw Mountain.

Gregory Kennedy has been an active naturalist since he was very young. He is the author of many books on natural history and has produced television shows on environmental and indigenous concerns in Southeast Asia, New Guinea, South and Central America, the High Arctic and elsewhere. He has also been involved in countless research projects around the world, ranging from studies in the upper canopy of tropical and temperate rainforests to deepwater marine investigations.